W9-BFC-260

Wilder Learning Resource Center
Northeast Iowa Community College
Calmar, Iowa 52132

	DATE DUE	
	W/O	

973
Cea   Ceaser, James W.   133462

Reconstructing America: the symbol
of America in modern thought

Reconstructing America

Reconstructing

★ ★ ★

America

The Symbol of America in Modern Thought

James W. Ceaser

Yale University Press
New Haven
& London

133462

Wilder Learning Resource Center
Northeast Iowa Community College
Calmar, Iowa 52132

Published with assistance from the Charles A. Coffin Fund.

Copyright © 1997 by Yale University. All rights reserved. This book may not be reproduced, in whole or in part, including illustrations, in any form (beyond that copying permitted by Sections 107 and 108 of the U.S. Copyright Law and except by reviewers for the public press), without written permission from the publishers.

Designed by Nancy Ovedovitz and set in Postscript Times Roman type by The Composing Room of Michigan, Inc. Printed in the United States of America by BookCrafters, Inc., Chelsea, Michigan.

Library of Congress Cataloging-in-Publication Data
Ceaser, James W.
Reconstructing America : the symbol of America in modern thought / James W. Ceaser.
p.   cm.
Includes bibliographical references and index.
ISBN 0–300–07053–5 (cloth : alk. paper)
1. United States—Foreign public opinion, European.   2. National characteristics, American.   3. Americanization.   4. France—Intellectual life.   5. Germany—Intellectual life.   I. Title.
E169.12.C38   1997
973—dc21   96–52890

A catalogue record for this book is available from the British Library.

The paper in this book meets the guidelines for permanence and durability of the Committee on Production Guidelines for Book Longevity of the Council on Library Resources.

10   9   8   7   6   5   4   3   2   1

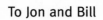

To Jon and Bill

Contents

Contents

Acknowledgments

I would like to thank the graduate students and colleagues who read and commented on parts of the book at different stages of its development: John Jordan, Joshua Dunn, Andrew Hall, Robert Stacey, John Dinan, Dennis Logue, Steven Lenzner, Daniel Mahoney, Richard Zinman, and Ralph Hancock. My late and dear friend Jean-Louis Seurin was a constant source of guidance on European sources, and Valentin Zellweger provided much-needed advice in translating some of the more difficult passages of German philosophy and poetry. My deepest debt of gratitude in this project as in so many others goes to my wife, Blaire French, who read the manuscript several times and risked pointing out all the errors and redundancies it contained.

Over the past few years I also benefited from the help of several institutions and foundations that provided support while I was conducting my research. In particular, I would like to acknowledge the Salvatori Center at Claremont McKenna College and its director, Charles Kesler; the George C. Marshall Center; the Harvard University Department of Government and the director of its Program on Constitutional Government, Harvey C. Mansfield; the Lynde and Harry Bradley Foundation; and the Center for Advanced Studies and the Department of Government and Foreign Affairs at the University of Virginia. A number of seminars sponsored by the Liberty Fund were also of great help in shaping many of my ideas.

Versions of some of the chapters were presented as lectures at Boston College, Harvard University, the University of Virginia, Claremont McKenna College, Washington and Lee University, the University of Massachusetts, and Michigan State University. I am indebted to many in those audiences whose probing questions and critical comments forced a rethinking of parts of my argument. Finally, at Yale University Press, I would like to thank John Covell, who was most helpful at a critical stage in the book's development, and Brenda Kolb, who performed a thorough and creative job in editing the manuscript.

Introduction

If it were acceptable in a work of modern scholarship to rise with indignation in the defense of one's country, I would begin this book with a simple call to arms: it is time to take America back. It is time to take it back from the literary critics, philosophers, and self-styled postmodern thinkers who have made the very name "America" a symbol for that which is grotesque, obscene, monstrous, stultifying, stunted, leveling, deadening, deracinating, deforming, rootless, uncultured, and—always in quotation marks—"free." I would ride from lecture hall to lecture hall warning my fellow citizens of the attack being launched against them and sounding the alarm: "One if by modern philosophy, two if by literary criticism!"

But given the strictures that bind us inside the academy, any such declaration of patriotism or profession of support for one's own is out of the question—unless, of course, it is made on behalf of a group that proclaims itself to be marginalized, victimized, or oppressed.

So, to reach my audience, I must start over again.

In a line of development that can be traced back more than two hundred years, some of the most illustrious thinkers of Europe have seized on the word "America" and made it into something more than a place or country. They have converted it into a concept of philosophy and a trope of literature. From Hegel to Heidegger in Germany (with passages through Spengler and Jünger) and from Buffon to Baudrillard in France (with passages through de Maistre and Kojève), a new America has been born. I shall refer to this America as the "metaphysical America" or the "symbolic America." And I shall try to distinguish it, so far as I can, from the real America, by which I mean the country where we live, work, struggle, and pray, and where we have forged a system of government that has helped to shape the destiny of the modern world.

The symbolic America is not, of course, identical for every thinker. But all have worked from the same concept, successively modifying and amending it with the previous meanings in mind. I could provide scores of examples illustrating the content of the symbolic America—in fact, every adjective I cited in the first paragraph comes from the work of one or another celebrated thinker. But I will spare my readers for the moment the pain of such a litany and confine myself here to a nice passage from the French writer Henry de Montherlant: "One nation that manages to lower intelligence, morality, human quality on nearly all the surface of the earth, such a thing has never been seen before in the existence of the planet. I accuse the United States of being in a permanent state of crime against humankind."[1]

Writers on America do not simply speak of the United States; they have also constructed the concept of "Americanism" or "Americanization," which refers to such fundamental developments of modernity as cultural homogenization, democratization, and degeneration. America so conceived may exist outside of the United States and involve no actual Americans. Once this point is reached, it becomes clear that the real America is no longer at issue: an idea or symbol called "America" has taken over. No other nation, so far as I know, has attained in anything like the same degree this status of a pure abstraction. No one, for example, speaks of New Zealandism or Venezuelanization. Yet for all this, the real nation remains the object of the symbol, and "America" always points back to the United States. In this respect America differs from other well-known geographical symbols where the object designated is not a political entity or society but a spiritual or intellectual activity, as is the case with "Jerusalem" (the biblical religion), "Athens" (philosophy), and "Rome" (the Catholic faith).

The symbolic or metaphysical America must be distinguished from the various images of America that circulate around the world today. Mass opinion, which generally holds a more favorable picture of America, derives from sources that are partly independent of the thoughts of philosophers and the musings of poets—a fact that no doubt accounts for some of the intellectual hostility toward America. The influence of America on public opinion comes from political events (above all, American participation in the world wars), from America's status today as the world's preeminent economic and military power, from America's identification with the idea of modern democracy, and from America's supremacy in the realms of popular entertainment, advertising, mass media, and computer language. The ascendancy of America in so many realms, which by accident happens to have followed upon Great Britain's reign as the world's foremost empire, has also elevated the English language—or "American," as many in the world now call it—to the status of the universal medium of communication in business, science, and diplomacy and on the Internet.

The spread of popular images about America in our era of globalization has made America into the nearest thing ever to an object of universal reference. America is spoken of with greater frequency and carries more meaning to more people than any other image in recorded time, including the biblical God or our own Madonna. From Mogadishu to Tbilisi and from Bogotá to Minsk, almost everyone has an impression of or an opinion about America. People may either love or hate America, but they almost never ignore it. The penetration of America into the consciousness of other peoples is well captured by the title of a recent book in France, *L'Amérique dans les têtes,* which, to take advantage of a colloquialism of our youth today, may be translated as *America Getting Inside Your Head.*[2] Foreign intellectuals and journalists often lament this preoccupation with America, but they still seem to underestimate its depth; for after delivering themselves of some weighty assessment about the meaning of America, they often work a conversation around to asking what the American perspective is on their nation's politics and culture—on the assumption that as they have a view about America, so too must Americans have a view of them. For the most part, however, there is no American view of France or Canada or Germany or England or Honduras in the same way that there is a French, Canadian, German, English, or Honduran view of America. This fact is less a manifestation of Americans' well-documented ignorance of foreign things than it is a reflection of the current asymmetry in the position of the nations of the world. Because America has a significant bearing on just about everyone else, yet because no other nation has this same effect on America, Americans have less need to build elaborate images of other countries.

Mass opinion about America, as noted, is not quite the same thing as the metaphysical or symbolic America. A congruence between the two would be impossible, if only because the foundations of the symbolic America were laid two centuries ago, well before the United States achieved its current status. The symbolic America has nevertheless exercised a significant, although indirect, effect on public thinking. Anchored in the works of some of the major thinkers of our age, the symbol continually impresses itself on the educated strata and on opinion makers, who in turn transmit bits and pieces of it to the public at large. Because the ideas of philosophers and writers have a staying power that cannot be matched by the evanescent images generated in the modern mass media, the influence of the symbolic America on public consciousness is sure to persist.

Irrespective of its impact on public opinion, however, the symbolic America is important in its own right and has become a central concept of contemporary thought. Open any book of modern intellectual history, and you are apt to see an allusion to America as the primary reference for such fundamental themes as technology (and rationalist thought or "logocentrism"), the end of history, political homogenization, cultural banalization, and (while it was still a respectable theme of intellectual thought) racial and ethnic homogenization ("mongrelization"). Whoever says "America" may mean any one of these things. Today America may not have a status equivalent to God in medieval thought or Being in classical thought, but it rivals any modern symbol for dominance in our time. In considering the symbolic America, a window is opened on modern thought itself.

Who discovered America? Why did modern thinkers single out a nation, and why America, to play so important a role in philosophy? I doubt that these questions can ever be fully or satisfactorily answered, for accident always plays a large role in the development of words and symbols. A study of the genealogy of the symbolic America should nevertheless show that while a term other than "America" might have been adopted, there is a certain logic to the selection of this country. Given that philosophy in the seventeenth century became more political in its horizons and aspirations, it is perhaps only natural that a political symbol should have become central to philosophy. America at its core has been a political symbol in the broadest sense. It has been connected not only with a particular kind of regime (a liberal democracy with a capitalist economy) but also with a new type of political community (one constructed from reflection and choice) and with the intellectual discipline that played the guiding role in its creation (political science).

Whatever its beginning, the symbol grew, and like other concepts, it began to take on a life of its own. With time, most thinkers no longer were aware of all that lay behind the concept but simply used it as an idea readily available to them. As modern linguistic theory has taught us, it is in the covering over or hiding of origins that a symbol acquires much of its influence. A loaded or partisan idea wins acceptance as a general concept, after which it comes to be thought of as being as real or meaningful as any other general idea or concept. Language, as Roland Barthes has observed, "encloses all literary creation like the sky, the earth, and the horizon sketch for man a familiar habitat."[3]

Of course, in the case of America we are not speaking of a symbol whose history is ancient. To search for its origins, we do not need to engage in the kind of etymological inquiry that traces the word back from its variants in the modern vernacular tongues to a medieval Latin source and thence to an original Greek or Indo-

European root. The invention of America is an event of the modern era, and its full symbolic usage became secure only in the twentieth century. As late as the 1930s, some of the key German thinkers who helped to develop the symbolic America were still aware of its constructed or "conventional" character. Conceiving themselves to be the masters of the symbol rather than mastered by it, they consciously sought to fashion the intellectual structure, or "house of being," in which we live and think.

They succeeded to a remarkable extent. Today the symbol of America is a part of the stock of intellectual ideas. A writer will refer as readily to Americanization or Americanism as to any other abstract concept. "America" has thus come to shape our thoughts and even the way we think. It is a symbol that threatens to control our destiny.

One objective of this book is to free the real from the symbolic America, thereby liberating a country from the mastery of a metaphor and the tyranny of a trope. Achieving this objective cannot be easy. If it were the case that propagators of the symbolic America were limited to a few European thinkers or that the symbol's influence were confined to the peoples of a few nations, the prospects for emancipating the real America might be quite favorable. But this symbol's grip on the modern mind is much too strong to warrant such hope. "America discourse" is no longer merely a Western European phenomenon. From its origin in France and Germany it spread to what used to be known as the East (the Communist empire); to Latin American nations, where people have special geopolitical and historical grounds to fear the United States; to the formerly colonialized nations of Africa; and, most noticeably in recent years, to parts of the Islamic world, where America, according to Bernard Lewis, is seen as "the diabolic opponent of all that is good."[4]

What is more striking still, the symbolic America is now regularly employed inside the United States, where intellectuals avail themselves of it with almost the same frequency as do their foreign sisters and brethren. Americans, who are the objects or victims of abuse in this discourse, make common cause with their abusers, producing a malady that should be known as the Battered American Intellectuals' Syndrome (BAIS). An echoing of European ideas of America is certainly nothing new; it reaches back to the origin of the Republic and was elevated almost to an art form by such literary figures as T. S. Eliot and Ezra Pound. But it is in our time, when America discourse has achieved such currency, that this syndrome has reached its zenith, penetrating into the disciplines of literary and cultural studies and philosophy.

One of the bastions of this syndrome inside academia is, of all places, the field known as American studies. This point was first brought to my attention in the 1980s, before the Fall of the Wall, by a number of then Eastern European dissidents who expressed their dismay at finding in Americans' writings on America many of the same notions that pervaded their own governments' official positions. I later confirmed this observation while visiting a number of American studies conferences in Europe. The American scholars imported to offer the latest thinking on America were invariably among the most earnest and graphic in their intellectual flagellation of their own country. The predominance of this view of America inside the field of American studies, while it may at first seem odd, is finally not surprising. American studies is not a discipline with a set of distinct scientific questions but a concentration, increasingly inside of cultural studies, held together by its focus on one thing: America. And where, one may ask, is it more likely that America discourse should ultimately gain ascendancy than in an academic enterprise devoted to this name?

Speaking as I have of symbols, metaphors, and tropes may create the impression that this book is the work of a literary or cultural critic—that highly sophisticated species of modern intellectual who roams without portfolio from culture to culture and era to era, foraging for "interesting" juxtapositions designed to shock us into looking at things in fresh ways. Cultural criticism, as one author has so nicely defined it, is "a genre of writing that aims not to anathematize or celebrate, but to understand, albeit with a dose of irony."[5] As much as I admire intellectuals of this type, I cannot hope to equal their erudition or sophistication. Besides, nothing could be further from my purpose.

I am a political scientist—a "traditional" political scientist, to be more exact. I add this adjective with reluctance, knowing that some may try to endow it with a negative or stodgy connotation. Still, the qualification is necessary, because the name "political science"—unlike "sociology" or "anthropology"—goes back many centuries and because much of the current academic discipline that now uses the name has little in common with the original form. What traditional political science consists of will become clearer as I proceed. For the moment, it is enough to observe that to be a political scientist means to apply oneself to the study of certain basic questions that derive, almost naturally, from an encounter with political life. Political science takes its bearings from what is recognized in developed societies as most important politically: the character or quality of different political systems. In its more theoretical aspect, which is sometimes called political theory, political science inquires into the quality of different regimes, asking how they contribute to justice, security, prosperity, and a more civilized life. In its more practical aspect, political science seeks to discover the factors that maintain and destroy different systems and international orders.

Traditional political science is also characterized by a distinct relation to its subject matter. It studies political phenomena in order not just to understand them but also to assist those who act in politics, with a view to improving the quality of political life. Political science rests on the assumption that we have been endowed with intellect in order not just to amuse ourselves or, as they say today, "keep the discussion going," but also to search for knowledge that may prove helpful to at least a portion of humanity. The political scientist, unlike our friend the literary critic, operates under no compulsion to be "interesting," let alone "ironic"; he may be allowed the privilege of being sober—I will not say boring—if sobriety is what is required to promote the objectives of the discipline.

It is because of my inquiries in political science, not in spite of them, that I have felt compelled to stray from the political scientist's usual path of studying constitutions and institutions and to enter into the unfamiliar territory of symbols. I have become convinced that to cede a monopoly of commentary on America discourse to the spokespersons of the various cultural disciplines would in the present context constitute a dereliction of the political scientist's duty. Any powerful symbol, in particular one designed with a political objective in mind, must have an effect on a society's way of thinking and on the well-being of its political system. This is surely the case today with the symbolic America, which distorts genuine analysis and serves increasingly to uphold the interests of an entrenched power structure within the republic of intellectuals.

There are, to be more specific, at least four reasons for the political scientist to study America discourse. The first and most obvious concerns its effect on how influential segments of the populace in many countries view the United States. I can begin to illustrate this point by recounting a personal experience. In the winter of 1990–91, during the months leading up to the Gulf War, I visited several German-language universities to lecture on American foreign policy. This was an unusually anxious time, when America's policy of risking war was subjected to the most intense scrutiny both at home and abroad. Strong arguments, passionately advocated, were what I expected to hear. Yet I was scarcely prepared for the reactions I encountered. Although there was passion enough in the exchanges, it was oddly disconnected from any of the strategic issues I had addressed. Instead, I found myself shadowboxing with a background idea: *Amerika*. It was as if the mere mention of this word elicited certain predetermined responses. On the canvas called America my listeners projected such themes as a wanton disposition to waste limited human resources, a blind indifference in the face of an ecological disaster, a total disrespect for all submerged cultures, and an unquestioning faith in technology. These putative characteristics, not Iraq's invasion of Kuwait or the West's vital strategic interests, were identified as the root causes of the impending conflict. America was the moral equivalent of the aggressor.

Nor was it possible to dismiss these attacks, as one might have a few years earlier, on the grounds that they were part of an orchestrated campaign set in motion by the Soviet propaganda machine. Not only was Communism in Europe at this point held in complete disgrace, but the United States was being singled out for special praise in Germany for its steadfast support of German unification. What I was encountering was no mere tactical ploy but a deep-seated preconception—what Walter Lippmann once called a "stereotype" and what may be labeled, to employ a more descriptive German word, a *Vorurteil,* or a prejudgment or prejudice.[6] It was the experience of meeting this symbol in all its force that prompted me to undertake this investigation. I had begun to see that it was no longer possible to speak merely as a political scientist without first confronting a way of thinking that was making the practice of ordinary political science impossible.

If one had crossed the Rhine into France a year later, it would have been possible to observe French intellectual reactions to America during the crisis period leading up to the opening of Euro-Disney outside of Paris. Here, as nowhere else, one could see the effect of this Vorurteil—better still, this idée fixe—at work. Jean Cau, a former personal secretary to Jean-Paul Sartre, called Euro-Disney a "cultural Chernobyl" and described the park as a "construction of hardened chewing gum and idiotic folklore written for obese Americans." Max Gallo, a former personal secretary of President François Mitterrand complained that Disney would "bombard France with uprooted creations that are to culture what fast food is to gastronomy." Disney was viewed by intellectuals on both the Left and the Right as the "Trojan Mouse" that had infiltrated the citadel of European civilization and was threatening to destroy it.[7]

That important intellectuals would risk going so far as to make themselves look ridiculous is proof enough that there is nothing really lighthearted in these criticisms. They are, on the contrary, vicious, and even more so in their depiction of America than of the Walt Disney Company. If these comments represented merely the isolated complaints of a few disgruntled intellectuals, their significance might readily be dismissed. But such attacks are standard fare among the high priests of intellectual life. The terms employed to describe America, down almost to the chewing gum, draw on the ideas of some of the world's most acclaimed thinkers, and the elevation of Disney to an object of high philosophical inquiry ranges from the work of the Frankfurt School's Theodor Adorno, who attacked Disney in a long exchange with Walter Benjamin, to that of Jean Baudrillard, for whom "Disneyland is there to conceal the fact that it is in truth the 'real' America, . . . just as prisons are there to conceal the fact that society in its banal entirety is prison-like."[8]

A second reason for the political scientist to consider America discourse is to study how a philosophic and literary symbol is able to ensconce itself in the political world, especially in the more subtle form in which the symbolic America appears today. For more than two hundred years this symbol has served as a rhetorical instrument employed against the United States, put to use first in the eighteenth century to try to forestall emigration to the New World, then in the nineteenth century to defend the cause of monarchy and the old regime, and again early in this century to promote the ideologies of fascism and Communism. Of greatest concern today is the contemporary version of this symbol that is found in postmodernist thought and in the various fields of cultural studies emanating from it. This symbol was fashioned by a string of German thinkers at the beginning of this century—Max Weber, Oswald Spengler, and Ernst Jünger—that culminated in the writings of Martin Heidegger, whose "America" has since been disseminated throughout the world.

For Heidegger, and for postmodern thought thereafter, America has stood for technologism and, even more fundamentally, for the mode of thought that gives rise to and sustains technologism, which is, roughly speaking, Enlightenment or rationalist thought. Americanism, in this view, has the effect of suppressing authentic culture, indeed of suppressing all cultures in their particularity, and of subsuming everything into one vast, boundless mass. "Americanism," as Heidegger characterizes it, is the "primacy of sheer quantity, . . . the emerging monstrousness of modern times"; America is "the site of catastrophe" (*katastrophenhaft*). It represents homogenization, one-dimensional life, the effacement of difference—in short, Wonder Bread.[9]

America in postmodern thought has thus become the symbol for oppression. The struggle for liberation—among those, at any rate, still opting for engagement over bemusement—is a struggle *against* America. On the international scene, it is a struggle to save the world's diverse cultures from American imperialism and hegemony and to protect the mostly nonwhite "others" from, in Edward Said's description, a "heady mixture of [American] patriotism, relative solipsism, social authority, unchecked aggressiveness, and defensiveness."[10] On the domestic scene, it is a struggle to recover the muffled voices of the suppressed "others" (women, Native Americans, African Americans, gays, Hispanics) and to revalorize the diversity stifled by the homogenizing effect of America's fundamental principles. In difference or particularism lies our salvation! (Incidentally, in the terminology of the new discourse, "Americanism," "Eurocentrism," "logocentrism," and "humanism" are often used as synonyms.)

The politics of difference, or multiculturalism, has emerged today as the intellectuals' chief rallying cry, taking the place of the ideologies that previously dominated intellectual discourse. The politics of difference derives in the first instance, not from a reaction to the political world itself, but oddly enough from the realm of metaphysical speculation. According to Iris Marion Young, author of *Justice and the Politics of Difference,* the position favoring difference is based on a critique of Enlightenment thought made by Theodor Adorno and Jacques Derrida. This critique—forgive me the abstractions—holds that "reason" or the "logic of identity" reflects an "urge to think things together [and] to reduce them to unity." In the realm of thought, the "logic of identity denies or represses difference"—a statement that echoes the modern epigram of Adorno and Max Horkheimer, "The Enlightenment is totalitarian."[11]

Translating this metaphysical or epistemological difficulty to the political plane, we arrive at the deepest problem of our society: repression and the marginalization of difference. The logic of identity, which lays down a bland universalist standard, also has the effect of excluding all that does not fit its norms. "The irony of the logic of identity," writes Young, "is that by seeking to reduce the differently similar to the same, it turns the merely different into the absolutely other." So here it is: America is repression, and the rationalism of those called our "republican fathers" has produced the various isms of subjugation endemic to our system, such as sexism and racism.[12]

Abstractions at this level, although they may be able to excite the passions of a few of the philosophically minded, are clearly too bloodless to move most intellectuals and professors, not to mention their followers. To establish America as a symbol of repression requires a more concrete discourse. Here is where the drones in the fields of American studies and American history must step in to feed the queen bees of philosophy and literary criticism. Their task, in the words of the historian Joyce Appleby, is to fashion a new "narrative" of America that is "faithful to the premises and methods of multicultural history." If the old narrative taught that the fundamental principles of liberty and natural rights were antidotes to oppression and that slavery, racism, and unequal treatment derived from other elements of the American experience, the new narrative must teach that America's fundamental principles are inseparable from oppression and racism. The new narrative will help us to see the "oppression exercised by [our] omnipresent cultural model" and enable us to understand how the founding principles are "America's peculiar form of Eurocentrism." From this perspective, the American founding becomes, if not a retrograde event, then at any rate a stage to be overcome in the quest for a higher "politics of difference," and those who rely on its political science are dismissed as proponents of an outmoded "founderism."[13]

A third reason for the political scientist to be concerned with symbolic discourse about America is that these discussions carry a political message, even when—or, I am tempted to say, especially when—they appear in a "cultural" form. Attacks on American culture are never as innocent as they seem. Whether one is aware of it or not, the object of the attack is the whole way of life of liberal democracy and its supporting principles. When the French poet Charles Baudelaire described America in 1857 as a "great hunk of barbarism illuminated by gas," his criticism was not just of American culture—as if a culture in any case can easily be disconnected from its political system—but of the vulgarity intrinsic to a commercially minded democracy. The originator of this critique whom Baudelaire cites is Joseph de Maistre, an early opponent of liberal democracy who launched one of the most influential assaults on rationalism and the political science employed by America's founders.[14]

The connection between politics and culture in America discourse was forged in the political and philosophical debates over the French Revolution. On the Left, defenders of the French Revolution sought to distinguish it from the American Revolution, which they argued was grounded on the principle of interest and on a defective understanding of modern thought. Given this flawed foundation, America must inevitably spawn a low, or inauthentic, form of politics and culture. On the Right, the conservatives opposing the French Revolution chose to view the American and French Revolutions as twin embodiments of modern rationalist thought, but America posed a special problem for these thinkers because it seemed to belie their claim, so clearly confirmed in the case of France, that no orderly and successful society could be based on reason and liberal democracy. From this embarrassment came the cultural-political attack on the United States: if America was not anarchic, it was at any rate banal. It had no art, no taste, no depth. Nothing built on the shaky ground of reason and rights could ever support an impressive cultural edifice.

Anyone who studies the history of America discourse must be impressed by the fact that, for two centuries now, Left and Right have expressed essentially the same criticisms of American culture. It is true that there have been notable differences in their diagnoses of the cause of the problem and important divergences in their prescriptions for reform. But in the central belief in the consummate vulgarity of

11

American life, Left and Right have stood steadfastly together. The symbolic America has fit the interests of both parties and has served on occasion as a common ground on which they have come together to forge their unholy alliances.

Today, in the time of the collapse of fascism and Communism in Europe (at least in their strong forms), it is more difficult to connect cultural critiques of America to a full-blown, revolutionary alternative to liberal democracy. Most contemporary critics of America profess to being democrats of some type seeking only a transformation of democracy from within, although the "only" of such transformations usually turns out to be something quite different from a liberal regime. But a few hardy souls are still willing to avow their hostile intentions. There is a new Right devoted to an intense nationalism (including racism) that despises the tolerance and openness of America's liberal principles. And there is a hard Left that is not content with merely a ritual slaying of the West, as found in American academic battles to remove courses in Western civilization from the core curricula of colleges and universities, but wants to see a real destruction of the Enlightenment rationalist project and "liberal democratic integrism," with America at its center.[15]

The reader may wonder at my speaking here of the connection between America and liberal democracy as part of "symbolic" discourse. Obviously, liberal democracy and natural rights are not ideas that foreign intellectuals have foisted on us but rather the proudest accomplishments of America's founders. In John Adams' expressive phrase, "We began the dance."[16] Originating liberal democracy is thus a claim Americans ought to be able to assert without difficulty, assuming they are willing to endure the obloquy that comes with it. Oddly enough, however, I have found from visiting American studies conferences that hazarding this claim, even in a context in which the creation of liberal democracy is presented as an achievement, is certain to provoke a hostile reaction. It is immediately charged that such an assertion bespeaks an arrogance bordering on insensitivity, that liberal democracy was probably begun somewhere else (perhaps among the Iroquois nation), or that the American founding, by permitting slavery and excluding women from full participation, can hardly be said to have initiated genuine modern democratic government. Yet the moment one shifts to a contemporary discussion of liberal democracy, in which liberalism is associated with its familiar repressive attributes of capitalism and logocentrism, the very opposite argument about America is heard, often from the same persons who raised the previous objections. Now the American origin of liberalism is not only admitted but insisted upon, and the republican fathers are forced to don the soiled mantle of defenders of "reason." Such displays of inconsistency, in which scholars first deny and then affirm the same point according to whether the response promotes the ideas associated with the symbolic America, show just how thoroughly the custodians of American culture have become ensnared in a discourse that has robbed them of their independence and good sense.

The final reason for the political scientist to be concerned with the symbolic America is of a more theoretical nature than the other three, but it is certainly no less important. For the duration of the life of this symbol, proponents of different intellectual disciplines have waged a battle for control over which body of knowledge would guide political life. America discourse has been instrumental to efforts to remove political science from a central position and to replace it with a rival discipline: first "natural history" (biology), then a deductive or abstract modern social science, then history, then aesthetics, and finally, today, postmetaphysical philosophy and literary and cultural criticism. The last effort has by now gone a long way toward being accomplished. One of America's leading philosophers turned literary critics has noted the "rise of literary criticism to preeminence within the high culture of the democracies" and of its place "as the presiding intellectual discipline." Ours, he tells us, is the age of "strong" poets, "strong" literary critics, and, I suppose, "strong" historians as well. Everyone has her narrative.[17]

Under the new model for the relation of knowledge to political life, the disciplines that embody a political or politico-cultural strategy—and they are not reluctant to admit it—are the various literary fields. Meanwhile, much of the academic discipline that goes by the name of political science rests content with a positivistic detachment and a newfound aesthetic delight in devising "elegant" mathematical models. We live increasingly in an academic environment in which the aesthetic disciplines are political and the political disciplines are aesthetic. No wonder contemporary political science is treated with such contempt by the more powerful literary critics—when, that is, they even bother to notice it.

No sensible person would ordinarily pause to worry over an academic turf war, the objectives of which are usually office space, research funds, and salaries. Yet in this case the issues at stake have important consequences for which body of knowledge will be listened to and how that knowledge will influence political life. The ascendancy of the cultural disciplines is based on a view of reality that excludes political things from the realm of primary phenomena. Political activity is seen as deriving from some other, more fundamental source, be it the movement of History or the mysterious emanations of Being. Politics is controlled by the reality of one of these realms, and political life is merely the stage on which a deeper drama plays itself out. Not only does this way of thinking represent a loss of dignity for political life, but it also suggests that the knowledge that should govern politics is inaccessible to those engaged in ordinary political activity. For all the claims being made today about the modesty of philosophy, the face of an imperious intellectual despotism seems to be lurking just beneath the surface.

By showing that America discourse has elevated cultural and literary criticism to a commanding intellectual role in the political world, I hope to persuade those who study political science today—they need not be members of the profession—to reclaim for political phenomena an autonomous place in our understanding of the world. I hope to enlist them in the task of rethinking the purpose of political science and of considering the discipline, as it once was considered, as an active force in human affairs. I hope to reawaken their sense of responsibility by reminding them that a healthy civil order relies on a certain relation between knowledge and political life in which political science helps to guide political action. Literary criticism and ironist philosophy, I am afraid, will simply not do. Until literary critics become political scientists or political scientists become literary critics, there can be no rest from the ills that trouble the university or the polity.

Political science is not a mere literary device that I have conjured up for my own purposes. It is the name that the founders of the real America used to identify the discipline that they consulted to guide politics. In their time the founders had already begun to distinguish political science from the hard scientific disciplines (both biological and mathematical) and from certain new philosophical and literary disciplines.[18] Political science did not make common cause with these disciplines but insisted on its own method and approach. However much modern rationalism may be held responsible for promoting homogenization in the realm of ideas—I leave this issue for the philosophers to debate—political science cannot be pronounced guilty of the crime. On the contrary, it aimed to carve out a place inside of rationalism to correct certain dangerous tendencies of universalism and to accommodate differences, all within a framework of a common human nature.

America's experience is bound up with political science to a degree that surpasses that of any other nation. The government was established with the assistance of political science, and America's founders can claim credit for reintroducing it as a practical force in the world for the first time since antiquity. Not modern medicine, not modern telecommunications, but the revival of political science has been America's greatest contribution to modern thought. This was the reason that the founders wanted foreign intellectuals and statesmen to learn English: "The great improvements America has made and will make in the science of government will induce the patriots and literati of every nation to read and understand our writings on that subject, . . . and [we] will take the lead in political knowledge."[19] No wonder, then, that political science has been a target of America discourse. Attacked from all sides, political science has barely managed to survive in this, its "home," country. In seeking to free the real America from the symbolic America, I am also hoping to restore political science to its rightful place in our way of thinking. The two objectives are parts of the same enterprise.

It is inevitable in this Introduction, where I am forced to speak in generalities, that I should be misunderstood on a few points, perhaps in ways that will cause others to take offense. Anticipating a number of these objections, I would like to offer some explanations. To begin with, I admit that today there is a clear problem in using "America" to refer exclusively to the United States. The word, strictly speaking, designates the entire landmass of the New World, which comprises North, Central, and South Americas as well as the Caribbean islands. Octavio Paz is therefore correct to say that "the United States of America is an abuse of language."[20] This abuse became a matter of controversy at the time of the commemoration (some insisted on the term "remembrance") of the five-hundredth anniversary of Christopher Columbus' discovery (some said "invasion") of the New World. The war of words extended to the term "America" itself, with many declaring that its appropriation by the predominantly white and Anglo-American population of the United States reflected a Eurocentric bias against marginalized groups and aboriginal peoples.

Some who advanced this argument were no doubt merely engaging in polemics, availing themselves of today's standard intellectual practice of seeking out any occasion to take offense. It seems disingenuous, after all, to make "America" a term coveted by native peoples when it is one imposed by European conquerors. And before anyone becomes too enamored of the term, it ought to be recalled that its origin involved a theft of credit by Amerigo Vespucci at the expense of Christopher Columbus—a crime, according to the eighteenth-century philosopher abbé Thomas Raynal, that was a "presage that America was to be the theater of future acts of injustice."[21] Finally, of all the nations and tribes of the New World, only the United States of America has elected to put "America" in its official name, a consideration that perhaps argues in favor of giving it some special proprietary claim to the word.

While these responses mitigate the charge of bad intentions, they cannot excuse the injustice. "America" by right should refer to the whole of the Americas, not to just one part of it. Yet I have been obliged by the subject matter of this book to set aside my scruples on this point, because those who created the symbolic America imputed almost all the attributes of Americanism and Americanization to the liberal democratic and advanced capitalist system developed in the United States.

On this score, however, there may be some grounds for satisfaction. None of those who have protested the linguistic appropriation of America wish to claim any of America's symbolic attributes for their own country or peoples; these they are more than happy to see attached exclusively to the United States.

On a different matter, some may object that I have unduly emphasized thinkers who express negative views of America. I acknowledge that many, perhaps even most, foreign writers who treat America have spoken favorably of this nation and have added to its image as a land of bountiful resources, unlimited promise, and unprecedented freedom. Especially at the time of the Revolution, democrats from one corner of Europe to the other sang America's praises. I could cite scores of laudatory comments, and not just from the late eighteenth century, when Goethe declared, "Amerika, du hast es besser / Als unser Kontinent, das alte" (America, you have it better than our old continent). I could point also to admiring remarks from the nineteenth century, when Richard Wagner pledged to perform his great operatic work, the *Ring*, "only on the banks of the Mississippi," and even from the twentieth century, when Sergey Rachmaninoff remarked, with compliments to Walt Disney, "I have heard my Prelude in C-Sharp Minor done marvelously by some of the best pianists, . . . but never was I more stirred than by the performance of the great Maestro Mouse."[22]

Yet all this said, it remains true that for the major thinkers who have made America an object of sustained attention or reflection, few have viewed America in a positive light.[23] What is more, in the case of the most notable exception—Alexis de Tocqueville—it is clear that he shared the American founders' concern for political science and regarded the symbolic America of his day as an attack on liberal democracy. There is a sound lesson here. When it comes to protecting political science and freedom, it is not the country that matters but the cause that is being defended. The true friend of democracy is not the flatterer but the one prepared to question and when necessary criticize its most cherished dogmas. For all the loud opposition to America today, few contemporary critics have gone nearly as far as the founders or Tocqueville in warning of certain dangers and excesses in equality and democracy. I therefore enlist any person—African, Asian, European, South American, Australian, or Antarctican—who would join an American in this enterprise.

Still others will object that, by seeking to free the real from the symbolic America, I am intending a whitewash of the real America. Even my language here may give cause for alarm in some quarters, for in the eyes of the dominant philosophical school, known as anti-essentialism or pragmatism, to use the term "real" is almost a provocation. The word implies that a thing has genuine being, while other things, not so qualified, do not; it thus illicitly privileges an object by connecting it to a putatively higher level of reality, which of course does not exist. Any implication I may have given on this account is inadvertent. Not being a teacher of philosophy, I can perhaps be permitted the latitude of using "real" in its ordinary sense to refer to what the average person has in mind when talking about a country—that is, the physical place organized under a certain form of government. And I can see no good reason why this meaning should provoke a quarrel with genuine pragmatism. In seeking to distinguish the real from the metaphysical America, I am only trying to eliminate the conceptual "reifications" that pragmatists once deplored and to follow John Dewey in attempting to "emancipat[e] mankind . . . from the errors which philosophy itself has fostered."[24]

A whitewash of America is in any case the furthest thing from my mind. The thinkers who developed the symbolic America offered some of the deepest reflections on the problems of modern times, and as a participant in modernity, the United States shares in these problems. Although one may mistrust the messenger, there is wisdom in one of founderism's most reliable maxims: "The prudent inquiry in all cases ought surely to be not so much from whom the advice comes as whether or not the advice be good."[25]

But there still remain grounds for caution, for much of the advice in America discourse that appears to be political does not proceed from a political analysis. What people call "modernity" or "postmodernity," important as it is, makes up only the historical circumstance or condition of our times, not the entirety of a political regime. To focus on a historical circumstance and ignore the realm of political choice is to reduce politics to the subpolitical, even if the subpolitical happens to go by the lofty name of intellectual history. Also, America discourse is often used as little more than a front for carrying on a theoretical discussion about modernity and the Enlightenment. "Descriptions" of America are not inductions from an examination of the real country but deductions from the premises of these philosophical positions. Here it is fair to ask, Are there not enough problems confronting the real America today without this nation being required to bear all the weight of these philosophic and literary disputes? Let the philosophers and literary critics cease trying to subsume all political phenomena to questions of metaphysics. Let them fight their battles on their own terrain, without holding captive the fate of a nation.

Finally, some will surely be dismayed at my tone, which they may find too strident. By way of justification, I could point out that displays of indignation at America's mistreatment by European thinkers represent the classic American posture of another age. So it was, for example, that Thomas Jefferson denounced the "wretched philosophy" of Europeans that belittled all American achievements, or that Alexander Hamilton bridled at the "arrogant pretensions of the European" who thought all things American to be degenerate.[26] Admittedly, times change, and a style of rhetoric appropriate to one situation may be ridiculous in another. Two hundred years ago, Europe stood at the center of the world in physical power and intellectual sophistication, whereas America was at the periphery. Now it is America that has the world's most powerful military and can boast of possessing some of the most prestigious universities. In this situation, the temptation is to ignore perceived slights. Complacency, however, is exactly what we do not need. Despite our power and prestige—or, rather, because of them—we risk missing the obvious. In the presiding intellectual disciplines of literary criticism and ironist philosophy, too many of our thinkers still play the part of good colonials, obsequiously bowing and scraping before their fashionable Continental masters. It is a lamentable spectacle to see so many of our best minds rushing to deconstruct all things American while failing to turn that method on those who gave them their marching orders.

If anything, then, the tone I have adopted may be too restrained. The theme of America discourse in the twentieth century is that the United States must, in one of those nice philosophical euphemisms, be "overcome." Thinkers once tended to express this idea in a belligerent or manly fashion, openly calling for this country's destruction. The contemporary practice favors purveying this message in the smug voice of irony, which is evidently the accepted manner in which the sophisticated now display their aggression. But the intent—to overcome—remains the same. As one side would make war rather than let America survive, so the other must accept war rather than let it perish.

1

★ ★ ★

America as Degeneracy

I was anxious to see the great men of Europe; for I read in works of various philosophers that all animals degenerated in America, and man among the number. . . . I will visit this land of wonders [Europe], thought I, and see the gigantic race from which I am degenerated. —Washington Irving

When America was founded—I am speaking here of the symbolic America— it rested on one of the most fantastic theories that the mind of man has ever conceived: the thesis of American degeneracy. This thesis, which dominated advanced scientific thinking in Europe during the second half of the eighteenth century, had two major components. First, it held that animals in America were inferior in variety, strength, and beauty to those found in Europe. This inferiority was no less true of the human species: the American Indian was a lesser being than the European or, for that matter, the Asian or the African. Second, it contended that everything that was transported from the Old World to the New—from plants to animals and again to humans—became stunted and lost its vigor. No sooner did Europeans set foot on American soil than they began a gradual decline—physical, intellectual, and moral.

The degeneracy thesis belongs technically to the period of the prehistory of the symbolic America, when "America" still referred to the whole of the New World. Even so, the tangible political stakes involved in this thesis were enormous, particularly for the United States. Promulgated on the eve of the American Revolution, the thesis left America's founders with little choice but to regard it as an attack on the new nation itself. American statesmen, who were then seeking diplomatic recognition and financial support from some of the European nations, could not allow the acceptance of a view that everything in this land was destined by nature to decline. After all, who would be willing to invest in such an enterprise?[1] Out of concern for policy as much as for truth, Benjamin Franklin, Thomas

Jefferson, and John Adams—all ambassadors in Europe during this period—waged a battle against the degeneracy thesis, a battle in which they were soon joined by the authors of *The Federalist.*

The degeneracy thesis was offered under the authority of "science" or "philosophy." In the late eighteenth century these two terms were used interchangeably to designate a mode of rational inquiry that sought to discover natural causes for natural effects. The degeneracy thesis was meant to correct certain nonphilosophic and literary views of America then circulating in Europe. These views, alternating between images of America as a "lovely garden and site for a new Golden Age" and a "hideous and desolate wilderness," had been drawn from accounts of early voyagers and then embellished by poets and other writers.[2] In contrast, proponents of the degeneracy thesis claimed to be relying on the most sophisticated techniques of data collection and the most rigorous methods of science. Degeneracy studies represented the cutting edge of research.

The theory underlying degeneracy was at the foundation of the first modern or positivistic social science—anthropology. The originator of anthropology was Georges Louis Leclerc, the Count de Buffon, who first propounded the degeneracy thesis. Buffon is well known to students of American political thought as Jefferson's chief antagonist in his *Notes on the State of Virginia.* Jefferson targeted Buffon because he was simply too large a figure to ignore; he was "the best informed naturalist who has ever written."[3] By a naturalist or student of natural history, Jefferson meant one who studied not merely subhuman phenomena but all living things, human beings included. Natural history was the name Buffon gave to his new science, the aims of which were to ascertain the factors that produce a species' unity (for example, what makes a horse a horse) and to discern the causes of a species' variation (why there are different types or varieties of horses). Buffon extended this inquiry to the study of man, thereby creating the field that shortly became known as ethnology or anthropology.[4] Buffon described man's common features and then turned to consider, to quote the title of one of his most famous chapters, "The Varieties of the Human Species." To do so he divided mankind into its different subgroups, using color or race as the initial criterion for the classification of difference. Anthropology accordingly began in conjunction with the thesis of American degeneracy (and Eurocentrism) and with the use of racialist categories as the basis for classifying the varieties of the human species. America discourse in European thought has ever since been bound up with the question of color, race, and ethnicity.

Others who promoted the degeneracy thesis at the time included the celebrated Encyclopedist abbé Raynal, author of *Histoire philosophique et politique des établissements et du commerce des Européens dans les deux Indes* (1770); the Scottish historian William Robertson, author of *The History of America* (1777); and the now forgotten abbé Cornelius de Pauw. Of these, de Pauw is for our purposes the most important, as he literally and figuratively wrote the book on America: *Recherches philosophiques sur les Américains,* a three-volume opus published in 1768.[5] This work, unlike Buffon's, focused almost entirely on America and discussed at length the political implications of natural history for the New World policy of European states. De Pauw was also more audacious than Buffon in articulating the degeneracy thesis, applying it without qualifications to the deterioration of European emigrants to America. De Pauw became so closely associated with the degeneracy thesis that he was often wrongly identified as its originator; John Adams, for example, once commented that "Jefferson exposed the mistakes of Buffon, so unphilosophically borrowed from the despicable dreams of de Pau."[6]

The degeneracy thesis did not go unchallenged at the time. It provoked what became known as the "dispute of the New World," in which scholars from Europe and America debated whether the discovery of the New World should be counted a benefit or a disaster to mankind.[7] The Americans answered the degeneracy thesis in two ways. One response was to question the empirical facts on which it rested, amassing a body of data that to any impartial observer refuted important parts of the thesis. This approach, employed by Franklin and Jefferson, had considerable success, although the original impression would linger in the European mind for a long time. But Jefferson's response, while answering the specific allegations of the degeneracy thesis, also took the fateful step of embracing the basic approach of natural history in the study of human affairs. In so doing Jefferson inaugurated an American school of ethnology that made racialism its central category in the analysis of politics and society.

The other response to the degeneracy thesis was adopted by the authors of *The Federalist* ("Publius"), who rejected the application of natural history to political life. Whatever might be the value of natural history for understanding the domain of plants and animals, *The Federalist* insisted that its categories of analysis and models of causality were inappropriate to the understanding of human beings and society. In its view, the most important influences on humanity's development are moral and political, not climatic and racial. People are shaped by their laws, their culture, and the political regime under which they live. The regime is caused by a series of political factors which include a human capacity to make governments "from reflection and choice."[8] In this task, political science, not natural history, provides the most helpful kind of knowledge. At the center of the debate over the degeneracy thesis, accordingly, was a struggle over what form of knowledge should guide political life: either the new social science based on natural history or political science. In this struggle, Publius was at odds not only with the European scientists of his day but also, in one of the most important conflicts of American thought in the late eighteenth century, with Thomas Jefferson.

As with any theory in the history of science, the degeneracy thesis won adherents in Europe because of the interests it appeared to serve. Its proclamation of the superiority of *Homo sapiens Europaeus* (Jefferson's term) represented the quintessential expression of Eurocentrism and was, as Publius points out, at the heart of the whole colonial mind-set: "The superiority she [Europe] has long maintained has tempted her to plume herself as the mistress of the world and to consider the rest of mankind as created for her benefit."[9] Given its connection to this political position, the degeneracy thesis seems to lend support to the position of the sociological school of historians who argue that scientific theories, far from being objective accounts of reality, are often ideological reflections that reinforce power relations in society. Yet even in this admittedly extreme case, the argument that things degenerated in America, while it was certainly affected by political considerations, had an independent theoretical life and was debated in part on philosophical grounds. Certain consequences of this idea, in the form of a reductionist approach to politics, remain with us to this day.

Cornelius de Pauw

Some of the most polite Europeans who visit the United States cast an incredulous eye on what is presented to them under the guise of coffee. The source of this peculiar prejudice can be traced to Cornelius de Pauw, who more than two hundred years ago declared the coffee beans of America to be of an "inferior quality to those of Yemen, Java, and even of Bourbon," so much so that the "rich people of Europe" would not deign to drink it. Much the same was said of American sugar, which de Pauw insisted was less sweet than that found elsewhere, and of course American wine, which he claimed came from shriveled, insect-ridden grapes.[10]

Cornelius de Pauw makes his most important appearance in American literature in the eleventh essay of *The Federalist,* wherein Publius (Alexander Hamilton) introduces and then responds to the degeneracy thesis. The passage in question, surely the most curious of the entire work, begins: "Men admired as profound philosophers have in direct terms attributed to her [Europe's] inhabitants a physical superiority and have gravely asserted that all animals, and with them the human species, degenerate in America—that even dogs cease to bark after having breathed awhile in our atmosphere." The "profound philosophers" Hamilton had in mind no doubt included the likes of the Count de Buffon and the abbé Raynal, but the specific work he cites is de Pauw's *Recherches philosophiques sur les Américains*.

Who was Cornelius de Pauw? Today, I suppose, de Pauw may be said to enjoy an obscurity altogether warranted by the quality of his work and the level of his talents. But his limitations were apparently not so evident to the intellectual world of the late eighteenth century, when his thesis on American degeneracy placed him momentarily at the center of attention in Europe. As one American historian has aptly observed, "History offers many examples of individuals who have occupied the center stage during their life-time, only to be forgotten by posterity; but in modern times few writers have risen so high, and then sunk so completely out of sight, as did the abbé Corneille de Pauw."[11]

De Pauw wrote a number of books besides his three-volume opus on America. They constitute a kind of series, all beginning with the phrase *Recherches philosophiques sur . . .* (*A Scientific Inquiry on . . .*). The other books are *A Scientific Inquiry on the Egyptians and Chinese* (1773), which earned de Pauw the notoriety of a public rebuke from Voltaire, and *A Scientific Inquiry on the Greeks* (1787). De Pauw wrote a final work, entitled *A Scientific Inquiry on the Germans,* which for some unknown reason he committed to flames just before his death in 1799. It was clearly de Pauw's book on America, however, that earned him his greatest renown. On its strength de Pauw was invited by Frederick the Great to serve as a personal reader at his court. (As was Frederick's wont with intellectuals, however, he soon tired of de Pauw and dismissed him—a fate that would shortly befall even the great Voltaire.) De Pauw's book was immediately translated into German and Dutch, and it quickly came to be considered the authoritative work on America. De Pauw was later asked to contribute two articles on America to the *Supplément de l'Encyclopédie.* His impact on the idea of America continued to be felt throughout the period. Biographical sources indicate an important influence on Kant (who developed some of de Pauw's ideas in his anthropological writings) and probably Hegel as well.[12]

Of de Pauw's personal life, little is known. He was of Dutch birth and a Roman Catholic, although hostile to the Jesuit order. He spent most of his adult life as a churchman at Xanten, except for his few forays to Berlin. To an American, the name de Pauw calls up that of DePauw University. According to a noted nineteenth-century historian of (and from) that university, John Clark Ridpath, the association is more than a coincidence. A major benefactor of that university was

Washington Charles De Pauw, a wealthy Indiana manufacturer who in Ridpath's account was the grandson of Cornelius. But quite apart from the indelicacy of an abbé fathering children, this genealogy is false: I have been reliably informed by a modern historian from DePauw University, John J. Baughman, that Cornelius left no physical legacy to degenerate on this continent.[13]

De Pauw's book was the fruit of a decade of research and drew on much of the existing literature on America. De Pauw claimed, however, to be making a new beginning in American studies by adopting a scrupulously scientific approach: "[I] never have given into my own prejudices or conjectures at the expense of the truth of the facts, for which I believe I have glimpsed the causes and principles in nature itself, and not in my own ideas." Yet a scientific approach for de Pauw, although it required one to "cite proofs, avoid declamations, . . . and be moderate," did not necessitate intellectual timidity, as the opening of his book amply attests: "It is," he observes, "a great and terrible spectacle to see one half of the globe so disfavored by nature that everything found there is degenerate, or monstrous."[14]

Surveying the animals of America, de Pauw notes that they are "for the most part inelegantly shaped and often so badly deformed that the first illustrators could scarcely grasp their shape." Many species lack tails, whereas others, notably the tapir and the anteater, exhibit an unseemly disproportion between the number of digits on their front feet and those on their back feet. De Pauw concedes that, for certain of the lower species found on both continents, the advantage lies on the American side: "The surface of the earth, covered with rot, is inundated by lizards, by snakes, and by reptiles and insects monstrous in their size and in the strength of their poison." De Pauw also lends credence to a report of a French explorer who described frogs in Louisiana that "weigh up to thirty-seven pounds and bellow like [European] calves." The source for this report was Louis Dumont's *Mémoires sur la Louisiane*. Although Dumont never lists a specific weight for the frog, de Pauw's overall characterization is accurate. For the sake of completeness, however, I should add that Dumont follows up his remark about the size of the frogs with a gastronomic evaluation: "They are excellent, and one can eat not only the legs but the entire body."[15] (I will later return to the fascination, not to say obsession, of European writers with the frogs of the New World.)

The principal cause de Pauw cites to explain the fecundity of the lower species and the stuntedness of the higher ones in America is the climate. The New World is more humid and damp than the Old. In certain zones in America, the earth is "covered with degraded water, unhealthy and often poisonous," while in others the forests and the mountains that trap clouds create "lakes and stagnant waters" and make the adjacent land "wet and filled with peat." All around, things on the earth are decomposing, giving off "vapors . . . extremely harmful to those who are not accustomed to them." These insalubrious vapors affected not only the higher forms of animals but also the indigenous humans. De Pauw dismissed as pure fantasy the idealized notion of the Indian as noble savage, which he believed was an invention of authors having the political purpose of promoting the colonial project. The real Indian, according to de Pauw, is a degenerated being: "Nature has peopled America with children, out of whom it is impossible to make men. . . . Even today, after three hundred years (since the Europeans arrived), not one of them can think. Their fundamental characteristic is stupid insensibility. Their laziness prevents them from learning anything. No passion can stir their soul. They have neither intelligence nor perfectibility." Notwithstanding their weakness, the Indians have wrought incalculable harm on the Europeans. From the Indian has come the scourge of syphilis, which has planted "the germs of death in the arms of pleasure." The stuntedness and deformity of American humans and animals thus point up an even more ominous characteristic of the New World: it is diseased. The human species can scarcely manage to reproduce. "America was the least populated region of the world."[16]

De Pauw does not stop with the assertion of a deformation of indigenous things but takes the logical next step. Since all phenomena are subject to the same natural causes, transported animals must suffer degeneration as well: "The animals of European and Asian origin that had been transplanted to America immediately after its discovery have become stunted: their size diminished and they lost a part of their instinct or of their capacity." Alexander Hamilton's canine reference, far from being an ironic invention, turns out also to be a bona fide scholarly citation. De Pauw writes, "It is known that dogs taken from our countries lose their voice and cease to bark in the majority of regions of the New continent." As with a few other of de Pauw's claims, his evidence was less then conclusive. De Pauw's source here was no doubt Christopher Columbus, who complained of the silencing effect of the New World on some European dogs. Yet insofar as there was any veracity to this claim, the cause could be traced not to the air but to behavior learned from the dogs of the Americas. American dogs, according to a recent scholarly investigation of this question, "did not bark like European dogs," although they were not *perros mudos,* or mute dogs; they could "yowl, grunt, and make other guttural sounds."[17]

De Pauw allowed certain exceptions to this general law of degeneration. Of the animals brought to America, at least one had fared better here than in Europe: the pig. Pigs "have acquired an astonishing bulk in America, because they thrive in a uliginous land, abundant in aquatic fruits, insects, and reptiles." Unfortunately for the European immigrant, the human being has not done so well. Not only is it the case that "native Americans are a race of degenerate men, . . . [but] the Europeans who came to live in America likewise degenerate." The effects of this process can be observed first in a lower rate of reproduction among Europeans in America: "The climate of the New World contains a secret vice that up until now opposes the augmentation of the human species. . . . The women of Europe become infertile in America far sooner than in their native countries."[18] America's inability to replenish its own population meant that the New World must remain dependent on Europe—a matter of growing concern for the German states that were losing population through emigration.

A further sign of the Euro-American's degeneracy appeared in his diminished physical capacity. De Pauw cites a book just off the press in Paris: *Histoire naturelle et politique de la Pensilvanie,* written by "the two acclaimed naturalists Bertrand and Calm" (John Bertram and the Swedish botanist Peter Kalm). These authors argue that during the French and Indian War the Euro-Americans proved inferior in strength, stamina, and ability to the Europeans and thus suffered much higher casualty rates than had their opponents: "In North America Europeans noticeably degenerate, and their physical constitution changes as the generations propagate." De Pauw then goes on to discuss the intellectual degeneration of the Euro-American: "In all of America, from Cape Horn to the Hudson Bay, there has never appeared a philosopher, a scholar, an artist, or a thinker whose name merits being included in the history of science or who has served humanity." He bases this claim at least in part on observations of the products of American education, which even then, evidently, was in crisis: "When very young, the Creoles learn readily, but once they have passed out of childhood they become more stupid than Europeans. The Academy of Saint Mark, the most celebrated school in America, has produced no one who could write even a bad book. The Jesuits . . . have not turned out a single great teacher, philosopher, physician, scientist or scholar whose fame has spread to Europe." De Pauw's charge of Americans' intellectual inferiority was given wider currency two years later, when it was echoed (copied, actually) by the abbé Raynal: "America has not yet produced a good poet, an able mathematician, one man of genius in a single art or a single science."[19] Without mentioning de Pauw, of whom he may then have been unaware, Jefferson cites Raynal's assertion in his *Notes* and spends pages indignantly refuting the famous Frenchman's conclusion.[20]

In a later article on America written for the *Supplément de l'Encyclopédie,* de Pauw continued the argument, concentrating much of his attention and criticism specifically on the United States. This focus is noteworthy because Buffon and

Raynal—accommodating themselves, no doubt, to Franklin's arguments—had modified their views to exempt Euro-Americans in the English colonies from degeneracy. De Pauw, however, remained adamant. Going beyond his initial theory of finding causality in climatic conditions, he linked intellectual degeneration in the United States to its culture and civilization. He dismissed reports of the merits of the "University of Cambridge in New England"—he must have meant Harvard—in terms worthy of the most partisan Yale graduate: "Could we really expect any such achievement from a handful of merchants and adventurers guided by a rapacious avarice in all of their actions? Alas, we doubt it very much."[21]

The Count de Buffon

Then as now, Georges Louis Leclerc, the Count de Buffon (1707–1788), was more famous than Cornelius de Pauw. Buffon had begun his life's work by 1749, when the first volume of his *Natural History* was published. Thirty-nine years and forty-three volumes later, he completed (with the assistance of a team of collaborators, including Louis Daubenton) his magnum opus, which dominated the field of animal natural history until it was replaced by Darwin's paradigm at the end of the nineteenth century. Buffon is generally considered the greatest biologist of the eighteenth century. Ernst Cassirer, for example, credits Buffon with having "established a new type of natural science and . . . [having] presented a companion-piece to Newton's *Mathematical Principles of Natural Philosophy*."[22]

Not only does the prodigious scope of Buffon's work make it a formidable challenge, but there is also the difficulty that he continually rewrote his books along the way, adding to and modifying earlier views in subsequent editions. Thus, while Buffon inspired de Pauw's work, we later find him (in 1777) questioning parts of the degeneracy thesis and criticizing de Pauw for his extremism.[23] Buffon had been persuaded to modify his views on America in part, it seems, by the evidence supplied to him by Franklin and Jefferson. That evidence came from their written works and from the steady stream of skins, bones, and sundry other animal parts that Jefferson sent to the great naturalist.[24]

Buffon was clearly a much larger figure in the development of science than Cornelius de Pauw. In describing Buffon in this way, one probably needs in the context of a discussion of natural history to pay attention to the physical as well as the figurative aspects of this portrait. Not to indulge too much in idle gossip, but it was widely rumored that Buffon took an inordinate pride in his personal appearance and carriage. David Hume once remarked that "it seemed as though the greater stature with which he himself had been endowed by nature made it difficult for

Wilder Learning Resource Center
Northeast Iowa Community College
Calmar, Iowa 52132

him to lower himself to the study of smaller things." Indeed, Buffon's view of nature is predicated on a hierarchy in which the larger animals occupy a decidedly higher rank than smaller ones. It was as if he held that greatness, nobility, and intelligence were stamped in nature in size and stature. For this reason, Buffon expressed the greatest admiration for the elephant, and he wrote many fine passages that evidence his esteem for that animal: "If the human species be excepted, the elephant is the most respected animal in the world." For the same reason, Buffon had little time for the insects and considered the study of them to be beneath the naturalist's dignity. Certainly, Buffon was not unimpressed with his own prowess, physical or intellectual. As his five most revered authors, he listed Newton, Bacon, Leibniz, Montesquieu, and himself.[25]

The issue of physical stature surfaced in this period in an amusing incident involving Benjamin Franklin and Buffon's disciple, the abbé Raynal. (Both Franklin and Jefferson used Raynal as the object of their most severe criticisms, thinking it prudent not to confront directly the more illustrious Buffon.) As Jefferson recounts the story, at a dinner Franklin hosted outside of Paris, Raynal "got on his favorite theory of the degeneracy of animals and even man, in America." Franklin thereupon asked his American and French guests to rise in order "to see on which side nature has degenerated." The six Americans, it so happened, were of the "finest stature and form; while those on the other side were remarkably diminutive, and the Abbé himself, was a mere shrimp." This story was embellished as time went on. In John Bristed's *Resources of the United States* (1818), which contains a spirited attack on the degeneracy thesis that begins to border on Amerocentrism, the Americans become "well-proportioned, tall, handsome," whereas the French degenerate to "little, lank, yellow, shrivelled personages, resembling java monkeys."[26]

Buffon had articulated the major elements of the degeneracy thesis before de Pauw, albeit in a more elevated style. In passages Jefferson cites, Buffon contends that "in this New World, there is some combination of elements and physical causes, something that opposes the amplification of animated Nature." Animals "shrink and diminish under a niggardly sky and an unprolific land." Indeed, "all the animals that have been transported from Europe to America . . . have become smaller, . . . and those which were not transported [and] which are common to both Continents . . . are also considerably less than those of Europe."[27]

Nor was Buffon much kinder to the Indian, whom he initially characterized as "a kind of weak automaton incapable of improving or seconding (Nature's) intentions." Although he would later introduce greater differentiation among the different peoples and tribes of the New World, his early summary is worth citing:

"Though each nation has peculiar customs and manners, though some are more savage, cruel, and dastardly than others, yet they are all equally stupid, ignorant and destitute of arts and industry." Buffon also discoursed at some length on the sexual prowess of the Indian, as this particular factor was an indicator—and in a sense an immediate cause—of the degree of civilization. The Indian males have "been refused the most precious spark of Nature's fire. They have no love of women." This "indifference," as he delicately put it, "is the original stain which disgraces Nature . . . and cuts the roots of society." Preoccupied as ever with the issue of size, Buffon observes that "in the savage the organs of generation are small and feeble. He has . . . no ardor for the female." Lacking this ardor, the Indian also has less attachment to parents, to children, and to society at large. The Indian's "heart is frozen," his "society cold," and his "empire cruel." Buffon concluded, "Nature, by denying him the faculty of love, has abused and contracted him more than any other animal."[28]

Buffon stopped short, however, of directly applying the thesis of degeneration to the Euro-American, and he later specifically rejected this idea. His new position on this point relied on his contention that a great flood had inundated the New World, making it physically younger than the Old World. The New World was not literally degenerating or getting worse; it was merely behind. Buffon accordingly left the door open for a gradual improvement for all things American, the Indian included.[29] Buffon also argued that beyond a certain stage of development, man no longer is subject to the rule of climate but can tame nature and assure his own progress.[30] The capacity of "perfectibility," unique to the human species, affords man this possibility. Yet only one portion of the species, "civilized man," who is essentially the European of middle latitude, has fully achieved this level of development. When Buffon finally accepted Franklin's figures on the increasing European population in North America, he incorporated them into his theory by arguing that the civilized Euro-American of North America had managed to overcome the physical obstacles that tended toward degeneration.

Causality in Natural History: Climate and Race

Natural history as a science had two broad objectives. The first was to describe and classify the phenomena of nature. The second was to explain the why of things—to provide the natural causes, or "laws," for why things developed as they did and for how they will develop in the future. This second part of the inquiry has been called "natural physics" and represents the truly modern and revolutionary element of the new science.[31]

The descriptive project involves a systematic analysis of the phenomena as they are seen and can be measured. The findings of natural history in the end are only as good as the quality of the observations that are available. The scientist is thus dependent on the representativeness of the samples examined, the reliability of the accounts of others, and the accuracy of the instruments and techniques of measurement employed to collect data. Mistakes could certainly occur because of faulty observations, and Buffon professed to "prefer as much a person who corrects one of my errors as one who teaches me a truth, for an error corrected is in fact a truth."[32] Still, a great part of Buffon's reputation derived from the impressive scope of his systematization of available data, which far eclipsed anything anyone else had previously accomplished. Buffon's overall prominence lent credibility to the degeneracy thesis. The case with de Pauw was different. Lacking Buffon's stature, de Pauw found that his observations were often questioned, and critics took him to task, even before an age in which field research was de rigueur for anthropologists, for never having visited the continent about which he wrote so profusely.[33]

Classifying phenomena is not as neutral or unproblematic a task as it may seem. It poses the difficulty of determining the basic categories into which individual things are placed. Within the animal kingdom, Buffon's subject is obviously not the sum total of all animals taken as individual beings, but groupings of individual animals (lions, tigers, dogs, and so on). Yet how does one determine such groupings, and how does one then distinguish between a primary group (or species) and a subgroup (or variety)? To refer to a group requires a criterion for identifying its members. This criterion may be something known a priori, through common sense, or by a constructed definition. Buffon was not always clear or consistent on such epistemological issues. At some points he defines a species according to a biological criterion of whether individuals can successfully mate and perpetuate the group. At other points he relies on commonsense notions of what constitutes a group, and he proceeds by describing the group's essential characteristics.[34]

The greater part of Buffon's effort, however, lay not in explaining the unity of each species but in accounting for the differentiation—the varieties—within each species. The search for the causes of the different varieties of a species, both as these causes have functioned over time and as they function today, constituted the core of the knowledge sought by natural history. The first cause that Buffon and de Pauw identified to account for variation was climate. Because climate is a result not just of meteorological patterns but of such topographical factors as the height of mountains and the number of lakes and rivers, the analysis broadens into a treatment of physical features.[35] Climate affects living things by the effects induced by sunlight and especially by air, which works its way into living beings directly by their breathing and indirectly by its impact on the whole food chain. De Pauw stressed the direct effect of climate, while Buffon emphasized the indirect factors: "The effects of climate and of food upon animals are well known, . . . and though their operation is slower and less apparent upon men, yet . . . their effects are not less certain . . . and manifest themselves in all the varieties we find among the human species."[36]

Varieties among animals, according to Buffon, develop over time and are a result of the effects of both the climate and a host of factors influenced by climate: food, the prevalence of certain diseases, and the way of living (or what we might call the cultural factor). Eventually, after repeated interactions of these factors and a continual intermixing of individuals who resemble one another, a "variety" of a species develops. A variety is a subgroup within a species that has acquired distinct physical and behavioral attributes. In the human species, the classification of varieties is based initially on physical appearance, of which the most important feature is skin color. The best-developed points in this schema are the basic color groups of white, black, yellow, and red, although Buffon also treats the gradations of color in between. The varieties of the human species are accordingly based on "race," where the word refers first to the major color groups and then to smaller subgroups inside each color group, which are determined by gradation of color as well as distinctive physical characteristics, such as height or facial configurations, and distinctive customs. Thus whites and blacks are referred to as "races," but so too, for example, are Finns and Lapps. Buffon sometimes calls the different human varieties "peoples" or "nations," by which he means not the legal entities but the putative biological or, as we sometimes say, ethnic groupings.

After defining a variety, Buffon had to determine its significance. The importance of the category goes well beyond grouping individuals according to their physical appearance. Varieties of the same species also exhibit different kinds of behavior, and they have distinct traits that relate not only to physical capacity but also to sensibility and intelligence. While great differences occur among individuals of the same variety (some are smarter or more beautiful than others, for example), huge differences also occur among the varieties. Buffon applies this theory about animals to humans, arguing that the varieties (the races) account for some of the most important elements of variation: intelligence, the moral sense, and the capacity for development. Part of the difference in the degree of development among the races is a result of accident (the color groups have tended to live apart and have developed distinct cultures), but the variety itself, understood as the biological properties of its members, has not become a primary cause that determines the stage of civilization.

Each variety acquires semipermanent or, as we would say, hereditary qualities. These are carried by some internal biological agent, which Buffon identifies sometimes as the blood, at other times as the "germs": "Certain characteristics are perpetuated and perpetuate themselves from generation to generation, as certain deformities or kinds of illnesses of mothers and fathers are passed on to their children."[37] Whatever the exact mode of transmission, however, the characteristics of a variety persist and do not immediately disappear with a change in environment, whether of climate or of culture. Each variety continues to carry its own previous history. Thus neither Buffon nor de Pauw believed that individual Indians who were moved to a European climate or placed in an Amero-European family would immediately (if ever) lose all Indian characteristics or that groups of Indians exposed to a different environment or influences would ever lose all of their native traits.

Even so, both men maintained that environmental factors continue to operate on human beings. If the races were exposed to different climates without taking prophylactic measures, they would gradually begin to change colors. Buffon thought that blacks would cease being black if they were to live in a northern climate for about "twelve generations," whereas de Pauw estimated that the transformation of white to black would take only about four generations, that of black to white somewhat longer.[38] Still, neither thinker held that a change of skin color was equivalent to a change of all their characteristics. The intellectual and moral properties of human beings are deeper and more abiding characteristics than color. For de Pauw, even the Euro-American living in the climate of the New World could not fall soon (if ever) to the level of the Indian, whereas the Indian could never attain the level of the European. For Buffon, the Euro-American could use his reason to seal himself off from the degenerative effects of the environment, whereas the Indian must remain different and developmentally behind, at least for a very long time.

The classification of the human species into its different varieties, biologically distinguished, is the starting point of Buffon's anthropology. It is an anthropology that emphasizes hierarchy. Not only are the varieties different, but they can be ranked. "Civilized man" stands at the apex of this hierarchy, having reached the height of human biological potential. There can still be progress, but it will not involve further physical change of civilized man. Civilized man is the European— indeed, for de Pauw, the European in Europe. And according to Buffon, "The most handsome and beautiful men are to be found between the fortieth and fiftieth degree of latitude [in Europe]." Civilized man is also white; although Buffon did not make too much of the importance of color per se, he regarded white as the "true or natural color of man" from which the other colors have derived. Below the European Buffon places the Asian, the black, and, at the bottom, the Indian.[39]

The three main points of natural history, as that science relates to the study of human beings, can be summarized as follows. First, human beings, while members of one species, are divided into different varieties that have developed over time. The varieties are classified by notable physical differences, beginning with skin color. Second, these varieties now have a strong internal or hereditary basis, even though they originally derived from, and continue to be subject to, environmental influences. Finally, the varieties contain not just incidental or secondary differences, but fundamental ones that relate to the deepest human qualities of sensibility and intellect. The biological characteristics of these subgroups make up the starting point for the scientific study of man and society.

Buffon and Modern Ideas of Man

Scholars, often quite unconsciously, tend to judge past thinkers on the basis of currently held assumptions or ideas. Because no major contemporary school of thought espouses the idea of different human varieties in Buffon's sense, one might think that he would be universally condemned as a protoracist. Surprisingly, however, Buffon has been quite widely admired. His foremost biographer and an eminent historian of science, Jacques Roger, argues that while Buffon was "a man of his time" (which accounts for some of his prejudices), his views on human variety are nevertheless "very modern" and "astonishingly close to those of modern anthropology." Buffon, in this view, helped to establish modern humanitarianism by providing the biological foundation for the unity of mankind.[40] To account for this quite unexpected judgment, I will need first to distinguish between the two dominant contemporary views of mankind—for only one of them celebrates Buffon—and then situate Buffon's position in the context of the debate of his own time between the proponents of monogenesis and polygenesis.

The near universal rejection of racial biologism today does not mean that all share the same basic conception of mankind. Modern thought falls into two quite different positions. The first I identify as the "humanitarian view." It emphasizes what is common among human beings and sees the variations as deriving from the different qualities of individuals. Of course, this view admits the existence of different groups and cultures, but these differences are seen as conventional and perhaps as even slightly regrettable. The deepest reality about man is the biological unity of the human species.

A frequent corollary of this view, which a large number of contemporary scientists have adopted, holds that as people are everywhere the same, political universalism of some kind is the natural or proper standard. Political and cultural barriers to universalism are regarded as primitive or atavistic. This idea was given its most famous expression in the "UNESCO Statement by Experts on Race Problems." Written in 1950 by a group of the world's leading social scientists, the statement looks at man from the supposedly objective perspective of the "hard" science of biology, which studies man outside of any particular context. The statement concludes with what amounts to an endorsement of a form of political universalism: "All normal human beings are capable of learning to share in a common life, to understand the nature of mutual service and reciprocity, and to respect social obligations and contracts. . . . Lastly, biological studies lend support to the ethic of universal brotherhood; for man is born with drives toward cooperation, and unless those drives are satisfied, men and nations alike fall ill."[41]

The other contemporary view, which I identified earlier as the "school of difference," enjoys a wide following among literary critics as well as many in philosophy, history, and anthropology. Although it does not deny the common biological basis of human beings, its proper starting point is not mankind in general but different cultural units. Added to this cultural perspective, which has a long history in anthropology, are elements of postmodern philosophy that emphasize and celebrate the differences among human groupings. Language in the broad sense is often seen as the most profound cause of cultural differences, because language structures different patterns of thinking. The differences among human groups run very deep, so deep that one may speak of virtually distinct human types. We are all first and foremost cultural beings, which means beings of particular cultures. The attempt to step "outside" culture and speak of mankind from some universal position (that of biological studies, for example) is artificial. Such humanitarian thinking tears people from the only place they actually live, which is inside a particular culture.

Proponents of the school of difference not only recognize but also prize the diversity among different groups or cultures. For many of them, a recognition of different cultures in their particularity constitutes the highest value or standard—a kind of philosophical and ethical absolute—leading to the commandment that all cultural differences should be respected. Others inside the school of difference, however, draw another conclusion. They deny that real diversity is ever promoted by a standard that values diversity, because the very act of valuing diversity bespeaks an acceptance of the supremacy of one culture—a Western and logocentric culture with its standard of tolerance. Particular cultures themselves have no idea of the concept of values or of the value of the respect for diversity, which are all rationalist constructions. Particular cultures act in accordance with their own distinctive ways, often in disregard of diversity. While there is therefore a dispute within the school of difference about who really has managed to escape the grip of Western logocentric thinking, its various strands nevertheless share a common antipathy to one culture: the bearers of modern rationalist thought. This culture is qualitatively different from all others. It constitutes a kind of nonculture because it envisages a universalism that threatens the very idea of diversity. It is the enemy of difference.

The favorable evaluation of Buffon in modern scholarship derives from the humanitarian camp, not the school of difference. This positive regard may seem strange in light of Buffon's emphasis on varieties, but it becomes understandable if one reconstructs the context of scientific thought of the eighteenth century. At that time, Buffon's theory was rivaled by an influential alternative that placed much *greater* emphasis than Buffon did on the differences among human groups. This view held that man did not descend from a common mold, as Buffon had argued, but that each race had been created separately.[42] This position, advocated by Voltaire and others, held that each race was in a certain sense a distinct species. Voltaire's position came to be identified by the term "polygenesis" (different groups of man originated from different sources), in contrast to Buffon's view of "monogenesis" (mankind originated from one source).

Modern science has all but forgotten the great debate between polygenesis and monogenesis. But it was the central point of contention in the study of man from the middle of the eighteenth century until the second half of the nineteenth century, when the terms of the debate were largely superseded by Darwin's account of human origins. (Traces of polygenesis nonetheless remained in certain strains of social Darwinism that identified different racial groups as the key units.) In archaeology and anthropology today, the old dispute is sometimes mentioned in the hotly contested argument about whether human beings have descended from one branch of hominoid or two or more. But this argument, although it has overtones reminiscent of the earlier debate, is in fact very different. In the monogenesis-polygenesis debate, the varieties of man were the different racial and ethnic groupings, whereas in the current dispute the inquiry focuses on whether mankind, fairly much *as a whole,* derives from one, or more than one, species.[43]

Monogenesis and polygenesis were also, perhaps even preeminently, theological terms. After much controversy in previous centuries, the church by the eighteenth century had adopted monogenesis as the orthodox Christian position. This view rested on the biblical account of creation, under which all of mankind was understood to have descended from Adam and Eve, the "original pair." A common

origin sanctioned the idea that mankind was a single species. Theological monogenesis did not, however, preclude further biblical interpretation that allowed for
the existence of different varieties within the human family. The most prominent
such view was that whites descended from Japheth (one of Noah's sons) and the
Semites from Shem (another son), whereas blacks descended from Ham, who had
been cursed by Noah. In contrast, those who endorsed polygenesis were deemed
antireligious, as their position contradicted the Bible. Some members of this
school took a certain pride in their iconoclasm, which they offered as proof of their
strictly "philosophical" or "scientific" approach.

As a philosopher, Buffon could not rest his position on the authority of the Bible.
He postulated instead the natural explanation of a "common mold" for man (although not a single original pair). All varieties of man derive from this common
mold and thus are members of the same species. Man developed into different varieties under exposure to varying environmental conditions. The differences
among groups were therefore in some sense not "essential," but "accidental" (in
Buffon's words). Presumably, too, differences that were environmentally made
may, as time goes on, be unmade. Man may somehow, at some time, become one
and the same. Although ambivalent on this point, Buffon did in a few passages
sketch a developmental idea according to which group differences may in the end
vanish and mankind become one.[44]

It is understandable, accordingly, why some liberal humanitarian thinkers today have developed a sympathetic view of Buffon. On the foundation of his monogenesis it is possible to construct a biologically supported idea of liberal humanitarianism. This step can be accomplished either by saying that all the existing
varieties of man are evolving toward one kind or by claiming that the different varieties are already fundamentally the same, the differences among them (physical
as well as intellectual) being the result only of current environmental and cultural
factors.

Buffon's position can also be used to support the vague, value-laden notion of
"humanity," which was one basis on which he denounced the atrocities against the
Indians and condemned the excesses of slavery, although not the practice itself.
The concept of humanity here rests on the idea that beings who are of the same
species "owe" something to each other; an awareness of this fact, whether by instinct or scientific knowledge, translates—or ought to translate—into a certain
gentleness and restraint in the way one human being treats another. Some nineteenth-century scientists who claimed to be Buffon's heirs attempted to construct
a humanitarian antislavery position on this ground. Polygenesis moves in the opposite direction, holding to the idea of essential distinctions among racial groups.

These groups cannot grow together because they are different species; or, rather, they *should* not grow together, because intermingling may lead to man's physical decline over time and, for the higher human species, will certainly lead to moral and intellectual degeneration. Intermingling of the different species of man is contrary to nature. Even so, not every eighteenth-century advocate of polygenesis was unsympathetic to the notion of a common humanity, and many opposed slavery and all forms of exploitation. But by the nineteenth century, many who claimed this label began to deride ideas of humanitarianism, and many of them became strident racialists and defenders of slavery.

All these factors help to account for the sympathetic treatment that Buffon has received from some modern humanitarians. But this evaluation should not cause us to overlook two important points about Buffon's thought and the position of monogenesis. First, monogenesis was not always linked to gentleness, freedom, and equality. In fact, the vast majority of those supporting slavery in the nineteenth century remained in the monogenetic camp; they may have done so partly because of religious scruples, but monogenesis imposed no compelling theoretical (or theological) reason to abandon slavery. And polygenesis was not always a defender of slavery. Indeed, Buffon's idea of varieties in no way eliminated—it rather tended to reinforce—the significance of practical distinctions among the races of man. Second, the often harsh form of nineteenth-century polygenesis which I described drew on the same methods of research and assumptions as Buffon had, arguing only that Buffon had adopted a faulty conception of a "species." Nineteenth-century polygenesis was as much the heir of Buffon's thinking as was the humanitarian view.[45]

Natural History as a Social Science

Natural history as it bears on the study of humans began as a purely theoretical inquiry. It sought to explain, for the purpose of knowledge only, the degree of unity and differentiation in the human species, bringing to this study many of the same categories and assumptions employed in the analysis of animals. In the case of the animals, Buffon expressed no interest in seeing natural history debased by association with the practical science we know today as animal husbandry. He would surely have shuddered at the kinds of projects, such as engineering beefier cattle and more productive hens, that are the focus of the science at major agricultural universities in the United States. At most, perhaps, we can imagine Buffon yielding to a few artificial measures for the sake of preserving his beloved elephant.

In the end, however, given the natural historians' claim to have discovered the basic determinants of human development, it could not have been long before many of them would seek to use this knowledge to guide public policy. At this point a line is crossed, and natural history is transformed from a body of knowledge with only theoretical aims to a social science that purports to have practical utility. Using the causal model developed in the theoretical part of the science, the practical part offers advice about how to alter and improve society. The practical application of natural history led in two quite different directions, depending on how amenable to change the main causes of human development—climate and human varieties—were thought to be. The first attitude was a progressive, engineering approach that envisaged people's conscious intervention in shaping their environment and guiding the path of their development. This position, with which Buffon came in many ways to be associated, corresponded to the great modern scientific view that the discovery of causality could unlock the key to man's mastery of nature. The second attitude was one that might be called conservative or, more accurately, fatalistic. It emphasized not just the uselessness of applying scientific engineering to human affairs, but something much more. Given the strength and intractability said to characterize the extra-political causes determining human development, many of the traditional political methods for trying to change society were futile or even dangerous. De Pauw was the spokesman, if not the originator, of this view.

Both Buffon and de Pauw believed that climate was the main external factor affecting the human situation, and America's excessive humidity was a primary cause of degeneracy. If, accordingly, the humidity in America could be reduced, human development could be promoted. Buffon thought that this objective could be achieved by a policy of deforestation and draining of wetlands—a fear of global warming evidently not being among his major concerns. The taming of nature that had contributed to the growth of civilization in Europe, Buffon argued, could now take place in America: "Some centuries hence, when the lands are cultivated, the forests cut down, the courses of rivers properly directed, and the marshes drained, this same country will become the most fertile, the most wholesome, and the richest in the whole world, as it is already in all the parts which have experienced the industry and skill of man."[46]

De Pauw also accepted the possibility of climatic manipulation. The situation in America, he acknowledged, was not as bad as it had once been: "Forests have been razed, waters drained, and the air purified by the smoke of many fires," especially in the English colonies.[47] When Europeans first arrived they could contract venereal disease merely by breathing the air, whereas by the eighteenth century more intimate physical contact was required. But although Buffon thought improvement in an absolute sense was possible in America, de Pauw held that climatic forces exceeded man's ability to dominate them. The best man could hope for was a slowing down of the rate of degeneracy, not a reversal of the process. America could never become self-sustaining as a developed or civilized region, de Pauw concluded, because its "complete independence [from Europe] is a thing morally impossible and will become no less so with time."[48]

Many of the best minds of the age, it is worth noting, accepted some version of the thesis that climate shaped man's physical and moral condition. It is certainly not against reason, for example, to observe that swampy lands and fetid air are injurious to human health and therefore to make a connection between humidity and disease or degeneration. Much early American forest policy was predicated on this view, although some, like Benjamin Rush, insisted on a balance between cutting and draining on one hand and preserving virgin forests and wetlands on the other. Perhaps the most ambitious suggestion for altering the climate came from Thomas Jefferson, who favored cutting a canal through the Isthmus of Panama in order to alter the direction of the Gulf Stream, thereby reducing the humidity on the eastern coast and improving man's moral condition.[49] Anyone who has suffered through a summer in Charlottesville can excuse Jefferson for this lapse of scientific rigor.

Race was the other cause on which natural historians thought a policy to transform society might be based. The options available here were either to encourage or to discourage a mixing of the varieties of man. Miscegenation would clearly affect the character of life—indeed, it was doing so even then on the American continent, where mixing had already occurred. Buffon and de Pauw addressed this subject indirectly, but their position clearly implied opposition to miscegenation. Unlike efforts to alter the climate, racial mixing offered no overall prospect of human improvement. In any exchange, a lower variety could improve itself only to the extent that it pulled down a higher one. Miscegenation would produce a leveling of the human species in which the higher is sacrificed to the lower. Because human progress is a function of what a small part of humanity does—is essentially the result of the activity of civilized man—miscegenation, whether by deliberate policy or by the natural course of affairs, would threaten what is best in the human species.

Cornelius de Pauw and European Isolationism

American commentators on Cornelius de Pauw have understandably focused on the theme of degeneracy and ignored the rest of his argument. Appreciating de

Pauw's subsequent influence on European thought, however, involves considering other parts of his work. De Pauw was a major spokesman for the policy of European isolationism and one of the first to develop a social science endorsing a kind of fatalism in human affairs. He was a scientist, but one who stood outside the "progressive" mainstream of modern science.

From the first page of his work, de Pauw makes clear that his purpose is not merely theoretical but political as well: "It is certain that the conquest of the new world, so famous and so unjust, has been the greatest of miseries that humanity has suffered." De Pauw urged his fellow Europeans to "cultivate our own" and appealed to them to withdraw from America and end all further colonial projects.[50] This position, he insisted, was grounded in scientific analysis. Natural history could speak truth to power. By showing the pre-political causes that determine social life, science could expose the false claims of the "political projectors" who had enticed European statesmen into their folly of investing in the New World. Science could demonstrate the case for the limits of political action by making clear the overwhelming force of physical causes that are beyond man's mastery.

De Pauw's support for a policy of European isolationism may at first seem surprising, given his claim that Europeans are superior to other varieties of human beings. Superiority, after all, has been a standard justification for colonialist policies. Yet de Pauw argued that climate and race, the two primary influences on society, imposed limits that human intervention could not overcome. He widened the gap between superior and inferior human varieties to such a degree that it seemed contrary to the interest, as well as beneath the dignity, of the superior to exploit the inferior.

America was weakening Europe not only by the steady loss of the populations emigrating to the Americas but also by a constant drain of Europe's wealth. Although the discovery of America initially brought huge profits from the mining of precious metals, these gains were temporary and detracted from the qualities of discipline and industry needed for genuine economic development. All empires that have yielded to the lure of precious metals, de Pauw argued, have been impoverished in the end. De Pauw also questioned the justice of the colonial project. The discovery of the New World tragically brought into contact two peoples who were wholly unsuited to each other. Never before in human history had there existed such a disparity between attacker and defender: "All the force and all the injustice were on the side of the Europeans. The Americans only had weakness; they had therefore to be exterminated and were exterminated in an instant." The tragedy inherent in this inequality of power was heightened when some Europeans adopted doctrines that denied their common humanity with the American Indian.

40

This view allowed the massacre of many Indians on the ground that it was not really humans who were being killed.[51]

De Pauw's book is a poignant indictment of the greed and brutality of the European conquerors, especially the Spanish. His analysis is consistent with the Enlightenment (and anti-Jesuit) theme of the "barbarism of civilization," which can be traced back to the thought of Montaigne.[52] This theme held that although superior knowledge gave Europeans a physical advantage over other peoples, it did not ensure them of a higher moral status. Civilization is not necessarily more just, only more powerful. Of course, the colonial mission also defended itself on the Christian grounds that it was devoted to saving the souls of the heathen. De Pauw allows that in theory this mission might be justified, but in practice it was seldom undertaken in good faith: "If those who preach virtue in advanced countries are themselves too vicious to instruct the savages without tyrannizing them, then we should allow them at least to live in peace." The Europeans had "strangely abused their superiority." Among their crimes were instances of not only the genocide of Indians but also the enslavement of black Africans, which was linked to the colonization of America and the need for reliable labor.[53]

Yet, one might ask, is not the corrective to an unjust policy of colonialism a just policy? Would not the proper course of action be to apply in the future the justice that had been wanting in the past? This was the position adopted by most Enlightenment thinkers, who argued that the progressive idea of science, hitherto ignored, could now be introduced to assure a positive result. A debased colonial project could be replaced by an enlightened one. It was on this point that de Pauw broke ranks with the other thinkers of his day. He did so not by rejecting science but by using it to demonstrate the "limits of science and knowledge" in supplying the means to master natural processes.[54] Europeans, he argued, undoubtedly had the power to conquer the world, but they would prove unable to manage that conquest. Unforeseen consequences, such as the spread of syphilis from the New World to the Old, always defied what superior power and planning aimed to accomplish. The conquest of the New World very nearly spelled the end of civilization and the re-barbarization of Europe, and further colonial adventures might yet produce that result.

Looking to the future, de Pauw predicted that the confident scientific project promoting the idea of colonization would one day spin out of control and lead to worldwide violence and war among the European nations. The forces of technology, once unleashed, could not be contained: "When Europe is at war, all the world is. All the points of the globe are successively shaken as by a great electric power, and the scene of massacres and of carnage is increasing, from Canton to

Archangel, from Buenos Aires to Quebec."[55] De Pauw's conception of the dangers of technologism and universalism, which he identifies with European Enlightenment thought, is precisely what European thinkers a century later called Americanism. And they did so with the same underlying theme in mind: Progress is a prelude to disaster.

De Pauw was among the first "conservative" proponents of the new social science. Whereas most who embraced science became progressives and had a general faith in the capacity of European civilization, de Pauw argued that the obstacles to schemes of social engineering were much greater than most realized. If this position sometimes paralleled a stance of political moderation, it was not because of any kind of systematic examination of political factors. De Pauw had no political science worthy of the name, and his counsels of restraint derived from reasoning about the effects of nonpolitical factors. In the end, his positions were not so much moderate as extreme in a different way. His doubts about human improvement went well beyond prudent reservations about the excesses of social engineering to unreasonable claims that progress is impossible outside the boundaries of Europe and that no successful society can be established in America. Because man is determined by his physical environment and race, nothing he can do through deliberate action, including the adopting of wise laws, can alter his basic situation. Such was the radical fatalism to which de Pauw's new social science led.

To postmodern thinkers who speak with such fondness of the differences among groups, Cornelius de Pauw must no doubt appear to be a quite sympathetic figure. True, some of his ideas about climatic effects may strike many as unusual; but scientific validity, as modern philosophers tell us, is only a matter of conventional agreement, and in any case de Pauw's climatological views are scarcely more extreme, and certainly no less politically inspired, than many contemporary theories of global warming. But it is less de Pauw's views about climate than his ideas about human beings and society that are apt to attract proponents of the school of difference. De Pauw's criticism of the hubris of Enlightenment thought prefigures the postmodern attack on rationalism and logocentrism, and his attack on Europeans' colonial policies foreshadows contemporary Third Worldism and multiculturalism. He is one of the great defenders of the marginalized "Other." Except for his comments on the superiority of the white European, Cornelius de Pauw would fit quite nicely into the mainstream of modern American academia and would make an ideal featured speaker at an American studies conference.

2

★ ★ ★

American Responses to the Degeneracy Thesis

No one today subscribes to the eighteenth-century biological theory according to which all things deteriorate more rapidly in America than anywhere else in the world. Yet, although the science behind the degeneracy thesis has been rejected, its basic conclusion has been widely embraced. In the softer disciplines of philosophy, history, and literary criticism, the word "America" has become a symbol of disfigurement, disease, and distortion. If anything, the European biologists of the founding era were more sympathetic to America than are the intellectuals of today. For them, only the frogs and pigs in America were overweight, whereas for our contemporaries the objects of repugnance in America are "obese" and "gum-chewing" people. The eighteenth-century scientists went only so far as to charge the American mind with mediocrity and unoriginality, whereas intellectuals in the twentieth century have identified America as a "crime against humankind" and as the "site of catastrophe."

Happily for America, happily for the human race, Americans of the founding generation saw fit to challenge the degeneracy thesis. Benjamin Franklin, Thomas Jefferson, Alexander Hamilton, George Washington, and Benjamin Rush (among others) raised their voices against this apostasy. Without their efforts, who can say how many more Europeans might have succumbed to the strange power of this theory or how much more damage might have been done to the cause of liberal democratic government?

But profound as our debt of gratitude to these patriots may be, it must not prevent us from an honest and critical inquiry into the soundness of their theoretical positions. Although all the Americans mentioned opposed the charges of American inferiority, Jefferson ended by joining the Europeans in proclaiming biology (or "natural history") rather than political science as the foundation for a new social science. The theoretical dispute over social science was thus not always between the Europeans and their American respondents, but sometimes among the Americans. The central debate in the United States found the two perennial adversaries of the founding era, Jefferson and Hamilton, arrayed against each other. Long ignored, this debate on the nature of social science is one of the most momentous in American political thought.

Thomas Jefferson

The discussion that follows contains what I acknowledge to be a most painful conclusion: Thomas Jefferson, an originator of the American experiment, was also among the first in America to undermine the influence of political science. Although this conclusion can only detract from Jefferson's reputation, I am convinced that presenting the full facts to a candid world offers the best way today to help restore political science to its proper place in our system and to maintain Jefferson's own political project. If it is impossible to save political science for Thomas Jefferson, it may at least be possible to save it from him.

From nearly the moment the degeneracy thesis was presented, American thinkers sought to disprove it by refuting the empirical facts on which it was based. One of the earliest and most effective arguments came from the pen of Benjamin Franklin. Franklin traced the demographic trends in Pennsylvania and showed that its population of native-born Euro-Americans was rapidly increasing.[1] This conclusion controverted the natural historians' claim that population in the New World would begin to decline because of a deterioration of physical strength and sexual prowess. Using the Europeans' own reasoning against them, Franklin concluded that the climate must be more agreeable in America than it was in the Old World. In 1782, in a pamphlet encouraging European emigration, Franklin called attention to the "salubrity of the [American] air and the healthiness of the climate."[2] Because of his renown in Europe, Franklin succeeded in compelling many proponents of the degeneracy thesis to modify their views, which most did not by abandoning the overall theory but simply by carving out an exception for the Euro-American in the British colonies.

The most systematic attempt to refute the degeneracy thesis by a recurrence to the empirical facts was made a few years later by Thomas Jefferson. In his only full-length book, *Notes on the State of Virginia* (1785), Jefferson sought to vindicate the New World against the Old. To the modern reader, who has difficulty even imagining that the degeneracy thesis could ever have been seriously entertained, much of the *Notes* seems tedious or even bizarre. Who but a naturalist will not weary of Jefferson's lengthy discussions of the elk and squirrel, or his detailed tables comparing the size and weight of quadrupeds in Europe and America? Who will not wonder at Jefferson's strange displays of indignation at the slight directed at the American mammoth? To appreciate these passages, we must recall that Jefferson's painstaking "observations" were designed not only to advance the cause of pure science but also to defend the political interests of his country.

The modern reader's interest is likely to be rekindled, however, when, about one-third of the way through the *Notes,* Jefferson turns his attention from the "brute animals" to the "man of America, whether aboriginal or transplanted." Entering now into the field of anthropology, Jefferson begins his discussion of man with a treatment of the American Indian. Once again Jefferson finds himself at odds with Buffon. The Indian, far from being the inferior individual that Buffon describes, possesses many admirable qualities. Indeed, in some respects the Indian is more praiseworthy than the European; to protect his honor, for example, the Indian is far more courageous in enduring torture. Where disadvantages do appear on the Indian's side, as in his lower rates of regeneration or in his brutal treatment of women, these can often be explained either by immediate physical influences (diet and mode of life) or by cultural factors. To add weight to his argument, Jefferson cites a long passage from a speech given by an Indian chief, Logan, whose eloquence in this case he claims to be the equal of anything found in Demosthenes or Cicero. Further research, Jefferson contends, would almost certainly confirm that Indians "are formed in mind as well as body on the same module" as Europeans.[3]

With this argument Jefferson conceived that he had cut down the degeneracy thesis at its root. In vindicating the Indian, he had vindicated his continent and his country. Now Jefferson could openly express his doubt, bordering on mild ridicule, of the inquiry into whether "nature has enlisted herself as a Cis- or Trans-Atlantic partisan"; and he could question whether the great Buffon had not displayed "more eloquence than sound reasoning" in support of his theory. As for Raynal's charge that America had produced not "one man of genius in a single art or a single science," Jefferson holds up the examples of Washington, Franklin, and David Rittenhouse, the astronomer and instrument maker, and he indignantly denounces, in words that even today must thrill any American, the "wretched philosophy . . . [that] would have arranged Washington among the degeneracies of nature."[4] Ever the proponent of empirical analysis, Jefferson proposes the production of a statistical index comparing number of geniuses per capita, which he was certain would favor America over the far more populous states of Europe. George Washington himself, writing with less mathematical precision a decade later, supported Jefferson's conclusion: "Although we are yet in our cradle as a nation, I think the efforts of the human mind with us are sufficient to refute (by incontestable facts) the doctrines of those who have asserted that everything degenerates in America."[5]

Had Jefferson ended his analysis at this point, his argument would have paralleled Franklin's refutation of the key findings of natural history while casting still further doubt on the basic assumptions of the science. But Jefferson took a new and fateful step: he adopted natural history as his guide, both in its method and in its categories of analysis. At the very point in the *Notes* where he defends the Indian, he makes clear his general agreement with the basic premise of natural history: "I do not mean to deny, that there are varieties in the race of men, distinguished by their powers both of body and mind. I believe there are, as I see to be the case in the races of other animals."[6]

Jefferson was widely criticized by his contemporaries in America as the American thinker who had yielded most to theoretical or speculative approaches to the study of political matters. Many of these criticisms, of course, were motivated by partisanship, as was most certainly the case in the young William Cullen Bryant's attack on Jefferson's obsession with natural history:

> Go, search with curious eyes for horned frogs,
> 'Mid the Wild wastes of Louisiana bogs;
> Or where the Ohio rolls his turbid stream
> Dig for huge bones, thy glory and thy theme.[7]

The serious charge reflected in such criticisms, however, was that Jefferson had followed the European philosophers in abandoning political science for a new "scientific" method of analyzing political phenomena.

The practical significance of Jefferson's acceptance of natural history becomes clear when he turns in the *Notes* to a discussion of the black race. This discussion, as many have pointed out, appears in a section in which Jefferson endorses a plan to end slavery. The plan called for freeing all newly born slaves, providing for their basic education, and then colonizing them in an unspecified place where they would become a "free and independent people" temporarily protected by the state of Virginia.[8] The proposal involved two interrelated objectives: ending slavery and separating whites and blacks into distinct political communities. As his theoretical foundations, Jefferson employed the science of natural rights linked to political science for the first objective, and the science of natural history for the second.

Before turning to natural history, I must say a word about natural rights. This "science" (Jefferson's term), which grounded the claim that all men are equal in respect to possessing rights, was widely endorsed by America's founders and was fully integrated into their general understanding of political science. Today, of course, social scientists generally dismiss any "scientific" (or "natural") basis for equal rights, insisting instead on viewing this proposition as a "normative" or ethical principle. (For some reason, however, many social scientists have not been reluctant to cite without embarrassment the unspecified "biological studies" that prove the "ethic of universal brotherhood.") To interpret natural rights analysis of the founding period as a purely normative or ethical doctrine, however, distorts the founders' understanding. To be sure, natural rights analysis carried a clear implication of ethical obligation, and nearly all the founders who employed it expressed a measure of responsibility—some more, some less—to rid the nation of the "barbarous policy" of enslaving blacks, a policy that "degraded them from the human rank."[9] But the foundation of natural rights analysis was understood to lie in what it revealed about the *facts* of human nature or the "constitution of man." In the discussion of slavery, the two pertinent facts were that there is a human nature, and that human beings by their natural bent—and surely when freed from superstition and enlightened about their position—will reject enslavement and assert their freedom.

Natural rights thinking was used not only to explain and justify the American Revolution but also to teach a highly realistic lesson about slavery. The argument from nature issued in the sobering appraisal that the time must come when the slave would rebel against his master and put him in danger of his life and liberty. This side of the natural rights teaching is evident throughout Jefferson's writings. In the well-known passage in which he warns that "God is just" and that "his justice cannot sleep forever," he also states that this possibility of "supernatural interference" clearly has a "natural" foundation in the factual situation at hand: "Considering numbers, nature and natural means only, an exchange of situations [between whites and blacks] is among possible events."[10]

The same kind of warning, based on human nature and connected to ethical considerations, is found in the natural rights analysis of many of the other founders. More than a decade earlier, for example, Benjamin Rush had written: "Human nature is now aiming to regain her dignity amongst the slaves in the Brasils, Surinam, and Chili who have at last asserted their liberty. Are not these insurrections the beginnings of universal retribution and vengeance upon European tyranny in America? and is it not high time for Britain to change her conduct and adopt some safe and equitable means of abolishing slavery in the colonies?"[11]

If the first part of Jefferson's plan (the proposal to free the slaves) generated the greatest controversy among southern whites of his day, the second part (the proposal of compulsory colonization for the freed slaves) clearly creates the greatest controversy today. Jefferson's defense of this provision follows from the impossibility, as he conceives it, of successfully incorporating blacks and whites into the same political community. He offers a mixture of "political," "physical," and "moral" reasons to explain this impossibility. The political consideration is based on the fact that American whites are prejudiced against blacks and that American blacks would always remember the injuries whites had inflicted on them. Any attempt to have the two races live together in the same political community, Jefferson concludes, must end in a race war and the "extermination of the one or the other race."[12]

Jefferson next points out that the division between the races rests on a "difference fixed in nature," which is the observable fact of color difference. But what is the character of this difference, and how important is it? At this point Jefferson leaves the realm of political considerations and turns to the new "scientific" ground of natural history, which now begins to guide his political analysis. The observed color difference, Jefferson asserts, represents a fundamental distinction delineating the different "varieties" of man. The concept of varieties, taken from Buffon, means that the differences between blacks and whites go beyond physical variations and include other human traits, such as intellectual capacity. The human varieties are "fixed in nature." Jefferson's summary thesis (or "suspicion," as he calls it) is that blacks are "inferior to the whites in the endowments both of mind and body."[13]

The same "wretched philosophy" that Jefferson had previously rejected in the case of whites in America he now endorses in the case of blacks. In an initial draft of the *Notes,* Jefferson borrowed the language about Americans from Raynal, who in turn had borrowed it from de Pauw, and applied it to the black race: "Never yet, so far as I have heard, has a black excelled in any art, in any science."[14] Jefferson's full survey of blacks finds them to be the superior of whites in musical ability, their equal in memory and in the moral sense, but their decided inferior in the most important human respects (reflection, creativity, and reason).

Jefferson admits to the difficulty of achieving certainty in scientific truths that relate to human faculties, as these faculties cannot be directly seen or manipulated in a laboratory. He accordingly calls for "further observation." He also admits to feeling a certain "tenderness" at a judgment "that would degrade a whole race of men from the rank in the scale of beings which their Creator may perhaps have given them." Science nevertheless must be pursued wherever it leads. In any case, as the word "perhaps" in the last quotation suggests, we do not really know what the Creator intended until we verify it by our own research. ("A patient pursuit of the facts, and cautious combination and comparison of them, is the drudgery to which man is subjected by his Maker, if he wishes to attain sure knowledge.") Jefferson accordingly calls for the establishment of an American school of natural history, of which he may justly be named the founder: "To our reproach it must be said, that though for a century and a half we have had under our eyes the races of black and red men, they have never yet been viewed by us as subjects of natural history."[15]

In advocating this new school, Jefferson reiterated the fundamental starting point of natural history in its study of man: namely, the significance of the category of varieties. "It is not against experience to suppose," he writes, "that different species of the same genus, or varieties of the same species, may possess different qualifications." The classification of varieties is based on color, and the "different qualifications" result not from conditions alone (not now, at any rate), but from qualities carried inside the group (in "nature," as he puts it). Jefferson, in fact, leaves open his position on monogenesis versus polygenesis; at a minimum, however, he placed greater emphasis than Buffon on the distinctness of the varieties understood as the different color groups.[16]

Jefferson proceeds from these theoretical investigations to develop a practical social science based on natural history to guide important aspects of political life. The new science of natural history, he believes, has much to say about no less fundamental a matter than who should be members of which political communities, or about what makes a people. Natural history contains a clear inference about the question of racial mixing. Nature, he argues, intends the separateness and hierarchy that have been found to exist: "Will not a lover of natural history then, one who views the gradation in all races of animals with the eye of philosophy, excuse an effort to keep those in the department of man as distinct as nature has formed them?" A mixing of blood, which Jefferson thought might have an instinctual origin in the urge of males of a lower species to have union with females of a higher species, was a danger to be guarded against.[17]

The partisan of "gradation," or human excellence, must accordingly take steps to prevent miscegenation and ensure that the black slave, "when freed, . . . [is] removed beyond the reach of mixture." As Jefferson later explained to Edward Coles, "Their amalgamation with the other color produces a degradation to which no lover of his country, no lover of excellence in the human character can innocently consent."[18] Although Jefferson does not say so directly in the *Notes,* the logic of his argument could hardly fail to apply to the free black population as well. The practical deduction from natural history was therefore that the United States should be made white—or at any rate not black. Jefferson originally had in mind Africa as the place of resettlement, although later, in 1824, he proposed Haiti.

Jefferson's scientific approach led him to a most extreme proposal for ending slavery. His final plan was to remove all slave children from their parents by the age of five, whereupon they would be brought up by the state and then shipped abroad.[19] The chain of family life would be entirely broken. Conceding here, as one must, the extremism of the condition of slavery that this plan was designed to redress, one still finds it impossible not to remark on the fantastic, experimental character of Jefferson's proposal, which is reminiscent of Plato's obviously utopian plan for founding the Republic. Nonpolitical analyses generate nonpolitical solutions.

It is no small thing politically speaking, even today, for the author of America's founding document to be associated with views that are an anathema to human equality. From the shock of this association, one can all too easily conclude that *all* of Jefferson's ideas, including those on equality and natural rights as expressed in the Declaration of Independence, are tainted and that the founders' ideas are at core racist. Such, in fact, has been the direction taken by revisionist historiography and by the new school of multicultural history. In response to this line of argument, some scholars, sensitive to the potential political repercussions of this conclusion, have soft-pedaled Jefferson's views on race, offering such pallid half-excuses as Jefferson's being "in advance of the Virginia gentry of his time." Dubious from the start, efforts of this kind to "save" Jefferson and the founding are clearly out of the question today. Jefferson's views on race cannot be hidden. They are continually being brought forward by historians, who, often with an adolescent glee, are only too happy to proclaim Jefferson's "negrophobia" and "hypocrisy."[20]

Simple good sense, as well as a concern for the truth, therefore argue for the need to treat Jefferson's views candidly and in light of their deepest source. That source was not Jefferson's prejudices—a view, incidentally, that minimizes what is at stake by reducing everything to one man's likes and dislikes—but his *theoretical* position adopting natural history as a guide for political analysis. This position helped to spawn an entire school of American social science based on racialist categories and to legitimate the formation of racialist ideology.[21] It is thus no accident that David Walker, the first black man in America to write a sustained assault on slavery, made Jefferson's embrace of natural history the chief object of his critique. Citing the passage from the *Notes* quoted above ("Will not a lover of natural history . . ."), Walker goes on: "This very verse, brethren, having emanated

from Mr. Jefferson, . . . has in truth injured us more, and has been as great a bar-
rier to our emancipation as any thing that has ever been advanced against us. . . .
Mr. Jefferson's remarks respecting us have sunk into the hearts of millions of the
whites and never will be removed this side of eternity."[22]

Placing the emphasis on Jefferson's theoretical position opens up a way of looking at the founding which is different from that so prevalent in recent historiography. Just as Jefferson's racialism derived from the theoretical premises of natural
history, so did much of the opposition to his thought have a theoretical foundation.
Many who disputed Jefferson did so not because of their concern for Negroes
("negrophilia"), but because they rejected natural history as the basis for social
science and maintained their adherence to political science. The significance of
this theoretical debate about man and social science has unfortunately been lost in
the efforts by historians either to shock us with Jefferson's prejudices or to shield
us from the stark implications of Jefferson's scientific ideas.

Thomas Jefferson's political thought as expressed in the *Notes* represents an attempt to combine the science of natural rights, which until then had been the principal foundation of his political thinking, with the new science of natural history.
Jefferson sought to graft natural history onto natural rights in an effort to create a
new and more complete social science. He is one of the few thinkers (as far as I
know, he may be the only one) to have attempted such a synthesis. If the *Notes*
shows that this attempt was conceivable, it also proves that it was implausible.
Other thinkers either embraced natural rights and ignored or rejected natural history, or they embraced natural history and ignored or rejected natural rights. Natural rights (often allied with political science) and natural history have almost always been in tension.

Setting aside Jefferson's scientific reasoning in the *Notes* and judging his argument only in terms of its political objectives, one must pronounce his effort a failure. The book did not create a broad movement for colonization, nor did it erode
support for slavery—indeed, it almost certainly had the opposite effect. By providing a new, scientifically grounded principle of racial hierarchy, the work allowed many to infer that the enslavement of blacks was according to nature. Jefferson's argument also damaged the case for natural rights and political science.
As the ideas of Jeffersonian natural history gained ground, natural rights came to
be widely regarded as merely a moral doctrine without any scientific foundation.[23]
According to mid-nineteenth-century social science, which was modeled on the
methods and approach of natural history, no truth became more self-evident than
all men were created unequal. Real social science, or so it was thought, started
from the varieties or races of man, not from the general properties of man as such.

This idea was widely used to support the slave-based regime of the Confederacy, which, some of its advocates claimed, represented the first genuinely scientifically founded political regime in human history.

In all of American political thought it would be difficult to find a more ill-advised or imprudent argument than Jefferson's contention about a natural hierarchy of the races. Two explanations of this error are possible: either Jefferson was political in the extreme, or he was extremely impolitic. The first explanation claims that Jefferson, mindful of how daunting was the political task of persuading slaveholders to end slavery, turned to a new and "harder" science to bolster his case. By appealing to nature in a sense that could supposedly be demonstrated by observations and experiments, Jefferson offered a scientific argument, with compelling emotional overtones, that he thought would promote his position against slavery. The unnaturalness of sexual union with an inferior race would induce whites to remove blacks from their midst, thereby also putting an end to slavery. According still to this explanation, whether or not Jefferson actually believed fully in the new science or trusted his observations, he offered the argument chiefly for its political effect. This interpretation makes Jefferson a profoundly political thinker, although one of profoundly dubious political judgment.

The other explanation attributes Jefferson's position to an impolitic cast of mind that derived from a doctrinaire application of modern science to politics. In this view, Jefferson proceeded on the assumption that modern science is a single, continuous form of knowledge that provides the best grounding for political life. Science in the modern sense takes precedence over "political" thinking, and a genuine thinker must follow science wherever it leads. There can be no defensible political science that claims the prerogative of instructing other scientific ways of thought or superintending how that thought should be presented. The truth of modern science and the political good are in harmony. According to this explanation, then, Jefferson, who accepted natural history as a bona fide part of modern science, sought to base his political thought in part on the premises of this new science. Although he hesitated before allowing the *Notes* to be published, in the end he saw no reason why a statesman should decline to speculate publicly on matters that a scientific researcher might discuss theoretically. By subordinating political thinking to modern science—and by holding that modern science and its methods could become the foundation of social science—Jefferson abandoned traditional political science and adopted a new view of what modern scientific thinking could accomplish in practical affairs. This understanding of Jefferson's cast of mind, incidentally, is the one expressed in *The Federalist*, albeit in a more political way.[24]

Judging from comments Jefferson later made in his letters, some scholars have suggested that he ultimately modified his view about the characteristics of the races. But while Jefferson always professed to keep an open mind on the subject, he never changed his view about the hierarchy of the races, nor did he ever repudiate his application of natural history to political affairs. His theoretical position remained the same. The most one can say is that he never restated his views publicly in anything like the way he had in the *Notes*.[25]

Many today take pleasure in trying to diminish Thomas Jefferson's reputation, hoping perhaps to ingratiate themselves with those promoting the agenda of the symbolic America. For my part, I confess to feeling only great sadness in recounting the theoretical error of one who did so much to lay the foundations of modern liberal democracy. To write this part of the book, I have come, as I often do at night, to one of the fine rooms that Jefferson designed around the magnificent lawn at the University of Virginia. Humbled by these surroundings, I can be assured that I have not yielded to the petty temptation to form an unjust judgment. Because Jefferson never entirely abandoned political science and natural rights thinking for ethnology, much excellent political analysis can be found in his writings. No greater document exists in the annals of human freedom than the Declaration of Independence, which bears no trace of the influence of natural history. At the same time, Jefferson must be charged with the dubious distinction of having contributed more than any of the other founders to the eclipse of the intellectual discipline that guided the creation of his country.

The Federalist

In 1787, the same year that Jefferson wrote a letter attacking the degeneracy thesis by claiming that the "European Reindeer could walk under the belly of our moose," another work of American thought, *The Federalist,* adopted an entirely different approach to the subject.[26] *The Federalist,* by almost every account America's greatest contribution to political science, rejected not only the basic proposition of American degeneracy but also any pretension of natural history to be a valid social science. At stake in the dispute between *The Federalist* and the natural historians is thus the decision about what kind of knowledge can properly claim to guide political life. The choice lay between natural history, with its factors of causality (the pre-political determinants of climate and race), and political science, with its emphasis on "moral causes," above all the laws and the political regime.[27]

Because *The Federalist*'s argument against the degeneracy thesis is not nearly as well known as Jefferson's, it is worthwhile to cite in full the passage in which

Publius offers his assessment. It is one of the most splendid texts in American literature:

> The world may politically, as well as geographically, be divided into four parts, each having a distinct set of interests. Unhappily for the other three, Europe, by her arms and by her negotiations, by force and by fraud, has in different degrees extended her dominion over them all. Africa, Asia, and America have successively felt her domination. The superiority she has long maintained has tempted her to plume herself as the mistress of the world and to consider the rest of mankind as created for her benefit. Men admired as profound philosophers have in direct terms attributed to her inhabitants a physical superiority and have gravely asserted that all animals, and with them the human species, degenerate in America—that even dogs cease to bark after having breathed awhile in our atmosphere. Facts have too long supported these arrogant pretensions of the European. It belongs to us to vindicate the honor of the human race, and to teach that assuming brother moderation. Union will enable us to do it. Disunion will add another victim to his triumphs. Let Americans disdain to be the instruments of European greatness! Let the thirteen States, bound together in a strict and indissoluble Union, concur in erecting one great American system superior to the control of all transatlantic force or influence and able to dictate the terms of the connection between the old and the new world![28]

This passage clearly has a strong rhetorical quality to it. Evoking the degeneracy thesis in 1787 was no longer necessary, as it had been a decade earlier, to protect American interests in Europe. Hamilton elects to discuss it here in order to rekindle Americans' anger and pride, sentiments that he then tries to harness and connect to the cause of the Union and the Constitution. The appeal to political sentiments is already a sign that *The Federalist* moves in a different world from that of the natural scientist—a world that speaks, not of the size of animal bones or the sexual prowess of different human groups, but of vindication, of overcoming disdain, and of teaching a lesson of moderation.

The Federalist's use of rhetoric confirms that it is a political book with a political purpose. It was written in a particular context, for a particular audience, with a particular objective in mind. Yet *The Federalist* is also a work of political science. It attempts, as far as possible, to ground its arguments in general principles. Even in its use of rhetoric, it does no more than put into practice what it explicitly teaches. Rhetoric, it argues, is a necessary instrument of any political work, not merely because good people must not forswear in advance the tools that bad people employ, but also because reason can go only so far in politics. Because "a nation of philosophers [is] an impossibility, the most rational government will not find it a superfluous advantage to have the prejudices of the community on its side."[29] Just as economics faces the basic condition of the scarcity of goods, so politics must accept a natural limit to the reliance on reason.

Yet the passage cited above is more than rhetorical. Hamilton introduces it with the observation that the matter at hand is a more theoretical topic than is "proper for a newspaper discussion" (*The Federalist* was published in a newspaper). The most striking aspect of the treatment is the way in which natural history is discussed. Hamilton refuses to engage it on its terms but insists on treating natural history by the canons of judgment of political science. There are, accordingly, no observations of the kind Jefferson had made in the *Notes* about the physical properties and intelligence of different groups. Instead, Hamilton proposes another kind of test for the validity of the degeneracy thesis: a political test. A decisive indicator of whether America is degenerating may be seen in what people accomplish in the political realm. If the United States can establish a just and viable republican constitution, it will have provided a refutation more convincing than anything that could be found in a scientific treatise of natural history.

In proposing this kind of test, *The Federalist* does not turn away from a study of nature. Rather, it proposes to study nature in a different way, a way that, given the subject matter, is arguably not less but more empirical. The part of nature in which political science is interested is human nature. Certain qualities of human nature reveal themselves through what people do concretely in their political activity in developed societies. What occurs in history, what is part of "that best oracle of wisdom, experience," provides the surest instruction about human nature.[30] There is therefore no discontinuity between the realm of political history and that of nature. To step outside the political realm into a world viewed from the supposedly more objective perspective of biological observations is to adopt an artificial starting point that ignores the most important source of empirical information about human nature.

The argument for the autonomy of political science goes a step further. According to *The Federalist,* there is no way to determine what constitutes political data—or to assess their significance—without recourse to political judgment. Phenomena in the world do not speak or label themselves as political; they become facts for a discipline only by their selection. But what method of selection is appropriate? Is it the method of a historical biological observation as proposed by the natural historians, or is it one that applies a continual refinement of political judgment, as suggested by *The Federalist*? The use of political judgment is found at the very outset of that work in defining what constitutes the central political fact of contemporary life: the experiment, still in the offing, to establish liberal democratic government. Grasping this "fact" requires making a judgment, for which even the study of history, which provides the data for formulating most general rules of political analysis, is inadequate. The sum of political phenomena is never exhausted by past events, and there are always new developments whose significance can be discerned only by a political assessment.

The rejection of the degeneracy thesis is part of *The Federalist*'s larger case against natural history as the discipline that should guide political life. Natural history's causal explanation of human development relies on the premise of varieties arrayed in a hierarchy. This view, Hamilton suggests, owes its ascendancy less to objective science than to the political predominance of Europe. Mentioning this point is already a way of beginning to call the validity of the thesis into question. But Hamilton is far too much the realist to think that theoretical criticism alone always carries the day. Political facts—in this case the predominance of Europe—inevitably have a certain weight. ("Facts have too long supported these arrogant pretensions of the European.") The degeneracy thesis must be challenged on the plane of politics as well as on the plane of theory. Just as events in theory sometimes influence politics, so too can events in politics sometimes influence theory.

According to *The Federalist,* modern rationalism is not—or at any rate must not be allowed to become—a mode of thinking that follows one generic method for all realms of human knowledge. The proponents of natural history, intent on having all sciences proceed according to the same model of explanation, are guilty of a grave theoretical error. Different *kinds* of sciences are appropriate to different kinds of phenomena. What is appropriate for studying animals and the relevant differences in that sphere is not appropriate for studying man and the relevant differences in the human sphere. The effort to collapse all sciences into one mold, using natural history as the model, produces a distortion of reality. This is the distortion of which admired philosophers—Buffon, Raynal, and Thomas Jefferson as well—are guilty.

But what, exactly, will have been disproved if America succeeds in its challenge? Here a fundamental theoretical choice must be made, for there are two possible answers. One is to say that an American success proves the superiority of the American to the European—that is, the superiority of one biological variety or tribe (the American) over another variety or tribe (the European). This conclusion, although it would refute the specific claim of Eurocentrism, would also confirm the theoretical premise of human varieties, on which it was based. The other possible answer is to assert, as Hamilton did, that an American success will "vindicate the honor of the human race." This is the position that *The Federalist* adopts: "Happily for America, happily we trust for the whole human race, [the leaders of the Revolution] pursued a new and more noble course [and] . . . reared the fabrics of government that have no model on the face of the globe."[31]

The American experiment interests the world not just because it may humble the European and cast doubt on the idea of a hierarchy of human varieties, but also because it offers an alternative account of the primary source of differentiation in human affairs. The most important differences derive not from distinctions among biological varieties of man, but from differences caused by moral and political factors. The political regime can be decisive. All peoples could take heart in an American success, because it would show what is possible for them to accomplish by political action.

Natural history and political science follow different models for how knowledge can be incorporated into human affairs and made active in human history. Natural history is a science of physical, pre-political factors, and the manipulation or engineering of these factors is the primary means of changing and controlling human societies. Statesmen and citizens, if they are to rely primarily on this science, must trust in the expertise of climatologists or biologists whose knowledge comes from tests that are beyond the statesman's or citizen's competence. At most, the political art is reduced to the task of deciding when and how to apply such knowledge. In contrast, political science constitutes a form of knowledge that is in principle intelligible to statesmen and to a substantial body of an enlightened citizenry, even if it is not often welcomed or easily accepted. Physical or pre-political factors must be considered, because they form part of the context in which politics takes place. But the primary determinants of societies derive from political actions and instruments—revolutions, laws, and constitutions.

The most fundamental difference between natural history and political science turns on the basic categories that each employs to study human beings and society. These categories govern how each science proceeds, because they define at the outset what is understood to possess primary reality, or being. The kinds of questions a science asks shape the answers that are given. In the case of natural history, the main category is the concept of human varieties, which is derived from the study of animals. Applied to the study of human society, this category makes the biological differentiation among groups the central point of inquiry. Research is then directed toward studying the basic biological limits and possibilities of each group.

The Federalist employs a different set of primary categories. It speaks first of "individuals" and "mankind," which are natural units in that they are biological entities. In between the individual and mankind *The Federalist* identifies other entities or units, which are derived from experience and observation of the political world. The two most important of these units are the "form of government" and a "people." For political science the form of government is the major object of study, because it is the unit that humans can use to give shape to a people. The form of government is not natural in the same sense that the individual and mankind are—it is not just "there" in a biological sense. Instead, it must be made or constructed. Still, government is natural in a different sense. It is an "indispensable necessity" for the good of man that responds to a basic predicament of the human situation. Humans wish to have a degree of security and justice in the conduct of affairs; yet because of the contrary effect of their own passions, they must construct an instrument of organization and restraint in order to achieve these objectives.[32]

Governments are not created in a vacuum, and many factors help to explain the shapes that they assume. One part of political science treats this question of causality. Its purpose is less to discover historical causality—why things have come to be as they are—than to devise general models of cause and effect that can prove helpful to political actors. One factor that *The Federalist* mentions to account for the forms of government is accident, which cannot be calculated within any deterministic system. The outcome of events and the fate of nations can sometimes hinge on a battle won or lost and a small step taken or not taken. (This indeterminacy is also one reason that political science does not focus on historical prediction but rather seeks knowledge that people can use under changing and unforeseen circumstances.) Another factor, and perhaps the most important one, is political action itself. Governments are in some measure the products of human beings attempting to influence political affairs by using such methods as force, fraud, and (potentially) "reflection and choice."[33] Political results are thus not always reducible to pre-political factors but must be studied and understood on their own terms—on the level of political passions and decisions and of the motives of political actors.

What occurs on the immediate political level is nevertheless conditioned by anterior factors. The most important such cause in political life is the existence of entities called "peoples" or "societies of men." These groupings of individuals have come to feel a common identity and are predisposed to act together, usually to form their own political system. Peoples display certain properties or characteristics; each people, in *The Federalist*'s vocabulary, has its own genius. What is possible or appropriate for one people may be impossible or inappropriate for another. The genius of a people constrains political action. It is also a partial standard for action, in the sense that any practical strategy must take account of the limits and possibilities deriving from the genius. As Hamilton remarked later (in 1799), "A government must be fitted to a nation as much as a coat to the individual, and consequently what may be good at Philadelphia may be bad at Paris and ridiculous at Petersburg."[34]

The Federalist goes one step further back in the chain of causality by considering some of the factors that condition the formation of a people: geography, stock (which one may suppose includes ethnicity and race), language, customs or cultural affinities, religion, an attachment to a common set of principles of government, and a common history of struggle for the same goal.[35] Taken as a whole, this list makes clear that a people is not exclusively defined by preexisting biological characteristics of race or ethnicity; a people may form as a result of factors that cut across biological characteristics. At least two of the factors on the list of what forms a people—attachment to principles of government and collective sacrifice for the same goal—may themselves have been subject to past political influence. The discussion of what causes a people thus has a circular character to it. Political action at some earlier point has created a people and formed its genius, after which the existence of that people with its own genius becomes a major constraint on present political action. In the case of most peoples, there is no history that is not already a political history.

A people, accordingly, is not necessarily a natural biological unit. Peoples form and change composition and character. Usually, this change results from the slow, unconscious effects of material factors or of accident, which is why the process is often described as organic. But the formation or transformation of a people is also subject to influence by deliberate political action. Political science aims to understand how peoples form, as the statesman may need to constitute or reconstitute a people. Steps may need to be taken, for example, to help different peoples occupying the same territory be induced to meld into one people. Such a process might be promoted by a common struggle, especially a military struggle, on behalf of the same principles. (The Revolutionary War certainly helped to solidify the American colonies into one unit.) The process of forming a people, known today by the expression "nation building," may also be promoted by a government that wins the respect and attachment of those living under it. *The Federalist* applies this lesson of political science in its own attempt to lay the foundation for a united American people: "A NATION, without a NATIONAL GOVERNMENT, is . . . an awful spectacle."[36]

At the time of the founding, the challenge of creating one people in America was left unresolved with regard to the division between the races. Although it is unclear what step could practically have been taken at the time of the Convention in 1787, it is interesting to consider the approach that Hamilton and John Jay discussed during the Revolutionary War. Hamilton at that point saw a rare opportunity to begin to knit together a single people by using large numbers of black soldiers to fight against the British. Hamilton's analysis represents a practical application of political science to the problem of making a people and invites comparison with Jefferson's analysis based on natural history:

> I have not the least doubt, that negroes will make very excellent soldiers, with proper management. . . . I foresee that this project will have to combat much opposition from prejudice and self-interest. The contempt we have been taught to entertain for the blacks, makes us fancy many things founded neither in reason nor experience; and an unwillingness to part with property of so valuable a kind will furnish a thousand arguments [against the scheme]. But it should be considered that if we do not make use of them in this way, the enemy probably will; and that the best way to counteract the temptations they will hold out will be to offer them ourselves. An essential part of the plan is to give them their freedom with their muskets. This will secure their fidelity, animate their courage, and I believe will have a good influence on those who remain, by opening a door to their emancipation. This circumstance, I confess, has no small weight in inducing me to wish the success of the project; for the dictates of humanity and true policy equally interest me in favor of this unfortunate class of men.[37]

The study of causality in *The Federalist* is guided by the overall purpose of political science. Political science is less concerned with developing an exhaustive account of historical causality—of explaining why things came to be as they now are—than it is with elaborating a body of knowledge that will assist those acting in the political world. The purpose of political science is not purely theoretical (knowledge for its own sake); it is practical as well. Political science is designed to help guide human interventions (including decisions to desist from action) for the benefit of creating a better society. Analyses of causality are partly offered from this perspective, as a way of understanding the factors that constrain political choice. The partial or qualified interest of political science in the theoretical question of historical causality also has a theoretical justification. Given the large roles that accident and human agency play in human affairs, there are limits to establishing laws of historical causality.

Returning from *The Federalist*'s broad discussion of causality to the immediate question of the degeneracy thesis, Hamilton aims to vindicate the human race against the European's claim of superiority (Eurocentrism). He proposes—to borrow contemporary terminology—that the United States lead a coalition of the marginalized or Third World peoples of Africa, Asia, and the Americas against the op-

pressors of the First World. But contemporary terminology is perhaps more misleading than helpful, for in contrast to the contemporary ideologies of Third
Worldism and difference, *The Federalist* stresses the common nature of human
beings. Hamilton proposes overcoming the arrogant pretensions of the European,
not by complaining of an unjust hegemony or by claiming the status of victim or
underling, but by accomplishing an objective that will surpass anything achieved
by those who believe they rank higher on the scale of human biology.

America is so far from being Eurocentric that it was founded on a rejection of
Eurocentrism. Fashionable thinkers who speak of America's Eurocentrism—by
which they mean, incidentally, about the same thing that Europeans mean by
Americanism—are expressing what is at best a confused half-truth, one that col-
lapses all strands of Enlightenment and rationalist thought into one hopelessly
homogeneous category. American intellectuals who adopt this way of thinking
swear allegiance to the first postmodern commandment: thou shalt not repress difference. How curious—no, how sad—it is that the only difference they refuse to
acknowledge is their own country's distinctive historical experience.

Particularism and Universalism

Contemporary literary criticism and postmodern philosophy have assumed as
their mission the task of exposing the awful homogenizing effect of rationalist
thought. Referred to sometimes as the logic of identity or logocentrism, rationalist thought is also known as Americanism. Americanism is held to be responsible
for promoting a stultifying universalism and for repressing particularisms and differences, both at home and abroad. Liberal democracy is the political form that reflects and promotes this universalist bias.

The conflict between universalism and particularism is certainly not a new
theme. It dominated debates in political theory after the French Revolution, when
European conservatives attacked abstract reason in an effort to save distinctive
and traditional communities. But even before the French Revolution, the conflict
was of concern to political science. Up to this point, I have emphasized the universalist side of *The Federalist*'s position: in rejecting the category of biological
varieties as the starting point in the study of human differentiation, *The Federalist* makes free use of the concepts of mankind, the human race, human nature, human reason, and the constitution of man.[38] Its universalism also supports the argument, rejected by proponents of the idea of human varieties, that the peoples of
any race on any continent possess the potential to develop free governments.

But the political science of *The Federalist* has another side, one that is highly suspicious of general ideas and doctrines that envisage the coming of a universal order based on political liberalism and the rights of man. *The Federalist* does indeed hope for the spread of free government, but it understands that the future will be decided by *political* actions. *The Federalist* rejects any source of movement in human affairs beyond politics, be it in history or sociology, that asserts the inevitable emergence of a new world order. Such theories are the precursors of ideologies and constitute a kind of philosophical demagogy; they are offered by "visionary and designing men" and "political projectors," who hold out the "deceitful dream" of a coming "golden age" of "perpetual peace." Political universalism is a doctrinaire mode of thought that purports to be rationalist because it begins, not with myths or supernatural causes, but with (allegedly) natural causes. Its conclusions, however, come from "speculations" devoid of concrete analysis based on the "history of mankind" and "experience." According to *The Federalist,* the political situation is one in which mankind is divided into different communities and regimes, where the potential for conflict is an enduring feature of the human situation.[39]

I have observed that political science rejects natural history's category of biological varieties as the source of difference among mankind. I now note that it also rejects those "idle theories" of science (abstract philosophy and history) that fold everything together into a single, controlling cause inaugurating the coming-into-being of a "happy empire" of united mankind.[40] Political science in the late eighteenth century was engaged in a two-front war: against a reductive hard science (natural history), which favored group particularism based on biological characteristics; and against an abstract philosophy of history, which favored a vague political universalism. Despite the clear differences between the two, they shared an important theoretical position: the political realm is controlled by something deeper or more fundamental than any political cause. In the one case it was climate or human varieties; in the other, a form of inevitable historical movement. Given this agreement, it is not surprising to find instances of the same thinker— Buffon and Jefferson are examples—going beyond political causality in both directions, at one moment espousing biological particularism and at another philosophical universalism.

The rejection of a political source of causality by the proponents of natural history and the philosophy of history leads to a final reflection. Contrary to a widespread assumption in philosophy today, the deepest theme in the study of human affairs may not be fully grasped by reference to the distinction between particularism and universalism. This distinction is too general or theoretical. There is a prior and more concrete actuality: what it is that actually generates and characterizes particularisms or universalisms in different realms. According to *The Feder-alist,* the realms of reality are not homogeneous: the laws that generate particulars and universals differ according to the different realms of being, according to whether the world in question is biological or moral and political. The political realm must be studied by analyzing political phenomena on their own terms, as a distinct and fundamental part of reality not derivative of or reducible to other realms.

Political Science and Modern Views of Man

The starting point of political science also invites comparison with the two dominant contemporary views of man: the humanitarian view and the school of difference. As with the two eighteenth-century opponents of political science, these modern views of man assume that the political realm is governed by a cause or reality beyond politics. The humanitarian view sees mankind as being ulti-mately unified or one—a position grounded in a supposedly established fact about human biology. Whereas in the eighteenth century biology favored the theory of different varieties, in the second half of the twentieth century it has insisted on the unity of mankind. From this fact humanitarian thinkers draw the conclusions that political or cultural differences are conventional (and should be respected only up to a point) and that the proper norm for all men is ultimately an "ethic of univer-sal brotherhood."[41] From biological unity—not from any kind of political analy-sis—comes a standard in favor of some form of political universalism.

In contrast, the school of difference (or postmodernism) boasts that it has iden-tified and exposed the homogenizing project of modern rationalism, including that contained in modern biological thinking. By making us aware of this project, the school of difference has laid a foundation for a new counterproject to escape ra-tionalism's control. It claims to have rediscovered and valorized human diversity, which it locates in some notion or other of culture, for which language and (in-creasingly) race and ethnicity are seen as the source. Many of those who consider themselves profound (as distinct from intelligent) have gravitated to this position. Put off, understandably, by the thinness and preachy superficiality of some liberal humanitarianism, proponents of difference argue that reality can be accessed only through distinct cultural perspectives. The old Enlightenment idea of humanism is a dangerous ruse—a category invented by modern rationalists to control others and to suppress difference.[42]

In literary criticism and philosophy, where the profound greatly outnumber the intelligent, the school of difference has clearly taken charge. According to its categories of analysis, to employ reason or the logic of identity makes one a proponent of an undesirable universalism; to favor difference (as one should) means that one has moved beyond rationalism to another mode of thinking, variously referred to as postmetaphysical thought or thought that embraces feeling. Accepting these categories has the unfortunate effect of pushing those with a certain faith in reason into a position of greater universalism and pushing those with an inclination toward the particular into a position of greater irrationalism. The rationalist begins to think she must despise patriotism, while the patriot begins to think he must shun rationality. Political moderation is left with no theoretical foundation. The emphasis on culture has also promoted political extremism, whether of the Right or the Left. Postmodernist thought in its harder form has led to the support of the *Volk* or nation as the only genuine source of community; in its softer form, it has led to the recognition of various racial, linguistic, and gendered groups as the deepest source of identity.

Political scientists would no doubt prefer to leave these theoretical debates about difference and being to the philosophers. The idea that such metaphysical categories are what govern political life, as if politics were nothing but inert matter pounded into shape by philosophical ideas, must strike any reasonable political scientist as a kind of madness. Practicing political scientists know from experience that the political realm has a certain autonomy from theory and that political life must be grasped by looking first at the political world. At the same time, however, no one can deny that theoretical doctrines have greatly influenced political thinking and have even prompted the formation of different parties in the real world. The political world is not sealed off hermetically from the theoretical world. Theory opens into politics, especially in the modern era (that is, since the sixteenth century), when philosophy has increasingly considered its function to be not merely interpreting the world but transforming it.

Postmodern thought has declared itself the foe of modern theory, seeking to overcome or put an end to this transformative project. But in so doing, it has embraced a political project of its own that is a mirror image of what it wishes to destroy. It proceeds on the view that a political world governed by theory must now be freed by an antitheory led by a literary project. Politics is the realm in which to change or deconstruct the past errors of theory. But the record to date shows that this literary-political project has been no less assuming than the project fashioned by Enlightenment theory. Literary critics, who were once content to interpret their texts, now are bent on changing the world. And like the thinkers they criticize, the postmodern program is derived from the realm of theory, not from a concrete analysis of the political world. The political realm is no more than a stage on which different theoretical ideas—previously metaphysics, now antitheory—play themselves out in history. Political affairs have no independent status within the primary categories of reality.

In the end, then, the political scientist cannot avoid all theoretical matters. Certain questions must be addressed, if only to save the autonomy of the political realm from being captured and reduced to the status of a mere reflection of the reality of another realm. Political science, although it accepts the empirical fact that different philosophic projects have been important moving forces inside political life, rejects the idea that political life simply follows theory. Politics has never been and can never become this theoretical; it is never merely the stuff of speculative projects. To free the study of politics from the pervasive grip of this purely intellectualist way of thinking, political scientists must take a step that no literary critic has yet dared to contemplate: they must put the political back into the study of politics.

Every important theme in the modern debate about the symbolic America was prefigured in the initial dispute in the founding era. First, there was the propagation of a discourse that depicted America as an alien place characterized by a diseased environment and a deformed culture. This discourse continues today. Second, many thinkers, American as well as European, sought to replace America's special intellectual contribution of political science with disciplines that were indifferent or hostile to the cause of free government. Such efforts are found everywhere in contemporary thought. And finally, against these hostile doctrines, there were the courageous actions of those who defended natural rights and political science. From this last example we can take heart. Faced today with the bemused contempt of those admired as profound intellectuals, it still belongs to us to vindicate the honor of the human race.

3

★ ★ ★

America in the Mirror of France:
The Two Revolutions

The classical historian Thucydides called the Peloponnesian War the greatest "motion" up to his day. The comparable event of modern times is no doubt the French Revolution, described by Alexis de Tocqueville as the "most momentous event of all history."[1] The importance of the French Revolution derives not only from its enormous political consequences, which shook the foundation of monarchy throughout Europe, but also from its extraordinary influence on modern thought. For many of the philosophers and writers of the late eighteenth and early nineteenth centuries, the French Revolution, viewed as the manifestation of the entire Enlightenment project, was the signal event of the modern age.

In the realm of political thought, the modern categories of "Right" and "Left" derive from the French Revolution. These words originally referred to the physical location of the various groups and parties at the Constitutional Assembly. On the right sat those who were opposed to the Revolution or were undecided, and on the left, those who supported it. After the Revolution, the Right came to designate the political forces who hated the Revolution and who regarded rationalist thought as the root disaster of modern times. The Left designated those who lamented the failure of the Revolution and who sought, under one form or another, to renew it. The development of the principal school of modern thought, historicism, was also connected with the French Revolution. The Right became conservative by adopting a version of historical thinking that provided a foundation of opposition to the Revolution, while the Left embraced first a doctrine of historical progress and then the full-blown historicism of Marx to support the Revolution.

Where, one might then ask, did this leave America and the American Revolution? Those on the Right initially saw the American Revolution as the source for the French Revolution and as a part of the same rationalist movement. As

Friedrich von Schlegel wrote in his *Philosophy of History* (1828), "North America had been to France and the rest of Europe the real school and nursery of all these revolutionary principles."[2] Given this similarity, those on the Right held that the horrible excesses of the Revolution in France or perhaps other evils, such as a lowering of standards or a homogenization of society, were bound to appear at some point in the United States. As time passed and the French Revolution receded in memory, America became for many on the Right the active symbol of revolutionary thought and served as a living reminder of the terrible consequences of rationalism and of democracy.

Those on the Left initially hailed the American Revolution as a precursor of the French Revolution. Indeed, in the first phases of the French Revolution, the group that pushed the process forward was sometimes referred to as the *américanistes*; it included such illustrious persons as Marquis de Condorcet, Baron de l'Aulne Turgot, and Emmanuel-Joseph Sieyès.[3] Even then, however, this group did not consider either America's revolutionary principles or its political science to represent the most advanced wave of the revolutionary cause. With the passage of time, this qualified approval gave way to growing opposition, as those on the Left began to find in America more to despise than to admire. America had stolen or coopted the modern revolutionary cause and brought it to a halt before it could achieve its higher goals. Later in the nineteenth century, when a return to the old form of monarchy seemed impossible and when capitalism was viewed as the primary engine of oppression, America for the Left became the symbol of the Right. In fact, America symbolized something worse than the ancien régime, for it lacked the old regime's charm and sense of community and was more methodical and brutal in its oppression. For the team of Jean-Paul Sartre and Simone de Beauvoir, America was the country where the "most odious form of capitalism had triumphed" (Sartre) and Americans were culturally a "people of sheep" (Beauvoir).[4]

America has been a symbol of the Left to the Right and of the Right to the Left. Perhaps, then, America should be placed in the Center. The Center, however, can refer either to a vague and undefined position between two poles, or it can designate a clear and coherent alternative in its own right. Neither the Left nor the Right in Europe wished to accord America the status of representing a distinct position. Whatever their differences, proponents of these two positions agreed on the basic terms of the debate. The modern age had only two options or parties: a party of revolution, rationalism, and democracy, and a party of restoration, traditionalism, and monarchy. In this scheme, there was no place for America and no space for political science.

America's founders had a different view. They asserted the distinctiveness both of the political system in the United States and of the intellectual method on which it relied. The difference with the Right was obvious. Although America would properly heed the opinions of former times, the founders took pride in breaking with past models of government and in leading a "revolution which has no parallel in the annals of human society."[5] The difference with the Left, although not as evident, was no less important. For America's founders, it was false to speak of a unified revolutionary party that everywhere wore the mantle of rectitude and justice. Inside the revolutionary movement were moderates committed to constitutional government and radicals whose views would lead to new forms of tyranny. For the founders the most fundamental of political distinctions—that between despotism and freedom—did not correspond, as the Left insisted, to the difference between the pre- and postrevolutionary eras. Postrevolutionary politics could also be despotic.

Just as the American founders could not embrace the traditionalism of the Right, which grounded societies in a veneration for antiquity and in some mysterious principle of organic development, so too they rejected the new philosophy (or ideology) of the Left, which grounded societies in an inevitable movement of progress in history. In the first case, societies did not "grow" spontaneously toward greater beauty or justice, like the fabled oak trees of which conservatives liked to speak. But neither did the advent of Enlightenment philosophy guarantee the evolution of just or prosperous regimes. Philosophy, moving by itself, did not control the realm of political activity. For the founders, the decisive events affecting each nation still depended on political actions taken in a world filled with contingencies and accidents.

In view of its distinctiveness, the American Revolution deserves more attention from philosophers than it has received. And although no one questions the momentousness—I will not say greatness—of the French Revolution, a bit more modesty about its significance is in order. The importance of the French Revolution depended not only on its character but also on the fact that, until a half-century ago, Europe was at the center of the world and France was at the center of Europe. The center of power in the world has shifted, and the fate of America is now of greater interest. If history (as some hold) is always being rewritten in light of our present consciousness projected back on the past, America's position today justifies a narrative that claims for the American Revolution a more prominent position in the realm of political thought. Events now suggest that America, not France, has become, in the strange terms of Continental philosophy, this epoch's "world historical nation" that has been entrusted with guiding liberal democracy "from its latent embryonic stage until it blossoms into the self-conscious freedom of ethical life and presses in upon world history."[6]

The Two Revolutions

The French Revolution could never have happened in America, and the American Revolution could never have happened in France. These events were so different, and the circumstances that produced them so dissimilar, that referring to them both by the term "revolution" seems to call attention only to the inadequacy of our language. The French Revolution was a war of one part of society against another; the American Revolution, a war of independence against a colonial power. France's Revolution had different and discontinuous phases, ending in the rejection of the Revolution itself; America's Revolution went through different periods, but these followed so consistent a line of development that the Revolution is generally understood to encompass both the War of Independence and the writing and ratification of the Constitution.

In light of these differences, why should anyone bother to compare the two events? Logical as this objection may be, everyone who has reflected on them—from Alexander Hamilton and Alexis de Tocqueville to Georg Jellinek and Emile Boutmy or Robert Palmer and François Furet—has been compelled to make some kind of comparative judgment. Fate seems to have decreed that the two Revolutions should be eternally measured, one against the other, for the honor of inaugurating modern politics.

However they may disagree about how to rank the two Revolutions, historians today tend to agree on two criteria for evaluation. The first is to judge the Revolutions according to their practical political results. By this standard the American Revolution is favored. The second is to judge the Revolutions according to their "moral" or "cultural" consequences and by the ideas or models for a just or good society that they have inspired. By this standard, the Left—but not only the Left—has accorded pride of place to the French Revolution. One historian, Paul Berman, has nicely summarized the standard view on both criteria: "The American Revolution was a political success, which showed the world that feudal systems could be overthrown and proper foundations for freedom . . . could be laid. But intellectually the American Revolution was less impressive. . . . The French Revolution went in the other direction. Politically it was mostly a failure. But precisely because of the calamities and heartbreaks that resulted, the French writers pored obsessively over the arts and science of revolution and kept asking what a revolution is supposed to be, and what is a proper revolutionary aim and how can things go better next time. This made the French Revolution a gigantic intellectual success."[7]

Relying on these two grounds of judgment, let me state first the case for the superiority of the American Revolution. It was clearly the more moderate of the two. It proceeded, all allowances being made for the circumstances, in a rather civilized way, avoiding most of the excesses of the guillotine and the Terror. The American Revolution produced a stable political regime, not a succession of empires and republics like that of postrevolutionary France. Finally, the memory of the American Revolution has generally worked to promote national unity (the Civil War period apart), whereas the French Revolution has operated, at least until the 1980s, as a divisive symbol; in addition to the intellectual battles for or against the Revolution as a whole, its adherents have also fought among themselves as partisans of its different phases—moderates, for example, aligning with the period of Comte de Mirabeau's influence, socialists lionizing the period of Georges-Jacques Danton's supremacy, and communists identifying with the period of Maximilien Robespierre's reign.

Historians have offered three reasons for the American Revolution's greater practical success. The first emphasizes the different conditions that existed in the two nations, which generally are said to have favored a happy result in America while virtually guaranteeing failure in France. America in the late eighteenth century had no privileged castes or legal orders of nobility, whereas France was burdened by centuries of feudal baggage and profound inequalities, both economic and social. In America, the Revolution's enemy was a foreign power, which united Americans in a common hatred; in France, the enemy was a domestic regime (the monarchy and the nobility), which divided the nation against itself and unleashed the passions of internecine conflict. In America, economic conditions at the time of the Revolution were fairly good; in France, ill-fed mobs roamed the streets of Paris, pressuring the National Assembly and offering ripe opportunities for demagogic appeals.

One of the clearest statements of the importance of material conditions in shaping the character of the two Revolutions is found in Georg Hegel's *Philosophy of History*. Hegel pointed to the abundance of open land in America, which he thought alleviated class tensions by allowing the poor to have access to a resource that might change their station. From this analysis comes Hegel's well-known remark: "Had the forests of Germany been in existence, the French Revolution would never have occurred."[8]

A second explanation offered for the greater practical success of the American

Revolution emphasizes the higher quality of American leadership. Judgments about leadership are notoriously difficult, especially when they involve evaluations of individuals from different nations. If we therefore confine ourselves to considering each nation's leaders separately, we are surely on safe grounds in asserting that the revolutionary period in America produced the country's most talented group of leaders, culminating in the Constitutional Convention, which assembled the "brightest minds and the noblest men that have ever appeared in the New World."[9] Likewise, no one questions that America was guided by a military leader and statesman of extraordinary capacity and moral stature: George Washington. In Chateaubriand's words, "This man who makes no great impression, because he is so just in character, merged his existence with that of his country: his glory is civilization's heritage, his fame rises like a public shrine whence flows the pure waters of an endless spring."[10]

On the French side, in contrast, it would be difficult to argue that the revolutionary generation produced the best political leaders France has had to offer, whether one wishes to measure quality in terms of political ability or of intellectual or moral worth. It has been observed by more than one scholar of French history that, "after Mirabeau and before Bonaparte, the only great figure in the Revolution was the Revolution itself."[11]

The third explanation for the greater practical success of the American Revolution emphasizes the ideas or modes of thought that guided the two events. The American Revolution produced a more favorable result because, along with its recourse to natural rights philosophy, it consulted political science in helping to construct its new government. The French Revolution was driven by ideology or by what Condorcet called the "new philosophy."[12] This was a new form of purportedly rational thought that derived its conclusions more from abstract speculation than from an acquaintance with the facts of a particular place and time.

As a body of rational thought, political science differed, as did the new philosophy, from pre-Enlightenment modes of thought that appealed to revelation or that sought to ground society in the authority of myth, superstition, or custom. Political science broke from this kind of traditionalism, even as it maintained its indebtedness to classical rationalism. The American system was established not on a "blind veneration for antiquity, for custom, or for names" but on the basis of "reflection and choice" guided by nature and political science.[13] The new philosophy's break with traditionalism and with the past was of a different character. Its adherents sharply distinguished between the old era of superstition and blind authority and the new era of enlightenment and reason. "The true science of society," wrote the abbé Sieyès, "does not date back very far."[14] Between the old regime and the new, there could be no continuities or connections. In the French Revolution, a new calendar would be inaugurated, Year One beginning in the postrevolutionary era. A huge temple in Paris was erected to Reason—La Madeleine—at which Reason's adherents would presumably worship (if such a scenario were not a contradiction in terms).

For proponents of the new philosophy, there were accordingly only two parties to the modern controversy: a party of the old regime and a party of the Revolution. All genuine human sciences belonged to the party of the Revolution, and political science (properly understood) therefore belonged to this party. If many American conclusions were flawed, it was only because the Americans had not gone far enough and divested themselves of all prejudices. By the time of the Constitutional Convention, however, it was clear to many Americans that political science differed not only from traditionalism but also from the new philosophy. Although *The Federalist* opens by distinguishing political science from traditionalism, it quickly set its sights on this new way of thinking, which in the modern age of rationalism represented a much greater temptation, and therefore a greater threat, than traditionalism. The new philosophy, according to *The Federalist,* moved in its own self-created world, taking its bearings from the "reveries of those political doctors whose sagacity disdains the admonitions of experimental instruction."[15] It was marked by its disregard of "experience." In one of its most dangerous tenets, the new philosophy held that theory itself, or some other material force that theory comprehended, was unfolding in progressive stages and controlled the course of history. An era of peace and universalism was in the offing. To this Publius responds, "Have we not already seen enough of the fallacy and extravagance of those idle theories which have amused us with promises of an exemption from the imperfections, the weaknesses, and the evils incident to society in every shape?"[16]

Although some referred to the political application of the new philosophy as political science, it was instead ideological thought that imposed its own structure on the political phenomena. Tocqueville later gave to this caste of mind the label of the "literary spirit" applied to politics, which "looks for the ingenious and the new, rather than the true, loves what makes a display rather than what is useful, . . . and [prefers] decisions made by loose impressions rather than by hard reasons."[17] Captivated by this spirit, French thinkers "philosophized without constraints on the origins of societies, on the essential nature of government, and on the primordial rights of mankind," but they knew nothing about concrete problems of governance or about how to build and sustain political institutions. The French preached Reason but scarcely ever applied reason. They had a political science in name only; they were instead foisting vague philosophic or aesthetic notions onto a fictive discipline that they called political science. Everything was "abstract and general theory . . . to which they blindly entrusted themselves."[18]

It makes a difference, of course, which of these three explanations of the greater practical success of the American Revolution one emphasizes. If physical or economic conditions were the principal cause, then the happier result in the United States was due not to any human quality or contrivance but to luck. It hardly seems edifying, after all, to praise or blame forests, however lovely they may be. If the quality of the leaders was the main cause, there is a great deal more to be learned, as one can analyze the statesmanship that contributes to political success and failure. Yet because various leaders act in such different contexts, deriving general lessons can be difficult. If, finally, the doctrines or ideas governing the two Revolutions were responsible for the different results, it may be possible to learn something about the kind of thought that can guide society. What contributed to the successful creation of liberal democracy in the past can perhaps help us to preserve it in our own time.

If the American Revolution was the more successful of the two events in a practical sense, many nevertheless insist that the French Revolution was the superior and the more praiseworthy. It offered something more compelling and admirable than anything grasped by the standard of practicality, and it aspired to a more just society and authentic existence than that sought by the American Revolution. This view has long been the argument of the Left, although the Left has borrowed freely from many of the images of the American Revolution created by conservative thinkers. As in the case of the argument for the American Revolution, there are three grounds for the judgment in favor of France.

First, the French Revolution is said to have been a more intense event than the American Revolution, one that revealed the character of the human situation at a more profound level and that more sharply exposed the extremes of human possibilities. Those who lived through the French Revolution experienced more, saw more clearly into the human condition, and drank more deeply of the cup of life. The superiority of the French Revolution on this score is confirmed by what occurred in the artistic realm. The American Revolution inspired no great drama, literature, poetry, or music, and it produced only modest accomplishments in painting. Compare this legacy to the artistic outpouring generated by the French Revolution, which includes—in addition to everything created in France—poetry by Wordsworth, music by Beethoven, and philosophy by Hegel. The French Revolution in its first phase inspired scores of works that either glorified or vilified the event. In a second wave, it prompted reflections that explored, sometimes with

73

irony but more often with disillusionment, what it meant to live after, and in the shadow of, so great a moment in history. Because they were so extreme, the passions unleashed by the French Revolution became a reproach to those poor souls living afterward in quieter times, when people could only dream of acting heroically. (Stendhal has his Count Altimira declare, "There are no more true passions left in the nineteenth century; that is why everyone in France is so bored.") Even many of those who hated the results of the French Revolution were captivated by the event and felt diminished if they had not taken part in it.[19]

Artists' neglect of the American Revolution might, of course, be attributed to nothing more than a dearth of artistic talent in America at the time, when the country lacked a large intellectual class and still looked to England for much of its culture. Whereas hundreds of poets, philosophers, and composers saw the French Revolution firsthand and were ready to comment on it, only a handful were similarly occupied with events in the Americas. The heroic exploits of those Americans who risked life, fortune, and sacred honor unquestionably deserve a more fitting poetic tribute than Philip Freneau's "American Independence" and a nobler musical score than "Yankee Doodle." Even so, it must be admitted that the American Revolution did not hold the same fascination for the artistic imagination as had the French Revolution. Say what you will, it is difficult—if one is speaking, for example, of the Constitutional Convention in Philadelphia—to make that much of a group of statesmen deliberating privately for three months about the nature of republican government and constitutionalism. In contrast, the public declamations of the speakers of the National Assembly, the constant meetings of intellectuals, the mobs roaming the streets—and all this taking place in Paris—make for much better theater. The French Revolution, at least in its initial stage, had the wonderful artistic advantage of unity of subject, time, and place.

In partial rejoinder, I should note that, by this reasoning, the superiority of the French Revolution turns more on aesthetic than on political criteria, and a case can be made that what contributes to the aesthetic often detracts from the political. What is interesting is not always politically sound, and what is politically sound is not always interesting. Of course this objection conflicts with the dominant views found in today's presiding intellectual discipline of literary criticism, where the tendency is to conflate the aesthetic and the political and to render political judgments on the basis of aesthetic criteria. To deny critics this prerogative would jeopardize such journals as the *New York Review of Books* or *Lire,* where those schooled in the latest literary theories deliver themselves of their witty and weighty political opinions.

Second, the French Revolution is said to be superior to the American Revolution because it was the more self-conscious of the two, spawning a degree of reflection and thought about the event that was never approached in the case of events in the United States. The French Revolution was more philosophic. This view was articulated at the time by Condorcet, who, in his *Sketch for an Historical Picture of the Progress of the Human Mind,* traced the ten stages of human progress, from man's origins to the imminent victory of the new philosophy. According to this work, philosophy now has as its function the guidance and direction of the course of human affairs. Statesmen and political actors are its servants. Philosophy produced the American Revolution, which was the first major instance of the new philosophy being applied directly to political history and which opened the eyes of the world to the possibility of change. But the American Revolution was only a prelude, so to speak, to the real event. The next and higher stage of philosophy was announced by the French Revolution, which was based on principles that were "purer, more precise, and more profound than those that guided the Americans." The authors of the American constitutions (state and federal) were still tainted by the "prejudices that [they] imbibed in their youth." The French, in comparison to the Americans, "more successfully escaped every kind of prejudice."[20]

One kind of prejudice that Condorcet had in mind was the principle of the separation of powers. Before the Revolution, many in France had read the constitutions of the American states, which Benjamin Franklin had translated in advance of going to France. By far the most acclaimed was the constitution of Pennsylvania, the only state that had a unicameral legislature. (It also had a very weak executive.) For Turgot and Condorcet, this constitution was the closest of any in America to serving as a model of good government, as it appealed to their sense of geometric logic and to their theoretical notions of what constituted pure sovereignty in a democracy. During the same period, America's founders, based on their observations and experience, had rejected the Pennsylvania constitution as a model for the federal government. Checks on the capacity of the people to put its will immediately into action was a healthy feature of constitutional government: "A dependence on the people is, no doubt, the primary control on the government; but experience has taught mankind the necessity of auxiliary precautions."[21]

The idea that the French Revolution is the truly philosophic revolution was later given its most general and famous expression by the most important philosopher of the nineteenth century, Georg Wilhelm Friedrich Hegel. According to Hegel, the French Revolution, not the American Revolution, revealed the fundamental truths about the unfolding of Spirit and self-consciousness in the world. In his *Phenomenology of the Spirit,* Hegel argued that it was through the French Revolution's claim of "absolute liberty" and "pure will" that one could now begin to glimpse the highest synthesis of civilization. History in a sense thus comes to an end with the French Revolution.

It is only fair to point out, however, that Hegel never argued that the participants in the Revolution themselves achieved this philosophic insight; this was accomplished afterward by certain philosophers reflecting on the meaning of the event. As for the participants, it would be difficult to claim that the leaders in France operated with a greater awareness than those in America or that the Parisian mobs possessed greater philosophic insight than the citizens of Philadelphia or Boston. If we take reason in its ordinary meaning, the American founding represented an equally self-conscious effort to employ reason. *The Federalist* opens by explaining that it was for Americans to decide the fateful question of "whether societies of men are really capable or not of establishing good government from reflection and choice, or whether they are forever destined to depend for their political constitutions on accident and force."[22] As for the French political leaders, Hegel readily conceded that, from the viewpoint of the history of the Spirit, they were acting unconsciously, being moved not so much by reason as by (in Hegelian terms) the cunning of Reason. And if one accepts the intriguing thesis of the French historian Augustin Cochin, those who "made" the French Revolution were swept along by an inner dynamic, born of the Revolution itself, that they could not control but only follow. They were marionettes acting out the roles assigned to them.[23]

The claim that the French Revolution is superior because it is the more philosophic of the two events is open to an objection like the one that applies to its supposed aesthetic superiority. What does it mean to say of a political revolution that it excels "philosophically" rather than politically? Is it not an abnegation of politics to act on behalf of philosophy rather than the common good? At the very least, the philosophic criterion distances one from concern with the fate of France or the French people. In fact, once nineteenth-century German philosophy appropriated the French Revolution as the climactic moment of world philosophic history, it became almost a matter of indifference that it had ever been a real event in the history of France. The French Revolution now had a higher function to perform. It became the general property of the intellectual, serving—rather as "America" serves today—as a category in philosophy and a symbol in literature. The French people expended their labor to produce a revolution, but it was the intellectuals who reaped the surplus value.

A corollary to the claim of the superior philosophic status of the French Revolution, but one that gives a larger billing to the actors in the Revolution itself, is that France rebelled not just for France but also for humanity. The French Revolution is therefore more "world historic," to use Hegel's formulation. Thus in

1902 Emile Boutmy indignantly rejected the notion that America's statements of rights, as in the Declaration of Independence, had an important influence either on French thinkers or on the world at large. These American documents, in Boutmy's view, were intended mostly for use in courts of law, whereas France's Declaration of Rights was designed for the "instruction of the world."[24]

Again, a reply is called for. Although America in the eighteenth century was admittedly very much at the world's periphery, Americans nonetheless conceived that their rebellion would fire, in Emerson's words, the "shot heard round the world." The writings of the founders are filled with prophecies of the importance of the American example for the whole of mankind. As George Washington noted in his first inaugural address, "The destiny of the Republican model of Government [is] justly considered as *deeply,* perhaps *finally* staked, on the experiment entrusted to the hands of the American people."[25] It is not clear that the Americans were wrong. Although the French Revolution became the favored theme of philosophers, the American Revolution continued to inspire liberal democratic movements in Europe and Latin America (albeit, unfortunately, with little attention to the teachings of the political science that guided it).

Third, the French Revolution is said to be superior to the American Revolution because it never accepted America's lowly standard of nature. The American Revolution, although it can claim the honor of being the first democratic revolution, must nevertheless yield to the greater glory of the French Revolution, which alone held out for the highest ideals. The American Revolution made its peace, somewhat ignominiously, with the lower side of human nature, embracing—or at any rate never attempting to suppress—man's drive for comfort and gain, settling for man as he was. The proof can be found in one of the most famous passages from *The Federalist*: "The latent causes of faction are sown in the nature of man. . . . [Because] the cause of faction cannot be removed, relief is only to be sought in the means of controlling its effects."[26] The American Revolution claimed to follow the laws of nature, but its understanding of nature was partial, flawed, and ultimately demeaning. It established liberal democracy on what Condorcet called the principle of the "identity of interests" or what others later contemptuously called "bourgeois" rights.[27]

In contrast, the French Revolution relied on and has kept alive the notion of a "higher possibility" for modern democracy. Its adherents have emphasized a standard that surpasses the calculation of interest by private individuals and the mere protection of private rights. The French Revolution added *fraternité* to the catalogue of essential democratic characteristics, and its leaders often spoke also of virtue and community. In other interpretations of the French Revolution, its higher possibility included genuine justice (understood as something approaching economic equality), the encouragement of human development, and cultural authenticity. Justice in the American sense—understood chiefly as the equal right to share in the fruits of a bourgeois or a mass culture—is hardly sufficient. What counts even more is "human development" or a "politics of meaning," which must lead us beyond a society rooted in a desire for gain. This higher cultural unity becomes for the Left a new standard of nature, which is now understood as a kind of project to be created and realized historically. Although it becomes confusing, this new understanding of nature in fact represented a rejection of solid nature in favor of human autonomy or freedom, in which human beings remake and recreate themselves according to their own various projects and designs. For rhetorical reasons—or from sheer confusion—many used the word "nature" to refer to this higher possibility.

The Left associates the French Revolution with a more just and genuinely democratic society that is at the same time devoted to a higher level of culture and meaning. This higher level, far from being undermined by greater equality, actually goes hand in hand with it; but it does so only when democracy renounces the low standard of bourgeois rights and embraces a project committed to authenticity. The great sin of American society is not just that it is unequal, but that it is prosaic. Stendhal makes the small town of America the standard of boorishness: "The tyranny of opinion in the smallest towns of France—and what an opinion!—is as stupid as that which is found throughout the United States."[28] It may also be recalled that if Louis XVI had not been guillotined, the punishment some proposed was to send him to America to live as a nice bourgeois in Philadelphia.

Talk of this higher possibility used to be heard in cafés all along the Left Bank in Paris but also, for that matter, in cafés (many with French names) in such places in America as Berkeley, Palo Alto, Cambridge, Princeton, and Charlottesville. It has unfortunately always been easier to speak vaguely of this possibility than to say what it would look like or how it might actually be brought into being. Nothing has been more characteristic of these partisans than a constant shifting of ground on the model said to embody the Revolution's deepest aspirations—from the Soviet model to Maoism, Castroism, the "third way," Eurocommunism, and finally a "new society." To dare suggest that this higher possibility is a chimera, or even to ask too many practical questions about it, is taken in some quarters as a sign of bad faith or, worse still, proof of moral complacency.

After a number of disillusioning experiences with different variants of this model, some of its adherents are now prepared to concede that the higher possibility should be conceived not as an actual model for guiding a society but rather as an ideal. To believe in this ideal is essential, for it serves the positive function of producing a creative tension or a dialectic without which liberal democratic society would sink to a lower level. The American Revolution, with its practical and realistic principles, cannot lead to anything higher; it needs the French Revolution to complete itself. The American Revolution may be the corporeal reality of modern democratic society, but the French Revolution is its conscience.

These two grounds for evaluating the Revolutions—the one favorable to the United States, the other to France—offer a fortuitous symmetry in which both Americans and the French appear to have half of the judgment in their favor. America receives the Oscar for practical success, which as everyone knows American civilization worships, while France walks off with the *Palme d'Or* for cultural achievement, which of course is all the French ever care about. But things are never quite so simple. Even though intellectuals may agree on the two basic grounds for judging the Revolutions, they do not accord them equal weight. And these two grounds do not so much separate the two nations as divide each of them from within. There is a "French" party in America which attacks "America" and the standard of the American founding and which urges America to move beyond the realm of rights to a higher realm of virtue or to a new politics of difference. And there is an "American" party in France which cautions against the dangers of ideal forms of democracy. It might even be said that among intellectuals today, the French outnumber the Americans in America, whereas the Americans outnumber the French in France.

Comparing the French and American Revolutions has been far more a preoccupation of the Left than of the Right. The Right, by which I mean nineteenth-century European conservative thought, originated not as a purely intellectual movement but as part of the political struggle to attack and discredit the French Revolution. For the Right, America and its Revolution became part of the discussion only as an afterthought, in terms of how America fit or did not fit with events in France. The Right has always seen America through the prism of the French Revolution.

For conservatives, the French Revolution was the result of a dangerous mode of metaphysical reasoning that wrongly tried to understand political phenomena from the perspective of abstract and universal principles. The consequence of this approach was to uproot all that was valuable inside the particular traditions of different nations. Abstract thinking, including thinking in terms of principles like natural rights, could only lead, as it had in France, to the destruction of the social fabric and to political chaos and disorder. The source of a nation's freedom and greatness is found not in this kind of metaphysical reasoning but in a deepening of its own traditions and history. It is in the histories of particular peoples, properly judged, understood, and cultivated, that one must look for political foundations, never in the new philosophic principles of nature or abstract reason.

Conservatives had two ways in which they could view the American Revolution. One was to see it as the metaphysical twin, or at any rate the philosophical first cousin, of the French Revolution. This view, which became the dominant conservative position on the Continent, assimilated the two events into one mold. What was true of France must also be true of America: both Revolutions were a threat to civilization. The other possibility was to distinguish between the two Revolutions and to say that America was not a manifestation of the new rationalist philosophy but a special case inside a primarily conservative outlook. Conservatism could then claim the American Revolution as its own. Elements of this view can be found in Edmund Burke's thought as well as in one strand of American conservatism. In neither of the two basic judgments of America, however, did conservative thought in Europe allow for a distinct position for the American founding and political science.

The assimilation of the French and American Revolutions can be traced to Joseph de Maistre, who helped bring conservatism to the Continent. De Maistre's writings represent a version of conservatism that goes well beyond—and arguably goes in a different direction than—that espoused by conservatism's first great spokesman, Edmund Burke.[29] What for Burke are nuances moderated by his ultimate liberalism often become dogmas for de Maistre.[30] In de Maistre's view, reason itself (not just metaphysical thinking) is suspect, and Providence now serves as the fundamental grounding for society. A nation's bearings must be found in faith, custom, tradition, and prejudice.

De Maistre's opposition to the French Revolution began with the claim that a nation's government can never be built on a rational foundation. "No constitution," he writes, "can be constructed from a deliberative [rational] process. . . . No assembly of men can constitute a nation."[31] There will always be some people, of course, who are foolish enough to attempt this experiment, but their efforts will fail, as the case of France so clearly proved. Healthy constitutions normally form by a process of germination, by growing rather as a tree grows. Alternatively—and de Maistre acknowledges the alternative, but only with great reluctance—a constitution can be instituted by a single legislator who seizes the moment and effects a transformation. In either case, however, rational discussion and deliberation play no constructive role. It is "circumstances that make everything, and men are only circumstances."[32]

De Maistre argues that it was folly to try to build a constitution for man in general or even to think about the political world with this idea in mind: "A constitution that is made for all nations is made for none. It is a pure abstraction, a work of scholasticism." The object of de Maistre's attack is Enlightenment political thinking, which obviously includes natural rights and contract philosophy. The proper starting point of political analysis is not the disembodied abstraction of man but the preexisting historical whole of a nation. In his most polemical attack on the concept of mankind—and strongest defense of a politics of difference—he even goes so far as to deny the existence of man: "The [French] constitution of 1795, like its predecessors, is made for *man*. Now, there is no such thing as 'man' in this world. I have seen in my life French, Italians, Russians, etc., and I even know, thanks to Montesquieu, that one can be Persian. But as for 'man' I declare that I have never met one in my life; if he exists, it is entirely without my knowledge."[33]

De Maistre continues his attack on reason by contending that theorizing about politics can offer no guidance for the practice of politics. Between a science or theory of politics and the activity of legislation, the same difference exists as that between poetics and poetry; and every poet knows how little true genius relies on abstract theory. For de Maistre, the few individual legislators who perform the task of constitution making "are never what one would call scholars. . . . They act more by instinct and impulsion than by reasonings." They are like artists, not under the wholly individualistic theory of one who creates according to his own design, but under a more community-centered notion of one who intuits the needs of a specific situation and crafts his work to conform to the "customs and character of the peoples."[34] These poet-founders are the only true legislators of a nation.

De Maistre concludes by contending that the French Revolution both reflected and revealed the catastrophe of modern rationalism. Modern thought is based on man's presumption that he can restructure political reality and create constitutions according to his own will. This is not only false but dangerous. It stimulates efforts at willful reconstitution of society that lead to tyranny, destruction, and disaster, for as long as man thinks he can remodel political orders, he will try to do so. In an effort to reinstill a sense of limits, de Maistre argued that people must be taught to regard the basic unit of political life as something that is beyond the control of rational direction or theory. In the largest sense, everything is subject to God's plan or Providence; in a narrower sense, each nation or people develops within God's plan according to its own organic path of evolution.

The American project of establishing government by "reflection and choice" clearly posed a special problem for de Maistre's entire argument, as he acknowledged. But not having studied the particulars of the founders' writings, he was unaware of just how far *The Federalist* had gone in anticipating some of his most fundamental arguments. He did not know, for example, that *The Federalist* had discussed whether constitution making must be the work of "one celebrated patriot or sage" or whether it could be accomplished by a "select body of citizens from whose common deliberations more wisdom as well as more safety" might be expected. Nor was de Maistre aware that the founders had considered whether the people ought to regard their lawgiver as a poet-founder who uses "violence with the authority of superstition" or as a "physician" whom they consult and listen to with deference but not with a full suspension of reason. But de Maistre did understand the basic character of the American founding and how its reliance on political science challenged his own philosophy. Knowing the American case would be raised against him, de Maistre himself elected to address it: "One could at most cite America; but I respond in advance by saying it is too soon still to cite her." De Maistre then goes on to argue that with time America will begin to manifest the evils of rationalist thought. To the extent that the Constitution relied on a rational process—"that chimerical system of deliberation and of political construction by previous reasoning"—it would fail: "All that is truly new in their constitution, all that results from common deliberation, is the most fragile thing in the world; one could not bring together more symptoms of weakness or decay."[35]

If de Maistre thought it too soon to discuss the political consequences of rationalism in America, he did not hesitate to pronounce on an analogous project that he considered even more fantastic in its pretensions: the construction, from scratch, of the new capital city of Washington. Here was an extreme case of man trying to use his reason to engineer a social venture, and so it must fail: "There is too much deliberation, too much *humanity* in this entire affair; and one can wager a thousand against one that the city will not be built; or that it will not be called Washington, or that the Congress will never reside there."[36]

A second line of conservative thought sought to incorporate the American Revolution and founding within the conservative tradition. De Maistre at a few points followed this path. Allowing that the American system might succeed, he argued that this result would only confirm his general theory. Successful regimes fit the constitution and laws to a people's character. A republican government in America conformed to this rule, because Americans had for a long time practiced democracy in their communities. The American founders were not trying to wipe the slate clean, as were the revolutionaries in France, but were only following the natural course of the historical evolution. Republican government was the conservative solution for the United States.[37]

This line of argument had been previously suggested by Edmund Burke in his three classic statements on the American crisis: "The Speech on American Taxation" (1774), "The Speech on Conciliation" (1775), and the "Letter to the Sheriffs of Bristol" (1777). Burke was one of only a few statesmen in England courageous and prudent enough to oppose British policy in the colonies and then to all but support a form of American independence. For this heresy, as he noted, "I am charged with being an American." Although Burke pleaded innocent to this charge, he proudly asserted: "I think I know America. If I do not my ignorance is incurable, for I have spared no pains to understand it." Burke's partial defense of the American cause came in political speeches and writings, which means that he often favored arguments that might prove persuasive in England. Ignoring the universalistic claims of the colonists, Burke elected to see events in America as a continuation of the movement for liberty begun in Britain. Each nation, he argued, has to be understood in terms of its "temper and character." In America's case, "a love of freedom is the predominating feature which distinguishes the whole." The Americans were "not only destined to liberty, but to liberty according to English ideas, on English principles." The foundation of the American Revolution lay in the Americans' effort to vindicate their historical rights as Englishmen, which the English monarch had not adequately respected.[38]

An American school of conservatism, led by Russell Kirk, has adopted the position that American liberty is the heir of the British tradition rather than of political science and natural rights theory. Inspired in its basic thought more by de Maistre than by Burke, this school seeks to connect Continental conservatism to the American founding. For these conservatives, evoking the idea of nature and natural rights in the American Revolution is worse than an error; it is a case of bad manners. According to Kirk, "The Declaration really is not conspicuously American in its idea or its phrases, and not even characteristically Jeffersonian." These conservatives wish to make the American founding into a "British thing," although unlike Burke they cannot offer the rationale of actually being British or speaking to a British audience.[39]

The effort to coopt the American Revolution for conservatism has been notable for the huge edifice it has tried to build on a flimsy foundation. One would expect, of course, that the words of the most speculative of the American founders, Thomas Jefferson, could be cited against this narrative. ("We had no occasion [in the American Revolution]," Jefferson wrote, "to search into musty records, to hunt up royal parchments, or to investigate the laws and institutions of a semi-barbarous ancestry. We appealed to those of nature.")[40] The problem for these conservatives, however, is that natural rights thinking ran the gamut of the American revolutionaries, including the great "conservative" Alexander Hamilton. ("The sacred rights of mankind are not to be rummaged for among old parchments, or musty records,"

Hamilton declared. "They are written, as with a sun beam in the whole volume of human nature, by the hand of the divinity itself.")[41] In turning to reason and man's natural rights, neither Jefferson nor Hamilton saw the need to deny the importance of Americans' historical rights as English citizens. For them it would have been a non sequitur to claim, as Kirk all but tries to do, that because the rights of Englishmen were violated, the rights of man were not. Even for Jefferson, after all, the English qualified as humans.

Further evidence of the distinctness of political science from conservatism can be found in the American response to the French Revolution. The most thoughtful American opponents of the Revolution did not become Continental conservatives but remained faithful to the method of political science. True, they sometimes exercised more care in talking about rights and nature, but in light of the enormous consequences of the French Revolution, it was only reasonable to rethink some of the lessons of political science. Still, American opposition to the French Revolution rested not on an attack on reason and rights, which was the form the opposition assumed in Europe, but on the political science that informed the founding. There was no need to abandon this position, because it supplied the ground for judging the new despotism, just as it had the old.

John Adams' reaction to the French Revolution illustrates this point. After studying Condorcet's *Sketch for an Historical Picture of the Progress of the Human Mind,* Adams condemned it as severely as did any of Condorcet's critics in Europe. Condorcet, he charged, "had waged a more cruel war against truth than was ever attempted by priest or king," constructing a doctrine of general principles that had no basis in experience or fact. Yet Adams based this critique not on a denial of the principles of nature but on a reassertion of them: "Principles drawn from nature are drawn from facts. What is nature but facts?"[42] Hamilton argued in a similar vein, decrying those in America who tried to assimilate the French and American Revolutions under the same cause so that both would have to be defended or attacked together. For Hamilton, the animating spirit and mode of reasoning of the two events were completely different; the French Revolution was conducted under "theories of government unsuited to the nature of man, miscalculating the force of his passions, and disregarding the lessons of experimental wisdom." No wonder it led to such an extreme result.[43]

American Political Science and the French Revolution

In the aftermath of the French Revolution, the attack on America by both Left and Right laid a second foundation, on top of the degeneracy thesis, for the subsequent construction of the symbolic America. In Europe the Left viewed America as backward and finally reactionary, while the Right considered America dangerous and revolutionary. Eventually, both parties agreed that America was also vulgar. For all the criticism directed against America, however, few acknowledged that American political science represented a distinct position inside of modernity. Adherents of both parties, each for its own reasons, adopted a theoretical framework that collapsed all modern rationalist thought into one category. The Left saw modern rationalism as leading the world into a new age of freedom, whereas the Right saw the same philosophy as leading the world into universal servitude and barbarism.

Political science offered an alternative that incorporated the most sensible elements of each position. In its critique of the Left, political science paralleled, indeed anticipated, many of conservatism's strongest arguments. Like conservatism, it appreciated the role of the historical situation and the importance of the fit between a constitution and the character of the citizens it governs. General rules had to be applied in ways that were mindful of the constraints of time and place. What political science considered here to be prudence, proponents of the new philosophy regarded as an unjustifiable sacrifice of reason and justice. "We cannot see," wrote Condorcet, why all states "should not have the same criminal and civil laws."[44] This way of thinking illustrated exactly the kind of doctrinaire approach that America's founders rejected. In the idea that philosophy should dictate terms to politics, the founders saw the outline of a new form of despotism. The aim of these doctrinaire thinkers was nothing less than to replace rule by political art as guided by political science with rule by ideology as defined by philosophy.

Like conservatism, political science also distinguished between abstract, speculative thinking about politics and genuine political reasoning. When Condorcet was not defending the vast claims of the inevitable movement of philosophy in history, he was extolling a new positivism that would make all forms of human knowledge follow the same techniques as the physical sciences or mathematics. Students of society could "follow the same methods, acquire an equally exact and precise language, and attain the same degree of certainty" as students of the natural sciences. In a remarkable preview of what modern academic political science would aspire to, Condorcet proposed changing the name "political science" to "social mathematics." Nothing could be further from the spirit of *The Federalist,* which insisted that political science was different in kind from the natural sciences and mathematics.[45]

But while opposing much of the thinking of the Left, political science also challenged the fundamental principles of the Right. For the founders, conservatism

sometimes appeared to have no standard at all other than the historically generated genius of each case. This approach left no basis on which to guide the proper
direction of prudent action. In actual fact, of course, conservatism on the Continent had not really defined its position by a rigorous analysis of the context but
had allied itself staunchly and dogmatically with monarchy and the old regime. It
was wedded to the old prescriptive rights and could not accommodate itself to any
general idea of justice. *The Federalist* had no hesitation in denouncing the "impi-
ous doctrine . . . that people were made for kings, not kings for the people," and
in laying down the standard of natural rights and constitutional government.[46]

Political science also differed from conservatism in its understanding of the
foundation of society and the mode of thinking that might guide it. Conservatism
tried to ground society in custom or tradition and argued that no general science
could assist political actors, who in the end could rely only on art, intuition, and
knowledge of their own situation. The founders offered political science to
thinkers and statesmen in other countries, believing that a body of rational thought
about politics could help statesmen to improve societies to the extent allowed by
local conditions and circumstances. The founders held that reason, looking as far
as possible to "experience," should judge tradition—just as it judged the claims
made on behalf of universal principles and philosophy. Proponents of political science never asserted that it could substitute for statesmanship or the political art.
Every application of political science occurs inside a particular country as part of
a political event guided by political actors, and it is for these actors to determine
ultimately how knowledge can be used. But political science can be of great help,
far more than those acting in politics are generally disposed to admit.[47]

Political science accordingly fit neither the Right nor the Left, but offered its
own account of the political world. It moved inside the horizon of the Enlightenment even as it rejected the leading ideas of modern social science and philosophy. An opponent of both of the great ideologies of the nineteenth century, political science was attacked and vilified in the successive portrayals of the American
Revolution and the founding. The fate of political science was bound then, as it
has been ever since, to freeing America from these symbolic representations.

4

★ ★ ★

America as a Racial Symbol:
The "New History" of
Arthur de Gobineau

Symbolic America has had a long-standing, direct, and intimate connection to racialist thinking. From the founding of anthropology in the late eighteenth century, which opened with a discussion of America, until the elaboration of Nazi theories about the United States in the 1930s, America has symbolized in various ways the meaning of race in human affairs. Although it is a fact sometimes overlooked today, the concept of race during this period was, in the words of George Stocking, the "central theoretical concern of pre-Darwinian anthropology" as well as a major theme of much philosophy, history, and literature.[1] In many areas of the West, racialist thinking in these fields had all but replaced political science as the intellectual discipline for the guidance of society.

America was employed to evoke two images that, although they rested on the same understanding of race, were nearly opposite in meaning. The first image was positive or optimistic, casting the United States as a young nation that would preserve Aryan blood in the modern world and help the remaining Aryan elements in Europe to maintain hegemony over the lesser races. ("Race" referred not only to the basic color groups—black, white, and yellow—but also to ethnic groups within each color group.) In this picture, America was founded, not on principles of natural rights and equality, as it proclaimed, but on the de facto supremacy of the white race in the form of its Anglo-Saxon element. America was successful because it ignored what it preached.

The second image was negative, depicting America as the source of the destruction of racial hierarchy. By its principles of equality and democracy and by its practice of wanton racial intermixing (especially among the various races of

Europeans), America was responsible for a leveling of the human species. Whatever the Anglo-Saxon race had once done to establish the greatness of America, that race was now, by a loss of will, abandoning its claim to rule as a distinct and self-conscious group. By allowing the increasing homogenization of blood types that sapped its vitality, America was falling to the ranks of the mediocre among the nations of the world. America, with its foundation in the rationalist ideas of equality and unity of the human species, was slowly destroying itself.

Racialist thinking of any kind rests on two basic premises: first, the fundamental human groupings are biological units, called races, which possess not only different physical but also different intellectual and moral endowments; and second, the races are hierarchically arranged. Western racialist thinking added a third premise: the white race (generally its Teutonic or Aryan element) stands at the top of the human scale, followed, in most accounts, by Asians (Native Americans were often put in this group) and then blacks. When people in the West today refer to racism, they usually mean a view that includes all these premises.

Although racism in this sense remains alive and well in the literature of various extremist groups at the edges of Western liberal democratic societies, it has disappeared from respectable intellectual thought.[2] This does not mean, however, that the old racialist discourse on America is without influence. Words and symbols acquire meanings over the years, like the layers of sedimentation that form on a geological surface. Even after a particular meaning has been covered over, traces remain. "Words," Roland Barthes has remarked, "contain an underlying memory that prolongs itself mysteriously in the midst of new meanings."[3] Much of the content of symbolic America today was worked out in racialist thinking and then applied to nonracialist discussions of technology and culture. Ideas influenced by racialism thus persist at the vanguard of progressive thought, which depicts the United States as the land of diminished intelligence, low tastes, and cultural homogenization.

The distinction of being the first racial theorist belongs to the nineteenth-century French thinker Arthur de Gobineau (1816–1882). This conclusion is supported not only by contemporary historians but also by those Europeans who made up the first intellectual and political groups that espoused racist principles. In this milieu, Arthur de Gobineau was referred to, with great respect, as the Father of Racism.[4] Among his progeny can be counted those in the "Bayreuth group" that gathered around Richard Wagner (a friend of Gobineau) and that actively promoted racialist theories in the second half of the nineteenth century. From this group it is possible to draw a direct line of influence to the thought of Houston Stewart Chamberlain, Oswald Spengler, Alfred Rosenberg, and Adolf Hitler. Gobineau's effect, while certainly greatest in Germany, was by no means restricted to that country. In France Gobineau's influence can be seen in the work of Ernest Renan and Gustave Le Bon, for example, and in America Gobineau's writings were enlisted in support of slavery and later of the racialist strain of social Darwinism.[5]

To link Gobineau and Nazism is not to dismiss the claim, insisted on by some of his recent admirers, that Gobineau's aristocratic viewpoint differed greatly from the crude, lower-class, populist racism of Hitler.[6] To be sure, Gobineau and Hitler are far apart in style (Gobineau was a novelist of some repute), and their racial policies bear no resemblance. But the categories of Nazi racialism derive from Gobineau's social science.[7] If Nazism is not the inevitable or only result of his thought, it is certainly a logical conclusion. Prescient thinkers at the time, among them Alexis de Tocqueville, easily foresaw the dangerous effects of Gobineau's ideas, although no one could begin to imagine the horrors that these ideas would be used to sanction.

Arthur de Gobineau is an intriguing figure. Besides being a novelist and a historian, he was a publicist, an orientalist, and, for more than thirty years, a diplomat for the French government, serving in such diverse places as Persia and Brazil. His writings on Persia have enjoyed considerable scholarly acclaim, and some of his letters analyzing the character of different groups in the Caucasus bear careful reading even today. Gobineau was a man of strong royalist sympathies, of a legitimist (Bourbon) bent. Although born in 1816, a quarter-century after the outbreak of the French Revolution, he resembled many of his generation in making the Revolution the starting point of his thought. Gobineau was an adamant foe of the Revolution. Although fate dealt him a cruel blow when it brought him into this world on July 14, Bastille Day, he managed to bear this misfortune philosophically, remarking on one occasion that it only "goes to prove how opposites may come together."[8]

Although Gobineau came from a modest noble background, this did not prevent him from extravagantly claiming to carry the blood of Ottar Jarl, a Viking pirate who raided the coast of Normandy. Gobineau's writings, especially his novels, evince a strong romantic current. Rejecting the Enlightenment's thin ground of universalism and reason, Gobineau immersed himself in the soul, blood, and mission of the Aryan nation. German romanticism, as Michael Biddiss has aptly remarked, cultivated the "world of the Scandinavian and Celtic north where it could manifest its growing interest in the primitive origins and purity of peoples as embodied in myth, saga, and legend. Thoughts of a return to nature were accompanied by fascination with primitive barbarism."[9]

Gobineau's romanticism was dark and brooding, not airy and hopeful. Some biographers have characterized his disposition as Gothic or medieval, which they attribute to a childhood scarred by his parents' notoriously tempestuous relationship. The breaking point came when the young Arthur, living with his mother in an old castle in Switzerland, began to suspect (rightly) an illicit liaison between his mother and his tutor. Upon the general discovery of this affair his mother was forced to quit the family, after which she went on to pursue other notable romances in aristocratic circles. Arthur evidently assumed the burden of trying to redeem the family name.

Whatever the cause, Gobineau's attachment to family and old nobility was unparalleled. To him the entire modern democratic movement, with its crass utilitarianism and commercialism, was an anathema. His racial theory was decidedly aristocratic, not nationalist or populist, as racialism in this century has generally been. For Gobineau, the hierarchy of race was reflected not only in the differences among nations but also in the classes within each nation. The pure race of a nation was its old nobility, which was usually Aryan, whereas the mass of the people was usually made up of a motley mixture of different races.[10] Thus, in France, the royalists were the "depositaries of the principles, traditions, and customs of a nation. . . . In a philosophic sense, one could say they are the nation itself."[11] Modern nationalism, by contrast, represented to Gobineau a perversion of the idea of race. Nowhere was this clearer than in France, which originated modern nationalism at the time of the Revolution: "There is no French race any longer; of all the European nations surely we are the ones whose original character has been effaced the most. And it is within this very effacement that we, physically as well as mentally, are now claiming to find our own character."[12]

The Objectives of Social Science

Gobineau's principal work as a historian and social philosopher, and the book for which he is best known, is his one-thousand-page opus *Essay on the Inequality of the Human Races* (1853–1855).[13] In this work, Gobineau claims to be among the first to pose systematically and to answer definitively the most fundamental question of social life: Why do civilizations rise and fall? Gobineau initially had great hopes for the impact of his book, believing that it would "give an electric shock to historical science and completely upset it."[14]

The originality of Gobineau's book, in his own estimation, was found in its elaboration of two major theoretical points. First, Gobineau identifies the proper object or unit of analysis of social science. That unit is not, as almost all previous social science had maintained, the government or the regime but the people, the nation, or the civilization: "I speak not here of a temporary prosperity or misery of a society, but of something more important: I speak of the existence of peoples and of civilization." A civilization is an entity or whole prior to and more important than the political form. Although the "influence of laws and political institutions is very great," Gobineau writes, "they cannot create powers where they do not already exist."[15] It is the race that fashions the laws before the laws, in turn, can fashion the nation.

Second, Gobineau claims to be the first to develop a full and complete science of civilizations. By a science he means a body of knowledge that could completely explain the life history or morphology of a given phenomenon, explicating its origin, its rise and fall, and its death. This science, which he calls "national biology," would leave nothing undetermined. Gobineau is seeking a "natural law of death which seems to govern societies as well as individuals," a "general, though concealed cause" that operates independently of conventional causes (laws, wars, accidents, the decisions of statesmen) and that determines the life and death of civilizations. The cause must be homogeneous and universal, operating in the same way in every case: "The principle of death in all societies is not only a necessary condition of their life, independent in a great measure of external causes, but is also uniform in all." Discovering and elaborating this scientific principle is the main object of Gobineau's work.[16]

An important connection exists between these two points. Gobineau is prepared to acknowledge that if the central unit of analysis in social life were the political regime, a pure science would be impossible. It is undeniable that man acts in the political realm, at least in some measure, on his own agency; the political realm therefore always contains a degree of indeterminacy or contingency that makes perfect prediction impossible. The prospect for a pure science for society is saved, however, by the fact that the most important thing about social life—the rise and fall of civilization—is not under the control of politics but obeys naturalistic laws of its own. In this realm, full prediction is possible. Moreover, the rise and fall of civilization in the end controls the political realm as well. Whereas political action enjoys a certain freedom in the short term, over the long term it is governed by the rise and fall of civilizations.

Gobineau operates with a self-consciously modern understanding of what constitutes a science in human affairs. Social science is a theoretical body of knowledge that sets forth the laws of historical development. These laws are not statements of probabilistic relations, of the type that if you select A (say, a certain set of political laws), then B (say, a stable monarchy) is likely to follow. Rather, laws are explanations of why things have come to be and of how they will develop. Science is not primarily a body of if-then causal propositions designed to assist man in shaping his environment; it is full knowledge that can account for everything. In this sense, "history is a science that is not otherwise constituted than all the other sciences"; it is the science "of what is happening and what is going to happen."[17]

Offering his new science as a critique of all previous forms of political or social science, Gobineau argues that past social science presupposed a nation's fate to be determined by factors, mostly moral or political, over which man in principle exercised control. This is untrue, at least with regard to the basic trajectory of civilizations. Of course social science could play a helpful, though limited, role inside the narrow interstices that remained subject to human control. It could assist man in making the best choices, just as a good physician might help a terminally ill patient by easing the suffering or prolonging a better quality of life. Even here, however, social science can play this role only by dropping all pretensions to full control and by acknowledging its subservience to another science that focuses on the deeper structure of causation governing the rise and fall of civilizations.

Although Gobineau charges all past social science with being guilty of this theoretical hubris, he distinguishes between ancient social science and modern Enlightenment social science. Ancient social science, although just as bold as modern social science in its theoretical claims, was as a practical matter "devoted to the point of exaggeration to the maintenance of the existing social system." It was conservative. In contrast, the practitioners of modern Enlightenment social science adopt the view that social matter is tractable and that man can readily transform society by his deliberate actions; these thinkers, "eager for novelty and bent on destruction," produce the most extreme consequences. Modern social science, what Gobineau calls the "Voltairian way," has become a "fearful weapon against all rational principles of government." With a propagandistic discourse that divides matters between good and bad, it has turned everything on its head and redefined all key terms of political thought to mean their opposite. To save us from what it calls the "ruin of society," it has proceeded "to destroy religion, law, industry and commerce under the pretext that religion is fanaticism, law is despotism, and industry and commerce are luxury and corruption."[18]

For Gobineau, as for Joseph de Maistre, Enlightenment social science has induced people to act without restraint to remake the world. It should therefore be curbed and prevented from influencing the policies of nations and statesmen. Yet although Gobineau's critique of social science follows that of de Maistre, Gobineau's system and approach are quite different. Whereas de Maistre turned from science to religion (and to providential governance of history) as the ultimate guide for political life, Gobineau looks to a new kind of science predicated on a full understanding of the laws of history. Gobineau claims to have corrected social science by scientific means. "We moderns," he contends, "are for the first time in a position truly to understand the laws of the rise and fall of civilizations; we can thus overcome the intellectual limitations of all previous social science."[19] The laws of history, scientifically understood, replace Providence.

Gobineau does not ask that anyone actually make use of his new science, although early on he expresses hope that it might exercise a moderating effect. By revealing the real springs of historical movement, national biology would presumably help people avoid the errors and excesses of existing social science, especially its fanatical projects to remodel the world. But this activist (albeit mostly negative) strand of Gobineau's thought is overshadowed by his fatalism and historicism. In his historical and philosophic writings, Gobineau never claims that he can save the world or alter the direction of historical progression. On the contrary, the course of history has already been fixed by forces beyond human control—forces that not even awareness of the truth can alter.

The Motor of Historical Causality: Race

For Gobineau, race (including ethnicity) is the force behind historical change, the hidden scientific principle that explains the rise and fall of nations. Everything is explained by this one factor. According to Hannah Arendt, "Nobody before Gobineau thought of finding one single reason, one single force according to which civilization always and everywhere rises and falls." Gobineau's primary law is that a nation is degenerated "when it has not conserved the same race as its founders, . . . when it no longer has the same blood flowing in its veins, but has been gradually modified in value by successive admixtures." This law is absolute: "A people will die definitively, and its civilization with it, the moment when its original ethnical element has become so subdivided or submerged by admixtures of foreign races that it can no longer give rise to sufficient impulse."[20]

Gobineau's definitive law of history parallels the thought of Hegel, whom Gobineau regarded for a time as his philosophical mentor. Substitute Gobineau's "ethnical" for Hegel's "ethical," and one has a good approximation of the generative cause of the rise and fall of civilizations. Race takes the place of *Geist*. For Gobineau, the in-flow, admixture, and then exhaustion of the blood of the founding race is a natural process that dictates the fate of nations, and the process cannot be influenced by human agency. When a nation "has completely exhausted its ethnical element," any defeat "will be its death"; at that point, "it has consumed the term of existence that Heaven has granted it."[21]

The history of all civilizations proceeds according to a dialectic between the conquering and the conquered races. The conquering race is the original nobility, which expands to bring other races under its sway. With this expansion, however, the conquering race begins to mix its blood with the subjugated peoples. Just when a civilization reaches its pinnacle, the purity of the master race begins to be eroded, leading to a gradual process of general degeneration. This cyclical process repeats itself in civilization after civilization.

Yet in the end Gobineau was interested in more than an account of the rise and fall of particular civilizations. His aim was to explain the entire history of man as a single or unified story. To do so he had to go beyond the pattern of cycles of distinct civilizations and find a common currency among them. He had to indicate which races are capable of forming civilizations, how high a civilization they could form, and which races are destined to prevail in the encounters among them. The explanation for these facts, he argues, is found in the "idea of an innate and permanent difference in the moral and mental endowments of the various groups of the human species."[22] The relevant groups are the different races, which are arranged hierarchically according to their moral and intellectual capacities. The core of his theory rests on the differentiation of the human species, grounded in the concept of race. Although Gobineau accepts the general notion of a common humanity to which all races belong, he denies any implication of racial equality. For Gobineau, the concept of humanity so conceived was at bottom a leveling and democratic idea that was meant to conceal a fundamental truth about mankind.

In fact, the very existence of the concept of humanity posed a problem for Gobineau. If differences among human types constitute the primary reality of social life, and if humans for the most part instinctively sense these differences, how did a general idea of humanity or equality ever emerge? Gobineau offers a sociological explanation. When conquerors and conquered enter a process of racial admixture, the offspring of these unions ("hybrids") begin from shame and interest to express reservations about the racial superiority and inferiority of their ancestors. After a time the hybrids deny the principle that "certain capacities are necessarily, fatally, the exclusive heritage" of distinct groups, and they come to embrace a notion of general equality or humanity, which they promote with such maxims as "All men are brothers." The idea of equality thus tends to be a product of the later stages of a given civilization. But this idea, according to Gobineau, has de-

veloped a special power in modern times; it has been elevated by science and philosophy into the "axiom" that "all men are endowed with the same intellectual
instruments, are of the same nature, of the same value, [and] of the same importance." The modern belief in equality accordingly goes deeper than ever before,
because it has acquired for the first time a theoretical and universal foundation.[23]

Gobineau's racial hierarchy applies to groups of people, not individuals. Race
captures the "aggregate power, moral as well as material, that is developed in the
mass of men." Gobineau makes clear that he does not wish to focus on the variation among individuals. It is a fact almost too obvious to mention that there is great
variation in individual talents, which means that the average for each race does
not describe every individual: "I emphatically reject the notion that consists of
saying that every negro is inept, because by the same logic I should be compelled
to admit that every European is intelligent," which is an absurdity. Whatever the
overlap among individuals from different races, Gobineau claims that it is irrelevant to the practical inquiry at hand. The average difference he found among
groups was more than sufficient to account for the different levels of civilization
and for what each group could accomplish on the stage of history.[24]

For the most part Gobineau's concept of race embraces both race and ethnicity,
ideas that we tend to distinguish today. At some points, however, he refers specifically to the color groups—black, yellow, and white—as the three "primary" or
"great" races (*les trois grandes races*) and calls the distinctions between these
groups the most fundamental of all. Blacks are the lowest on the scale, never having initiated any great civilization. They have limited intellects, are largely indifferent to distinctions between virtue and vice, and are easily enslaved. They are
nevertheless endowed with great artistic talent, which is foreign to all other races
and was acquired by them "only after the intermarriage of White and Black." Next
in the hierarchy is the yellow race, whose members lack originality but are remarkably adept at copying and perfecting what others have discovered. In fact,
Gobineau is so impressed with this imitative quality that he comes close in a number of passages to predicting that the yellow races will one day dominate the world.
Finally, at the apex, stands the white race, which is physically the most beautiful
of the races and the only one that possesses the power of invention. Its most important quality, however, is its capacity for honor: whites alone have nobility, the
willingness to do certain hard things for their own sake, without regard to mere
utility (which was the continual preoccupation of the yellow race).[25]

But the concept of race does not end with the distinctions between the three primary varieties. The further subdivisions within the races, though more complex,
yield fundamental differences that are essential for explaining the evolution of his-

tory, and in fact most of Gobineau's effort is spent in discussing the relations between the various "races" of white people. In the final analysis, the most important distinction for the movement of history is not the one that separates the three
primary races but the one that separates the only pure white element, the Aryans,
from all the others, be they red, yellow, black, or the rest of the whites.

Monogenesis Versus Polygenesis: A Reformulation

In method and approach Gobineau was far more a historian than an anthropol-
ogist. He proceeded by inferring properties of the races from an analysis of the historical record rather than by conducting scientific observations of the physical
properties of different peoples. Even so, his position was fully dependent on the
supposed fact of permanent biological differences among the races, and he therefore had to consider the findings of natural history.[26] Yet although Gobineau drew
freely on the observations of the natural historians, he pronounced himself an opponent of the prevailing school of natural history, which had come to be associated with environmentalist assumptions that denied the idea of fundamental and
ineradicable differences between human types.

Gobineau gives the position adopted by the natural historians of his day a new
name: unitarism. Unitarism held that differences among recognized human
groups were secondary and could be overcome relatively quickly if the groups
were exposed to the same environmental conditions. In order to reinforce the idea
of sameness, unitarists adopted the biological definition of a species which relied
on the capacity for successful interbreeding. But the core of the unitarist position,
Gobineau argues, is best captured by a political argument, not a technical or biological one: "All mankind is, for them, capable of the same improvement; the original type, though more or less disguised, persists in unabated strength and the Negro, the American savage, the Tungussian of northern Siberia, can attain a beauty
of outline equal to that of the European, and would do so, if they were brought up
under similar conditions."[27]

The unitarist position foreshadows the dominant contemporary position in anthropology, which ascribes predominance in the matter of group behavior to nurture (culture or socialization) rather than to nature (heredity). In this view, variation in intellectual and moral behavior may theoretically be eliminated in one
generation, because nature itself (heredity) supplies no special trace that distinguishes one group from another in moral and intellectual endowments. The unitarism of Gobineau's day was not quite the same. Although it emphasized the importance of immediate culture, it allowed for hereditary variation among races or

varieties; but this variation was itself subject to alteration by environmental influences within a reasonable time period (say, a few generations). Assuming the
same conditions, differences that now exist among varieties will begin to disappear. The unitarist view, according to Gobineau, was intended to lend scientific
support to the general idea of sameness or equality; it was the biological parallel
of the Enlightenment philosophical position regarding humanity.

Gobineau rejected unitarism. He was a biological pluralist for whom the hereditary differences among the races was fundamental. These differences were, for
all intents and purposes, permanent and ineradicable; they could not be altered beyond a certain point by cultural or environmental factors. Of course, Gobineau did
not deny that alterations in manners of life (culture) and the environment could
produce significant changes in behavior. For example, Indians brought up under
the Europeans' religion and law were very different from Indians who had been
left undisturbed. But there remained fundamental traits and characteristics carried
by the races that could not be altered by any environmental changes, whether over
one generation or several. Environmental changes could therefore never bring the
results that unitarists assumed or expected.

The old debate between monogenesis and polygenesis, if we understand these
terms in their strict sense as doctrines referring to a single or plural human origin,
did not do justice to the issues involved in the conflict between unitarism and pluralism. But the old terms could not be ignored. They had continuing theological
significance, and the question of man's origins seemed to have some probative
value for determining the present character of man. The position of monogenesis
lent somewhat more weight to the unitarist view, and it was often loosely used as
a synonym for unitarism—even though many who embraced monogenesis also
thought that the races over time had developed into highly differentiated varieties.
In contrast, polygenesis lent credence to the pluralist conception of unbridgeable
differences between human types, and it was often used as a synonym for pluralism.

This terminology presented certain embarrassments and difficulties for Gobineau. Because the church considered polygenesis to be heretical, believers were
pulled in the direction of unitarism. Although Gobineau thought the polygenetic
hypothesis was plausible, as a believer he could not allow himself to accept it, because it "impugns a religious interpretation sanctioned by the church." Gobineau's
strategy was to decouple the classical theological debate from the contemporary
debate over unitarism and pluralism. Even, he argued, if one were to grant the
premise (as one must) that mankind descended from Adam and Eve, this fact in
no way supported a conclusion of an equality among all groups today. Creation

occurred so long ago, and the factors that generate differences among groups have had such a long time to develop, that the original condition had no bearing on the present situation. In all the time we have had observable data, there have always been different races, and "no race has changed its peculiar characteristics" because of an alteration of environmental circumstances. The racial composition of man has been altered only by intermixing.[28]

The unitarist position, Gobineau argued, led to some highly dubious and even untenable conclusions. If, as unitarists claimed, the current differences among the races, both physical and intellectual, were a result of environmental factors, then by this line of reasoning the races could change colors within a relatively short period. Indeed, some of the most progressive and humanitarian scientists took this view. Benjamin Rush, for example, thought that white was the one natural or basic color of man and that the existence of other skin colors represented a diseased deviation, a kind of leprosy, which could be eliminated or cured with a change in environment.[29] Claims of this type, Gobineau declared, had no empirical foundation and revealed the real ideological impetus behind the unitarist position.

Another conception that Gobineau began to question was the modern biological construct of species, on which unitarists relied. This conception, which defined a single species to exist whenever individuals could interbreed without loss of number, was used to try to prove much more than it actually did. The term "species" suggests a fundamental unity that is connected to all sorts of moral and ontological connotations. Here, according to Gobineau, lay the little trick of unitarism: it defined a species in a technical and biological sense but then relied on the term to evoke other meanings that had no scientific foundation. Gobineau denied that the notion of a species, biologically defined, makes mankind "one" in the most important respect.[30] The biological criterion, he argued, is quantitative, not qualitative. It therefore misses the most important point. Human types may indeed be able to interbreed and multiply in number, but when they do so the higher types degenerate in quality. Compared to their purer ancestors, the hybrids are inferior or lesser beings. For Gobineau, therefore, the relevant category for judging the question of the unity of man is not the quantitative one of "species" but the qualitative one of "types." By this criterion, the fundamental and observable fact about mankind is not its unity but its differences.

On Difference

Gobineau's racialism (and de facto polygenesis) led him to emphasize the differences between human groups. Being an observer of the fact of human difference is not, of course, the same thing as being a proponent of difference or even an advocate of tolerance. Indeed, in his account of the rise and fall of civilizations, Gobineau was in no way tender or sentimental in his view of the interrelations among racial groups, for he believed that subjugation on the basis of racial distinction was the warp and woof of history. At the same time, however, he conceived his position to be one of moderation and respect for difference, especially when compared to the position inspired by Enlightenment humanism.

The Enlightenment view, Gobineau argued, promoted a project of homogenization that went well beyond anything ever conceived by man when governed by his brute instinctual drive for conquest. Enlightenment social science proceeded under the axiom of the equality or sameness of man. It reasoned that if men were at bottom equal and if all that separated them were their living conditions, then all groups could be made the same. Stated differently, if all groups were pacified and environments made more favorable, mankind would begin to evolve toward its natural condition of unity. Under the auspices of this premise, Gobineau believed, Europeans had adopted the project to "remodel" all peoples and nations: "We try to recondition them, but we succeed only in destroying them; we do not succeed in transforming them."[31]

Gobineau had a clear explanation for why this effort at reconditioning must fail. Human types or races are fundamentally different from one another and therefore cannot attain the same standards of civilization. At certain moments Gobineau seemed to think that his new science might exercise a moderating influence on political affairs by fostering a sense of limits of what man could expect to change in the face of immutable biological differences. Racialism might help to reestablish, on a scientific basis, something akin to the older instinctual feelings of difference that had been submerged by Enlightenment rationalism and the concept of one humanity. If people would only accept that human differences were encased in biology, then an end could be put to the foolish and tyrannical project of remodeling all of mankind. Gobineau sometimes drew the conclusion, which is as close as he ever came to offering advice, that Europeans should leave native peoples alone. This counsel appears, paradoxically, in some of the most racist parts of his book—passages that emphasize the unique properties of different races and the incapacity of certain races ever to attain certain standards of civilization.

Here Gobineau's argument is reminiscent of the theories of de Pauw and de Maistre, which identified Enlightenment social science with a form of fanatical imperialism. Gobineau's position—to employ terminology he does not use—is that intolerance is allied with unitarist or humanitarian thought and is an Enlightenment trait, whereas tolerance is allied with racialist thought and is an anti-

Enlightenment trait. Gobineau offered a hard teaching that recognized and even justified racial conquest and racial subjugation; yet in the past, he argued, these acts reached a kind of limit imposed by man's natural instincts. Modern humanism destroyed that limit. By substituting reason and theory for instinct, it opened the way to a more extreme kind of interference than mankind had ever seen. For no matter how much humanists and unitarists preached peace and harmony among peoples, they were in fact excited by one idea: the sameness of man. It was this idea that led them to their universalistic interventions to remake all of mankind according to a single model.

The European Crisis and the Myth of America

Gobineau analyzed history in terms of a single, universal scheme: the cyclical rise and fall of individual civilizations.[32] One common phenomenon, akin in his system to Hegel's Spirit, ties together the whole story of mankind, giving it a beginning, a middle, and presumably an end. That substance is Aryanism. "I am convinced," writes Gobineau, "that everything great, noble, and fruitful in the works of man on this earth, in science, in art, in civilization, derives from a single starting point; . . . it belongs to one family alone, the different branches of which have reigned in all the civilized countries of the universe."[33] The extinction of the Aryan "family" would therefore mark the extinction not just of a single civilization but of civilization as such, and Gobineau believed this was the point that civilization in Europe was fast approaching. The drama of European history was being played out in blood. Race is the substructure; thought and culture are parts of the superstructure. Viewed in these terms, Enlightenment rationalism and humanitarianism were nothing other than the signs of the continuing dilution of Aryan blood into a vast sea of inferior races.

Gobineau's treatment of modern times then turns to an analysis of the racial situation of Europe. The predominant fact of contemporary Europe is the growing "romanization," meaning amalgamation or interbreeding, of Europe's races or ethnic groups.[34] Only in a limited geographic area does Aryanism still exist in what could be called at best a semipure condition. This area includes Austria, some parts of Germany up and down the Rhine, certain regions of northern Europe, and much of Great Britain: "In this area are the last elements of the Aryan race, doubtless very distorted, eroded and withered, but still not completely vanquished."[35]

Like a cornered animal, the Aryan nation has instinctively sensed the peril of its situation and the terrible fate that awaits it inside Europe. Out of desperation, Aryans have sought a place of renewal, a haven where they might once again invigorate their race and reassert control over the world. That haven is America: "The present successes of one of the states of America seems to herald this most necessary era. The Western world is the vast stage on which they imagine the blossoming forth of nations which . . . will enrich our own and accomplish things of which the world has yet only dreamt."[36] For many Aryans of Gobineau's day, America was a wondrous myth of deliverance and redemption. America was the Great White Hope.

America in Gobineau's analysis assumes a world-historical or universal significance, for it is in America that Aryanism will either renew itself (and history will continue) or deplete itself (and history will end). Gobineau's last task, contained in the final part of his work, is to assess the future of the New World and to analyze the hopes contained in the prevailing Aryan myth.[37]

Gobineau begins his account of the New World with a survey of the native peoples, whom he identifies as mainly offshoots of the Asian race with occasional infusions of Finnic and Scandinavian blood. These Aryan elements accounted for the major civilizations of the New World, but as the "infusions of noble essence put into circulation among the Malaysian-based masses was too weak to produce anything vast or durable, the resulting societies were few and very imperfect, and were very fragile and very ephemeral."[38] What remained in the wake of the decline of these civilizations was an inferior race (or inferior races), which the Europeans encountered when they came to the New World.

Gobineau's concern then shifts to the fate of Europeans in America, as only the white man offers history the chance of renewing itself. His survey begins in the South, with the Spanish and Portuguese areas of the New World, but these he dismisses with the briefest of considerations. Having interbred extensively with the Indians, the Spanish and Portuguese were clearly in decline: "South America, with its Creole blood corrupted, has henceforth no way to stop the fall into crossbreeds of all variety and all classes. Their decadence is without remedy."[39] For serious study this left one nation only: the United States, which Gobineau treats as synonymous with America.

Gobineau presents two pictures of America, one that applies to the past and another that is more descriptive of the future. In his first and positive picture, he develops the traditional characterization of America as a Teutonic (or Anglo-Saxon) nation. The Anglo-Saxons founded America and gave it its vitality, enabling it to become the dominant power of the New World. The Anglo-Saxons, the people "who are the furthest removed from both the blood of the natives and that of the Negroes," are the superior type in the New World—superior both to the other color groups and to the romanized whites from the other parts of Europe: "The Anglo-

Saxon core existing in the United States has no difficulty at all in having itself recognized as the most dynamic element of the new continent. It is placed in relation to the other populations, in a position of overwhelming superiority in which formerly all the branches of the Aryan family were placed . . . in regard to the multitude of mixed-race peoples."[40]

The example of America affords the historian a unique opportunity to observe how the process of conquest takes place. The subjugation of inferior races that has occurred in America presumably provides a model for how dominant races in the past must have prevailed. But as Gobineau continues his account, he increasingly remarks on what he supposes are the unique elements of the American experience. These derive from the fact that the conquest of America is taking place in the modern age, which brings into play two new elements: systematization (science) and hypocrisy. Thus in his relation to the Indian, the Anglo-Saxon has managed to conquer all with an efficiency unknown in the past. Even more striking is how the Anglo-Saxon race has rationalized this miserable treatment, "inventing words, theories and oratory to absolve itself of its guilt. Perhaps it recognized, in its innermost conscience, the impropriety of its sad excuses." Gobineau's treatment of the black only adds more detail to this picture. Enslaved and systematically forced to do much of the work, the black race in America has been placed in a frightful condition. Slavery is all the more appalling for its hypocrisy, "because it is contrary to the humanitarianism preached by those responsible for it."[41]

Everything the Anglo-Saxons have accomplished has been in the service of their narrow understanding of utility. The character of their conquest, though supposedly part of Gobineau's positive picture, is hardly flattering. America has been created by the dominant Aryan element, but the Anglo-Saxons, being the last to carry the banner of Aryanism, are already infected by all the corrosive fruits of modernity. Their victory appears to be more dishonorable than noble: "Our own civilization is the only one which has ever possessed this instinct to destroy and the complete capacity to carry it out; it is the only one which has constantly striven to wreak general destruction, while advocating limitless gentleness rather than anger, and even thinking itself indulgent. The reason for this is that it exists only to discover what is useful to it."[42] Still, even though the Anglo-Saxon race is guilty of these moral failings, nothing can prevent it from fulfilling its imperative of controlling the continent. The Anglo-Saxons "are men suited to dominate, . . . and [they] willingly dominate their inferiors." They are modern barbarians. The most sophisticated of the Latin Americans saw the Anglo-Saxons in just that light: as narrow and utilitarian representatives of an unseemly culture, but as too powerful to resist.

Such, then, is Gobineau's "positive" picture of America. Unhappily for America, this description applies best to the past and is now well on the way to becoming obsolete. Gobineau's second picture of America—of the nation he now sees emerging—shows the Anglo-Saxon element losing its will to rule and beginning to yield to principles of humanitarianism and democracy. The Anglo-Saxon race can no longer maintain the delicate, hypocritical balance on which its dominance had hitherto depended.

The loss of Aryan control of America may be seen in the nation's changing demographic composition. Hundreds of thousands of immigrants have been allowed to enter without regard to race: "The American Union is in fact the one nation in the world which, from the beginning of this century, and especially in these last few years, has seen the greatest mass of heterogeneous elements flowing onto its territory." In a short period, probably before the end of the nineteenth century, America "will be in the hands of a mixed family, in which the Anglo-Saxon element will play only the role of a subordinate part." Gobineau has nothing positive to say of the new immigrants, whom he characterizes as the "rubbish" (*détritus*) of Europe: Irish, Germans (most of them impure), and Italians (people of even more dubious stock). The meeting in one place of all these degenerated races will lead in some instances to violent racial conflicts. But to the degree that these races intermingle in the future (along with those, in the Southern states, of Indian, Negro, Spanish, and Portuguese blood), Gobineau foresaw nothing but "an incoherent juxtaposition of the most degraded kind of human beings."[43]

For Gobineau, America is thus hardly the young nation offering a chance for the revival of Aryan civilization. On the basis of his study of the facts, he pronounces all such hopes to be "inanities." The Great White Hope is pure illusion. America is only replicating the process of democratization and romanization that had been going on for so long in Europe. If anything, Gobineau sees more hope in the short term for Aryans in Europe than those in America, and Aryans would probably do better to put their efforts into preserving their bastions in the Old World than "to pour out their blood" to no good effect in America. In a more general sense America was not improving on anything in Europe but taking that continent's defects and intensifying them: "All the effort of this country [America] is limited to exaggerating certain aspects of European culture, and not always the most beautiful, to copy as best it can the rest, and to ignore some of the best."[44]

Americanism and Europeanism are the same thing, with America being only an extreme version of Europe's worst tendencies. America is the monster Europe has created out of its own modernist vision—a monster without any of the restraints still to be found in Europe. Here are echoes of de Pauw's Euro-isolationism, which

Gobineau later corroborates by concluding that the discovery of America had been a terrible mistake.[45] Later, in a series of newspaper articles, Gobineau developed these themes further, depicting the United States as a land of rapacious brigandage, rootlessness, ethnic intermixture, and, increasingly, decadence and decline. European immigrants who sought in America the "temple of virtue and happiness" were sorely disappointed. There was nothing new in the New World.[46]

Far from being a symbol of the reversal of the process of European degeneration, America for Gobineau represents the final and sad end of civilization. The end of history—which is the end of Aryanism and the end of the idea of race—has another name: democracy. In a letter Gobineau wrote from Persia in 1856, he noted that he no longer found it possible to discern that people's racial makeup, so far had the process of intermixing proceeded: "This people has no racial prejudices and cannot have any. Democracy has been fulfilled."[47] His description fit perfectly the condition America presaged for Western civilization and eventually for history as a whole.

The End of History

Gobineau's discussion of America leads directly to the conclusion of the *Essay*, where he presents his arresting idea of the end of history. In a letter he wrote a few years later, he summarized the message of his book's conclusion: "I am not telling people, 'You are acquitted' or 'You are condemned'; I tell them, 'You are dying.' The causes of your enervation are gathering and they will continue to gather. . . . No one in the world will replace you when your degeneration is completed. I am not a murderer; neither is the doctor who announces the coming of the end."[48]

The end state Gobineau describes is characterized by both homogeneity and universalism. All mankind is moving to the same end: "The definitive end of the suffering and toil as well as the pleasures and triumphs of our species is to attain, one day, supreme unity." For Gobineau, this state of unity carries no hint of fulfillment; on the contrary, it is a "sad spectacle" that seems to have left Gobineau suspended between anger and melancholy. Mankind will have degenerated to the last stages of leveling, displaying the "greatest mediocrity in all fields: mediocrity of physical strength, mediocrity of beauty, mediocrity of intellectual capacities— we could almost say nothingness." Nor is there any prospect of revival: "I am convinced that the present enfeeblement of the mind is not only universal, but that its spread is inevitable, irreparable and unlimited."[49]

As intolerable as this end state may have seemed to Gobineau, it is not clear whether he thought it similarly depressing or objectionable to the subjects themselves—"our descendants," as he bemusedly calls them, suggesting that they have evolved into another form. In the coming age, "each person will possess an equal portion; no motive will exist for one man to seek a portion any greater than anyone else's. . . . All people will have the same amount of physical force, the same instinctive aims, [and] similar amounts of intelligence." Filled, it seems, with a kind of dumb satisfaction, these beings will roam the surface of the earth as "human herds" that are "numb in a state of nullity, like buffalo grazing in the stagnant waters of the Pontine marshes." No longer possessed of any yearning for distinction or conquest, they will live in harmony not only with each other but also with their natural environment, to which they will relate as "guests, like the inhabitants of the forests and the waters."[50]

The striking idea of the end of history, made famous in our day by Francis Fukuyama, naturally raises the question of who originated this concept. Fukuyama took it from Alexandre Kojève, who in turn attributed it to Hegel, although some interpreters have insisted that Hegel was far less certain about the idea than Kojève maintained. Hegel's reservations appeared in his discussion of America, where he declared that "America is therefore the land of the future, where, in the ages that lie before us, the burden of the World's History shall reveal itself."[51] Perhaps, then, it was Arthur de Gobineau who was the first to speak definitively of an end to history. He surely was the first to take America out of the realm of possible dreams for the future and to incorporate it into the existing scheme of universal history. Gobineau in this sense completed Hegel's thought by foreclosing any idea of an uncharted future on a new continent. For Gobineau, there is nothing new about America; it represents a working out, in a more rapid and extreme fashion, of the trends of modern European degeneration. It is Europe on fast forward.

Near the end of his life, Gobineau observed that his thought would come to be genuinely appreciated only in a century's time. Almost exactly a century after the publication of the *Essay,* Kojève wrote that the "American way of life is the type of life proper to the post-historic period." The transformation of mankind from a human to an animal nature appeared to Kojève no longer as "a possibility still to come, but as a certitude already present." If Kojève was the first to spot the "human herds" in New York City, it was Arthur de Gobineau who a century earlier foresaw that they would be there.[52]

5

★ ★ ★

From Ethnology to
Multiculturalism

The use of America as a symbol in racialist thought, which Arthur de Gobineau inaugurated in the 1850s, became widespread by the end of the nineteenth century. Both in Europe, in a line of philosophical-historical thought that stretched from Richard Wagner through Oswald Spengler, and in the United States, in a new positivistic school of ethnology, America was the place where the meaning of race in human history was being played out.

The picture of America alternated between the two polar images Gobineau had sketched. The first was the positive vision (in the racialists' thought) of America as a white, Anglo-Saxon country constructed on racialist ideas that ignored the nation's founding principles. This view served as a foundation for the Confederate States of America—the regime Hitler later characterized as the lost "embryo of a future truly great America." The other, negative image of America was of a nation in decline that had abandoned racial hierarchy and that was yielding control to the inferior races, understood to include not only blacks and Asians but also Jews and various white peoples of southern Europe. This America was fast becoming a land where, in the words of Louis-Ferdinand Céline, "negroes will go to New Harlem to see the 'pale faces' dance the polka."[1]

But whichever image racialist thinkers attached to America, the aim was the same: to develop a new intellectual discipline, or a new theory inside the existing disciplines, that would serve as the authoritative guide for political life and establish the supremacy of a master race. The American people's acceptance of the principles of natural rights and equality was seen as one of the greatest mistakes of modern history, and the founders' recovery of political science one of the major intellectual errors.

For intellectuals, no body of thought stands in greater disrepute today than this doctrine of "classical" racialism. If one looks at various disciplines before 1950, important books in many fields employed racialism as a fully respectable approach, and many scholars considered it an advanced concept of modern science. Racialism remained a key concept in anthropology, history, and philosophy. After World War II, when the horrors of Nazi race policies became known, racialism lost all respectability in intellectual circles (although obviously not in every popular forum). In the ensuing decades, it was treated as not just an error but an intellectual pathology. Science made a complete turn, with some going so far as to proclaim that biology had disproved the validity of all racial hypotheses. This reaction against racialism arguably became an ideology of its own, immediately labeling as pseudoscientific virtually any kind of inquiry into heredity-based group differences.[2]

Although classical racialism has been rejected—and although the dominant voices of the hard sciences have sought to eliminate racial considerations completely—racialist thinking has reemerged at the vanguard of modern intellectual discourse under the aegis of the school known as multiculturalism or the politics of difference. At the same time that this school has been an inveterate foe of classical racialist ideology, it has made racial categories the common currency of contemporary thought. While this school claims in one breath that the source of difference in society is cultural, in the next it closely links these cultures to biological, and especially racial, groups. Its image of America as a society controlled by a Eurocentric Anglo-Saxon hegemony reestablishes race as the central theme of America's historical experience and follows the descriptive account—even as it rejects the evaluation—of the old positive image of America as sketched by the classical racialists.

The American Ethnologists

The establishment of an American school of ethnology, which Jefferson had urged in the 1780s, became a reality by the 1830s. And by the 1850s ethnology was greatly influencing scientific thought not only in the United States but throughout Europe as well. American ethnologists were the primary spokesmen for a new polygenetic theory that became for a time the leading scientific doctrine in the study of man and society.

Important connections existed between the American school and the thought of Arthur de Gobineau. In 1855 American ethnologists prepared a translation of Gobineau's *Essay,* which was supplemented with extensive notes and commentaries by Henry Hotz and Josiah Nott. The American ethnologists regarded the publication of this work as an important event in their quest for greater standing and legitimacy. The theories of Gobineau, who was touted by the editors as one of the era's greatest philosophers, were shown to be moving in the same direction as those of America's scientists. And the lines of intellectual influence were running in the opposite direction as well. Gobineau was well acquainted with the work of some of the Americans, and in the *Essay* he cited with qualified approval the cranial anatomy studies of Dr. Samuel Morton, whose writings had been widely circulated among other European scholars.[3] Had Gobineau known about the other research conducted in America, he would undoubtedly have relied on it more. As it happened, however, Gobineau's *Essay* was published in 1854, the same year that saw the publication of the magnum opus of the American school of ethnology: J. C. Nott and George Gliddon's *Types of Mankind*. These two books were the most significant works of racialist theory of the nineteenth century.

Ethnology, strictly speaking, was another name for the branch of natural history that dealt with the study of human beings. Originated by Buffon, this science developed throughout Europe in the late eighteenth and early nineteenth centuries and received the attention of such well-known figures as Gustave Flourens in France, Johann Friedrich Blumenbach in Germany, and James Cowles Pritchard in Great Britain. Most of these thinkers, who preferred the old label "natural historians," argued for a position that was closer to the unity of mankind. In contrast, the American version of this science fell under the domination of those espousing a racialist position. These scientists favored the new terms "ethnology" and "ethnologists," which they thought helped to differentiate themselves from the more established unitarist and environmentalist position. Adopting this terminology was a signal that they were breaking with unitarism and striking out in a new direction.

Not all American scientists, to be sure, supported a racialist position. Some, following in the path of Benjamin Rush, argued strongly for the unity of mankind. Two scholars in particular merit mention for their extensive critiques of the *Types of Mankind*: the Reverend John Bachman and Professor James Cabell. Cabell, who taught comparative anatomy at the University of Virginia, published a memorable book, *Testimony of Modern Science to the Unity of Mankind* (1859), which sought to refute the entire ethnological school.[4] In one of history's little ironies, at the University of Virginia, an elegant building named Cabell Hall is today situated opposite the famous Rotunda that Jefferson designed, on a site that Jefferson planned to leave open. It stands as a quiet symbolic reminder of the other side of the debate on race and the unity of man.[5]

The ethnologists, many of whom were fervent nationalists (an issue that would shortly lead to support for the Confederacy), proudly insisted that America was the best place in which to pursue the study of man in its positive or empirical aspects. For what America might lack in great universities and libraries, it more than made up for in the real-life laboratory it offered for observing the different racial groups. American scientists, able to view and study the empirical phenomena, could more easily free themselves of the prejudices of humanitarian thinking and begin to see matters in a genuine light. Repeating Jefferson's point about the obligation of Americans to develop ethnological studies, the opening section of the *Types of Mankind* declares that "there are reasons why Ethnology should be eminently a science for American culture. Here three of the five races . . . are brought together to determine the problem of their destiny as they best may. Extraordinary facilities for observing minor subdivisions among the families of the white race are also present by the resort hither of immigrants from every part of Europe."[6]

The American ethnologists praised Gobineau as one of the first Europeans to emphasize the plurality of human types. At the same time, they noted how their method and approach differed from his. According to Nott, Gobineau, "view[ed] the various races of men as a historian," whereas the Americans looked at the same questions more as natural scientists would.[7] The Americans relied in the first instance on experimental studies—anatomical measurements and the like—that were "outside" history, whereas Gobineau drew his conclusions from his account of the story of mankind. These differences, however, were relative, not absolute. The Americans defined ethnology as having a historical as well as an empirical component, and Gobineau had high praise for much of the anatomical research, even if he could never quite bring himself to survey, for example, the hat sizes of different races, as Nott had done.[8]

If the Americans were arguably narrower in their scope than Gobineau, they were bolder in their claims. Nott mildly took Gobineau to task for stopping short of advocating the original diversity among the races. Gobineau hesitated, Nott claimed, because of "religious scruples" and because of a "want of accurate knowledge in that part of natural history which treats of the designation of *species* and the laws of *hybridity*."[9] In contrast, the Americans had freed themselves of religious orthodoxies and had elaborated a new conception of a species that enabled them directly to challenge the views of natural historians.

The most important figure in the American school of ethnology (albeit more for his prowess as a publicist than his skill as a scientist) was Josiah Nott, a physician from Mobile, Alabama. Nott took the lead in persuading the more prestigious physician Samuel Morton to declare himself in favor of polygenesis, and Nott was the driving force in the production of the *Types of Mankind,* which is less a book in the usual sense than a compendium of the views of the major American ethnologists. *Types of Mankind* is a huge work of nearly eight hundred large-format pages replete with tables, drawings, and figures. Its immense size and scope are prefigured by its imposing title, *Types of Mankind; or, Ethnological Researches, Based upon the Ancient Monuments, Paintings, Sculptures, and Crania of Races and upon Their Natural, Geographical, Philological, and Biblical History.* The book went through ten editions and was used by students for three generations as a seminal text in anthropology.[10]

Types of Mankind elaborates and defends the main characteristics of the American school of ethnology. The first characteristic was an emphasis on a highly scientific or positivistic approach. Using the most advanced and rigorous techniques of their time, from cranial measurements to statistical studies, the ethnologists circulated their findings throughout the world. Even before the publication of *Types of Mankind,* they were gaining ground within the scientific community, if not by convincing everyone of the case for the new polygenesis, then by finding weaknesses in the unitarist position.

A second characteristic was the American school's religious heterodoxy. The ethnologists took the lead in attacking the unity of man, an idea then supported by religious authorities. Nott, for example, promised to deal with the subject "purely as one of science . . . [and to] treat the Scriptures simply in their historical and scientific bearings." Admitting that he had once tried to reconcile science with theology, he now declared that he had had his fill of being "vilified by self-constituted teachers of the Christian religion." Science alone would henceforth be his standard: "The banner of science is now nailed to the mast."[11] Recalling previous battles between religion and science in matters relating to astronomy, cosmogony, and geology, Nott likened himself to a modern-day Galileo, but one who would not recant: "The last great struggle between science and theology is the one we are now engaged in."[12]

A third characteristic of the school was its break with the views of the previous generation of natural historians—Flourens, Blumenbach, and Pritchard. These men had argued that the human species was one and that the different race groups were different varieties of humans, resulting from different (and alterable) physical and cultural factors. The Americans claimed that this position was false and could be disproved by using the same positive or scientific methods used by natural historians. The key to allowing for a fresh look at the phenomena was to adopt a new definition of what constitutes a species. According to Morton and Nott, a species is best defined as a "type, or organic form, that is permanent; or which has remained unchanged under the opposite climatic influence for ages. The Arab, the Egyptian, and the Negro; the greyhound, the turnspit, and the common wild dog . . . may be cited as examples." Louis Agassiz, the famous Harvard professor of natural history, considered this definition to be a conceptual breakthrough that revolutionized the study of man; it constituted a "true philosophical definition of species, the first to bless the world of science."[13]

The novelty of the definition was its decoupling the concept of a species from hybridity, the prevailing biological criterion of successful reproduction. The new concept stressed the persistence, despite environmental influences, of an observable form. The question of hybridity, the ethnologists argued, should be studied apart from the question of a species, because hybridity was not an essential characteristic of a species. Instead, there were a number of possibilities for hybridity among species. In most instances interbreeding between species could not occur at all; in some instances it could occur with limited success; and in a few instances, between closely related species, it could occur with apparently great success. But successful interbreeding in no way altered the fact that the things interbred might be of two different species and that the hybrid produced was something different from either of the originals. This was the case, Nott insisted, in the interbreeding of the races of man. Although intermixing between the races was biologically possible, the races were different species. Even in America, Nott thought, the mulatto population showed signs of physical decay, and he especially doubted that the rates of hybridization could be high when the "distance" between the intermingling races was too great, as when higher whites, such as Anglo-Saxon Americans, mixed with blacks, as distinct from when lower whites, such as the Spanish or Portuguese, mixed with blacks.

But Nott's main argument was that, whatever the rates of hybridity, the new types produced by intermixing were of a different kind than the originals who created the mix. The ethnologists drew what became the classical racialist conclusion about the effects of interbreeding. Intermixture between races produced, on average, beings that were at once more intelligent than the original lower race and less intelligent than the original higher race. Intermixing, although biologically possible, was undesirable. The portion of mankind enlightened by science should take the practical steps necessary to respect and protect the natural principle of hierarchy, for on this point all future progress of civilization depended. "The infusion of even a minute proportion of blood of one race into another produces a most decided modification of moral and physical character," Nott declared. "It is evident, theoretically, that the superior races ought to be kept from all adulteration, otherwise the world will retrograde, instead of advancing, in civilization. . . . The human family might possibly be exterminated by a thorough amalgamation of all the various types of mankind now existing upon earth."[14]

The ethnologists' concept of a species was designed to show that contemporary biology could not, on the basis of its empirical criterion of successful hybridity, settle by fiat the question of the unity of mankind. Nott claimed that modern proponents of the unity of the human species had used the biological definition to help them *think* they had resolved the issue of unity by positivistic criteria; but in reality their reasoning was circular and rested on a definition that produced a predetermined conclusion. Anyone who examined the issue closely, he insisted, would see that the term "species" was vague and even somewhat arbitrary. A species "is but a simple *abstraction of the mind,* and not a group, exactly determined by nature herself."[15] If Nott could not necessarily prove the case for the ethnologists' own conception of a species as a "primordial organic form," he could at least claim to have posed the philosophical problem of how one can know whether individual things make up a "kind," whether one calls that kind a "species," "type," or something else.

Finally, like Gobineau, the American ethnologists did not stop at dividing mankind among the basic color groups (or "primary races"), but went on to elaborate racial differences within these groups. Their attention naturally focused on the white race, where their views paralleled Gobineau's theory of a Teutonic and Anglo-Saxon element at the top of the hierarchy and many of the southern European groups (and Jews, treated as a Semitic type) at the bottom. Nott does not use the term "romanization" to describe intermarriage among these white groups, but he has in mind exactly the same idea when he speaks of "amalgamation." Without explicitly making the argument, Nott pointed in the direction of policies that would try to restrict the white part of American society to Nordic elements.

American ethnologists of the nineteenth century believed they offered not just a theoretical science but a body of knowledge that could help to direct society and establish political standards. *Types of Mankind* begins by stating its two purposes: to "investigate the mental and physical differences of Mankind" and to "deduce from these investigations principles of human guidance in all the important relations of social existence."[16] At the time, the crucial issue in American political life was slavery, and the ethnologists became deeply involved in the debate. Although it was possible to subscribe to racialist views and still oppose slavery—Jefferson, as well as many European thinkers, had done so—the ethnologists in America generally allied themselves with a defense of slavery. Ethnology, Nott observes, clearly had "practical implications," and he proudly describes how ethnology's research had influenced the thinking of John Calhoun.[17] Ethnology also provided a powerful defense of slavery based on the scientifically established proposition that slavery represented, in the words of one modern scholar, the "natural relation of the races—the mere external adaptation of natural law."[18]

Given the clearly political use to which ethnology was put, it was often attacked at the time—as, of course, it has been ever since—as a politicized science. But the ethnologists refused to allow themselves to be placed on the defensive. Throughout their writings they insist that it was not they but the unitarists who were guilty of politicizing science. Time and again the ethnologists took the natural historians to task for preaching the unity of the human race in order to promote universalist and philanthropic political ideas. It was the unitarists' political beliefs, the ethnologists argued, that prevented them from viewing the facts in a dispassionate and scientific light.

The ethnologists' advocacy of pluralism went beyond a defense of slavery to an attack on parts of the Enlightenment. In search of allies, the ethnologists tried to connect their argument against unitarism to the general conservative critique of universalism and equality. Even though conservatives did not rely directly on racialist theories, the ethnologists stressed that the two groups had a common foe: democratic or humanistic rationalism. Echoing the views of opponents of the French Revolution, the ethnologists charged that the natural historians were seeking to impose unity and homogeneity on the world. Two excerpts from the leading ethnological magazine of the time, *De Bow's Review,* show the direction of this line of thinking:

> If the whole race have but a common original, then common systems may be applied to all; and the greatest license is given to "later day" theorists, who would organize the world upon certain uniform bases and fit the same institutions and laws to every stage of civilization. If, on the contrary, this assumption be false and groundless, these mad dreamers will at once be refuted, and the world discover that parliament and congress are unsuited to the Hottentot and the African.

> The Proudhons and Fouriers, French Socialists, Continental Republicans, Northern Abolitionists, who, setting out with the perfect equality in every respect of all the nations and families of men, proclaim the doctrines of universal republicanism, . . . stand ready to fit . . . Hottentot and Bushman, semi-civilized Negro and Caucasian, to institutions of a common shape and character![19]

In contrast with conservatism, however, the American ethnologists did not question modern social science; instead, they made it the very foundation of their position. In this respect they joined Gobineau, who also claimed to ground his theory in modern science. Yet between the ethnologists and Gobineau there was also an important difference: the ethnologists, whose foundational science was biology and not history, rejected Gobineau's notion of the laws of history that direct the future to a predetermined end. Rather like the proponents of Enlightenment thought, the ethnologists saw their science as playing an active role in changing the course of history. The ethnologists did agree with Gobineau in regard to his fears of human degeneration, but they saw their science as providing the knowledge that could help governments to avoid this result.

The activism (or "voluntarism") in the ethnologists' thought is revealed by their highly selective translation of Gobineau's *Essay*. The editors, Hotz and Nott, omitted the chapter on America, which predicted the decline of American Anglo-Saxon rule, and they excised much of the material that spoke of an end to history. They wanted an ally, not a critic, and they even went so far as to dedicate the translation "to the statesmen of America," thereby suggesting that Gobineau wished to create a political science to found racialist regimes. (Gobineau, in fact, disavowed any such aim.) With its extensive notes and careful selection of passages, the American edition of the *Essay* was actually more a work by the American ethnologists than it was one by Arthur de Gobineau.

By the 1850s the ethnologists had gained a large following within the scientific community in America and had begun to exercise an impact on opinion in educated circles in the South. Eric McKitrick, a leading intellectual historian of this period, includes Josiah Nott among a handful of influential proslavery thinkers "known for their writings throughout the literate South."[20] But McKitrick acknowledges that, because of their religious heterodoxy, the ethnologists produced the "nearest thing to an intellectual schism in the pro-slavery ranks."[21] Ethnology was objectionable to many defenders of slavery who wanted to remain Christians and who saw no need to go all the way to polygenism in order to find sanction for the institution.

As the Civil War approached, however, ethnology won more adherents. Of the existing defenses for a race-based slave regime, ethnological polygenism supplied the surest and most confident justification. Its enhanced status is illustrated in the "Corner Stone Speech" of Alexander Stephens, vice president of the Confederate States of America. Delivered in 1861, this speech was the most serious attempt of a Confederate political leader to enunciate the basic principles of the new regime. In it, Stephens tried to join together the religious and the scientific (ethnological) arguments in favor of slavery, giving much greater weight to science. Stephens began by rejecting as "fundamentally wrong" the idea of the American founders that slavery "was in violation of the laws of nature." This understanding of the laws of nature "rested upon the assumption of the equality of the races. This was an error." Stephens continued, "Our new government is founded upon exactly the opposite idea; its corner stone rests upon the great truth that the negro is not the equal of the white man; that slavery—subordination to the superior race—is his natural and normal condition." Acknowledgment of "this great physical and moral truth," Stephens allowed, "has been slow in the process of its development, like all other truths in the various departments of science." But now, at last, it is known: "This, our new government, is the first, in the history of the world, based upon this great physical, philosophical and moral truth." Stephens' speech, as Harry Jaffa has pointed out, made the Confederate States the first political system to rest on a "doctrine of the master race . . . set forth *on the authority of modern science.*"[22]

The defeat of the Confederacy put an end to the ethnologists' hope of having their science serve as the official doctrine of American politics. Yet ethnology by no means lost all its influence. In the postbellum period it led the defense of racialism, and its prestige grew along with the increasing authority of science generally in the late nineteenth century. Even the advent of Darwinism worked in a curious way to reinforce the racialist ideas of the ethnological school—contrary, perhaps, to the pure science of the matter. Darwinism, technically speaking, called into question the idea of "fixed types" on which the ethnological definition of species rested. But Darwinism also suggested that the path of evolutionary development contained less developed and more developed varieties of a species; this idea was broadly consistent with the ethnological literature. In any event, many thinkers in Europe and America found ways to join Darwinist precepts with ethnology, creating a race-based social Darwinism. This marriage of two distinct families of thought constituted the scientific (or positivistic) pillar used to support racialist opinion and policies in America from the second half of the nineteenth century until the Massive Resistance of the 1950s.

After World War II, in reaction against this kind of science and especially the policies of the Nazis, some leaders of social science took it upon themselves to issue an official response under the auspices of the United Nations Educational, Scientific, and Cultural Organization. The UNESCO Statement on Race, which was issued in 1950 by a group of scientists led by Ashley Montagu, argued for a liberal, humanitarian view of man. Like the unitarists from which it descended, this school claimed that a hard science (biology) was the source of its proof of the unity and equality of man. Of course, the importance of the political context in which the UNESCO statement occurred was undeniable, but this did not mean, according to its authors, that politics dictated the results.[23]

The UNESCO statement argued that biology could not only disprove the bold claims of racialism but also establish positively the case for unity: "Biological studies lend support to the ethic of universal brotherhood." The statement did not assert, in the fashion of the strange arguments of some nineteenth-century unitarists, that changes in physical environments would actually eliminate all physical differences among human groups. Instead, it handled the matter of difference by the expedient of redefining terms. Since so much mixing had taken place among humans, the authors of the statement expressed doubts about whether races actually exist and thus whether race is a meaningful term: "Race is not so much a biological phenomenon as a social myth." It was therefore suggested that the term "race" be dropped and replaced with "ethnic group." (This term had a more friendly connotation in 1950 than it does today, in the wake of what has become known euphemistically as "ethnic cleansing.") Whatever differences now remained among these ethnic groups, the statement went on, were physical only: "The scientific evidence indicates that the range of mental capacities in all ethnic groups is much the same." Finally, to solidify its case for humanism (and universalism), the statement concluded with another biological fact: "The whole of human history shows that the co-operative spirit is not only natural to men, but more deeply rooted than any self-seeking tendencies."[24]

Not all scientists in the fields of ethnology or biology were content with this presentation of what was called scientific evidence, and some of them attempted to draft a restatement. Nevertheless, although research about group differences has continued in out-of-the-way places, the views expressed in the statement became the accepted public idea of what "science" has proven. Everyone was given to understand that biology lent its cloak of support to the universalist thesis, and anyone who suggested otherwise was defined as outside of the mainstream. Stephen Gould's widely read *Mismeasure of Man* represents the classic expression of this view, and the book received all of the honors appropriate to a work that articulates so well the prevailing wisdom of the day.

Into this comfortable consensus marched the modern-day heirs of pluralism, Richard Herrnstein and Charles Murray, authors of *The Bell Curve* (1994). Their book was responsible, as its jacket copy proudly proclaims, for breaking a "taboo" and reintroducing the idea of a connection between race and certain nonphysical characteristics, specifically "cognitive intelligence" as defined by social science. The tremendous controversy this book engendered when it was published—it was featured on the covers of two major newsmagazines—confirmed in one sense the tenacity with which the liberal humanitarian position was still held. But the situation in 1994 was more complicated than it was in the 1960s, when all rushed to support a scientifically blessed universalism. By the 1980s, those in the cultural fields had abandoned liberal humanitarianism and were celebrating the new value of difference. As a result, many who attacked the book for its racism spoke at the same time of the strong differences between groups, but always characterizing the differences in positive terms.

The maelstrom of criticism that greeted *The Bell Curve* led Charles Murray— Richard Herrnstein had died in the interim—to express annoyance that so much attention was being devoted to only one part of a very long book. "In the 845 pages of this book," Murray stated, "there is one chapter on race and I.Q. There is, within that chapter, twenty pages, out of 845, which deal with the question of the source of the difference. Now, may I suggest to you that if we put that discussion in such a small place, buried in the middle of the book, maybe we didn't think it was that important." Either this complaint resulted from a fit of amnesia or Murray was just whistling "Dixie." No prominent social scientist in our times, in this country, could possibly have made the kind of argument that *The Bell Curve* makes about race without expecting to provoke a reaction. In fact, the authors clearly knew they were inviting controversy, admitting in their book that the "topic of genes, intelligence, and race in the late twentieth century is like the topic of sex in Victorian England." Having made this not quite felicitous analogy, could Murray and Herrnstein have really thought that twenty pages of a steamy bedroom scene in the middle of *Middlemarch*—itself a book of some length—would have gone unremarked by George Eliot's contemporaries?[25]

In the chapter entitled "Ethnic Differences in Cognitive Ability," which is the longest in the book, Herrnstein and Murray begin by observing that there are notable differences among large population groups in respect to measurable criteria of intelligence. The authors mention several different kinds of groups, but they devote most of their attention to race-based categories. The data show that "East Asians" (their term) do slightly better than white Americans on intelligence tests and that whites ("European Americans") do significantly better than African Americans. The authors discuss next whether (and to what extent) the causes of these differences derive from environmental or genetic factors. Although Herrnstein and Murray make clear that the data can supply no definitive answers to these questions, they argue that the weight of evidence suggests an important role for genetic causes.

Assigning a significant role for genetic causality is, of course, the claim that ignited all the controversy. As in the case of the unitarist-pluralist exchange of the nineteenth century, the authors met with severe criticism for a supposed science that employed racialist categories, only to respond that it was the adherents of the prevailing orthodoxy who relied most on unexamined premises and practiced a political use of science. But in contrast to the nineteenth-century racialists, Herrnstein and Murray have no wish to use their findings to separate the races or attack liberal principles. At one point they write, "We cannot think of a legitimate argument why an encounter between individual whites and blacks need be affected by the knowledge that an aggregate ethnic difference in measured intelligence is genetic instead of environmental," and at another point they claim that even if it were known that all differences were genetic rather than environmental, "nothing of any significance should change."[26]

But these statements, which contain such phrases as "legitimate argument" and "should," reveal the authors' uneasiness about the impact of their presentation. In the real world, as Herrnstein and Murray concede, there is an "impulse to think that environmental sources of difference are less threatening than genetic ones" and therefore a danger that their research may be misunderstood. They give no examples, but a few points come readily to mind. If a belief in the primacy of genetic differences were to guide public policy, would whites and blacks continue to view each other in the same light? Or would the nation's foreign policy (toward Africa, for example) be conducted in the same way? To escape charges of irresponsibility—charges that they in effect raise against themselves—Herrnstein and Murray go on to offer an extraordinary justification of their approach. On the basis of personal observations (but not one piece of data), they maintain that Americans hold views about race that are far more extreme than almost anyone admits. The "underground conversation" about race in America, among not just racists but almost everyone, "is increasingly shaped by privately held beliefs about the implications of genetic differences that could not stand open inspection." Not to put too fine a point on it, the "private views" of most Americans are thoroughly racist. Given this supposed state of opinion, Herrnstein and Murray can now present themselves as paragons of responsibility. Social science is not only true, it is salutary. *The Bell Curve* will serve to correct false ideas and promote better race relations by moderating people's views: instead of people thinking that there is huge genetic inequality (which is a prejudice), they will know that there is only significant genetic inequality (which is a fact).[27]

Murray's public retreat from even talking about this argument concedes that *The Bell Curve* did not have anything like its intended beneficial effect on the question of race. Its failure on this score reflects the fact that the categories governing the book's discussion of race and difference begin not from political phenomena but from psychological and biological data—or "observations," as Jefferson would have called them. Only in the conclusion of the book, when the authors present their justification for liberal democracy, do they turn from social science to political science. At this point they cite *The Federalist*. But these passages, which concern individual rights and individual differences, have nothing to do with the racialist categories that *The Bell Curve* has reintroduced. Publius would no more bless *The Bell Curve* than he blessed *Notes on the State of Virginia*. No writer of political science, using political categories as the guiding criteria of a work, would approach the subject of race in the way Herrnstein and Murray do. Political science, as *The Federalist* showed, has another way of treating the question of groups and race in human society.

Racialism in Twentieth-Century European Thought

If racialism in America has traditionally rested on positivist grounds, relying on measurements of one sort or another, the racialism of Europe has generally been grounded in a philosophical and historical approach. The categories that Arthur de Gobineau introduced in the 1850s had an enormous impact on subsequent European thought, finding their way into philosophy, literature, art, and music. Gobineau's racialist philosophy only became important, however, insofar as it was transformed from a fatalist doctrine that accepted the demise of civilization and Aryanism to an activist or voluntaristic theory that emphasized a project of social transformation. Even Gobineau's great admirer and disciple on the question of race, Richard Wagner, pronounced Gobineau's fatalist outlook to be unacceptable and argued that steps could be taken to rescue mankind from impending doom. For this reason, too, Hitler rejected Gobineau and turned to Wagner for his inspiration. As he told Hermann Rauschning in 1933, "The problem is this: How can we arrest racial decay? Must what Count Gobineau says come true? . . . For myself, at every stage in my life I come back to Wagner. Only a new nobility can introduce the new civilization for us."[28]

The rejection of Gobineau's fatalism also opened the door to the most pernicious effects of racialist thought, bringing it out of the study and into the streets. Once fatalism was denied, it seemed that the best way to improve human societies was to set proactive policies for manipulating the racial composition of society. Particularly in Germany, Gobineau's conservative racialism was replaced by an activist racialism that proposed measures designed to alter the ideas, practices, and laws affecting race. The measures ranged from racialist immigration policies to laws enforcing segregation and banning miscegenation and finally to racial enslavement and the infamous final solution. These interventions were guided by a body of thought that claimed to understand race and the means by which different races could be preserved. (Sadly, in Germany during the 1930s, this pseudoscience was for a time known as *politische Wissenschaft,* or political science.)[29] In Germany, one can trace the line of racialist thought from Gobineau to Richard Wagner, the historian H. Stewart Chamberlain (Wagner's son-in-law), the Nazi "philosopher" Alfred Rosenberg, and Oswald Spengler, by far the most famous thinker of the group.

Oswald Spengler was the author of *The Decline of the West* (1917), an epoch-defining work that catapulted him from the obscurity of an academy teacher to the status of a leading international intellectual.[30] So much do we associate Spengler's name with this one book, we tend to forget that he continued to write afterward and became one of the most influential thinkers in rightist intellectual circles of the Weimar Republic. Spengler, who favored the business elite and the aristocracy, initially viewed Adolf Hitler with contempt, although Spengler also saw him as a useful tool, if kept in his place. As National Socialism emerged as the strongest force on the Right, Spengler shifted toward the movement and supported Hitler for president in 1932. At this time Spengler was widely thought to be a member of the Nazi party, but he withheld a strong public endorsement of the new regime. He met privately with Hitler in 1933, apparently hoping—in some version of the dream of philosophy instructing power—to become a high-level adviser to the new leader. (Martin Heidegger seemed to have had similar aspirations.) But Hitler refused to meet certain conditions that Spengler had set for the relationship, and the two men broke off their talks. The next year the Nazis began to attack Spengler for his pessimism and denied him the honor of being a prophet of the new order. Spengler died in 1936.[31]

Although Spengler briefly discusses America in *The Decline of the West,* there is nothing unusual in his treatment. He viewed the United States merely as one country among others, not as a symbol. But in two of his later books, written more than a decade after *The Decline of the West,* he elaborated the themes that proved so important to German thought on America.[32] These books were *Man and Technology* (1932), an extended essay that was little read at the time, and *The Year of Decision* (1933), which was widely distributed but has since fallen into obscurity. Although Spengler's ideas can be fit into a single picture, these works emphasize, respectively, two quite different themes: technology and race. In this chapter I focus on race (at some cost in coherence to Spengler's thought), postponing treatment of Spengler's views on technology until Chapter 7.

If the Spengler of *The Decline of the West* was known for his gloomy outlook, the later Spengler must be considered downright despairing, for his theme was nothing less than the impending collapse of civilization and the return of mankind to a state of barbarism. The cause for this collapse was the unwillingness of the natural leaders of society to continue the struggle for industrial and technological development on which civilization depended. This analysis rested on the idea (which Spengler adapted from Friedrich Nietzsche) that the only way for man to create and sustain anything noble or great, either within a nation or among nations, was to embrace the principle of hierarchy: "There is a natural distinction between men born to command and men born to service, between the leaders and the led of life." Life, Spengler intoned time and again, is struggle, and this struggle can be waged only by the "few," by those "born to command," by the "few creative heads."[33] Society can be successful and civilization can survive only if this hierarchy is respected, if those who can lead do so, and if those who cannot step aside. What form the government takes—monarchic, aristocratic, or democratic—is not important, nor is the form of the international order. What counts is whether the society's organizing and animating principles allow for the de facto leadership of those fit to command. Otherwise, failure is certain.

Spengler expressed this thesis about the "natural" condition of leaders and followers in different ways. In *Man and Technology,* he linked it to the capacity of certain creative minds to continue the process of technological development. In *The Year of Decision,* he connected it to the theme of race. As the title suggests, *The Year of Decision* was meant to be a practical book addressed to the leaders of the day. It focuses on the political situation of the world as it might be viewed by statesmen, leaving open (in contrast to the more fatalistic argument of *Man and Technology*) the possibility of corrective action, provided that action is taken soon. The hierarchy needed to ensure the survival of civilization, which is also the hierarchy that constitutes the nobility of man, is reflected in the relations among the various races of man. In the final analysis, the world crisis is a matter of race: "For behind the world wars and the still unfinished proletarian world-revolution there looms the greatest of all dangers, the *coloured* menace, and it will require every bit of 'race' that is still available among white nations to deal with it."[34]

Spengler's practice of putting the word "race" in quotation marks was meant to introduce ambiguity. In some contexts he employs the term in a metaphorical rather than strictly biological sense, using the word as a synonym for the principle of hierarchy and nobility. To be of good "race" refers to one who recognizes his rightful position as a superior and who is willing to assume the responsibility of commanding. Spengler writes that "for centuries all stocks and species have been mixed. . . . Healthy generations with a future before them have from time immemorial always welcomed a stranger into the family if he had 'race,' no matter what race it was to which he belonged." In his papers, he went even further: "There are no noble and ignoble races. There are only noble and ignoble types and specimens in *all* races." Notwithstanding such statements, Spengler's practical analysis always seemed to come down to racial and ethnic groups in the ordinary, biological sense, and he sketched a hierarchy of the races that fully corresponded to the precepts of classical racialist thought. At the top stood the white race; beneath it (in no particular order) were the yellow, red, and black races. Among whites, Spengler delineated the usual hierarchy, with the Germanic or Anglo-Saxon races at the apex and the Slavs, southern Europeans, and Jews at the bottom. As he put it, "The Celtic-Germanic 'race' is the strongest-willed that the world has ever seen."[35]

In his analysis of the world situation, Spengler argued that, now as before, it is a "group of nations of Nordic blood . . . that still commands the situation."[36] Included in this group are Germany, the United States, France, and Great Britain. These nations constitute the natural leaders of the world and the only countries fit to command. Yet they are rapidly yielding power to the colored peoples. The triumph of the colored races would mark the end of any real hierarchy and the beginning of mankind's descent into chaos and barbarism. As a last-ditch effort to reverse this decline, Spengler suggested a grand coalition among the nations of Nordic blood. But even he was dubious that such a coalition can take place. The fault lies not with the colored races but with the white race, which, as the ruling element, bears the responsibility of maintaining its preeminence by a continual reassertion of its status. A loss of control follows from a loss of will, which derived from either exhaustion or ideological blindness. Spengler contended that ideological blindness was the chief problem among the commanding nations. Because of their acceptance of democracy and equality, these nations are unwilling to affirm the natural fact of hierarchy. Dupes of insipid and debilitating democratic ideas, the Nordic nations had lost sight of the truth of racial hierarchy and were abandoning their place of world leadership.

At this point Spengler turns to America, for the great crisis of civilization is prefigured by its development. The United States had been created and made into a great nation by a "ruling Anglo Saxon type," but America was now on the verge of slipping into mediocrity. The outward sign or cause was the Anglo-Saxon's loss of control to the lesser races: "Quite apart from the Negroes, the immigrants during the twenty years before the War included—with only a small proportion of Germans, English, and Scandinavians—no less than fifteen million Poles, Russians, Czechs, Balkan Slavs, Eastern Jews, Greeks, inhabitants of Asia Minor, Spaniards, and Italians."[37] Largely because of its acceptance of the ideas of democracy, America was becoming a nation without "race," and here Spengler meant both senses of the word. Not only had America lost an ethnic center and ceded control to inferior peoples, but it had also lost sight of the principle of nobility and hierarchy. America's internal crisis was emblematic of the crisis facing the world as a whole: the loss of "race" prefigured the collapse of civilization.

Any treatment of European racialist thought would be incomplete without mentioning the person who put into practice the most extreme, yet fully "logical," conclusion to this philosophy. Adolf Hitler was at least roughly familiar with the views of these racialist theorists, and his thinking about the United States paralleled the dominant ideas in racialist discourse, alternating between its positive and negative images of America. In fact, Hitler found a certain way of combining the two. In *Mein Kampf* (1925), his references to America were highly favorable, if not envious. His assessment was largely shaped by the racial issue. America was not only one of the leading nations of the world but also a nation of Nordic blood.[38] Hitler also saw in America some signs of a country that wished to maintain its racial standards against empty Enlightenment ideas of equality. In this respect, America offered a glimpse of a model for the proper kind of "national state": "The American Union, by principally refusing immigration to elements with poor health, and even simply excluding certain races from naturalization, acknowledges by slow beginnings an attitude which is peculiar to the national state conception."[39] Hitler also seemed to admire America for its technological development; the private train that sped him from Munich to his vacation retreat in the Alps bore the name *Amerika*.

By 1933 Hitler's largely positive view began to yield to a more negative image of America. Although it contained the same racialist premises, the new image relied on a different empirical analysis that reflected the views of Gobineau, Rosenberg, and Spengler. America, in this interpretation, had begun to lose its way by abandoning its truest and deepest racial instincts and giving in to its democratic spirit. Hitler summarized his views in an informal speech he gave in 1933: "Since the Civil War, in which the Southern States were conquered, against all historical logic and sound sense, the American people have been in a condition of political and popular decay. . . . The beginnings of a great new social order based on the principle of slavery and inequality were destroyed by that war, and with them also the embryo of a future truly great America that would have been ruled by . . . a real master class that would have swept away all the falsities of liberty and equality."[40]

The greatest problem with America was its political regime and political principles, which were corrupting and destroying the deeper spirit of its *Volk*. Rosenberg, National Socialism's official philosopher, traced the problem back to the American founding, where the idea of the rights of man was first introduced, which then became the model for the French *droits de l'homme*. The error was compounded with the Civil War, when these rights began to be extended to blacks. Later, of course, Jews were also admitted in large numbers and began to exercise more influence as time passed.[41]

What distinguished Hitler's view of America from that of Gobineau and Spengler was his belief that America could be turned around and renewed. Hitler was no fatalist. America could yet be saved by appeals to the instincts of average white Americans against constitutional principles of equality and democracy. According to Hitler, the "wholesome aversion for the Negroes and the colored races in general, including the Jews," provided the basis for hope. The kind of awakening that had taken place in Germany could occur as well in America: "National Socialism alone is destined to liberate the American people from their ruling clique and give them back the means of becoming a great nation."[42]

Multiculturalism

Today the slogan that American intellectuals have embraced and exported to the rest of the world is "multiculturalism"—or, for those who prefer the more philosophical version, the "politics of difference." Multiculturalism is being addressed everywhere in the international republic of letters—in symposia presentations, books, lengthy essays, and classroom discussions. It has been called the most important ideology of Western intellectuals since the collapse of Communism. Inside America, where multiculturalism more or less has its home, it is also the most difficult to define or characterize. The term has been used to designate proposals as mild as those that ask American students to learn more about non-mainline European groups and as controversial as those that would amend the Constitution to guarantee political representation for groups officially designated as "oppressed or disadvantaged."[43] On the campuses of American universities, its meaning can range from support for new departments of cultural and ethnic studies to assaults on what is called the "canon" of Western thought.

It may be an indication of American dominance in the world—or, more likely, of American self-centeredness—that so many in the United States proceed as if specifically American issues immediately merit the status of an ism. It is hard to imagine intellectuals in any other nation today moving with such blithe assurance that what counts in their own country has such worldwide significance. There is accordingly merit in looking at how multiculturalism has been conceived outside of its American context, for then an effort must be made to broaden and clarify its meaning. Such is the case, for example, in an essay by the Canadian political theorist Charles Taylor, who traces the origin of multiculturalism to the human need for recognition as supplied by a fixed group identity. In treating the politics of his own country, Taylor focuses much of his discussion on the claims of French-speaking Canadians, who prefer to be called Québécois.[44]

The German philosopher Bazon Brock has attempted to broaden the conception of multiculturalism to a European context. In a long essay in *Der Speigel,* Brock describes the essence of multiculturalism as the elevation of a people's "culture" (which he roughly equates with a linguistic or nationality group) to the extent that the culture is the most important part of the people's identity and social attachment. He argues that multiculturalism comes in two forms: a rightist version, which asserts that each culture has a claim to political sovereignty over its own group and territory and a right to exercise it, if need be, by fighting for ownership of the state; and a leftist version, which holds that a number of cultures should live under the same political authority, with each culture enjoying and profiting from its contacts with the others. (These designations of Right and Left reflect the postwar tendency of identifying nationalist movements with the Right and antinationalist ones with the Left.)[45]

The accounts of Taylor and Brock, while agreeing on the meaning of culture, end in strikingly different assessments of multiculturalism. Taylor is sympathetic to the idea of group recognition, at least up to a certain point, and he argues that humans acquire a good part of their identity from their feeling of belonging to a particular cultural group. Brock could not be more critical of multiculturalism, judging its rightist version to be atavistic and its leftist version to be incoherent or even destructive of its own objectives. Rejecting culture as the preferred basis of community, Brock argues instead for "universal civilization"—meaning the formation of community on the basis of common principles of humanity as suggested by reason. He takes this position all the way to its logical conclusion, calling for what amounts to a worldwide community.

These analyses of multiculturalism from outside of the United States highlight certain issues that may have been insufficiently noticed here. First, they point up that American conceptions of multiculturalism move within the orbit of leftist thinking, which advocates that different cultures abide together within a single political state. Calls for independence and political sovereignty, such as those made by the different cultural movements in Quebec and in parts of Eastern Europe, are presently confined in America to a handful of native American groups, a few extremist white groups, and the New African People's Organization, which calls for the "freeing of a piece of territory from the colonial power."[46]

Next, these analyses of multiculturalism force attention to the foundation of "culture" in America. Whereas European accounts generally focus on traditional national, ethnic, or linguistic groups—Serbs, Croats, Germans, Gypsies, and so on—American accounts tend to equate culture with racial groups (or sometimes gender). Amy Gutmann, in her introduction to a collection of essays on multiculturalism, offers a fairly typical list of the cultures said to exist in the American context: "African-Americans, Asian Americans, Native Americans, and women."[47] When it comes to defining America's cultures, the groups that multicultural theorists have foremost in mind are characterized generally by biological criteria. After World War II, science reacted to the horrors of traditional racialism by seeking to banish racial distinctions (except to condemn them), but today race has returned as a major category.[48] It has returned, moreover, in a particular way—not as an obstacle to be removed or even as an important but secondary characteristic, but as the primary feature of social identity and the deepest source of authenticity. Race classifications have been reinstated as an ordinary part of the legal framework, and race is widely viewed as the most important element of social identity. If we are cultural beings and if race is a defining element of cultural identity, we cannot escape its importance. Race not only matters but is fundamental.

American multiculturalism has also succeeded in joining together two terms—"race" and "culture"—that many once labored to separate. At the beginning of the twentieth century, Franz Boas, the pioneer of modern anthropology in America, adopted the concept of "culture" in order to eliminate racialism as anthropology's central organizing category. In Boas' conception of culture, differentiation in groups of humans resulted from diverse patterns of socialization, not innate biological characteristics: "Culture is the result of innumerable interacting factors and there is no evidence that the differences between human races . . . have any direct influence upon the course of development of culture."[49] Cultural anthropology, in other words, meant nonracialist anthropology. Today multiculturalism has reconnected the concepts of culture and race, if not inside anthropology itself, then in such disciplines as history and literary criticism. To be sure, the theorists of multiculturalism do not embrace a simple biological foundation for culture, and they often point to the historical experiences of different racial groups, not the biological aspects of race per se, as the material that furnishes cultural identities.

The overlap between race and historical experience in America is an old theme of American history, and it is especially true for whites, blacks, and Native Americans. What is new about multiculturalism is not this point but the elaboration of a general theory or ism that connects culture and race to the study of society. The tendency to generalize can be seen in the assigning of racial qualities to other race groups besides Native Americans and blacks, as in the frequent and casual designation of "Asian American" as a culture. If national origin and language were the criteria, one could speak, not of Asian Americans, but of Japanese Americans, Korean Americans, Chinese Americans, Vietnamese Americans, and Cambodian Americans, and so on—all of which, incidentally, are often described as distinct and sometimes adversarial cultures in their countries of origin. What makes them all members of one culture in America today is the racialist preconception of multicultural theory; it is culture by intellectual ukase and bureaucratic decree.[50] The case of Hispanics or Latinos, often mentioned on cultural lists, is more complicated, since the word "Hispanic" refers not to a race but to a group who share a common language. Its members (once) spoke Spanish, but the vastness of the Spanish-speaking world means that they no more share a common culture than do the many cultural groups who speak English. What many proponents of multiculturalism really have in mind by the "Latino" designation, however, is not so much the linguistic grouping as the racial image of "brown." The "authentic" Hispanic is thus a "person of color"—a point illustrated by the awkwardness of situations when calls for diversity turn up Hispanics who are blond and blue-eyed.

The connection of race to culture in multicultural discourse can be seen by considering the groupings generally disqualified as cultural units. Hegel once wrote, "Religion is the sphere wherein a people gives itself the definition of what it regards as true,"[51] and many sociologists routinely refer to the "culture war" looming in America between the secularists and the religiously orthodox. But these units, lacking any kind of racial or ethnic dimension, are seldom if ever mentioned as cultures by proponents of multiculturalism, and any attempt to include these groups within the call for "diversity" would not be taken seriously.

Although multiculturalism does mark a return to racialism as the basis of thinking about culture and society, it obviously is quite different from classical Western racialism. Classical racialism insisted on a biological hierarchy of the races, and its political objectives were either to keep the races apart (to avoid any pollution of the higher races) or to justify the rule or enslavement of the lower by the higher races. Multiculturalism has had the political objective of overturning classical racialism. Because of this opposition, one might suppose that multicultural thinkers would stress their common ground with liberalism, which has also opposed classical racialism. Yet this has not been the case. One reason is no doubt liberalism's tendency to subordinate cultural or racial identity to individual identity as connected to a common political community. But a more important reason is that liberal democracy is seen as the carrier of the project of reason and the Enlightenment, and the philosophical foundation from which multiculturalism derives has made this project its chief opponent. These legacies of the eighteenth century are said to bear primary responsibility for oppression in modern society, and as the most important liberal democratic state, America is regarded as the symbol of a repressive and racist order.

Multiculturalism or the politics of difference cannot be understood apart from the philosophical foundation that supplies their categories for analyzing politics. To be sure, few who use the terms have this (or any other) philosophical position explicitly in mind, but the structure of their arguments has nonetheless been shaped by these philosophic ideas. Once this philosophical component is brought into the open, moreover, multicultural political theory is seen to be a misnomer. For just as it was once said of the Holy Roman Empire that it was neither holy, nor Roman, nor (in its later stages) an empire, so it may be said of multicultural theory that it is neither multi, nor cultural, nor genuinely theoretical.

In the first instance, multicultural thought is fundamentally binary rather than multi. The schema under which it constructs the world is a division between two theoretically defined categories: the Oppressor and the Oppressed, or (to use current terminology) the Hegemon and the Other. The Hegemon-Other distinction, as explained by Charles Taylor, captures the situation in which those who possess hegemonic power are in a position to bestow or withhold recognition. The failure to recognize another culture "can inflict a grievous wound, saddling its victims with a crippling self-hatred."[52] The victim, misrecognized and marginalized, is the Other, the voice that is submerged. Iris Marion Young, author of *The Politics of Difference,* makes this distinction the center of social analysis. The pervasive experience of "cultural imperialism" in America is one in which the "dominant meanings of society render the particular perspective of one's group invisible at the same time as they stereotype one's group and mark it out as the Other."[53]

The spirit of multiculturalism, a movement pervaded by this Hegemon-Other distinction, is revealed as much by certain activities or events as by theoretical writings. On college campuses, proponents of multiculturalism regularly demand that more people of color and women be hired as faculty members to overcome the male, Eurocentric bias of the current educational system. Multiculturalism here refers to the repression of different groups, the members of which are said to possess a distinct outlook and value system. A provocative example of the spirit of multiculturalism unfolded in 1992 with a major exhibit at the Whitney Museum of American Art. A requirement for each artwork to be included was that it focus on the experience of being "marginalized." White males who visited the exhibit were asked to wear buttons proclaiming their guilt.[54]

Although the primary criterion of categorization in multiculturalism is binary, not multi, a multi or plural dimension is subsequently introduced. After the societal pie has been cut into its two primary pieces (the Hegemon and the Other), multicultural theory goes on to divide up the Other into a multiplicity of cultures. By this means is the impression conveyed that it is a view based on plurality. Even so, the subordination of multiplicity to the more fundamental binary distinction is easily observed. The multiplicity of cultures, welcomed as a good, is admitted to exist only inside the category of the Other, not inside the category of the Hegemon. The Other is always plural, a veritable cornucopia of skin pigmentations and alternative sexual preferences. Meanwhile, the Hegemon is for all practical purposes seen as an undifferentiated unity: whites, or white Europeans, or white European males, or white Euro-American males, or what have you. Lost, somewhere, under this veil of whiteness are the subtle shades among, say, Minnesotans of Norwegian, Finnish, and Swedish origin, not to speak of the differences between the blond Aryans and the various peoples of eastern and southern Europe that Gobineau and the classical racialists so despised.

According to proponents of multiculturalism, the source of the oppression that creates the Hegemon-Other distinction is the Enlightenment project. Adapting a major thread of modern or postmodern thought, they claim that Enlightenment thought—indeed reason itself—has led to an essentializing difference that has created a favored and a marginalized group. According to Iris Marion Young, the mental process we call reason conceptualizes matter as "substance" or a "selfsame entity . . . that can be identified, counted, measured." It creates a "logic of identity" that separates everything into categories of "a/not-a": "Reason seeks essence, a single formula that classifies concrete particulars as inside or outside a category." This way of thinking is flawed; it "flees from the sensuous particularity of experience with its ambiguities, and seeks to generate stable categories." It thus misses multiplicity (or even "denies or represses difference") and constructs a political field in which there is imperialism and marginalization. Cornel West, although not making the connection quite as exclusive, emphasizes the "oppressive deeds done under the ideological aegis of the notions" of "necessity, universality, rationality, objectivity, and transcendentality."[55] The implication is that the whole Enlightenment project is the source of repression.

The Hegemon is the name given to the carrier of the imperial idea. In its largest sense, it can be identified with Western civilization or Eurocentric thinking. On the international scene, this theory has become the foundation of what is called Third Worldism, in which the First World (European and white) was arrayed against a colonialized and exploited Third World (non-European and of color). In philosophy and literature, and then increasingly in political discourse (especially after the Vietnam War), the symbol for the First World became the most powerful of the Western nations, "America," from which correct-thinking Europeans and Americans could, as it were, distance themselves.[56] This philosophic idea gives rise to an interpretation of American foreign policy, as in the work of Edward Said, the self-styled cultural intellectual, that purports to show how every use of American military power in the Third World, beginning with the wars against Native Americans, represents an example of an unjustified imperialism against various nonwhite enemies or Others. Said's political analysis here is a perfect example of a literary or cultural model. In the land of symbolic discourse, "America" must be a certain way, so in the real world that is exactly how it is said to be.[57]

The same analysis is then applied to social relations inside America. Indeed, the foreign and domestic are almost always connected, for America's imperial adventures and militarism are always undertaken to divert us from the domestic blights of, in Said's words, "racism, poverty, ecological ravages, disease, and an appallingly widespread ignorance." In the domestic version, the Hegemon now becomes the political regime of the United States as conceived and founded by a specific group—white European males. The Other consists of the various marginalized racial-biological groups. According to Young, the "republican fathers . . . explicitly justified the restriction of citizenship to white men on the grounds that the unity of the nation depended on homogeneity and dispassionate reason." The most "American" things in the nation's heritage are the sources of the repression of difference, which must be overcome by a new narrative of the country's history—designed to remind everyone that the basic American creed is, as Richard Sennett has described it, a nationalist myth that "legitimates attacks on peoples whose lives are different."[58]

A closer look reveals that this new multicultural historical narrative has striking parallels to the positive image of America as depicted in classical racialist discourse. The glory of America, for the latter, was the white Anglo-Saxon's dominance of the inferior races, who were properly repressed; the principle of natural rights was only window dressing that the Anglo-Saxon elite used to make its hegemony appear more palatable, while political science was merely a cover to hide the rationalist project. With a change only in the evaluation of this account, it has now become cutting-edge multicultural history. America is exactly what the old racialists hoped it would be: a white Anglo-Saxon nation whose ruling group will permit no real inroads into its control. At the same time, the negative picture of America under classical racial thought also enters multicultural historical analysis. America is seen to be an homogenizing culture, at least with reference to the white and Eurocentric America responsible for political liberalism.

Every traditional ideology or discourse contains a standard for allocating honor and distributing praise and blame—for "valorizing" and "devalorizing," as one says today. Multiculturalism is no exception. Its system of honor, based on this binary distinction, accords praise to the Other and blame to the Hegemon. The "Other" in multicultural discourse is more than a term of description; it is a term of distinction. The Other is the one who, having had her voice silenced for so long, will now at last be heard, whereas the Hegemon, having long misrecognized her, should now be silent. The two passions that multiculturalism most encourages derive from this same distinction: aggressive resentment (on the part of the Other) and supine contrition (on the part of the Hegemon).

The praise or valorization of the Other has naturally encouraged groups to try to include themselves in this favored category. The condition of so many claimants to this one status tends to level the injustice experienced by various groups and to miss the differences that exist among the histories of African Americans, Asians, Hispanics, and women. The same is true for those pushed into the category of the Hegemon. Certainly on a worldwide scale, identifying the Hegemon with the white European male vastly oversimplifies our reality. There is almost no form of oppression said to occur between the Hegemon and the Other that has not occurred—and fairly recently—among groups within the category of the Hegemon (and, for that matter, among groups inside the category of the Other). White "tribes" have decimated each other with as much savagery and fury as they have people of color, and people of color have oppressed each other with no less brutality than have white people. If there is any indicator of a common human nature, sorry as it is, is it not the universal tendency of peoples of all colors and stripes to oppress and abuse one another, regardless of color? To open the question of oppression to this kind of analysis, however, would upset the coalition of allies that the proponents of multiculturalism have labored so hard to construct.

There is something surprising in the multiculturalists' proclamation of a simple value standard that favors the victim and condemns the oppressor, given that they reject all previous standards on which such judgments are based—be it a view of human nature, of natural justice, or even of a direction to history. Indeed, most multicultural accounts begin from the theoretical premise of antifoundationalism or pragmatism, according to which there is no reality (except under one or another description) and no privileged position or ground (only alternative narratives); and they freely employ this premise to call into question any previous essentialist or metaphysical position, above all a position that supports the republican fathers' political science and regime of liberal democracy. Yet when multiculturalism's own narrative is presented, claims are made on its behalf in a way that begins to sound suspiciously like the proclamation of essentialist truths. Suddenly, we have exited the realm of narratives and have touched a real ground. Thus, according to Martha Minow, "those with less privilege may well see better than those with more," and according to Mari Matsuda, victims of racial oppression have "distinct claims to normative authority."[59] As one analyst, William Weaver, has so aptly observed, it is as if "being on the bottom gives one a view of reality, whole or distorted, while being on top or in the middle gives one only a perspective."[60] Given the multiculturalists' rejection of reason and their emphasis on the experience of being Other, their standard presents itself more or less as a passionately held moral conviction. Victimization is the transfer point where theoretical relativism is laundered and turns into moral absolutism.

The emergence of a standard from a starting point that denies standards has created controversy inside contemporary philosophy. Why should the victim be privileged rather than the oppressor, and why should tolerance be favored over a further round of victimization? The nation's leading pragmatist, Richard Rorty, has denied that philosophy can support the privileging of the Other and has criticized multiculturalists for using pragmatism when it suits their cause, only to ignore it when it does not. He invites them to "consider the possibility . . . of dropping the claim that there is something called 'right' or 'justice' or 'humanity' which has always been on their side, making their claims true." Although their cause may be worthwhile—Rorty himself, under his categorical recommendation to "avoid cruelty," espouses some of the same political positions—their narrative, like any other narrative, has no foundation other than that "we" happen to have chosen it. To ask philosophy to do more is to demand more than it can give. Rorty's position has met with fierce opposition among critical theorists and proponents of difference. Seyla Benhabib has called Rorty's position "sad" and has suggested that his position fosters a new form of conservatism. Others have gone so far as to accuse him of being a bourgeois white male. Philosophy, it appears, has once again been put on trial.[61]

Multiculturalism obscures its own meaning for a second reason. Multiculturalism is not a culture, and cultures are usually not multicultural. Cultures are almost always described as involving something deep-seated—a distinctive language or religion, for example. Although multiculturalism has certainly developed an elaborate jargon of its own, this still falls well short of constituting a language. The only possible basis for the formation of a multicultural culture would be around the poles of the Hegemon and the Other. But this foundation lacks the "thickness" to uphold a genuine culture. In some forms it may even tend to dissolve genuine culture by fostering a mishmash in which, so to speak, one eats kosher on Monday, Italian on Wednesday, and Chinese on Friday. Fortunately for the maintenance of culture, however, this constant "tasting" of other cultures tends to be the province mostly of a cosmopolitan elite sophisticated enough to delight in the customs of peoples who themselves have yet to become so sophisticated.

At most, therefore, multiculturalism is offered as a kind of add-on to the real cultures. Each culture, while remaining itself, agrees to respect the worth of every other culture (as well as, many hastily add, the rights of individuals). Here, however, a difficulty appears. If the only standards are cultural, on what ground can a culture be asked to abandon its ways when they are inconsistent with these requirements? Any demand to change begins to look like a form of metacultural imperialism—indeed, because multiculturalism is itself a Western intellectual movement, an imperialism with a Eurocentric bias. No response to this difficulty has been forthcoming, other than perhaps a vague hope that once the prime cause of repression (reason or the logic of identity) is eliminated, a respect for difference will naturally flourish. Although this idea fits nicely into the narrative, the record of cultures that have been untouched by reason does not inspire much confidence that tolerance will be universally upheld.

Cultures themselves are usually not multicultural. Cultures tend to be proud of their particularity, which they often regard as superiority. They can be intolerant not only of other cultures but of individual rights, and they can be closed, dividing the world between "us" and "them." Given these tendencies, many have worried that multiculturalism will end up encouraging what it does not really want. Its result may not be a *multi*culturalism that endorses the value of multiplicity or difference. Instead, its result may be a culturalism pure and simple, which emphasizes the particular beliefs of distinct and sometimes hostile cultures—in short, tribalism, balkanization, and racialism. The culturalists would seem to hold the advantage over the multiculturalists, because the culturalists' convictions are more authentic, deriving from simple prejudice rather than reason, and because they often hold their beliefs with greater resolution. When cultural prejudices are displayed by groups from inside the Hegemon (for example, white nationalists), multiculturalists have not hesitated to condemn them. But when expressions of culturalism emanate from inside the Other, the tendency is to back down and excuse the gesture.

The encouragement of culturalism, along with the simultaneous wish to place certain limits on it, is the ground on which multiculturalism has been accused of incoherence. Either culture is primary, or it is not. The American version of multiculturalism is unclear on just this point. It claims to put culture first, yet in its hope for tolerance and intercultural respect, it relies on traits that derive from rationalism and liberalism. At the same time, multicultural theorists attack the foundations on which rationalism rests. Multiculturalism draws on the capital of liberalism, while refusing to repay any of the loan.

Finally, multicultural theory is not really a political theory at all. Political theory is not merely a set of ideas applied in the political realm; instead, it is a certain way of thinking that treats the phenomena of politics on their own terms, seeking to understand the structure or nature of the political realm, including its possibilities and limits. This assumes, of course, that political reality has a structure—and one that is not merely "constructed" but has a character to it. Understanding what that character is and how human beings can best fit into it is the aim of political science. In contrast, multiculturalist thought attempts to replace political science with a species of literary-philosophical speculation whose categories emerge from distant philosophical premises, not from a study of regimes and their properties. It is not, finally, a truly political mode of thought at all.

Anyone, of course, can produce any kind of historical narrative that she wishes. But it is another matter entirely whether a narrative connects to the political world in a way that sheds lights on how it operates and that can therefore serve as a body of knowledge to assist in guiding political affairs. The philosophy of difference often disconnects us from the political world. Under its aegis, the core of political thinking becomes an examination of the record of historical injustice, and the study of politics begins to resemble a new Star Chamber with the sole aim of determining who is Oppressor and who is Victim. This concern for the history of injustice, important as it is, is no substitute for an analysis of the political good or of what will promote it. Even in the realm of its own specialty of injustice, moreover, the school of difference employs abstractions that distort the phenomena, putting all the strands of Enlightenment thought into one whole and pronouncing it guilty of oppression. So it is that the American founding and political science are placed together in the same category as classical racialism and then contrasted with a second category of difference and liberation. If, as philosophers of the school of difference argue, binary logic has been the scourge of Enlightenment reason, none are more guilty of this way of thinking than the proponents of multiculturalism.

For two centuries, America has been an object of constant attention in racialist discourse. For traditional racialists, America was sometimes a symbol of hope, more often a symbol of degeneration. This degeneration was traced to America's founders and their misguided efforts, undertaken in the name of reason and natural rights, to establish a political regime on principles that disregarded the primacy of race and racial hierarchy. Today a new philosophy has emerged to dominate the discussion of intellectuals. This philosophy, although it is the enemy of classical racialism, has introduced a new cultural-racialist discourse of its own. It, too, has chosen America as a symbol of degeneration—this time with the claim that America's founders and their principles are the source of both homogenization and racial and sexual oppression.

There is no reason to dwell on these curiosities or ironies of intellectual history. For the political scientist the objective is instead to search for a way of thinking about culture and race that can be of help in maintaining constitutional government. But this objective can be realized only after we have escaped the grip of a symbol of America that makes a political analysis impossible. As the ethnologists observed—and on this point alone, perhaps, were they correct—America is the best place in which to study race. For it is in America, with a diversity unmatched by any other nation, that more of the world's cultures and races have come together in one place to determine their destiny. The question is not whether race is to be studied, but how. The use of America as a symbol of racialist discourse has appeared in the disciplines of racial history, then ethnology, and now philosophy. It remains now for race to be considered politically.

6

★ ★ ★

Racialism Versus Political Science: The Tocqueville-Gobineau Exchange

Each time in the past two centuries that America has been attacked and political science challenged, a voice has emerged to take up their defense. In the late eighteenth century it was the founders, above all Publius, who responded to the degeneracy thesis of the Count de Buffon and Cornelius de Pauw. In the mid–nineteenth century, it was Alexis de Tocqueville who replied to the racial theories of Arthur de Gobineau.

These two "dialogues," separated by more than half a century, contain striking parallels. Not only were Publius and Tocqueville trying to save America and liberal democracy from the charges of sickness, decay, and mediocrity, but both were also seeking to defend political science from new and supposedly more advanced forms of social science. If Tocqueville's discussion of these issues tended to be more theoretical than that of the founders, it was perhaps because of the different audience he addressed. *The Federalist* was a book with a particular political purpose, written, as Tocqueville put it, "with the object of pointing out to the nation the advantages" of adopting a new constitution. Tocqueville's writings—excepting his state papers and political speeches—were directed more to the thinkers and statesmen of his age.[1] This distinction, by Tocqueville's own account, explains a great deal. "There is a difference," he observed, "between the art [of politics] and the science; practice often diverges from theory."[2] The elaboration of general theory, including a systematic political science, requires abstracting somewhat from reality and positing a greater degree of regularity than actually exists. By the same token, the more one is immersed in practice, the more it is necessary to qualify general theoretical points.

136

I should add that I have no reluctance in turning to a Frenchman rather than an American for a defense of political science. In one sense I have no choice, for no American theorist of stature ever responded to the new racial science. In fact, by the mid–nineteenth century, political science as a major discipline in the United States had been driven to the sidelines, having been replaced in part by ethnology. Where it did exist in name—in the works of John Calhoun, say, or Francis Lieber—it had taken an important turn from the founding period and had begun to incorporate substantial elements of racialist thought.[3] In another sense, the defense of political science should not be considered an ethnocentric enterprise. Political science can just as easily be practiced by a Tanzanian or Malaysian as by an American or Frenchman. As for America's founders, they never claimed political science as an exclusively American science but reintroduced it to assist in establishing a free government, hoping it might also contribute to that cause elsewhere in the world. What concerned the founders most about the future of political science was how it was threatened by new movements within contemporary philosophy and science.

Much the same can be said about Tocqueville. His main objective, as he described it in a famous passage in *Democracy in America,* was to elaborate a "new political science for a new world" in order to assist political cultural and political leaders in averting despotisms and establishing free regimes.[4] Tocqueville defined political science as the "science that treats the guidance of societies," which he helped to develop not just for the benefit of France alone but for "mankind."[5] Finally, like Publius, Tocqueville feared that political science was in danger of being replaced by modern intellectual systems that would undermine the cause of free government. Gobineau's new racial history was a primary case in point.

Severing any ethnic or racial connection between America and political science, as I hope by now I have done, frees me from the need to construct one of those historical half-truths, known today as "narratives," which claims that Tocqueville learned all his political science from Americans. In fact, many of his teachers were Europeans and also the classical philosophers of ancient Greece and Rome. But Tocqueville did greatly enrich his understanding of political science through his encounter with America—not only by observing American practices but also by studying American political thought as found in its constitutions, laws, court cases, and theoretical writings. Tocqueville was one of only a few Continental thinkers of the nineteenth century who seriously engaged this thought, of which *The Federalist* for him was the foremost work.[6] He was also one of the few to offer a friendly, although by no means uncritical, treatment of America. Most thinkers of this period were either antiliberal or antidemocratic and therefore hostile to

America. Tocqueville, following in the same path as the founders, defended liberal democracy—indeed, he may have coined the term itself.

The Tocqueville-Gobineau dialogue on racialism began just after the publication of Gobineau's *Essay on the Inequality of the Human Races* in 1853 and lasted until 1857, two years before Tocqueville's death. The exchange is increasingly referred to as a classic of early social science. Raymond Aron, the great French political thinker, chose to discuss it when receiving the Tocqueville Prize in 1980. And the English translator of the correspondence, John Lukacs, ranks it "with the great dialogues of modern history, with the dialogues between Machiavelli and Guicciardini, between Proudhon and Marx, between Burkhardt and Nietzsche."[7] In spite of these judgments, however, the dialogue has been largely ignored in America. This is probably because Tocqueville's analysis of racialism fits with neither the moralistic and multicultural approaches that dominate the discussion of this issue in America today nor the new social science approach as illustrated by Herrnstein and Murray, the authors of *The Bell Curve*. Tocqueville's method is different: it is political.

The Tocqueville-Gobineau exchange is something of an accident of intellectual history. On his own, Tocqueville would probably never have discussed Gobineau's theories so extensively. He did so only because Gobineau was a friend—indeed, Tocqueville was a kind of mentor to Gobineau. In 1843 Tocqueville selected Gobineau, who was eleven years his junior, as a research assistant for a study of European mores and habits in the era of social democratization. Although the study was never executed, Tocqueville appointed Gobineau as his official secretary in 1849, when Tocqueville became minister of foreign affairs under the regime of Louis Napoleon. On leaving the government six months later, Tocqueville helped to secure Gobineau's continuance in the foreign service, which began the younger man's long diplomatic career. The two men obviously had discussed much together, and many of Tocqueville's ideas appear in Gobineau's writings, although invariably distorted and "racialized" to fit Gobineau's thesis.

Yet even with, or rather because of, this friendship, Tocqueville might never have commented on Gobineau's theory had not Gobineau insisted that he do so. Gobineau seemed to be seeking, if not Tocqueville's approval, then at least a kind of recognition. He never received it. Although Tocqueville admitted to admiring the vigor and erudition of the *Essay,* he could not hide his disapproval of its central argument: "I am opposed in the extreme to your doctrines. I believe they are probably quite false; I know that they are certainly very pernicious. . . . There is an entire world between our beliefs."[8] Tocqueville offered his criticisms reluctantly, knowing that they would damage the closeness of their relationship. In fact, at one point, in order to save what remained of their friendship, Tocqueville cut off further discussion on race: "When one deals with grave questions and with new ideas, one should not discuss them with one's friends when one has no hope of persuading them."[9] But he would not compromise his principles. One instance reveals the delicacy of his situation. Tocqueville agreed to help Gobineau have one of his papers presented before the Academy of Moral and Political Sciences in France, but he would not agree to introduce it. "I could not do so," he wrote to Gobineau, "without strongly attacking your ideas."[10]

Tocqueville stated his major objections to Gobineau's thesis at the outset of the exchange: "Your principal idea . . . seems to belong to the group of materialistic theories. Moreover, it is one of its most dangerous members, for it applies fatalism not merely to individuals but to those perennial conglomerations of individuals we call races."[11] His criticism of Gobineau's thought thus focused on what he took to be its two basic doctrines: its new social science (fatalism or historicism) and its understanding of the fundamental cause of historical movement (racialism). Tocqueville would argue for a different kind of social science—that is, political science—and for a different starting point, in which political and cultural factors, not race, were the causes of social action.

Tocqueville's Critique of Historicism

Tocqueville began the exchange by noting a view that he and Gobineau held in common. Both men believed that the modern political and intellectual crisis in Europe originated in the French Revolution, and even more fundamentally in the philosophy and social science that helped prepare the way for the Revolution. The central flaw of this thought was its activism or excessive voluntarism—the notion that man, with the aid of a new rational science, could remodel political life according to universal norms. "The last century had an exaggerated and somewhat childish trust in the control which men and peoples were supposed to have over their own destinies; it was the error of those times."[12] In fact, when Tocqueville wrote these words, he was working on his own critique of the effects of *philosophe* rationalism on European political life, an examination found in *The Old Regime and the Revolution*.[13]

Tocqueville initially characterized Gobineau's project as an effort to control the voluntarism of philosophe social science. Tocqueville even allowed that, for strategic reasons, he might have been more friendly to a fatalist argument had voluntarism still been the dominant tendency of modern thought. But it was not. Gobineau, Tocqueville contended, remained fixed on the origins of modern thought and had completely misdiagnosed the contemporary democratic era. The central problem today, he argued, was an underestimation of man's ability to change his world: "After having felt ourselves capable of transforming ourselves [in 1789], we now feel incapable of transforming ourselves. . . . We thought we could do everything, now we think we can do nothing. . . . This is the great sickness of our age."[14]

For Tocqueville, the current crisis could not be lessened—it could only be made worse—by a theory that denied man's capacity to control part of human affairs through conscious political action. The real danger of the dawning age, notwithstanding the revolutionary claims made at its origins, was a diminution of man's belief in his power to shape his own destiny. Historicism or fatalism, including a conservative historicism that proclaimed its hostility to all things democratic, promoted the worst of these modern tendencies. Writing to Gobineau, Tocqueville declared: "If we were to suffer from excessive enthusiasm and self-confidence, as did our ancestors in 1789, I should consider your book a salutary cold shower. But we have disgracefully come to the opposite extreme. We have no regard for anything, beginning with ourselves. . . . A book which tries to prove that men in this world are merely obeying their physical constitutions and that their will power can do almost nothing to influence their destinies is like opium given to a patient whose blood has already weakened."[15]

In this critique of historicism Tocqueville elaborated his distinctive, political method of intellectual analysis—the same method he used in *Democracy in America*. Any body of thought must be assessed according to not only its own internal logic but also its likely effects on society. The deepest and most lasting of these effects often derive less from an author's surface argument than from his underlying presuppositions about the nature of reality, for these presuppositions shape the way people think. For Tocqueville, accordingly, the core of Gobineau's thought was not his opposition to the French Revolution but his system of historicism. Far from helping to oppose democracy, which was the surface argument, Gobineau's system actually promoted an extreme and dangerous form of democratic thought. The "doctrine of fatalism" teaches that the destiny of man is beyond the control of any human action and instead unfolds through some form of automatic—and in Gobineau's case, material or nondivine—process. This view is the opposite of the one grounding an aristocracy or a healthy democracy, both of which assert that what individuals and peoples do can make a difference. Fatalism encourages a "weak" or "self-pitying" disposition and teaches nations "that they are bound to obey some insuperable and unthinking power, the product of preexisting facts, of race, of soil, or climate."[16]

The dispute here between Tocqueville and Gobineau went beyond their differing assessments of the historical situation in the mid–nineteenth century and focused on their contrasting view of social science and its possibilities for guiding society. If it were true, as Tocqueville argued, that the thinkers of his day claimed too *little* control over man's destiny, then there would clearly be a role for political science in helping to guide and shape the future.[17] Gobineau denied any such possibility. Tocqueville again surmised that this position might be the result of Gobineau's fear of social science as it had been constructed at the time of the French Revolution. But whatever Gobineau's motive, Tocqueville argued that Gobineau had erred by casting all rationalist or scientific thinking (up until his own new historicism) in the same mold. Although Tocqueville could appreciate the practical reasons for waging a campaign against rationalism in the aftermath of the French Revolution, he felt it was a great mistake to turn this kind of campaign into an ideological war. Victory on these terms would in the end not only sacrifice the truth, but sacrifice it in such a way that later it would be impossible to develop effective solutions for the practical problems of the day. Gobineau, in Tocqueville's judgment, had become a victim of this propaganda.

Tocqueville's approach to rationalism was different. Although he was as unsparing as Gobineau in his critique of the thought that prevailed at the dawn of the French Revolution, he argued that another strand of rationalism—political science—was free of an immoderate voluntarism. The flaws within rationalism were no reason to condemn rationalism as a whole. Political science could point out the excesses, and it could offer a balanced view of what a body of knowledge could hope to accomplish in human affairs, claiming neither more nor less than was reasonable for a science.

The dispute between Tocqueville and Gobineau was not about whether reason should be consulted but about the sort of reason that was appropriate to the study of human affairs. Gobineau was not in the camp of thinkers who rejected reason outright in favor of tradition or submission to Providence. Although conservative in his political position, Gobineau spoke as the originator of a new, more accurate, and more comprehensive form of science—a "science of history" akin to the positivistic sciences of geology or medicine. It was on the basis of this science that the inadequacy of all old rationalist social sciences could be demonstrated.

Gobineau's idea of an historical science, although it must ultimately be judged on its own merits, clearly grew out of earlier conservative arguments against rationalism. Conservatives had originally attacked not only metaphysical thinking as it was applied to politics but also reason itself, and they had tentatively turned to historical thinking as an alternative to reasoning about nature. Gobineau radicalized this turn by claiming he could validate the antidemocratic (and anti-American) position by a rigorous *science* of the historical process. What conservatives had once tried to establish by attacking science, they could now defend on the basis of science. Indeed, Gobineau's claims for the explanatory power and comprehensiveness of science went well beyond anything that the first generation of conservatives had ever attributed to Enlightenment social science. This point explains why Tocqueville could consider Gobineau's turn to historicism to be, not a reversal of philosophe rationalism, but a more extreme manifestation of its excesses.

Tocqueville introduced his comparison between historical science and political science by raising a question about the scientist's responsibility to political life. Is the writer obliged to take into account the "practical effects" of his thought on human behavior and somehow craft his science with this fact in mind? This question can only be discussed in connection with the theoretical issue of the status of free will. For if man cannot influence the course of affairs in important ways by his own efforts—if man is faced, as Tocqueville characterizes Gobineau's position, with "a vast limitation, if not a complete abolition, of human liberty"—then it makes no sense even to inquire into the "practical effects" of thought.[18]

From what Tocqueville already knew of Gobineau's thinking, he could not at first accept Gobineau's fatalism at face value. A decade before, Tocqueville had taken the measure of Gobineau's ambition: "Your need is to change the world and you will not be content with less. I am more modest." Yet as the dialogue proceeds, Gobineau insists that he has now renounced any intention of influencing the course of human affairs. For him to say anything different, of course, would have meant abandoning the logic of his system, which held that social science can have no effect. Gobineau ultimately elected to save his consistency at the expense of claiming any influence for his thought. Science in its highest form, he argued, can change nothing. Science ("truth") is knowledge that unlocks the key to why things happen one way and only one way: "By telling you what is happening and what is going to happen, am I taking something away from you? I am not a murderer; neither is the doctor who announces the end." There is accordingly no point in considering whether anything, including his own labor, will produce a salutary effect: "If I am wrong, nothing will remain of my four volumes. If I am right, the facts will not be subdued by the desire of those who do not want to face them."[19]

Still, Gobineau was clearly dismayed at being forced to profess his own insignificance. Put in this corner, he came as close as he ever did to attacking his mentor, suggesting that Tocqueville was a moralist who was more concerned with effect than truth. Gobineau sardonically allowed that he would admit to being immoral only if truth had nothing to do with morality: "If truth and morality are not connected, I shall be the first to agree that my book is devoid of the latter, but then it is also devoid of anti-morality, as are geology, medicine, archaeology. My book is research, exposition, presentation of the fact. There is nothing else to say."[20]

But Gobineau's attempt to end the discussion ("There is nothing else to say") works only if one accepts his characterization of the relationship between truth and science. In Tocqueville's view, Gobineau wrongly conflated all forms of knowledge into one mold, equating truth in social science with truth, for example, in geology. For Tocqueville, reality was not so homogeneous. Political science is a different kind of science from geology, because political phenomena are different from geological phenomena. Human beings do not stand in relation to laws of social science as stones do to laws of geology. Political science is a moral science, because the outcome of history changes as a result of human actions freely made. Included among these actions is the propagation of an intellectual doctrine, which can have important consequences even when the author disavows any such intention or denies that possibility. A political writer is one who will fit the truth inside the requirements discovered to be true by his discipline. Gobineau saw no merit to this "second-order" view of truth; he told Tocqueville that his *Essay* would be better received in Germany, where his readers were more concerned with "intrinsic truth."[21] Tocqueville did not use the same terminology, but he certainly agreed with the sentiment.

The influence of Gobineau's doctrines on slavery in America illustrated the point. Gobineau himself introduced this issue by calling attention, with some pride, to the notice his work was receiving across the Atlantic: "In America, . . . three distinguished persons whom I did not previously know honored me by writing. One of them translated the entire systematic argument of the volume and requests my opinion about a second edition."[22] Tocqueville responded, not with the congratulations that Gobineau hoped for, but with a reminder of the pernicious effects of the *Essay*: "Those Americans whom you mention that translated your book are known to me as perfervid leaders of the anti-abolitionist party. They translated the part of your book which suits their prejudices, the part which tends to prove that the Negroes belong to another, to a different and inferior race." Tocqueville later strengthened this criticism: "Your doctrines are being approved, cited and commented upon by whom? By slaveowners and by those who favor the perpetuation of slavery on the basis of racial differences."[23]

Intellectual doctrines are not passive testimonials but actions that can shape the historical process, and that contention led Tocqueville to insist that political science must consider effects as well as truth. In fact, the two cannot be thought of as being entirely distinct. The degree of rhetoric is always going to be determined by the situation—by the era, by the problems faced, and by the audience. Political science applies the truths of its teaching to the age, making clear in a general work why a particular rhetoric may be more appropriate in one context than another. The need to combine and synthesize effect and truth, accordingly, is based on the nature of human and political phenomena. Assessing the entire school of historicism, Tocqueville wrote: "I have not yet become enough German to be captivated so much by the novelty or by the philosophical merits of an idea as to overlook its moral or political effects."[24] Tocqueville did not try to resolve here the question of how exactly to blend effect and truth. Assigning the proper weight to each cannot be the work of a simple formula but varies according to time and place. The balance can be seen and judged only in the product of an actual work of political science, such as *Democracy in America*.

Tocqueville's critique of historicism on this point helps to explain the different character and purpose of political science as compared to scientific history. For Gobineau, the object of the new historical science is truth, understood as knowledge of what has happened and why. A scientist's work is judged by whether its prognostications turn out to be right or wrong, not by how it might benefit society. The scientist changes nothing. In contrast, Tocqueville criticizes thought that "becomes impassioned with what [are] considered abstract truths, without taking account of their practical consequences."[25] Such truths are in fact not as true or as neat as they appear in systematic treatises, given the roles that freedom and accident play in human affairs. There is accordingly a space open for political science in a scheme of human knowledge as a discipline that aims not only at truth for its own sake but also at assisting human action in behalf of the human good. Political science may be regarded as a discipline different from geology or, for that matter, from abstract or general philosophy. It enters into history, insofar as man chooses to bring it in, as a tool to assist man in action for the human good. It is not an ideology that prescribes a program of action, but knowledge that can educate and assist "those who direct societies."

The second element of Tocqueville's critique focused on Gobineau's claim that race is the main determinant of social and political life. Tocqueville located the source of differentiation among groups of human beings in political and moral factors. Although Tocqueville did not foreclose the possibility of certain differential hereditary traits among ethnic or racial groups, he argued that elevating race to the status of the chief cause in social and political affairs blinded social science to what experience had already shown to be the fundamental influences. Not only was racialism dangerous in its effects, but it lacked any convincing scientific proof.

Tocqueville's general method was to illustrate the case for the importance of political factors, not to engage in polemics about race or biology. Yet he could not entirely ignore the debate on unitarism and pluralism. As he had observed earlier in *Democracy in America,* a position that emphasizes the primacy of political and moral factors already takes a side in this debate. It is because mankind is one species that general ideas can be transferred from one context to another and that people can receive encouragement from the experience of others. Without the unity of man, political science was impossible: "If men turned out differently in America from what they are elsewhere, . . . what happens in the American democracy would teach me nothing about what might happen in democracies elsewhere."[26]

Obliged to elaborate on this position in his exchange with Gobineau, Tocqueville began by presenting the modern biological idea of a species, which he thought offered some evidence in favor of the idea of the unity. When Gobineau was still working on the *Essay*, he asked Tocqueville to summarize what Buffon and Flourens had written about the unity of mankind, and Tocqueville reported that they believed in the "diversity of *races* but the unity of the human *species*." Their conception of a species was defined by the biological notion of the "faculty of reproduction that demonstrates fundamental unity of animaldom." Tocqueville endorsed this view as far as it went, although he did not believe that biological criteria alone could be decisive in establishing the idea of unity.[27]

More important for Tocqueville was the religious case for unitarism, particularly since he was speaking to a professed believer. Here he relied less on the scriptural account of the original pair (Adam and Eve) than on the general "spirit" of Christianity, which affirmed the existence of "one human race." Polygenesis was incompatible with Christianity, he insisted, not just in a technical sense, as Gobineau had conceded, but at its foundation. Christianity could not be reconciled with a "doctrine that makes races distinct and unequal, with differing capacities of understanding, of judgment, of action, due to some original and immutable disposition which invisibly denies the possibility of improvement for certain people." Instead, Christianity taught that all members of the human species "were equally capable of perfecting themselves and resembling one another."[28]

Tocqueville's most important argument for a common human species, however, rested on an understanding of nature and specifically human nature. In fact, it is only because of human nature that man can recognize the existence of a common species in the first place. Through his faculty of observation, aided by his reason, man has access to the world and can know certain things. This is the basis—the only basis, other than faith—on which one can begin to determine which individual beings or things make up a group that is fundamentally alike: a species. Man is a species because the different individuals we know to be men are endowed with a common nature or constitution. The fixed part of the human "is founded in the very nature of man, on his interests, his faculties, the needs revealed by philosophy and history, the instincts which change their objects with the times, but never change their nature, and are as important as the race itself."[29]

The aspect of human nature Tocqueville chose to emphasize to Gobineau was the universal and profound aversion to being enslaved or degraded. Responding to Gobineau's claim that the fate of racially corrupted Europeans was despotic governance, Tocqueville wrote: "No, I will not believe that this human species which is at the head of visible creation has become that degenerate herd of which you speak, and that there is nothing left but to surrender, with no future and no recourse, to a small number of shepherds who are after all no better and often worse animals than we are."[30] Tocqueville acknowledged, of course, that people were regularly degraded or forced into slavery and that they might be conditioned, by extraordinary and unnatural methods, to (almost) accept their lot. Indeed, he had described in *Democracy in America* the elaborate system that American slaveholders had used, with some success, to build a psychological foundation for their despotism. Yet both the extremity of these steps and the impossibility that they could ever be accepted as legitimate demonstrated how contrary slavery was to human nature.[31]

A further proof of the unnaturalness of enslavement is found in the fact that appeals made against it will ordinarily meet with receptivity. Addressing Gobineau, Tocqueville asked, "Would you offer your own bare back [to the whip] in order to render personal confirmation of your principles?"[32] The rhetorical technique of appealing directly to his reader, which Tocqueville used elsewhere, is predicated on the existence of a moral dimension that Tocqueville thought informs all human encounters. The writer should not deny or ignore this dimension but use it as a means of adducing evidence about human nature. A writer-reader relationship that in the name of objectivity tries to place itself entirely outside a direct moral response—as if we were all neutral observers—can miss what is most important. Only humans have certain responses, and one of the best ways to learn about them is for an individual to look into his or her own reactions.

Tocqueville's support for the unity of the human species brought him into conflict with a fundamental claim of Gobineau and his followers. One instance when Gobineau may have conceded that doctrines had a practical influence was when he charged that the concept of humanity helped to promote the fanatical project of attempting to subject all men to the same mores and laws. Unitarism as a dogma was at the source of the modern process of homogenization and universalism. For Gobineau, the only way to retard this process was to propagate the scientific truth that the different races were different types of beings. But for Tocqueville there was no incompatibility between the concept of humanity and the existence of a large degree of particularity in human societies. The fact that man was one species did not mean that all people were destined to live—or should live—in a universal and homogeneous state. It was perfectly possible, even reasonable, to support national communities and a moderate patriotism to sustain them: "Man has been created by God (I do not know why) in such a way that the larger the object of his love the less directly he is attached to it. His heart needs particular passions; he needs limited objects for his affections to keep these firm and enduring. There are but few who will burn with ardent love for the entire human species. . . . I am convinced that the interests of the human race are better served by giving every man a particular fatherland than by trying to inflame his passions for the whole of humanity."[33]

Tocqueville, too, was deeply concerned about the prospect of homogenization in modern times and was among the earliest to warn of its dangers—partly, one suspects, as a way of getting people to take notice. Well before Gobineau ever spoke of the "herd," Tocqueville had offered his own picture of the evolution of developed societies into a dreary, egalitarian mass. He even appeared to acknowledge that the idea of humanity was a precondition for homogenization; for this reason he carefully sought to limit its interpretation and application, and there is no concept or general idea that he treated with more circumspection. "Variety," he wrote, "is disappearing from the human race; the same ways of behaving, and feeling are found in every corner of the world. Men are . . . getting closer to what is essential in man, and that is everywhere the same."[34] Yet this sameness, insofar as it resulted from the elimination of structures of domination and inequality, was not a bad thing. As regrettable as Tocqueville sometimes found the loss of difference and charm to be from an aesthetic standpoint, he realized the greater justice of a world in which permanent castes and hereditary classes were eliminated.

This condition of sameness, however, had to be distinguished from a more extreme form of homogeneity produced by a political society that sought to enforce a pervasive equality of condition. Uniformity of this kind went well beyond what the natural concept of humanity required or suggested; it resulted from a powerful yet restrainable passion for equality and from modern theories that insisted on eliminating any sort of difference or distinction. Uniformity in this sense was the great danger that degraded human beings, and it was the defining characteristic of the soft despotism that Tocqueville so abhorred.

Tocqueville was accordingly no less concerned than Gobineau with the possibility of homogenization. But he had a different view of its causes and character. In the first place, it had nothing to do with a mixing of the races. Although racialist doctrines might temporarily strengthen certain lines of differences among human groups, they would do so not by ennobling people but by promoting unjust political orders. On one hand, racialism would be used against "lesser peoples living in abject conditions of barbarism or slavery to persuade them that, such being their racial nature, they can do nothing to better themselves, to change their habits, or to ameliorate their status." On the other hand, racialism would embolden those seeking to maintain a reign of enslavement and tyranny: "Inherent in your doctrine are all the evils produced by permanent inequality: pride, violence, the scorn of one's fellow men, and abjection in every one of their forms."[35] "Difference" purchased at the price of injustice was unacceptable. Indeed, difference itself could not be a starting principle. One first had to inquire into the kind of difference that contributed to the benefit of man.

Racialism, in any case, was not the bulwark against homogenization that Gobineau maintained. Tocqueville thought it actually contributed to a kind of egalitarian mass order—at least inside each race group. Racialism was fundamentally a populist theory. It proclaimed that the source of human distinction is ultimately found not in any efforts men make (which is an aristocratic principle) but in an automatic and material factor (which is an egalitarian principle). The more groups came to think in terms of race, the more they would become mass societies. The only thing that would separate such societies would be color. Difference would then be no more than skin-deep.

When Tocqueville turned from these speculations about the future to a concrete analysis of the past and the present, he drew a picture of a world filled with variety, and his writings try to supply some of the categories that account for this variety. On this very point, in fact, the dialogue between Gobineau and Tocqueville had commenced long before their exchange of letters about race. The great distinction between the two men lay in their views of the causes of human difference. Although Gobineau rarely cites Tocqueville in his published work, he clearly intended the *Essay* as a response to *Democracy in America,* which he considered an unphilosophical and unsystematic work.[36]

For Gobineau, fundamental human differences are traceable ultimately to the single factor of race, which allows for a systematic and deductive science of history. In contrast, Tocqueville lists a number of factors to explain difference, no one of which is completely reducible to another. In addition to such immediate political causes as the general form of regime (for example, despotism or liberal democracy) and the particular nation, he presents a set of pre-political causes: civilizations, national characters (or peoples), and the different families of man (or races).[37]

From the twin facts of the unity of the human species and the variety of human groups comes the dualism that is so characteristic of Tocqueville's analysis. On one hand, because human beings share a common constitution, certain principles apply to all peoples, and there is the possibility that any group can both instruct and learn from any another. On the other hand, because human beings fall into distinct groups, principles must always be adjusted to fit particular cases and circumstances. The distance between groups can sometimes be so great as to make practical transfers of institutions between them all but impossible, or at least until many preliminary steps have been taken.

The broadest lens Tocqueville used for showing the differences among human groups was that of the variety of civilizations. A civilization is a loose group or whole that shares a basic outlook. A civilization is connected, in the first instance, to a religious-intellectual tradition. As examples Tocqueville mentions the classical Greeks and Romans, early Christianity, Islam, and the world of modern Christianity and the Enlightenment. A civilization, in an even more general usage, refers to "wholes" at different stages of development—for example, man in a nomadic, agricultural, or commercial condition. Civilization in this last context had a specific and conventional meaning, referring to the stages of development beyond barbarism. For Tocqueville, the distinguishing feature here was man's use of reason to plan for the future; the savage is one for whom the "expectation of future advantages has only a feeble effect."[38] Civilization in this respect did not equal moral superiority, however, and Tocqueville described with great poignancy the barbarism that the European revealed in his treatment of the Indian and the black in the New World.[39] But if the moral superiority of European civilization was open to question, its advantage in terms of power and force was not. For better or worse, the European had for now the upper hand.

A second lens that Tocqueville used to examine different groups was "national character." This category identified the commonalities of a group that had lived together in one area, generally under the same government (for example, the French, the English, the Spanish), and that had developed certain characteristics regarding habits of industry, patterns of risk taking, and norms of governing and being governed. Because these traits tended to persist for some time apart from the immediate form of government, national character had special relevance for analysis of colonies. Where large groups of people leave their home nation and settle elsewhere, the national character traits they bring with them help to account for subsequent patterns of development. Tocqueville relied extensively on this concept in explaining the differences in the Americas. Dividing the Europeans in America into three major groups—Anglos, Spanish, and French—he sketched broad generalizations about their development in different areas of the New World. He was confident in predicting, for example, that the Anglo-Americans would establish an "immense preponderance" over all other Europeans, as they were "far superior to them in civilization, industry and power."[40]

So heavily does Tocqueville rely on traits of civilization and natural character that some have seen him as favoring cultural or sociological causes over immediate political causes (in particular, causes that emphasize deliberate acts of "constituting" human communities, such as the American founding). Whether or not this portrayal of his thought is accurate, Tocqueville never argued that national character could be understood apart from political factors. Politics and foundings were for him among the main causes that shaped national character: the Anglo national character is different from the French or Spanish national character largely because each of these peoples carries a different concept of political rule (Anglos were decidedly more republican than the others). What the concept of national character emphasizes is the staying power of previous events and foundings, which constrain the degree of choice in current political actions. Tocqueville's concept of national character is roughly the same as the founders' idea of genius or Burke's notion of temper.[41]

Civilization and national character were the two main pre-political categories Tocqueville used to account for differences among groups. These categories are only names, however, and they do not explain why differences emerged in the first place or what keeps them going. Tocqueville gives no systematic answer to these questions about causality, because none was possible. He lists, to be sure, a variety of variables that account for difference, among them geography, intellectual and technological developments, political forms, and specific decisions of men and governments. But from the standpoint of a theory that tries to relate everything to a reproducible pattern of cause and effect, Tocqueville's account is deliberately nontheoretical. The mix of factors that has created each civilization will not be repeated, making the development of a given civilization largely a story unto itself. Social science in this instance can do little more than identify something as it is—however it came to be—and then treat it as a cause for exploring other questions.

Tocqueville sought greater rigor when discussing what kept civilizations going. The deepest cause is what he called "mores," which consist of a group's habits, its beliefs, and above all its patterns of thinking and reasoning, its way of seeing and processing the world. Tocqueville used this concept to account for much of the distinctness among groups and to explore the problems encountered in attempts to transfer patterns of behavior from one group to another. Groups, of course, are always changing and adjusting to circumstances, including those of their encounters with other groups. But this is a different matter from consciously trying to change in order to achieve a planned result—transferring democratic institutions from one nation to another, for example, or transferring patterns of industry from one group (such as the Europeans) to another group (such as an Indian tribe). Planned changes are difficult to achieve, especially when the mores of the nations or groups involved are poles apart. The things that can be inserted into a group from the outside (a new set of laws or even a new physical environment) are always processed or digested in terms of the group's own mores. How something works in one context will thus never work the same in another, and in certain instances changes may have the opposite effect from what was intended. A formal constitutional arrangement that functions well in one place may function very poorly in another.

From a strictly logical perspective, attempts to effect any change in behavior should start with a transfer of mores rather than of laws or conditions. But in practice this logic proves difficult to follow. Mores cannot be simply exported; they are generated and maintained internally in ways that are not easily duplicated. The distinctness of groups can thus be traced back largely to the differences and intricacies in how each group transmits its mores by means of the thousands of signals and experiences embedded in the group's institutions, stories, laws, and practices. The centrality of this process—what we today call "socialization"—accounts for why Tocqueville emphasized it in his political science, analyzing the institutions and agents in society that deal with socialization and beginning, of course, with the family.

To say it is difficult to export or alter mores, however, is not the same thing as saying it is impossible to do so. Tocqueville was not a conservative in the Continental sense. He rejected de Maistre's view that "circumstances make everything, and men are only circumstances."[42] At the same time, he mistrusted an analytical approach, employed by certain contract theorists, that placed too much emphasis on nature and that treated people as if they existed in some fictive nowhere outside of a specific group context. The great object of practical political analysis in comparative politics was to help people know when, how, and by what means transfers of mores and institutions could take place from one place or time to another. This analysis relied on an intimate knowledge of the different contexts, informed by an idea of nature that stood inside or behind all the variety.

One means of transferring mores between groups is by intermarriage, although this is feasible only in certain circumstances, usually where the two groups live near one another. Intermarriage seems to offer a good prospect for success, for it brings individuals together inside the family, the unit that performs the initial function of transmitting mores. Tocqueville accordingly paid close attention to intermarriage in America, and particularly to the most "extreme" cases, where intermarriage occurred between those of simultaneously different civilizations and different races. His analysis reveals the complexity likely to be encountered by any plan to alter mores. Both groups in these unions play a part in the transmission of mores, of course, so it is not always clear which side will prevail. In the case of the intermixture of Indians and Europeans in Latin America, Indian mores were transferred to the European (the Spanish and Portuguese) as much as European mores were transferred to the Indian. In North America, intermarriage proved more successful in transferring European mores to Indian populations, but compared to Latin America, it did not occur nearly as frequently. Within North America, similar distinctions existed between the Anglos and the French. The French were more likely to intermarry than the Anglos, but they were also more likely to give up their European ways for the Indian mores, which had a certain attraction for them.[43] The Anglos were the most stubborn in maintaining their European mores and prevailed most often in bringing the Indian to European ways, but the same stubbornness also made them the most reluctant group to intermix.

These cases involving intermarriage illustrate the difficulties of deliberate social policy. Even where the family, the primary socializing unit, is shared and created together, the planned changes do not always and easily occur. A full transfer of mores from one people to another is harder still to achieve where there is no intermarriage and where the two groups come from two civilizations. As long as any group remains even partially intact, its members will be socialized in distinct ways, and identifiable patterns will persist, even when the groups live side by side. As Tocqueville summarized the results of the relation of the European and the Indian in North America, "The Europeans have not been able to change the character of the Indians entirely, and although they can destroy them, they have not been able to establish order or to subdue them."[44] Of course, in most instances this failure resulted from the Indians' unwillingness to follow the European, whose mores they thoroughly despised. Yet even when tribes wanted to make the change, as the Cherokees did, it proved exceedingly difficult and succeeded only after a number of generations. Obviously, when the peoples were from the same civilization and were separated only by their national characters, it was easier to exchange political and social institutions. European nations, for example, were continually trying to adopt practices and mores from other European nations. But even in these cases failure was more likely than success.

Race Versus Racialism

Gobineau's system explained the difference of mores by the deeper biological cause of race. Tocqueville's response was not to reject the possibility of hereditary, nonphysical differences among human groups. A categorical assertion that all groups were exactly the same in all nonphysical respects was to him an unknowable proposition, probably even an unreasonable one: "Surely among the different families which compose the human race there exist certain tendencies, certain proper aptitudes resulting from thousands of different causes."[45] But such biologically grounded differentiation, if it existed, had never been shown to be the decisive source of nonphysical differences among human groups, let alone the basis for hierarchy among them.[46] Racialism was thus nothing more than speculation posing as science.

But Tocqueville's rejection of racialism was not a denial of the significance of race. An obvious fact about human beings is the physical differences that exist among population groups, with color differentiation generally being the most notable feature. In *Democracy in America,* Tocqueville refers to the "natural differences" that are both "physical and permanent." His idea of unitarism was therefore different from that of such biological unitarists as Benjamin Rush, who based his idea of unity on the claim that all races, but for environmental factors, were the same and hence would revert under similar conditions to the same color. This is the kind of absurd conclusion that follows from efforts to use physical science to achieve political objectives, even where the aim might be laudable. Not only does Tocqueville observe that there are physical differences among groups, but he also notes that people inevitably remark on these differences and ascribe to them a role in human relations. People are not color blind.[47]

Tocqueville's view here differs from the tortured modern ideas that seek to deny the natural fact of race and the natural fact that people see race. Henry Louis Gates, who has surveyed these ideas, finds that in one such view, all reality is historically constructed, including one's race or gender; in another, race is said be a fiction; in another still, deriving from literary criticism, race is a trope. As Gates summarizes these variations: "Who has seen a black or red person, a white, a yellow, or brown? These terms are arbitrary constructs, not reports of reality."[48] Obviously, no meaningful political analysis could ever begin from such an absurd account of "reality." Tocqueville's position, without insisting on the significance of every hue and shade, acknowledges the differences of basic color groups that he, along with almost everyone else, readily and normally perceived.

Observing differences among the races, however, is altogether different from racialism. Race is a natural fact, whereas racialism is man-made or conventional. Racialism is an intellectual doctrine that proclaims a fundamental nonphysical differentiation among the races and that makes the differentiation the rationale for a rigid hierarchy among them. But, Tocqueville asks, with what logic? There was no doubt, of course, that his European contemporaries ascribed great significance to race. This was partly the result of the coincidence that the different colors of groups or "families" correlated—by no means entirely, but substantially—with other important factors of differentiation. Living in some cases physically apart from each other, sometimes even out of contact, the races had developed different civilizations. People could thus more easily confuse cultural and racial factors, assigning causality to race. Yet the existence of different races had been known to Europeans long before they had developed the idea of systematic racial hierarchy. The primary factor that accounted for racialism, Tocqueville argued, was not the existence of different races, but the need for a doctrine to rationalize subjugation and enslavement. Slavery in the classical world had been based on conquest, but this doctrine, along with slavery itself, had lost legitimacy. When slavery was reintroduced into Europe, it needed a new foundation, and that foundation was the doctrine of racial inequality: "In the modern world, the insubstantial and ephemeral fact of slavery is most fatally combined with the physical and permanent fact of the difference of race."[49]

When the first volume of *Democracy in America* was written in the 1830s, Tocqueville could at least contemplate the possibility of a decline of racialism (the United States remaining the great exception). With slavery now all but abolished in most of the Christian world, something might be done to begin to eradicate the "prejudice of race and the prejudice of the white."[50] The publication of Gobineau's *Essay,* however, forced Tocqueville to reassess his position. Not only would Gobineau's doctrine help to revive racialism, but it would place it on a far more solid foundation. Racialism had previously grown mostly out of people's interests, which were then attached to their prejudices and to a few haphazardly developed religious and intellectual ideas. Now, however, racialism had been given a place inside science, the highest source of intellectual authority in modern society. Scientific racialism, Tocqueville feared, would become a full-blown ideological doctrine that would enter onto the stage of history.

Tocqueville's discussion of the relations between whites and blacks in the United States provides further insight into his general views on race.[51] From his observations as well as from his reading of Jefferson's *Notes,* he concluded that the American whites' opinion of their racial superiority was so deeply ingrained that a full integration of blacks as equals into American society was highly improbable. In the North, where the black population was relatively sparse (and becoming sparser), the treatment of blacks, although highly unjust, did not threaten the existence of society. The situation in the South, where the population of whites and blacks was more equal, was entirely different. With an increasing concentration of blacks in the slave states and with very little new white immigration, the question of racial conflict hung eerily over the whole society. For Northerners the possibility of racial conflict in the South was a "common topic of conversation, . . . but in the southern states there is silence; . . . One avoids discussing it [even] with one's friends; each man, so to say, hides it from himself. There is something more frightening about the silence of the South than about the North's noisy fears."[52]

Tocqueville speculated on what might happen in the South, subject to his usual qualification that "in any vision of the future, chance always forms a blind spot which the mind's eye cannot penetrate." (As it turned out, the future of the South was determined by an alignment of forces so improbable that Tocqueville never even considered it: namely, whites from the North would fight against whites from the South to end slavery.) For the immediate future, Tocqueville foresaw that the beleaguered whites in the South, resisting all trends of the modern world toward ending slavery, would take more strenuous and devious measures to maintain it. Even those who understood the economic limitations of slavery would support it, fearing the consequences of adopting any other policy. Notwithstanding all these efforts, the status quo could not be maintained. A major rebellion of the slaves would probably take place, followed by an all-out race war. Either the whites would exterminate the blacks, or—the balance of forces proving somewhat more favorable to the blacks—the territory would be divided, a black rump state possibly being formed somewhere along the Gulf coast. A resettlement of black and white populations would then ensue, with whites moving out of these areas and blacks moving in. Perhaps with a continuing increase of black population, whites would begin to move to the North and cede more of the South to the blacks.[53]

In his scenarios for the South, Tocqueville's discussion closely followed the political part of Jefferson's analysis, from the latter's view of the desperate situation of the whites (and blacks) to his fear of a catastrophic war between the races. Given this analysis, Tocqueville saw only one way to resolve the situation short of a race war: miscegenation. (The plan of colonization, he thought, was for demographic reasons alone impracticable.) Miscegenation was an option that Jefferson, on the basis of the racialist premises he derived from natural history, had rejected as unthinkable. Without mentioning Jefferson, Tocqueville disagrees with him on the theoretical question of adopting natural history (and racialism) as the science to guide politics. It was not that Tocqueville thought a mingling of the European and the black to be likely. He "saw no evidence for this in the facts" and felt that those who envisaged mixing as a simple solution to the race problem were indulging in a chimera. American whites, with their pride of origin and prejudice of superiority, would spurn any open policy of intermarriage, fearing above all that it would cause their offspring to be despised by society. (Almost all sexual congress between the races therefore took place outside of marriage between white males and black females, and white males rarely acknowledged their progeny.) The Southern white, Tocqueville observed, "is afraid of resembling the Negro, once his slave, and he is afraid of falling below the level of his white neighbor."[54]

Tocqueville's analysis is based entirely on a reading of the attitudes and prejudices at play in America. Unlike Jefferson, he never argued that miscegenation would be a violation of a putative racial hierarchy. Tocqueville was so little impressed by the idea of racialism that he kept returning—at least three different times—to mixing as the only means for a peaceable resolution of the race problem. Each time he observed that the white race would resist this approach, he suggested that it was the only sensible policy. At the least, before any kind of social equality could be achieved, what would have to yield was the idea that a race's first priority is to save the race—which was of course exactly the teaching of racialism. A solution that would encourage a mixing, he observed, would be the favored policy of a ruler who did not need to govern by consent: "Some despot subjecting the Americans and their former slaves beneath the same yoke might perhaps force the races to mingle."[55] For Tocqueville, the idea of miscegenation was improbable, but it was certainly not unthinkable.

Tocqueville's repudiation of racialism in *Democracy in America,* which Gobineau tried to answer in his *Essay,* became a major theme in their exchange of letters in the 1850s. It is arguable that no one has ever improved on the cogency of Tocqueville's two positive criticisms of racialist theory. These criticisms, like Hamilton's opposition to natural history, proceed by arguments which show that there is a political approach for treating the subject of race which is quite different from the method of either the biological or cultural schools.

Tocqueville's first argument is that racialism excludes any fundamental role for the individual in influencing the course of human affairs. Tocqueville does not deny here the importance of groups in human history; rather, his point is to indicate the role that the individual plays in shaping the group. Individuals on occasion are decisive in altering civilizations and national characters. The success of empires, he observed, can often be attributed to the "influence of certain men" who act in politics and whose qualities are not determined by the previous characteristics of the group.[56] Racial theorists admitted, of course, that there was great variation among individuals and that a genius could appear from within an inferior race. But these theorists in fact limit the realms in which geniuses can operate to art and science, thus excluding politics: no individual from an inferior race is great enough to be able to decisively alter his group's traits and change its fate in the world. Racialism therefore denied the real importance of the individual political actor.

Tocqueville's second criticism is that there was no way to prove a racial hierarchy by analyzing the performance of groups in history other than by claiming to know the "end of history." Without making such a claim, it is impossible to conclude that a given group or race that is on top at one time will occupy the same position at another time. The idea that the biological capacities of groups are insuperable "has not only never been proved, but no one will be able to prove it, since to do so one would need to know not only the past but also the future."[57] The pretension to knowing the final outcome of history—which Tocqueville considered implausible on its face—was therefore not just a peculiarity of Gobineau's thought but a necessary assumption of any kind of historical argument in behalf of racialism.

Tocqueville's reasoning here was not based merely on a skeptical premise (just because something has held true in the past, there is no certainty that it will hold true in the future), but on a much simpler point. In order to claim today that the group now on top is in fact superior, one would have to know how everything turned out. To illustrate this argument, Tocqueville observed that if anyone in the past had tried to judge group capacities from their performance up to that point in history, their prognostications would have been wildly inaccurate: "I am sure that Julius Caesar, had he had the time, would have willingly written a book to prove that the savages he had met in Britain did not belong to the same race as the Romans, and that the latter were destined thus by nature to rule the world while the former were destined to vegetate in one of its corners." Again, if performance to date had been the criterion for judging permanent racial characteristics, no historian writing long ago and using racial analysis would ever have been able to foresee the rise of the European race: "A few million men who, a few centuries ago, lived nearly shelterless in the forests and in the marshes of Europe will, within a few hundred years, have transformed the globe and dominated the other races."[58] And just because Europeans were now on top did not mean they would remain there forever.

Tocqueville argued the point in another way. Even if one accepted that there were important hereditary differences among groups, how would one know exactly which qualities make for dominance? Is a certain attribute always decisive? Accepting for the sake of argument one of Gobineau's racial characterizations, Tocqueville asked if the white race was not itself certain to be displaced by the Asians. If the great virtue of the Asian race, as Gobineau claimed, was its rigorous and systematic implementation of methods of production, and if this quality seemed to fit so prominently with the requirements of dominance under modern conditions, then might not the future belong to the East?

The Sociological and the Political

In my discussion of Gobineau and Tocqueville, I have contrasted how they viewed the broad patterns of human development. As different as their accounts are, if Tocqueville had ended his analysis at this point, he would have shared Gobineau's predominantly sociological approach to the study of man and society. But this was not Tocqueville's last word. In the final analysis what most distinguishes Tocqueville and Gobineau is how differently they viewed the status of a sociological approach itself. For Gobineau, the political is subordinate to the sociological, whereas for Tocqueville the sociological is subordinate to the political.

The term "sociological," as I am using it here, refers to an analysis that explains political developments in terms of pre-political factors. This approach is characteristic of Gobineau's social science, which uses the concept of civilization (and then, in turn, race) to account for the emergence and maintenance or decline of different political regimes. The political is explained by the pre-political. Gobineau takes this sociological or cultural analysis a step further. For him the character of political regimes is ultimately unimportant. The truly significant unit or whole is the civilization, which accounts for the movement of history. Political regimes come and go, but they have no bearing on what will happen to the higher and more embracing whole of civilization. A sociological or cultural approach, in this sense, is one that focuses on a realm more important than politics.

In contrast, for Tocqueville, what mattered most was the specific shape people give to the system that governs them: "To me, human societies, like persons, become worthwhile only through their use of liberty."[59] The highest objective of his social science was to offer instruction for this task. Tocqueville was certainly interested, as both a theoretical and a practical matter, in what I have called sociology. In his study of the broad aggregations of civilizations and national characters, as well as in his discussion of the category of the social state and the historical movement from Aristocracy to Democracy, he probably did more to develop the field of sociology than any thinker before Emile Durkheim and Max Weber. Yet he did not stop at sociology. He employed sociological analysis to help explain the context in which politics operates and to explore the constraints that deliberate political actions might encounter. The final object of his scientific analysis was the political regime. Even if it were true that these pre-political categories account for the outcome much of the time—or, as we would say, that they explain most of the variance—this fact would not justify making a sociological approach the central focus of social science. The highest purpose of social science is not maximizing the explanation of variance according to scientific modes but acquiring knowledge that can help to guide people in establishing better societies.

Tocqueville therefore differentiated between what he called the search for "abstract truth" in the study of society and "political science." Each approach had its own purpose, and that purpose influenced the mode of explanation one adopts and even one's account of the character of reality. Purpose is neither epistemologically nor metaphysically neutral. Once a thinker makes the aim of abstract truth (or explaining variance) the object of social science, he will seek to build a "system" and will become increasingly disposed to hypothesize a single, irreducible cause of human action. Only then will the objective of system building be met in all its rigor. In Gobineau's case, that factor was race, but it could be something else—such as climate or class or spirit—and the structure of explanation would be the same. This is what Tocqueville meant by what he called "German" thinking, referring to how German philosophy since Hegel had favored just this approach of historical system building.

There is an additional temptation for those who follow the search for abstract truth. Theoreticians who want to build systems that explain "why things have developed as they have and could not be otherwise" tend to avoid studying phenomena that undergo too much unsystematic change,[60] focusing instead on more general categories, such as civilizations, that are not as subject to contingency. If one cannot fully explain the flux at the political level, the best approach is to depreciate the status of the political and impute to social reality a higher category.

From this lofty perspective, the question of the particular constitutions of different societies is of minor concern and will wash out in the grander scheme of things. The ordinary science of politics is beneath the dignity of the theorist, who now becomes a doctor of civilizations.

By his own account, Tocqueville himself often felt tempted to veer too far in the direction of this kind of theorizing. For one thing, it was easier to construct a system that displayed the necessity of matters being as they are than it was to offer a more modest science of how matters might be encouraged to turn out differently. For another thing, the system builder might win a kind of renown that was impossible for the political scientist to ever achieve. Partly for these reasons, Tocqueville saw sociologism as not just an intellectual error but a character flaw: "The author is made to appear great, but humanity small."[61] Tocqueville mistrusted his own tendencies toward broad sociological explanations, and time and again he reminded himself and his reader of the limitations of general theorizing. His own theory forces one to heed political things as independent phenomena in their own right.

In the nineteenth century, Arthur de Gobineau was one of the first to use "America" in its modern sense as a symbol in a mode of thought that looked for something deeper than political activity as the main factor controlling human destiny. In his account of the rise and fall of civilizations, America represents the inevitable and sad end of the Enlightenment project: a herd of racial hybrids living under the uniformity and mediocrity of a liberal democratic regime. Alexis de Tocqueville was one of the few important European thinkers of the era to defend liberal democracy and America. This defense was also part of a more general argument for the importance of the political realm and thus, to speak more abstractly, for the need to consider political phenomena as a primary part of reality. Political science was the intellectual discipline most appropriate to understanding these phenomena.

The category that Gobineau proposed as a replacement for politics was civilization, whether in its explanatory sense as the cause that accounts for politics or in its higher sense as the whole that is more important than politics. Although mindful of the significance of this category in both respects, Tocqueville refused to make political activity a mere response to or appendage of civilization. On the contrary, he argued that the fate of civilization often depended on political action. One great theme of his work was that the future character of the "Christian world"—what we loosely call the West—would be decided in no small measure at the political level, in the outcome of the contests between free government and the regimes and ideologies that threatened to destroy freedom.

Quite apart, however, from such lofty concerns about civilization, Tocqueville insisted on the significance of the political realm in the more ordinary sense of the importance of the differences among the various forms of government. He could appreciate this point not only in the oldest teachings of political science but also in his personal experience. The regime of the French Revolution, the first modern or ideological tyranny, had introduced into political life a new form of fanaticism whose many victims included members of Tocqueville's own family. It thus made a difference—a real difference—whether one lived under a despotism or under a constitutional form of government. The possibility of a recurrence of another such ideological regime was reason enough for Tocqueville to consider the question of the forms of government as no merely secondary inquiry; on the contrary, it was a decisive matter for human beings. Tocqueville could only wonder at the abstraction of modern theoretical writers who disconnected the study of society from the question that occurred first to those who think politically: whether the governments men create and live under are despotic or free. If this question is beneath the dignity of social science, then, it is fair to ask, what is social science is for?

Our own century, one might have thought, should have settled this question decisively in favor of this commonsense appreciation of the importance of the political realm. After the experiences of Nazism and Communism existing side by side with liberalism—all, incidentally, inside the same civilization—the differences among political regimes should hardly seem inconsequential. What could count more? Yet the sad truth is that many of the best minds of our time have obscured the importance of the political question, skipping quickly over the differences among regimes and affixing blame for the horrors of our era on the West, or America, or Enlightenment civilization—as if civilizations, not political regimes, acted directly and governed human affairs. And if it is our civilization that is responsible for the crimes of our era, so this argument runs, then the guilt must be apportioned among its parts more or less equally: for the Nazis, it is Auschwitz; for the Communists, it is the Gulag; and for America, it is Hiroshima. Political differences wash out; it is all a matter of civilization. Such are the irresponsible distortions that follow from the failure to include political phenomena as a distinct part of reality.

7

★ ★ ★

From America to Americanization: Images of America in German Thought

O Freiheit! du bist ein böser Traum!
(O freedom! what an awful dream!)
—Heinrich Heine

In 1930, Otto Basler, a German philologist, published an article entitled "Americanism: The History of a Term" in the intellectual magazine *Deutsche Rundschau*. Noteworthy less for its insight than for its subject matter, the article focused on the ubiquity of the term "America" and its cognates in German discourse of the time. "In the practical professions, in scholarship, in ordinary life, and in the newspapers," Basler wrote, "one daily hears the terms Americanize, Americanization, and Americanism."[1] "America" had become a vehicle by which ideas generated in philosophic and intellectual circles in Germany were transferred to the realm of common opinion.

The symbolic America of the turn of the century serves as a bridge between the America of the natural historians and racialist thinkers (Buffon, de Pauw, and Gobineau) and the America of postmodern thinkers (Heidegger, Kojève, and Baudrillard). The natural historians and racialists built their symbol on the idea of degeneration, which referred to a shrinking, diminution, or enfeeblement of physical things. The America of the turn of the century was different. It was seen as a powerful, almost irresistible force, degenerate, if you will, in the sense of being grotesque and often blindly destructive. The earlier thinkers had attributed degeneration to the physical causes of the environment or the mixing of the races. At the turn of the twentieth century the cause of deformation was intellectual or spiritual. America represented the political idea of a constructed political order based on individual freedom and democracy, the economic principle of the pursuit of well-being, and the cultural idea of the common man's taste influencing society's artistic horizons. America became the emblem for the technological and scientific project of modernity, which prepared the way for the contemporary identification of America with the themes of the end of history and the totalitarianism of the Enlightenment.

The meaning of America that emerged early in the twentieth century paralleled certain linguistic changes. The simple name "America" of the nineteenth century metastasized into the abstractions "Americanism," "Americanization," and "Americanness." Until the middle of the nineteenth century, America had been discussed as a place or country—although it was clear that its qualities were often serving political and philosophical purposes. By the second half of the nineteenth century, it was also being seen as a process or a worldview capable of being separated from its physical home and transferred elsewhere. America was entering the realm of spirit. The abstract meaning of the word "Americanize" grew out of a more concrete usage. The earliest references appear among German immigrants in America in the 1850s, who lamented the "Americanization" of the German community, meaning its loss of identification with the homeland and its full-scale adoption of the ways of the new country. In 1877, Emil Dubois Reymond, the German intellectual and author, extended this idea to refer to the "overrunning of European culture with realism and the growing preponderance of technology."[2] In this view it was still America that promoted this development, indirectly at least, by the sheer force of its economic might. But Dubois Reymond took the next step by suggesting that the American way of life struck a natural chord with the European masses. Americanization was a powerful and attractive idea, not in the sense of offering people a fully developed ideology but in awakening the common man's deep-felt desire for political, economic, and cultural democratization.

Paul Dehns elaborated on this abstraction in 1904 in an article entitled, significantly enough, "The Americanization of the World." Dehns offered one of the first explicit definitions of the process: "What is Americanization? Americanization in an economic sense means the modernization of the methods of industry, exchange and agriculture as well as all other areas of practical life. Americanization in its widest sense, including the societal and the political, means the uninterrupted, exclusive, and relentless striving after gain, riches, and influence."[3] Others added to this the related idea of a rationalization and standardization of the processes of production, undertaken in order to reach the mass of consumers, where the greatest buying power was now to be found. Thus well before World War I and the passions it engendered, Americanism in Germany had developed into a significant symbol.

Although the elaboration of this notion of Americanism occurred in Germany and was most pronounced there, a parallel development took place in France. There the locus of activity was among the clergy rather than the secular intelligentsia. Near the end of the nineteenth century, a number of French prelates began a campaign to have the Catholic Church declare "Americanism" an official heresy, to be ranked in obloquy with such past great heresies as Albigensianism and Jansenism. The leading voice in this campaign was the abbé Charles Maignen, who wrote a series of articles and a book criticizing the theology of an American priest, the Reverend Thomas Hecker. The book's self-proclaimed "lofty motive" was "to save the Church from grave and imminent peril." The threat was Americanism: "We have thought it well to raise our voice boldly against contemporary Americanism and its avowed or secret leaders."[4]

The target of Maignen's campaign was less American Catholicism than America's political principles. Father Hecker, in the tradition of John Carroll, had tried to reconcile Catholic faith with liberal democratic principles, and American Catholics generally had begun to be more assertive in church circles in behalf of a more progressive or liberal Catholicism. (In an echo of the politics of the French Revolution, the clergy sympathetic to this reformist spirit called themselves *américanistes*.) If there was a logic to Maignen's attack, it lay in the old argument that any regime based on the principles of rights and democracy is inimical to Catholicism. For Maignen, America now assumed the place of revolutionary France as the despised object of modernity, and his chapter on the American heresy begins by recalling Joseph de Maistre's critique of America. To those who had offered America as a model to de Maistre, "heaping tiresome praise on that infant in swaddling clothes," he had responded, "Wait till he grows." One hundred years have now passed, Maignen observed, since that "great philosopher" had uttered this phrase, and a grown-up America has now confirmed all of his doubts. The chaos of a nation built on rationalist principles and composed of different races was now manifest to everyone. What America lacked, above all, was an organic connection to the past and a sense of rootedness: "You know nothing of old nations settled for ages on the banks of the same rivers, in the shadow of the same mountains, plunging their roots deep into the soil, and silently bringing forth under an identical sun for each passing generation the ripe fruits of labor, the flowers of art and poetry."[5]

The debate on Americanism raged for the next two years. Journals likened Americanism to an "invasion of barbarism": "It is the assault of money against honor, bold brutality against delicateness, . . . machinery against philosophy." Fulminations against America reached a height of obscurantism in *Americanism and the Anti-Christian Conspiracy,* by the abbé Henry Delassus.[6] The book outlined an alliance among liberal forces (Jews, Freemasons, and Americans) to undermine Catholicism. America was now viewed as a Protestant and therefore essentially secular state bent on the destruction of Christianity. President William McKinley, during whose administration America seized some of Spain's dominions in the Spanish-American War, was named the sinister leader of this unholy conspiracy. (Some of these ideas were picked up later by various American extremist movements—absent, of course, the specifically anti-Protestant and anti-American charges—and were used to bolster attacks on Jews and the Left.)

In the end, Pope Leo XIII sidestepped much of this issue. In a papal letter of 1899, the pope condemned the excesses of certain radical modern ideas known as Americanism, but he did not directly accuse the leaders of American Catholicism of promoting such doctrines. American Catholics seemed to have considered themselves warned rather than rebuked.[7] So ended this odd attempt to forge a linguistic connection between a nation and a religious heresy. Had this campaign succeeded, it would have been necessary to speak here not only of the metaphysical and symbolic America but also of the theological America, albeit one quite different from John Winthrop's image of the shining "city on the hill."

Aside from the seminars given by Cornelius de Pauw in the court of Frederick the Great, the development of the concept of America in Germany was a product of nineteenth-century thought. There were, of course, discussions of America in the German states at the time of the American Revolution, and some writers, swept up in the spirit of the Enlightenment, spoke warmly of America. But in Germany, the emphasis of Enlightenment thought was on France, not America, and the French Revolution was the focus of inquiry.[8]

One of the first extended images of America in German thought is found in Hegel's *Philosophy of History.* The passage occurs not in the body of his history proper but in the introduction, which focuses on nature, not history. In this section, Hegel divided the New World into two parts, North America and South America. What separated them was not only their colonizers' countries of origin (England on one hand, Spain on the other) or the degree of European colonization (greater in North America than in South America), but also their religious foundations. North America was predominantly Protestant, whereas South America (including Mexico) was Catholic. For Hegel, the religious difference was fundamental, as only Protestantism allowed for the kind of mutual trust among citizens that could sustain a limited constitutional form of government: "Among Catholics, on the contrary, the basis for such confidence cannot exist, for in secular matters only force and voluntary subservience are the principles of action."[9] Free or republican government in the New World was therefore possible only in the United States, to which Hegel then turned.

Whereas America's constitutional form of government may seem to put it in advance of the nations of Europe, Hegel quickly qualified this impression. The theory underlying American republicanism, he argued, was incompatible with constitutionalism for a society under developed conditions. Public authority in America had no greater role than the protection of property. America's fundamental character lay in its profoundly individualistic and contractual nature, in the "endeavor of the individual after acquisition, commercial profit, and gain; and in the preponderance of the private interest, which devotes itself to the general interest only for the protection of particular interests." America—this is his central point—had no "state" in the real meaning of the term. Genuine politics presupposes conditions in which the resolution of issues requires both the development of a community consciousness and the use of collective approaches. These conditions occur in a developed society that faces certain communal problems: class differences, which focus political attention on the division of property; a scarcity of land, which compels people to turn to one another and resolve matters together; and threats to national security, which require the establishment of a large military force. The state is the great instrument man has created to deal with these issues.[10]

America, however, had not yet reached the point where it needed or had developed a state. With its sparse population, abundance of land, and lack of powerful neighbors, America still remained a kind of frontier country. Here we find one of the earliest versions of the thesis of American exceptionalism. America's constitutional forms and freedom were tied to unique (and temporary) conditions, and for this reason, the American republic could not serve as a model for Europe. Whatever praise Hegel gave to America for its constitutional government, he more than took away with his criticisms of American liberalism and individualism. Although these comments were ostensibly offered as mere descriptions of a stage of development, they nevertheless carried clearly ethical overtones, and they have served ever since as the basis for a straightforwardly moral critique of American political principles and culture.

It is remarkable, in fact, how the terms of this critique have persisted. Thinkers on both sides of the Atlantic have charged that America remains frozen in a primitive liberal form that has never adjusted to the more advanced idea implied in the notion of the "state." The word in this sense was brought into the American lexicon by Progressive thinkers, who were directly influenced by Hegel's thought. Woodrow Wilson entitled one of his major works *The State,* and his own political thinking became a powerful appeal to the establishment of a state in the Hegelian sense, replete with its attendant instrument of administration. (The state would, of course, be democratized to fit the American context.) As Wilson put it: "The idea of the state is the conscience of administration. Seeing everyday new things which the state ought to do, the next thing is to see clearly how it ought to do them."[11] The state has remained a concept of supposedly empirical or positivistic analysis ever since, although it has consistently conveyed the hidden implication that limited or liberal government is regressive. Thus it was often said in the 1970s that America had failed to develop the industrial policies of mature neocorporatist states, and today one often hears that welfare policies in America are behind those of the more advanced welfare states in Europe.

Hegel concluded his discussion by indicating why he would not provide a systematic account of the United States in his survey of world history. History is the realm of what has occurred, and the essential story of America had not yet taken place. Until now, he observed, America had been tied to the politics and civilization of Europe. But as America moved to center stage of world historical development, it would reveal its distinct characteristics: "America is the land of the future." Without endorsing the idea that America represented a land of hope, Hegel noted the power that this idea held for many Europeans in search of a new beginning. America "is a land of longing for all those who are weary of the historical lumber-room of old Europe. Napoleon is reported to have said, 'Cette vieille Europe m'ennuie' [This old Europe bores me]."[12]

It is with romanticism proper, however, that the image of America was constructed in German thought. Romantic thinking on America contained two strands. One developed from the just-mentioned longing for something new—for a release from the burdens of history and for a chance to start over. Goethe gave expression to this theme in his poem "The United States," which opens with the line "America, you have it better." "Better" here means to be free of the past, with its "ruined castles" and "useless memories." A variant of this hopeful view was the idea of America as a young people or a young race, robust and full of vitality.

In America history might begin again—precisely the idea against which Gobineau had so strongly reacted. Finally, there was a fascination with images of wild and unspoiled nature, which appealed to a desire for what was untamed by any kind of convention.[13]

The other, and dominant, strand of German romantic thinking offered a strikingly different, indeed almost opposite, picture of America. The triumph of this view by the middle of the nineteenth century reflected a working out of the stronger philosophical and political implications of romanticism, especially as they were found in Germany. German romanticism grew in reaction against universalist and Enlightenment ideas. It opposed societies created by reason or contract, preferring instead forms that grew organically, and it opposed the calculating rationality of the individual, favoring the deeper bonding of individuals inside a historical community. America in its founding political principles came to be seen as the embodiment of the despised Enlightenment characteristics. This political element was of great importance in Germany, where the romantic writers assumed much of the burden of defining the idea of the nation in the uprisings against the Napoleonic occupation, which was also viewed as an extension of Enlightenment ideas. Popular and nationalist ideas in Germany therefore emerged in opposition to rationalism, the blame for which was quickly transferred from France to America.

The two fundamental conceptions of the "nation" still in use today derive largely from this period. As defined in present-day scholarship (and arguably a bit too rigidly), one conception, which is based on the model of America and France, grounds the nation in the acceptance of certain principles. The other, which originated with German romanticism and which has tended to dominate in the central European states, defines the nation as a distinctive community sharing preexisting ethnic or cultural characteristics said to embody a deeper spiritual meaning. Each *Volk* is a nation. Those who adopted this understanding, even when they saw themselves as democrats, viewed the American idea of *liberal* democracy as alien. Theirs was a *völkisch* conception of democracy.[14]

The dominant strand of the romantic image of America is best seen in the writings of one of the most famous poets of the age, Nikolaus Lenau, sometimes referred to as the German Byron. Lenau's picture of America could claim more than the usual authority because Lenau, unlike so many others who wrote on America, actually visited the United States, in 1832–1833. Lenau's picture of America is all the more striking for having resulted from a conversion. In the period before his visit, Lenau expressed all the positive notions about America. Lenau told a friend he planned to remain in America for at least five years in order to experience its "gigantic stock of the most magnificent scenes of Nature"; he would also escape the dreary despotism of Austria and breath the air of "you my dear new world, you my dear free world."[15]

Lenau arrived in America just as Tocqueville was leaving. But although these two observers looked at the same country, they hardly saw the same thing. Notwithstanding Lenau's proclaimed romantic proclivities, he proved far less adventuresome in his journey than the supposedly more sober French traveler. Whereas Tocqueville went all over America from North to South, venturing even into the wilds of the upper peninsula of Michigan, Lenau confined himself to a much smaller geographical area, spending most of his time in Baltimore, parts of Pennsylvania, and New Lisbon, Ohio. For Tocqueville, the natural habitat of America exercised a powerful and at times mysterious effect, and some of the most beautiful passages of *Democracy in America* and his diaries recount his impressions of the vast and largely uninhabited lands of the West. Given the narrow radius to which Lenau restricted himself, it is perhaps understandable, although certainly not justifiable, that he was less enthusiastic. In fact, he complained incessantly about the landscape, grumbling, for example, that the "formation of the mountains and the indentation of the valleys is all monotonous and unimpressive."[16]

Lenau's America marks the transition from the degeneracy thesis of the late eighteenth century, where decay in America was tied to physical forces, to the nineteenth-century idea of disfigurement, where deformation is attributed to America's political principles and culture. This transition occurs in Lenau's first letters from America, in which he suddenly—and inexplicably—becomes disenchanted with the land he had only recently celebrated. He despairs at the absence of the sound of "any nightingale, indeed no true Songbirds," a fact that must have a "deeper and more serious meaning." Might it not, he wondered, be a "poetic curse" placed on a nation of "disgusting shopkeepers" who bring "death to all spiritual life"? Perhaps the nightingale "was right not to show up among these wretches."[17]

Considering the matter further, Lenau recalled a more scientific explanation of the deficiency: "Buffon was right that in America man and animals degenerate from one generation to the next." Although he would not go as far as de Pauw and aver that all American canines were mute, he did claim never to have "seen here any spirited dog, fiery horse, or passionate man." Lenau was not the only one to still be insisting on the idea of the physical inferiority of the new world. A philosopher of no less rank than Friedrich von Schlegel, in his *Philosophy of History* (1828), took it as a matter of common knowledge that the animal kingdom in

America "is far inferior to the other and more ancient continents" and that "many of the noblest and most beautiful species of animals did not exist there originally and others were found most unseemly in form and most degenerate in nature."[18]

To these observations, grounded in the science of natural history, Lenau added a new line of speculation that focused on the defects of America's way of life, or "culture" (*Kultur*). Lenau developed his theme, tracing the lineage of this term while applying it as a category of analysis. He began by using the term in its original and literal sense—the care and cultivation of plant life. Here he found American horticulture to be remarkably crude. He then moved to the term's newer meaning, referring to the level of a people's spiritual and intellectual development. America's culture, he observed, "has in no sense come up organically from within" but was imposed from the outside. American culture, from business to education and all other endeavors in between, was *bodenlos,* or without any ground or roots of its own. America could not grow or nurture its human resources any more than it could its plants: "The education of an American is no more than a business and practical one. Here the practical man is developed in his most frightful matter-of-factness."[19]

Lenau concluded his survey by referring to a nominative form of bodenlos, which he thought captured the essence of America: "With the expression *Bodenlosigkeit* [rootlessness] I think I am able to indicate the general character of all American institutions, including political institutions." His political critique, which is reminiscent of some parts of Hegel's analysis, focused on the way in which the society was put together. America is a country in which the bond among people is based on a rational calculation of personal interest, not on some more fundamental, natural (in the sense of organic and preexisting) connection. Missing in America, Lenau complained, was the idea of the "Fatherland": "Each individual lives and takes part in the republican association, only because and as long as his private property is secured. What we call Fatherland is here merely a property insurance scheme. The American knows nothing, he seeks nothing but money. He has no ideas; consequently the state is no spiritual or customary institution (Fatherland), but an artificial convention." Lenau ended his stay by referring to America as the "true land of the end, the outer edge of man."[20]

Lenau spoke of America in some of his poems but more often in his letters, which were published in 1855. These were for the most part intended as poetic essays, and they made a deep impression at the time. Even so, his views might have remained fairly restricted had it not been for the movie version, so to speak, of Lenau's trip, which appeared in *Der Amerikamüde,* one of the most widely read novels of the time. Written by Ferdinand Kürnberger, a fellow Austrian, the story is roughly modeled on Lenau's trip, tracing the American travels of a German poet who goes to New Lisbon and grows increasingly disenchanted with America. This novel, which is otherwise unremarkable, is worth mentioning because, as I note later, it served as a point of departure for Max Weber's classic work, *The Protestant Ethic and the Spirit of Capitalism.*

Better known than Lenau was Heinrich Heine (1797–1856), who wrote what is probably the most famous of all romantic German poems, "Die Lorelei." The poem is named for a fabled rock on the Rhine where, legend has it, a beautiful siren once sat and combed her golden hair. Even today it is a kind of ritual pilgrimage in Germany to take a boat trip past the rock while singing the lovely lyrics of this poem. Heine's verses on America, however, contain no such enticing images. America is the anti-siren and symbol of all that romanticism detested: "Sometimes it comes in my mind / To sail to America / To that big pig-pen of freedom / Inhabited by boors living in equality." In the end, Heine reported, he thought better of such a voyage, admitting that he would be disturbed to find himself among people "who spit tobacco without using spittoons." In his prose, Heine employed the same technique of joining liberal democratic ideals to the worst of nightmares. America now becomes a "gigantic prison of freedom" where the "most extensive of all tyrannies, that of the masses, exercises its crude authority." Following this comment comes the now standard criticism of liberalism as thoroughly materialistic and selfish: "This-worldly utility is the American's true religion, and money is his God, his only, almighty God."[21]

Revolutionary Conservatism

The romantic view of America became the foundation for the abstract notion of Americanism developed in Germany in the latter part of the nineteenth century. It was most often the conservative thinkers who elaborated the theme of America as a threat to European life, and especially to its higher cultural achievements. As the historian Fritz Stern noted, "From the 1870s on, conservative writers in imperial Germany expressed fear that the German soul would be destroyed by 'Americanization,' that is by mammonism, materialism, mechanization and mass society."[22] The protection of the "German soul," according to Stern, was seen as the sacred mission of a cultural elite which had to protect Germany, if not against all forms of democratization, then at any rate against the liberal form, Americanism, in which the tastes of the people became the governing force in cultural affairs.

But conservative thinking about America in Germany was not entirely negative. A distinction must be drawn between the traditional conservatives, who defended an older, more aristocratic order (and for whom America seemed hostile to high culture), and a group of thinkers referred to as the revolutionary conservatives or the reactionary moderns.[23] These thinkers stressed above all else the need to be realistic and forward-looking. They attacked traditional conservatives (and romantics) for their inability to confront the forces shaping the modern world. For the revolutionary conservatives, what loses a struggle, simply because it has lost, is untrue; what emerges victorious, because it has won, is true. Americanism as the dominant force in the world therefore held an obvious appeal for these thinkers, for America had proven its mettle in the only arena that counted: real history.

Revolutionary conservatives nevertheless found reason to be highly critical of Americanism—indeed, to make it the main threat to sustaining civilization. Americanism was a force lacking in all self-understanding. Wedded to the shallow materialistic, universalistic, and liberal democratic ideas of the Enlightenment, America would prove itself incapable of maintaining its own achievements. Left to its own principles, it would destroy civilization. This being the case, civilization's survival depended upon its foundation being renewed and transformed. Not America, but only a nation endowed with spiritual depth and philosophic awareness could accomplish such a transformation. That nation was to be found in Europe and, specifically, in the "center." A reformed Germany would alone be capable of harnessing the forces of technology and submitting them to the discipline of a political principle that could meet the demands of a new era.

The revolutionary conservatives—among them Arthur Moeller van den Bruck, Oswald Spengler, and Ernst Jünger—have all been considered as in some sense disciples of Friedrich Nietzsche, although some scholars today, noting the revolutionary conservatives' simplifications and distortions of Nietzsche's thought, prefer to call them "vulgar Nietzscheans." Vulgar or not, their development of the symbolic America owed much to Nietzsche's discussions of America. In his initial presentation in *Human, All Too Human,* Nietzsche described America as an extension of Europe and a "daughterland" of European culture.[24] Yet, although part of that culture, America embodies certain of its most troubling elements, and in their most intense form. Modern European culture is characterized by a restlessness or agitation that is more fully in evidence in America. This restlessness is a threat to higher culture, which above all needs contemplative habits. Modern culture, in the way of life exhibited foremost in America, threatens to lead us into a new barbarism.[25]

Nietzsche's subsequent discussion of America shifted the focus in one important respect. In *The Gay Science,* America appears as something more distant and alien, sending its powerful influences back to Europe. America represents the coming future in its most disfigured form, displaying a preoccupation with the material and a total systematization of work and production: "The breathless haste with which they [the Americans] work—the distinctive vice of the new world— is already beginning ferociously to infect old Europe and is spreading a spiritual emptiness [*Geistlosigkeit*] over the continent." American culture, which consists of a "constant chase after gain," seeks to reduce everything to a kind of numeric calculation: "One thinks with a watch in one's hand." The finer or higher things are crowded out ("prolonged reflection almost gives people a bad conscience") or else treated under a calculus of quick consumption ("one lives as if 'one might miss out on something'"). The effect of this culture is to give the great moral term "virtue" a new meaning: "True virtuousness now consists in doing something in less time than someone else." Everything is reduced to efficiency and work: "Work more and more enlists all good conscience on its side," whereas leisure brings a bad conscience.[26]

Nietzsche saw in the American spirit a confidence in the individual's capacity "to do just about everything and manage every role." Whatever positive aspects are detectable in this assessment are overshadowed by more sinister and destructive elements. "Role playing" here refers to a thin individualism. Society is now composed of those who are unwilling to join into a genuine community and who are incapable of planning and building for the future. Along with its lowering of cultural standards, therefore, Americanism appears to be incapable of sustaining its own project. It is Americanism in this sense that is now returning to infect Europe: "The faith of the Americans today is more and more becoming the faith of the European as well."[27] As briefly outlined here, the picture Nietzsche sketched became the metaphysical America of the revolutionary conservatives.

The most influential of the early figures among the revolutionary conservatives was Arthur Moeller van den Bruck (1876–1925). Van den Bruck was an extraordinarily prolific writer, endowed with a talent for expressing his thoughts in phrases that captured the popular imagination. He might best be described as a "public intellectual" but for the fact that he was on the radical Right. He is remembered most today for having reintroduced into modern German thought the term "Third Reich," the title of his widely read book published in 1923.[28] This book initiated a new category of German thought—*Reichsideologie* (Reich thinking)—which tried to define a specifically German concept of the nation in opposition to the liberal ideas embodied in the Weimar constitution. In this respect at least, Van den Bruck expressed a sentiment that was, or would shortly become, widely shared among German thinkers of the period.

Van den Bruck's most extensive discussion of Americanism occurred in an ear-

lier work, *Contemporary Times* (1906), in which he surveyed the national characters of the different countries of the world and sought to outline their philosophic
and historical import.[29] He continued thereafter to comment on the meaning of
America, Americanism, and *Amerikanertum* (Americanness)—apparently a term
he coined. Van den Bruck was perhaps the first writer to explicitly draw the distinction between the actual or geographic America and Americanism understood
as an abstract principle. America, he noted, is a "new land," whereas Americanism, "not locally but spiritually understood," represents a distinct posture toward
the material universe; it is the "decisive step by which we make our way from a
dependence on the earth to the use of the earth, the step that mechanizes and elec-
trifies inanimate material and makes the elements of the world into agencies of human use."[30] Americanism so understood was an essential step forward, and without it man could not progress or even survive.

Van den Bruck continued, however, by insisting that America's political principles—its idea of rights, its reliance on reason, and its individualism—could not
assure its own successes. If progress were to continue, if the world were to avoid
collapse, a new principle of governance would have to be discovered and instituted. That principle could not be based on a return to aristocratic forms (going
backward is never possible); rather, it must build on, while moving beyond, the
ideas of the democratic age. Instead of rejecting such terms as "democracy" and
"socialism," Van den Bruck sought to redefine them in ways that pointed to a new
and popular form of conservatism and particularism. Democracy, rather than being tied to certain institutional forms, becomes for him something more spiritual.
It is the "participation of a people in its destiny."[31] A shared sense of mission in
History, rather than an adherence to the principles of nature or reason, is the new
foundation of a popular political order.

Decrying liberalism, Van den Bruck looked instead for a new form of collective solidarity (a Reich) that relied on understanding and feeling more than reason. American principles did not provide the requisite degree of community but
produced a mass society that lacked the bonds to sustain a common national effort: "In America everything is a block, pragmatism, and the national Taylor System."[32] Van den Bruck's search for a principle of solidarity led him to embrace a
form of socialism that was clearly not a Marxist or international variant but of a
kind that builds unity inside a particular nation. In *The Third Reich* he called for a
"German socialism," which he described as a "corporate conception of state and
society, that may need to be brought about by revolution, but then will become
conservative." Redefining the term to fit his purposes, Van den Bruck wrote, "Socialism for us is: rootedness, proper order, and structure."[33]

In one of his last writings, Van den Bruck discussed America according to the older romantic distinction between young and old peoples. Under this distinction, a young people was equated with robustness and vitality (of which the German nation, recently come into its own, was the prime example), whereas an old people was identified with decay and "civilization" (used pejoratively). Exactly which nations were classified as old depended on the author, but the list invariably included the Latin and "Jesuit" peoples. The young-old distinction roughly paralleled the racial distinction between Aryan and non-Aryan peoples and was another, albeit less biological, way of evoking the same theme. For Van den Bruck, America was at heart a young people; this, at any rate, represented America's deepest tradition and instincts. The qualities of youth in this description, however, referred not to America's political or constitutional forms, but to the deeper and more essential aspects of the character of the people revealed in the pioneering spirit of the settlers of the West. In this view, the real America—if I may use the term— consisted of American mores and character as they existed in spite of or against all the influences of her form of government and official political principles. America, Van den Bruck argued, had unfortunately betrayed her deeper instincts in World War I, siding with the coalition of the older nations against Germany. The great question for the future was whether America would choose to be true to herself and join with Germany in a new coalition to help revive the West.[34]

Van den Bruck and the conservative revolutionaries set the stage for Oswald Spengler, one of the most idiosyncratic yet influential German thinkers of the early twentieth century. Spengler is difficult to place in any school. Like Van den Bruck, he was a disciple of Nietzsche, but unlike Van den Bruck, he often embraced fatalist principles that made deliberate human action appear futile or inconsequential. This standpoint set his thinking apart from the "voluntaristic" perspective of the earlier revolutionary conservatives, who recommended decisive and vigorous steps to change the course of history.

Spengler treated America in relation to two major themes: race (discussed earlier) and technology. His discussion of technology began in a short book entitled *Man and Technology* and continued in *The Year of Decision. Man and Technology,* published originally in German as *Der Mensch und die Technik,* is one of the first book-length, philosophical treatments of the subject of *die Technik,* or technology, which Martin Heidegger later elevated to a central theme of modern philosophy. The German word "Technik" has a broader meaning than the English word, which refers mostly to the application of science to the production of things for practical use. The German term points beyond the things science produces to the ideas and the posture toward reality that makes possible their production. "Die Technik" refers as much to a set of philosophical ideas and a mindset as to a process of scientific research and invention. Because of this difference, Charles Francis Atkinson, who translated Spengler's book into English, elected to render "Technik" by the neologism "technics."[35]

Spengler helped to introduce and develop this broader meaning of "Technik" into modern thought. In *Man and Technology,* he defined technology as the sum of the tactics that man from the very beginning developed in an attempt to ensure his survival and prosperity. These tactics included not just the tools man invented but also the thinking and strategizing that lay behind their development.[36] Since Spengler conceived life in terms of struggle and conflict, originating with the struggle of primitive man against nature, a survey of technology covers all of human history. Technology is not only a fact in the study of human history but the key to the whole story of man. In contrast to his view of history in *The Decline of the West,* where he presented the notion of eternally repeating cycles, Spengler here elaborated a single world history into which all cycles fit. The common line of development is driven by an ever-increasing "mechanization of the world."[37]

The modern age is characterized by the highest development of technology, which is ultimately the product of the mind-set or worldview of Western thought and science. Ours is thus the age of technology proper. The domination of the world by technology, which means the domination of the world by Western thought, is the central event of our era and the fact that will determine the future. Society today is characterized not only by an increasing reliance on mechanization (and thus a growing artificiality in man's relation to nature) but also by a new way of viewing the world. Man today looks at and evaluates all things solely in terms of their potential application for mechanization: "Civilization itself has become a machine that does, or tries to do, everything in mechanical fashion. We think only in horse-power now; we cannot look at a waterfall without mentally turning it into electric power; we cannot survey a countryside full of pasturing cattle without thinking of its exploitation as a source of meat-supply."[38]

The present age is the penultimate stage of world history. It is the period before the end, where the "end" is conceived as either the physical extinction of the human race or the collapse of civilized life. The end is at once man's final glory and his final tragedy. It is man's final glory because he will have taken his Faustian dream of controlling and subduing nature to its farthest limit. It is man's final tragedy because it spells man's inevitable doom. Spengler offered a number of reasons for the collapse of civilization. In one version, which prefigures the thinking of part of the modern environmental movement, he hinted at a physical or natural reaction in the form of ecological disaster. The artificial control of the world can be pushed only so far before Nature calls a halt by way of a "catastrophe":

> The mechanization of the world has entered on a phase of highly dangerous overextension. The picture of the earth, with its plants, animals, and men, has altered. In a few decades most of the great forests will have gone, to be turned into news-print, and climatic changes have been thereby set afoot which imperil the land-economy of whole populations. Innumerable animal species have been extinguished. . . . Whole races of humanity have been brought almost to a vanishing-point. . . . This machine technology will end the Faustian civilization and one day will lie in fragments, forgotten—our railways and steamships as dead as the Roman roads and the Chinese wall. . . . The history of this technology is fast drawing to its inevitable close. It will be eaten from within, like the grand forms of any and every Culture. When, and in what fashion, we know not.[39]

On further analysis, Spengler argued that the impending catastrophe would result, not from man's going too far against nature, but on the contrary from his failure to go far enough. Man cannot sustain his Faustian drive, which falls victim to his growing intellectual, moral, and political weakness. Spengler cited a number of signs of decay. The talented and the geniuses, on whom all technological development depends, have begun to grow bored with technology and have turned to idle, speculative thinking: "The flight of the born leader from the machine is beginning. . . . It is precisely the strong and creative talents that are turning away from practical problems and sciences towards pure speculation. Occultism and Spiritualism, Hindu philosophies, metaphysical inquisitiveness under Christian or pagan colouring . . . are coming up again."[40] In a parallel development, as technology becomes more complicated, the intellectual gap increases between the laborer and the promoters of mechanization (inventors, entrepreneurs, and industrial leaders). Laborers find themselves unable to understand the work of industrial leaders; the laborers suspect that, being more intellectual than physical, this is no longer work in the genuine sense, and they no longer respect or willingly defer to the industrial leaders, whom they grow more and more to resent. This resentment in turn feeds their democratic envy and becomes further grounds for the spread of democratic ideas.

The most important sign of decay, however, is a political failure. Societies have lost sight of the real sources of their development and achievement. Life is struggle, and this struggle can be successfully carried on only by the few, those "born to command" and those "few creative heads." But modern Western societies, democratic to the core, prefer to deny or evade this truth. Living under the sway of Enlightenment and utilitarian ideas, people attribute the achievements of these creative heads—to the extent they even recognize them—to lower motives: either a philistine desire to acquire more personal comforts or a social concern for promoting progress. But the real driving force of the great inventors and leaders "has nothing whatever to do with its practical consequences"; it is pursued for its own sake, for the personal satisfaction it brings to those of a superior type or race.[41] Until or unless this fundamental and undemocratic fact of human existence is recognized, there can be no hope for rebuilding society on a sound and sustainable foundation.

The fatalism that dominates *Man and Technology* yields at this point to a few speculations about a saving course of action. Man can perhaps avert the disaster that awaits him, not by renouncing the technological project and attempting to enter into a harmonious relationship with Nature, but by developing new and more powerful forms of mechanization. Most important is not the control over any particular energy resource but the control of those who know how to create or find new energy sources. Whether further technological development can finally make a difference, Spengler never says. We are told time and again that it may, only to be told time and again that it cannot. The inconsistency here, glaring as it may appear to us, was not so important to Spengler, for he insists that his ultimate concern is neither the accuracy of his prognostications nor even the survival of the outward physical forms of civilization, but the nobility of man. From this standpoint, what counts most is not the outcome but how man confronts it. Man's greatest glory is to understand the story of his existence on earth—to see in it the struggle that it is—and then, on the basis of this truth, to construct a society that recognizes the inherent difference between leaders and the led, taking the struggle for existence to its highest plane. Man's worth lies in the pride he takes in facing the end—knowing it is the end, yet acting to the last and without illusion to do all he can to prevent it. *Man and Technology* ends on a note that one commentator has labeled "fatalistic fortitude" but that may just as well be called pompous platitude: "Optimism is cowardice. . . . Our duty is to hold on to the lost position, without hope, without rescue, like that Roman soldier whose bones were found in front of a door in Pompeii, who, during the eruption of Vesuvius, died at his post because they forgot to relieve him. That is greatness. That is what it means to be a thoroughbred. The honorable end is the one thing that cannot be taken from a man."[42]

In *The Year of Decision,* Spengler adopted a more "practical" approach to the crisis of modernity. Although he continued to predict an ominous end for mankind, he also held out the possibility that things would be salvageable if the right *political* choices were made. Although the world's problems have their origin in factors that go much deeper than politics as ordinarily understood—in ideas and in technological developments—the only place that these problems can be effectively addressed is in and through the realm of politics. Politics is the arena in which the philosophical-technological problems that dominate society must be worked out. The knowledge that can help to direct society, however, is not political science but a historical science that comprehends the movement of philosophical ideas and technological developments.

It is in the context of discussing the political situation in the world that Spengler turns his attention to America and Americanism. The entire West, Spengler insisted, is sick. Its sickness derives from a worldview that denies the natural principle of hierarchy (or "race"). All Western isms, beginning originally with rationalism and then following with the political ideologies of liberalism, socialism, pacifism, and Marxism, are based on an insipid egalitarianism: "'Equal rights' are contrary to nature [and] are the beginning of the irrevocable decline of societies. . . . Society rests upon the inequality of men. That is a natural fact. There are strong and weak natures, natures born to lead or not to lead."[43] Of these various egalitarian isms, the two major political models of the day are Bolshevism (Russia) and Americanism (the United States). In a deeper sense, however, these systems are not really alternatives at all but variations on the same theme. "There is an inner relationship," Spengler writes, "between Bolshevism and Americanism." The underlying way of life in both societies derives from materialism: "Life is organized exclusively from the economic side." Neither regime has a concern for man's spiritual side or his nobility, and both have abandoned themselves without understanding to the process of mechanization. "It is the Faustian will-to-power, but translated from organic growth into soulless mechanization," that governs these regimes.[44]

Spengler enunciated here what would become a major theme of modern philosophical thought: differences among traditional political regimes hardly matter, for the real force that shapes life—the real regime of our time—is technology (Technik). This regime takes precedence over the traditional political questions of who rules and for what ends, because the process of technology and the ideas that stand behind it make up the real government of society. The traditional arrangements of governance are merely the facade or superstructure.

Despite the insistence of the propagandists of Americanism and Bolshevism that the two systems are different, Spengler found them to be remarkably similar in their effects. In neither society is man free in any meaningful sense. Both regimes are mass societies that effectively operate as tyrannies: "There is the same dictatorship of public opinion in America as in Russia (it does not matter that it is imposed by society instead of a party) that affects everything that is left in the West to the free option of individuals: flirtation and church-going, shoes and make-up, fashion in dance and novels, thinking, eating, and recreation." Both regimes impose a numbing standardization on life from control centers that operate in the United States through the private economy (the system of trusts) and in Russia through the party (the system of state socialism). These two systems promote essentially the same kind of standardization of marketing and production: "Everything is the same for everyone; there is one recommended type of male and especially female when it comes to a prevailing idea of the body, the clothes, and the mind; any deviation from or criticism of this type arouses general attention, in New York as in Moscow."[45]

Spengler added to this general description some particular observations about America that derived from an analysis of its history and situation. Reiterating the major Hegelian themes, he argued that America lacked a state in any meaningful sense and thus possessed no instrument for forging leadership, political or cultural. Society's energies could not be galvanized, and a genuine community did not exist. Spengler ascribed this statelessness to not only its historical foundation in liberalism but also the absence of any neighbor powerful enough to threaten America's existence. This seemingly fortuitous circumstance adversely affected the American character, which lacked any tragic dimension or depth.[46] Everywhere he looked in America, Spengler found a want of that fatalistic fortitude which for him constituted life's highest virtue.

Whether Spengler saw any practical course of action by which the West could escape collapse is unclear, as it is in all of Spengler's discussions about the future. If there were to be a revival, however, it must come from the vital principle of hierarchy being regenerated in such a way as to confront the challenges of the modern world. Neither Bolshevism nor Americanism was capable, finally, of meeting that challenge. Although both societies were among the most advanced in the world, they lacked the awareness and philosophical competence to master the technological forces of modernity. Indeed, it was in one or both of them that the catastrophe of the modern world would most likely begin to play itself out. Only one country offered a chance for regeneration: Germany. Spengler declared, "Germany is the key country of the world not only because of geographical situation . . . but also because Germans are still young enough to experience world-historical problems, to form them and solve them inwardly."[47] Of course, this regeneration could take place only if Germany itself underwent a profound change and adopted the new principles of a new Reich.

Although the preeminent philosopher of technology and the originator of the postmodern symbol of America was Martin Heidegger, much of what he wrote on these themes was drawn from the works of Oswald Spengler and especially Ernst Jünger. Twice in the early 1930s, Heidegger formed reading groups to study Jünger's major political-philosophical writings of the late Weimar period: the essay "Total Mobilization" (1930) and the best-selling book *The Worker* (1932).[48]

A well-known work on German political thought of this period, Walter Struve's *Elites Against Democracy,* lists Ernst Jünger in the index as having died in 1960. This date sounds plausible when one considers that Jünger was born in 1895 and that his fame as a war hero and a novelist stretches back to the 1920s. But while Jünger seems to be a figure of the first part of this century, as of 1996 (Struve's index notwithstanding) he was not only still very much alive but also still writing and publishing. Jünger's examination of America ceased sometime in the 1930s, when he turned from the political world to the world of insects, where he is known today as a leading specialist in the study of beetles, with more than forty thousand of these creatures reputed to be in his private collection.[49]

Jünger's novels about World War I won him great admiration in conservative and nationalist circles, where he was considered one of the most accomplished writers of the time. He expressed what Walter Benjamin called an aesthetic fascination for the qualities that enable both individuals and nations to wage war. "The essential point," Jünger wrote, "is not what we fight for, but how we fight." This fascination was not, however, built on a romantic idea of a single soldier, standing with sword in hand, but on a "new type of man"—the warrior that could endure modern mechanized warfare in all its terror: "The spirit of material warfare has . . . created men such as the world has never before seen." Such men made up a "new race, embodying total energy, charged with the greatest might, . . . able to overcome, forged of the nature of steel, and adaptable to battle in its most ghastly form."[50]

More than any of the other revolutionary conservatives, Jünger showed that the guiding spirit of this movement was far more revolutionary than conservative in any conventional sense. Jünger's conservatism, if one can use that label, lay in his rejection of the bourgeois and liberal (individualistic) foundation for society coupled with his embrace of a collectivist society based on the idea of the nation and run by an elite. His advocacy of these views, however, had supposedly nothing to do with any personal preference for conservative ideas; it derived instead from an analysis of what was required for a nation to survive in our technological age. Only those societies that can adapt to modern technology—those societies that are totally mobilized from top to bottom—can prevail. In fact, Jünger considered any judgments on the basis of a person's "values" to be mere bourgeois sentimentality. Jünger's literary style certainly illustrates this approach: writing with a clinical realism, he treats his own role as a thinker as a part of the reality of the age, as a single piece in the process of total mobilization.

The new age, according to Jünger, demanded wholesale change. The old society—not just the aristocratic society but the bourgeois era that succeeded it—had to be destroyed to prepare the way for another kind of society. To wage the struggle for existence, a society must prepare itself for war in every element of its organization. Because modern power rested on total production, all of society should be formed on the model of an army, and no member of the upper class, aristocrat or bourgeois, should hold himself aloof from the worker, on whom all else depended. The shape of the future was revealed by America's example in World War I: it lay in a democratic capacity to involve the entire society. This was the aspect of Americanization that Jünger lauded: not the liberal America but the strapping, technological, and fully mobilized democratic America. "In the United States with its democratic constitution," Jünger wrote, "mobilization could be executed with a rigor that was impossible in Prussia, where the vote was based on class. And who can doubt that America, the country lacking 'dilapidated castles [and] basalt columns,' emerged the obvious victor of this war? Its course was already decided not by the degree to which a state was a 'military state,' but by the degree to which it was capable of Total Mobilization."[51]

Jünger saw some of the same virtues in postwar Bolshevism, with its mass planning and mobilization. Indeed, all manner of the modern world's popular movements against the old society of class and hierarchy displayed some signs of a capacity for involvement of the masses: "In Fascism, Bolshevism, Americanism, Zionism, in the movements of colored peoples, progress has made advances that until recently would have seemed unthinkable." These isms, despite their differences, rested on the same fundamental principle. Everywhere in them, "esteem for quantity is increasing: quantity of assent, quantity of public opinion has become the decisive factor in politics." There is thus no real difference between the modern Left and the modern Right. The character of this new order, whatever its specific form, is a regime of mass tyranny: "Even the dream of freedom is disappearing as if under a pincer's iron grasp; the movements of the uniformly molded masses trapped in the snare set by the world-spirit, comprise a great and fearful spectacle." A terrible beauty was born.[52]

No way existed to escape the hard requirements of the new age, and to think otherwise was sheer romanticism: "There is no exit, no turning to the side or going backward."[53] The nations that survive will not only embrace the character of the age but also understand how to master and control it. Bolshevism and Americanism point the way, but they are both ultimately inadequate. They put man under an "empty concept like humanity" and view labor in its material or wage-earning, rather than moral, capacity.[54] This view, finally, must fail. The only real moral unit is a national or organic one, not one created by an intellectual concept; and the only way to mobilize fully the forces of our time—"the machine, the masses, and the worker"—is through a discipline in a new kind of national order. Jünger offered a third way between Communism and Americanism, a way that embraced technology but sought to divorce it from the fatal materialism of these two Enlightenment ideologies. The proposed third way—the German way—would tie technology to the idea of a national community, forging a new ethic of steel and blood that would bring "victory of the soul over the machine."

Jünger's proposed regime can be described as either national socialism or Bolshevism without Marxism.[55] At its core was the worker, commanded from the top and mobilized for continuous struggle. This was the point that drew Jünger to Bolshevism. The worker represented the new man, even the new race of man.[56] (It was perhaps on the basis of this idea of race, founded on a functional rather than a biological or racial category, that Jünger maintained his distance from the Nazis, who very much wanted his support.) Jünger called this society a "worker democracy." It certainly was not a liberal democracy. Its democratic character consisted in the transformation of the whole of civil society into a mass collective army: "The huge image of war as armed combat merges more and more with the vastly expanded image of a gigantic work process. Alongside the armies that meet each other on the battlefields, there arise the new armies of transportation, food, production and the armaments industry—the universal *army* of work."[57]

Important as the conservative revolutionaries were for fashioning the modern symbol of America, other major thinkers in Germany also contributed significantly to its development. At the political center was Max Weber, for he supported a kind of constitutional government, albeit in the dangerous form of *Führer-Demokratie* (leader democracy). It was Weber who added to America the striking and now frequently employed image of the iron cage.[58] One scholar has called the image Weber's "most telling figure of speech," and it is found in the title of at least two recent works of scholarship, sociologist Lawrence Scaff's *Fleeing the Iron Cage* and multicultural historian Ronald Takaki's *Iron Cages*.[59]

The attention given to this image today results in part from a major shift in the interpretation of Weber's work. Weber's thought was originally presented to the English-speaking world under the guidance of the famous sociologist Talcott Parsons, who emphasized empirically tested causal analysis as the core of Weber's thought. But many scholars have recently depicted Weber in a different light, as a "theorist of modernity" whose horizon was defined by the thought of Nietzsche and whose chief concern was the problem of "rational life-conduct" in a lifeless, disenchanted world.[60] This new focus in Weber scholarship has emphasized the parts of Weber's work that have been most influential for symbolic thinking on America. Weber, as is well known, wrote some fine accounts of the workings of the real America, especially his descriptions of the American political parties, which he made after visiting the United States. In general, too, he held a quite positive view of America. But in 1904, before Weber had visited the United States, he published his classic work *The Protestant Ethic and the Spirit of Capitalism,* which introduced his concern with the dilemma of modern man and which portrayed America in a quite different—and symbolic—way.

The Protestant Ethic is in a sense framed by America. It opens with a long quotation from Benjamin Franklin, whose worldview, Weber remarks, "contains what we are looking for in almost classic purity." Franklin's mind-set is taken to be the perfect presentation of the "Protestant ethic" in its secular form, which Weber thought was the driving force in the development of modern capitalism. The passage, which is three pages long, contains vintage Franklin: "time is money"; "money can beget money, and its offspring can beget more"; "the good paymaster is lord of another man's purse."[61] Almost everything that Weber wishes to develop in his thesis on capitalism is illustrated in this passage, to which he returns time and again. The Protestant ethic in its original religious meaning held that all was for the glory of God, not for one's own enjoyment. With the secularization of this view and its displacement onto economic affairs, acquiring money becomes an object of duty, not a means of pleasure; saving becomes more important than consumption; and work becomes a task honored for its own sake. The controlling ideas in this ethic of secularized Protestantism are discipline and a joyless pursuit of duty. Capitalism, in Nietzschean (and Freudian) terms, is built on the repression or the denial of the pleasure principle.

Weber has often been roundly criticized for his reading of Franklin, whose own life can be described as anything but ascetic. Indeed, Franklin had far fewer hangups, sexual and otherwise, than did Weber, who wrote some odd things about sex and who suffered from acute mental disorders. Nor can any serious reader of Franklin fail to notice the irony and playfulness in many of his writings. Weber may be partly excused for his presentation, however, because the passage he cites is not really his own selection, as he indicates in his notes, but is taken from an early scene in Ferdinand Kürnberger's novel *Der Amerikamüde,* a book that Weber characterizes as a "paraphrase of Lenau's impressions of America." In the scene in question a young American schoolboy is forced as a punishment to learn morality from Franklin's passage, which may account for Weber's unsubstantiated claim that this text is "used for school reading in America." More important than such incidental details is the infamous summary Weber gives of this passage: Americans "make tallow out of cattle and money out of men." Again, this conclusion is made not by Weber but by a character in Kürnberger's novel. But Weber appropriates it as a perfect expression of the "philosophy of avarice." By his circuitous route Nikolaus Lenau managed to extract his revenge on America for the bout of depression he suffered during his unhappy stay in Ohio.[62]

As much as Weber's thesis about the rise of capitalism has been debated by sociologists, it actually has remarkably little to do with his famous description of the modern human condition. In the final analysis the argument about the Protestant ethic does no more than prepare the ground for a stunning new image that Weber introduces at the end of his work, literally on the last page. Here we learn that the whole ethos of Protestantism is, or will shortly become, a thing of the past, to be replaced by the era of modern rationalism. "The tremendous cosmos of the modern economic order," Weber writes, "is now bound to the technical and economic conditions of machine production which today determine the lives of individuals who were born into this mechanism, with irresistible force, including those not directly concerned with economic acquisition." This is the "iron cage," which succeeds capitalism and, being a "mechanism," is controlled not by an internal human motivation but an external force. This "cage of the future" is found in its fullest form in America, "where the pursuit of wealth, stripped of its religious and ethical meaning, tends to become associated with purely mundane passions, which actually often give it the character of sport."[63]

Weber then offers his famous summary judgment on life in the cage: "For the 'last men' at this stage of cultural development, it might well be truly said: 'Specialists without spirit, sensualists without heart; this nullity imagines that it has attained a level of civilization never before achieved.'"[64] Weber depicts a cold world where the process of rationality has ended in a system that no one controls, a system that controls us. The means have become the end. This bleak result is what Weber calls the "fate of our time." One might just as well call it the end of history—it is certainly the end of history inside the Enlightenment—except that Weber leaves open the possibility of change by the intervention of a "new prophet."[65]

It would be hard to overestimate the influence of the metaphor of the iron cage in modern thought. Oddly enough, however, its power in the English-speaking world is the result of an accident, for "iron cage" is a mistranslation of *stahlhartes Gehäuse,* a phrase that should be rendered as "steel encasement."[66] This poetic mistranslation is the product of Talcott Parsons, who made every effort to portray

Weber as a positivist and system builder rather than a cultural philosopher brooding over the fate of modernity. Parsons even went so far as to omit Weber's mention of "last men" in the passage cited above.[67] Nevertheless, by his translation of "iron cage," Parsons helped to call far more attention to the conclusion of *The Protestant Ethic* than it would otherwise have received (or than it has received in Germany). Although the metaphor of the cage has been ignored by the positivists in sociology (the "fate of our time" is a difficult variable to operationalize), it is nonetheless a radically "sociological" interpretation of our condition: the cage is more important than any political regime in structuring social life and provides the key to understanding the deepest social reality. It is this image or idea, associated with America, that governs us.

By the third decade of the twentieth century, the symbol of America in German thought—and German thought has served as the foundation for modern philosophical thought—began to assume the quality of pure abstraction. Americanism came to represent modernism in its most advanced, and usually most grotesque, form. The only dispute seemed to be between those who thought Americanism should be condemned for its destruction of culture and rootedness and those who, dismissing such value judgments as outmoded personalism, saw Americanism as the blind force of modernity that had brought "progress" to its most advanced point—a point at which it had to go beyond anything American in order to survive.

To ordinary Americans concerned with the fate of their country, the transformation of America from a nation and a political regime into a metaphysical category representing modernity may seem cause for relief. For what, or how much, does "America" so conceived any longer have to do with the real America? It is now, it would seem, only a neutral term of development, affecting all the world. Alas, to escape the effects of the symbolic America on this ground is impossible. The expansion of the symbol from a country to a stage of historical development does not eliminate the focus on America but only emphasizes it all the more. Under the enlarged symbol, we live in the regime of modernity—a cage called America—and all of political life has been subsumed under the force of an inevitable movement of history. Here truly is a constitution that depends on "accident and force," not on "reflection and choice." The symbolic America is not just beyond all hope; it is beyond all guidance.

8

★ ★ ★

Katastrophenhaft:
Martin Heidegger's America

No thinker in this century has had greater influence on the development of the idea of America than Martin Heidegger. Although he borrowed much from his predecessors in Germany, particularly Spengler and Jünger, Heidegger went well beyond any of them in fashioning a symbol that has ever since connected the themes of desolation, horror, and homelessness to America. With Heidegger, America was transformed from a country to a major literary and philosophic category that intellectuals have since been unable to ignore.

The importance of Heidegger's legacy in shaping modern thinking about America derives from two facts. First, as the most acclaimed philosopher of the twentieth century, he has had a profound effect on almost all the nonpositivistic disciplines, from philosophy to art to literary criticism. In political thought, Heidegger, who was an active supporter of German National Socialism in the early 1930s, has left an imprint not only on the thinking of the far Right but even more on that of the Left, in the form of existentialism, a strain of Marxism, postmodernism, and ecology.[1] Second, Heidegger gave a prominent role to America in his writings, a fact about which English-speaking readers will become increasingly aware as more of his texts are translated. America for Heidegger is the symbol of the crisis of our age, which is also the deepest crisis of all time. America represents the greatest alienation of man, his profoundest loss of authenticity, and his furthest distance from Being. America thus stands as the supreme impediment to spiritual reawakening. It must be overcome or destroyed if any kind of renewal is to take place.

My purpose is not to suggest anything so absurd as that Heidegger's thought can be reduced to a fit of anti-Americanism. His elaboration of America must be considered in terms of how it functions inside his overall philosophy, in which it becomes readily apparent that certain symbolic dimensions of America can be separated from the real, geographic place. It would nevertheless be an error to suppose that Heidegger ever wished to completely decouple the two. Heidegger, more than any other modern philosopher, is known for the attention he paid to language and its effects. Revelations of reality, he tells us, often come through poetry or the poetic use of language: "Poetic composition is truer than exploration of beings."[2] Poetry for Heidegger relies on the resonance that attaches to particular things. America, as a particular thing, carries the full weight of his poetic discourse. It would stretch credulity, therefore, to think that he could have employed this symbol without being conscious of its impact, both cultural and political. America in Heidegger's thought designates not only a way of life, but also the political form of liberal democracy. Heidegger's philosophy includes a treatment, albeit an unusual one, of alternative political systems in which America (liberal democracy) occupies a conspicuously low place.

A well-known Heideggerian theme is that the beginnings of concepts fix their essential meaning and establish their subsequent power over human thinking. Special attention should therefore be given to Heidegger's own first use of the symbol of America, which occurred in a series of lectures he gave in 1935 and published in 1953 under the title *An Introduction to Metaphysics*. In contrast to many of Heidegger's other writings, where the reader must work hard to follow the argument, the passage in which he first refers to America is highly accessible. One does not need a background in philosophy to grasp the basic meaning of Heidegger's America, and it is a striking image, especially when one imagines how it must have been understood in the Germany of 1935 or, for that matter, of 1953. The following long passage vividly illustrates the point:

> This Europe, in its ruinous blindness forever on the point of cutting its own throat, lies today in a great pincer, squeezed between Russia on one side and America on the other. From a metaphysical point of view, Russia and America are the same, with the same dreary technological frenzy and the same unrestricted organization of the average man. . . .
>
> We have said: Europe lies in a pincer between Russia and America, which are metaphysically the same, namely in regard to their world character and their relation to the spirit. What makes the situation of Europe all the more catastrophic is that this enfeeblement of the spirit originated in Europe itself and—though prepared by earlier factors—was definitively determined by its own spiritual situation in the first half of the nineteenth century. . . . The lives of men began to slide into a world which lacked the depth from out of which the essential always comes to man and comes back to man, so compelling him to become superior and making

him act in conformity to a rank. All things sank to the same level, a surface resembling a blind mirror that no longer reflects, that casts nothing back. The prevailing dimension became that of extension and number. Intelligence no longer meant a wealth of talent, lavishly spent, and the command of energies, but only what could be learned by everyone, the practice of a routine, always associated with a certain amount of sweat and a certain amount of show. In America and in Russia this development grew into a boundless etcetera of indifference and always-the-sameness—so much so that the quantity took on a quality of its own. Since then the domination in those countries of a cross section of the indifferent mass has become something more than a dreary accident. It has become an active onslaught that destroys all rank and every world-creating impulse of the spirit and calls it a lie. This is the onslaught of what we call the demonic (in the sense of destructive evil).[3]

So impressive is this image of America that one can only conclude that Heidegger must have wished to construct a powerful new symbol. It is true, of course, that at this point, in 1935, he spoke of two nations embodying the two main variants of the modern situation: America and Russia. For Heidegger, these two variants were essentially the same. Americanism and Bolshevism both applied indiscriminately the driving principle of modernity, technology; both were shaped by that principle; and both were utterly oblivious of the ground on which the principle rested. Yet, although Heidegger would continue after 1935 to note the essential "metaphysical" similarity of these two nations and regimes, America emerged as the sole symbol of modernity and of its crisis. Americanism, he wrote in 1942, is the purest form of modernity: "Bolshevism is only a variant of Americanism." Americanism is the "most dangerous shape of boundlessness, because it appears in the form of a democratic middle-class way of life mixed with Christianity, and all this in an atmosphere that lacks completely any sense of history."[4]

After World War II, Heidegger spoke less about specific countries. When he did so, however, his references to the nation that represented the age of technology were usually to America. Moreover, it was in America, not in the Soviet Union, that a confident scientism ("logistics" or "cybernetics") dominated philosophical thought and made impossible any chance of a spiritual reawakening. The point here is not that he believed the Soviet Union was more successful than America, but (if anything) the opposite. America, as the foremost embodiment of technologism, emerged as the greatest carrier—and symptom—of the crisis of modernity. In a *Letter on Humanism* (1948), another of his most accessible writings, Heidegger drew a further distinction between Americanism on one hand and Marxism and Communism on the other—again to the detriment of America. Americanism, he pointed out, is trivialized as an idea if it is viewed as merely representing a lifestyle. Americanism is something much deeper: it is a way of thinking about reality that most fully embodies the mindset of the modern age. With Marxism there is at least the prospect of having a "productive dialogue" on our situation, largely because of Marx's appreciation, through Hegel, of a sense of history.[5] But Heidegger never mentions the possibility of a dialogue with America's founders or with any strain of liberal thought. Such a dialogue was evidently out of the question. For this reason again, America trumps the Soviet Union as *the* symbol of the modern crisis.

Only one statement in Heidegger's work appears to contradict the idea of the essential equivalence of the two regimes, but it is easily accounted for. In a 1948 letter to his former student Herbert Marcuse, Heidegger explains his support for National Socialism in 1933 and notes that at the time he had expected from National Socialism a "spiritual renewal of life in its entirety, a reconciliation of social antagonisms and a deliverance of Western man [*Dasein*] from the dangers of communism." Although from this comment one might construe Communism as representing the greatest threat to a spiritual renewal, a more accurate reading is that in 1933, Heidegger (along with a majority of German intellectuals) believed that the only real choice in Germany was between Communism and National Socialism, liberal democracy at that time having been totally discredited.[6]

In view of Heidegger's highly rhetorical use of America, it seems reasonable to pursue an interpretive strategy that expands examination of America's symbolic resonance to passages in which America is not explicitly mentioned but only evoked. Each time after 1935 that Heidegger refers, for example, to the dominance of technology or consumerism, one may make a connection to America and assume that other readers will also make—were, indeed, intended to make—that connection. (In fact, Heidegger in these contexts often does mention America, although he perhaps became more circumspect after the war.) It is even reasonable, I would argue, to project the symbol of America back into parts of Heidegger's earlier thought, where the images he created parallel descriptions of what later became America. This approach would be most relevant to the well-known section of *Being and Time* (1927) that elaborates the theme of "mass man" or "collective man" (*Das Man*). This passage strongly influenced a variety of later Continental writings about America, from Herbert Marcuse's *One-Dimensional Man* to Jean Baudrillard's *America*.[7]

America functions as a major theme in Heidegger's account of the history of Western philosophical thought (*Seinsgeschichte*). History here is divided into different epochs defined by the relations that man has to Being. The history of Western thought since Plato has been a working out or unfolding of Plato's original understanding of reality. From this beginning, which is to say from the origination of metaphysics, reality or Being has been interpreted in a partial or incomplete way. It has been understood as ideas or as objects that could be fully apprehended by man's thought, not as things having a mysterious power of revealing or disclosing themselves to us. Prefigured in this classical metaphysical view, Heidegger contends, was already a certain attitude toward reality: everything is or exists first and foremost as an object for our domination and use.

This attitude did not immediately manifest itself; instead, it remained hidden as a kernel inside a mode of thinking and a language that still retained many elements of an older, premetaphysical view. In the older view reality was more mysterious in the way it opened itself and came into the presence of man. The unfolding of the full implications of the newer, metaphysical view proceeded in stages and took much time. It was greatly advanced by the translation of metaphysical terms from Greek into Latin, which then became the standard language of metaphysical discourse. Greek had the property of bringing man closer to the particular character and quality of things, of creating poetic resonances with the hidden aspect of reality. Latin, in contrast, had a more abstract and surface quality, which strengthened the objective view of reality. Moreover, contrary to what one might have thought, the emergence of Christianity in no way reversed this process. Christian theology adopted and intensified the essential modes of metaphysical thinking, and it also employed Latin to express them. Christianity thus further developed the Western metaphysical view, preparing the way for the next step.

The decisive moment in the unfolding of the utilitarian implications of Western metaphysics came with the advent of modern physics and mathematics in the seventeenth century, and particularly with the work of René Descartes. Although the modern scientific mode of thinking in one sense overturns classical metaphysics, in a more basic sense it continues the metaphysical tradition and develops its implications. Heidegger therefore emphasizes the similarities rather than the conflicts between classical metaphysics and modern science. The major discontinuity he sees in Western thought is between the pre- and post-Socratic thinkers, not between classical metaphysics and modern science.

Under the sway of modern physics and mathematics, man, who is the thinking subject, conceives reality as an object meant for man's use; or, to be more precise, he conceives reality as a series of ideas or categories that he has deliberately constructed and projected onto the world. Because man constructs and projects these categories onto the world, this process is often referred to, both accurately and misleadingly, as subjectivism. Heidegger clarifies this paradox. The goal of this deliberate representation, or subjectivism, is an extreme kind of objectification: to control and use the material universe. Heidegger thus shows that subjectivity (man making things according to his own representation), far from being the antithesis of the modern scientific view, is its core: "Today's society is only modern subjectivity made absolute."[8]

The current stage of the history of thought is the age of technology. It brings the scientific (or metaphysical) view to completion, which is why Heidegger also calls it the age of the "end of philosophy" or the "end of metaphysics." Here "end" means not just the final stage temporally but a completion of the essential core of what is contained in philosophic or metaphysical thinking; no further step of any importance can be taken.[9] Technology in its concrete manifestation confronts us as a set of material facts: machines, modes of organization, and systems of communication. But in a deeper sense, technology inheres less in any material fact than in a way of thinking about the world, which itself is a product of how man conceives of the world. Reality (Being) consists of things or beings—calculable entities—that we seek to control ("command") for our own use. As a result of modern, seventeenth-century philosophy, reality is conceived as forces ("standing reserve" or "raw material") and "nature now becomes a gigantic gasoline station, an energy source for modern technology and industry."[10] Technology creates consequences that determine the way of life in modern times and is the decisive factor, the controlling regime, that governs the modern world, not just in the realm of scientific and technical matters but also in the realms we classify as culture and politics. Technology or completed metaphysics includes "nature in its objectified image, culture maintained in motion, directed politics, and constructed ideals." Man is the agent who ushered in the technological way of thought, but technology has now become his master: "Man does not have technology under control; rather, man is its play thing."[11]

The way of life most characteristic of the age of technology is captured by the symbol of America (or Americanization). America embodies all the effects of the rule of technology over production, culture, and politics. The material things themselves are less important than a way of "calculative thinking" that reckons everything in quantitative terms and that represents the culmination of metaphysical thought. Here Heidegger offers the closest thing to a definition of Americanism: "The primacy of sheer quantity is itself a quality, i.e., an essential characteristic, which is that of boundlessness. This is the principle we call Americanism." American thinking is characterized by total unawareness of and complete indifference to the question of man's encounter with Being. In America prevails a mode of thought that Heidegger calls *Logistik* (logistics), which purports to take the place of the deepest kind of thinking: "In many places, above all in Anglo-Saxon countries, logistics is today considered the only possible form of strict philosophy, because its result and procedures yield an assured profit for the construction of the technological universe. In America and elsewhere, logistics as the only proper philosophy of the future is thus beginning today to seize power over the spirit."[12]

The triumph of logistical thinking in America spells the end of any intellectual depth or spiritual awareness: "Logistics is the calculative organization of absolute ignorance over the essence of thinking." America is the place where what claims to be thought makes real thought impossible: "[Americans] are still bound up in a way of thinking, viz., pragmatism, that furthers control and manipulation, but which at the same time blocks the way to a serious consideration of the particular properties of modern technology."[13] The worst part of this situation is not the failure to pose the question of Being but the confident belief that this question is in fact being posed and answered. Americans are oblivious to their situation. Inured to their homelessness, they feel no need for a home: "Man today is in flight from thinking. . . . But part of this flight is that man will neither see nor admit it. He will say—and quite rightly—that there were at no time such far-reaching plans, so many inquiries in so many areas, research carried on as passionately as today."[14]

The Catastrophe of No Catastrophe

Heidegger identifies the current age as the one in which man has moved furthest away from a genuine encounter with Being and in which he has all but lost any awareness of that loss. Our time is an age of crisis, and we stand on the verge of catastrophe. But what is it, Heidegger asks, that constitutes a genuine catastrophe? He takes up some of the usual meanings or scenarios, noting the possibility of technical scientific developments leading to the depletion of such traditional energy sources as coal, oil, and timber. But he then appears to dismiss these scenarios, arguing (to use Spengler's terminology) that man is sufficiently Faustian to continue his technological development whatever the result. Man will discover new kinds of energy that will dispense with the need of renewable sources (Heidegger had atomic power in mind).[15] Heidegger has full "confidence," if one can use that word, in man's capacity to make the physical world serve his projected purposes: "The earth and the atmosphere become mere raw material."[16]

Heidegger next discusses a more radical kind of scientific development in the field of biophysics or human genetic engineering. Man now views himself as an object of production, as raw material. Man makes man: "Man can be produced in accordance with some determined end, just like the making of any other technical object." When man develops "factories for artificial breeding of human material," he will then have it in his power to produce a new human type and to create a new form of nationalism based on this biological construction rather than on, for example, ethnicity. Technology commands us not only in the realms of applied science but also in the political and cultural realms. It leads to political systems of total planning, a world economy, a world communication system, and the formation of a world public opinion. Although Heidegger does not necessarily foresee a single world state in the strict sense that all people would live under the control of one sovereign entity, all the advanced forms of government are subject to the same imperative, which is the transformation of everything into the uniform and calculable. In this sense, all mankind falls under the control of one order or regime. Ours is the age of the hegemony of technology.[17]

The existence of different sovereign political entities means that conflict and war remain possibilities in the modern world. With the onset of the Cold War, Heidegger observed that a preoccupation with planning for war had become a characteristic of our age and that the difference between war and genuine peace was no longer clear. World War II "eventuated not in a peace of a traditional kind, but rather in a condition in which warlike characteristics are no longer experienced as such at all, and peaceful characteristics have become meaningless and without content."[18] The world wars settled nothing essential but only hastened the completion of nihilism and confirmed Jünger's thesis of a world of total mobilization.[19] America is completely caught up in this destiny, with its current reality characterized by the "collusion of industry and the military, with the economic development and equipment that it requires."[20]

The annihilation of man through nuclear war therefore remains a distinct possibility, yet even this is not the catastrophe Heidegger has in mind. The real catastrophe, in the ordinary meaning of the term, is no catastrophe at all. It will occur when the "danger of a third world war has been removed [and when] . . . calculative thinking comes to be accepted and practiced as the only way of thinking." We would then have entered into an age of "total thoughtlessness" in which "man would have denied and thrown away his own special nature [as a] meditative being."[21] We would then be witnessing the physical survival of a creature who resembles man but who would no longer be man. Man ceases to be human in either or both of two ways: when he will have changed biologically and become a new species, or when he will have reached the reign of "total thoughtlessness" wherein all human intelligence, as calculative thinking, exists solely to serve the animal or the instinctual. This moment is reached when the "impulse of animality and the *ratio* of humanity become identical."[22] A combination of these two developments—a fabricated being programmed to serve the instinctual—marks the outer limit of technology. America is the land of the living dead.

The "real catastrophe" of humanity has its analogue in man's relation to nature. Technology does not fail us, in the sense that it depletes all resources. Rather, it fails us by succeeding: "Everything is functioning. This is exactly what is so uncanny, that everything is functioning and that the functioning drives us more and more to even further functioning, and that technology tears men loose from the earth and uproots them."[23] Technology destroys a genuine encounter with nature. After the first space probes, Heidegger commented that "there is no longer either 'earth' or 'heaven,' in the sense of the poetic dwelling of man on this earth."[24]

Today some view Martin Heidegger as a kind of antitechnological romantic who stands Spengler and Jünger on their heads. Without question, his lament at the loss of nature (earth and heaven) and his account of the frightening effects of technological dominance have helped to inspire a modern strand of antitechnological ecologism.[25] But Heidegger objected to such a characterization: "I have never spoken against technology or against the so-called demonic in technology. Rather I am trying to understand the essence of technology."[26] He sometimes spoke of getting technology under control, an idea that might have included the use of technological methods for serving simpler or more environmentally friendly ends (another strand of the modern ecological movement). In a larger sense, however, he insisted that to ask whether he was for or against technology, as if his personal tastes or preferences could change things, was beside the point. The age of technology is our fate. What, if anything, can be done about it is part of a much broader inquiry into what, if anything, thinking itself, including Heidegger's own thinking, can do for mankind.

The real catastrophe that awaits us is not one brought about by the scarcity of material goods. The real catastrophe is man's spiritual extinction and the elimination of nature, including the possible change of man's nature through biological engineering. This is already at hand in America, the site of catastrophe.[27]

The spiritual emptiness Heidegger saw in America is captured in an anecdote told by Heidegger's confidant and chronicler, Heinrich Petzet. Once, after World War II, Heidegger and his circle of friends had gathered together, and the discussion turned toward America. The tenor was one of bemused contempt, with everyone enjoying a good laugh at the account told by one of the group's members, who had been asked by a jovial, back-slapping American college president to tell "all about Mr. Heidegger—in five minutes." Heidegger then inquired about Americans' posture toward death. Upon learning of some of the "repulsive customs" for dying and burial that were common among the well-off—the embalming, the makeup, and the like—Heidegger fell silent, convinced, as Petzet describes it, that the "American attitude toward death . . . was at the same time a revelation of American life."[28]

The Symbolic America

Among all the modern thinkers, Heidegger draws the bleakest picture of America. At the same time, in at least some of his formulations, his America is the least American of all the representations. "Americanism," in one of his definitions, is "something European. It is the not yet fully understood variant of the still unfolding and not yet full or completed metaphysical essence of the emerging monstrousness of modern times."[29] Americanism is not something born on the rocky shores of Massachusetts and nurtured on the broad plains of Kansas. It represents a working out of modern European thought; or, tracing matters back all the way to their origin, it is the culmination of the entire Western metaphysical tradition. The founder of America is not Publius, but Plato; it was refounded not by Lincoln, but by Leibniz.

The "place" of America in Heidegger's thought is less geographical than temporal. America is a moment in history; it is the spatial manifestation of the temporal fact of the "darkening of the world" and the "forgetting of Being" that is the characteristic of our age. Our age is the "final state" (*Endzustand*) of the development of the West, which eventually becomes the developed world as a whole, Asia included. Yet if Heidegger sometimes de-Americanizes America, it seems only to be a part of a larger strategy. For had he wished to separate the symbolic America from the real America, he could have dropped the symbol and relied on his two developmental terms for the modern era: the "Way of Technology" and his neologism *Ge-Stell* (construct or enframing). In fact, however, he goes in the opposite direction and Americanizes these concepts. The Way of Technology and Ge-Stell take on concrete meaning by their association with America. As proof that modern man has reached the final state, Heidegger offers as evidence any "encounter in a discussion with Americans"; when one speaks to them about the fate of mankind in our age, "they do not even know where they are."[30]

While linking his picture of catastrophe to a nation, Heidegger also evokes many of the emotions that exist on the level of nations confronting each other in the real world. Why he wishes to maintain these particularistic and even primal associations can better be answered after surveying the characteristics he assigns to America. First, Americanization represents the transformation of language into nonlanguage. This transformation largely results from the flatness or thinness of mass communications. Modern technology enables information (including news) to flow faster and faster, but when it reaches people it is out of any context or grounding in authentic experience: "Any incident whatever, regardless of where and when it occurs, can be communicated to the rest of the world at any desired speed, . . . [and] the assassination of a king in France and a symphony concert in Tokyo can be 'experienced' simultaneously."[31] The circulation of information is accordingly either leveling or without meaning.

Information has a fundamental relation to the age of technology. Far from being merely neutral, information already contains within itself the technological orientation of man's plan to dominate the world: "The key word for this fundamental attitude of contemporary man goes by the name: information. We must understand that word in its American-English sense. . . . Information as a message is also already an arrangement which puts before mankind all objects and material in a form that suffices, in order to secure man's dominion over the whole earth and even over that which is beyond it."[32] Information is thus itself a kind of "language," but one that destroys all the possibilities connected with the deeper function of language, foreclosing any chance that language can disclose a genuine encounter with Being: "Language today, just like everything else we use daily, is merely an instrument, an instrument for the acquisition of information. . . . Information dominates the public mind, so much so that we can scarcely even realize its worrisome power."[33] Projecting this point onto the contemporary scene, one could say that the scientific mode for the communication of information is computer language, as expressed in pidgin American; the political mode is the news, as broadcast by CNN; the entertainment mode is the movies or television serials, as created in Hollywood; and the commercial mode is advertisement, as developed by Madison Avenue.

The name that Heidegger gives to the modern language of information and technical communication is "American" (or sometimes "English-American"). American is the foreign language that people learn today in order to communicate for purposes of business and science. In another (and metaphorical) sense, however, "American" is the name Heidegger gives to the deformation of all the advanced languages. It changes language from its poetic function as a medium able to capture the particular and the distinctive into a bland vehicle for technical communication, no matter what the supposed language (French, German, Italian) one happens to be speaking. "Our language is 'German,'" Heidegger writes, "but we actually talk 'American.'"[34] American is the enemy from within, the name for that which is slowly destroying what remains of the German language and the German nation.

The transformation of language into American is nothing short of a disaster. Language, for Heidegger, is the "house of Being," the means by which we grasp our world, "that alone which gives us an access and passage to all will to think."[35] The deformation of language accordingly goes hand in hand with a deformation of thought. To be able to think meditatively, one must be able to use language poetically, in a way that sinks roots into something particular. In American this is impossible. American stands for the triumph of the uniform over the particular.

Second, Americanism represents consumerism, which is more than a mere desire for material ease or security. Consumerism embodies a fundamental attitude toward reality. In modern technological society, life is characterized by the "reign of the ersatz": "Everything is replaceable, in a game in which everything can take the place of everything else." Consumerism is the expression of this attitude in relation to the things around us. We replace goods not because they are worn out or defective but because we value them only temporarily, until something new can be had to take their place: "Being today means being-replaceable." Consumerism's frenzied undertone, which we reveal in our continual dissatisfaction with objects and our yearning for their replacement, is symptomatic of a void in our lives: "The emptiness of Being can never be filled up by the fullness of beings (things), especially when this emptiness can never be experienced as such." Modern society is based on economic production that is ever more rational but at the same time ever more aimless: "Consumption for the sake of consumption is the sole procedure that distinctively characterizes the history of a world that has become an unworld."[36]

The false or artificial in modern consumption (the ersatz) is characteristic of America, although the American element (technology) has long been inside Europe. "Not the American way of life alone threatens us today," Heidegger tells us, "but already the way of technology threatened our ancestors and their things."[37] Heidegger quotes a letter from Rainer Maria Rilke, where Rilke speaks of the American way of life in which all products have lost their connection with anything real or human: "Still for our grandparents was a 'house,' a 'well,' a familiar tower, even their own pieces of clothing, something intimate and meaningful for them. . . . Now is emerging, from out of America, pure undifferentiated things, mere things of appearance, sham articles. . . . A house, in the American understanding, an American apple or an American vine has nothing in common with the house, the fruit, or the grape that had been adopted in the hopes and thoughts of our forefathers." Rilke's statement, which antedated by a half-century the availability of plastic fruits from K-Mart, emphasizes the homogeneity of mass-produced items in America and the standardization of its culture. Rilke also anticipated Heidegger's central metaphors of home and homelessness. In modern society, Heidegger comments, we find "constructed lodgings and urban concentrations . . . but no longer a home."[38] Homelessness represents the spiritual condition of modernity, exemplified in the character of the American way of life.

Third, America is the place where philosophical development has moved furthest toward specialization. This parceling of knowledge into different domains reflects the governing idea that knowledge exists for mastering reality and making objects calculable. Each discipline is assigned its own area and objects to study and discover how to use or control. Man himself is treated as such an object, not only in biology but also in psychology and economics: "We will soon be able to read in tables and charts what the Americans have already sought for decades in the field of psychology: the establishment of what man is and how he can most efficiently, without loss of time and energy, be brought into a position of most effective use." This understanding of man is part of what Heidegger calls "American pseudo-philosophy" (*Scheinphilosophie*), which had come to dominate American universities and was increasingly being copied by German science, as if American thought "had already established the truth about man." Like consumerism, however, American science is a deformation, leading us away from genuine thought and toward the situation of homelessness or the "dead end" (*Ausweglosikeit*).[39]

Finally, America symbolizes the ahistorical, the incapacity to be situated meaningfully in time. The relation of ahistorical man to time parallels the relation of the consumer to things. Homelessness is the metaphor that connects these two senses. To be homeless is to have no place, either in a physical dwelling or inside a genuine tradition. The absence of a sense of history results in an attitude in which nothing is viewed as permanent and in which nothing exists to be transmitted or handed down. Persons in the sway of this posture live in a perpetual present; the only permanent condition is a continual quest for the "always new of permanent change": "The past can no longer exist, unless it is in the form of that which is considered to be outmoded (and thus in a sense a nullity or a non-occurrence)."[40]

The absence of a historical sense is even more damaging to the collective or the public than it is to the individual. A shared history is what makes a group of persons into a larger whole—into a people (*Volk*). Without a history, there can be no people.[41] America, in its blindness to history, is a collectivity of persons that is not a people. America is a monstrous nonbeing, thoughtlessly stumbling about and trying to annihilate what it cannot understand. America's entrance into World War II is part of that blindness: "We know today that the Anglo-Saxon world of Americanism is resolved to destroy Europe, which is to say the homeland, which is to say the origin of the West. . . . The entry of America into this world war is not an entry into history, but is already the last American act of American absence of historical sense and of self-devastation."[42] America, spiritually representing the absence of the historical sense, is waging war on the historical sense. America is now the enemy of Germany and, through Germany, of Europe and of all that is worthwhile in the West.

The references to America in the preceding paragraph appear in a series of commentaries that Heidegger wrote during World War II on the works of the German poet Friedrich Hölderlin, whom Heidegger considered to be the "poet of all poets."[43] It may seem strange that these passages on America should appear in a discussion of a poet from the last century who never mentioned America. Yet, as many scholars have recently observed, Heidegger's poetic commentaries are the most political of all his works, if by "political" we understand a discourse aimed at altering the ground of thinking as a way of ultimately changing the ground of politics as well.[44] In these commentaries the political realm is synonymous with a people's spiritual-cultural mission that is articulated by the poets. There is a "Greek-German mission" in the world, an appreciation for which constitutes "'politics' in the highest and most authentic sense."[45] In and through the efforts of its poets (and now, presumably, commentators on poetry), Germany must seize for itself a genuine meaning: "The planet is in flames. . . . Only from the Germans can come the world-historical reflection, provided that they find and preserve their German element."[46]

Heidegger here is developing a new mode of poetic-philosophical discourse that replaces his more direct political-philosophical discourse of the early 1930s.[47] In this new mode, he creates a historical narrative or mythology that focuses on the dichotomy of home and homelessness. On one hand, there is the home or homeland, Germany, which is joined to the "fire" of pre-Socratic Greece and to the spirit of "originary" or first thinking, which is connected to the poetic and to the rooted, which in turn is linked to the capacity of a people to seize and make a destiny for itself. On the other hand, there is homelessness and uprootedness, which is linked to the absence of the poetic and of any genuine encounter with the historical, which in turn is connected to America. The confrontation between Germany and America is nothing less than the struggle over the soul of humanity—indeed, over whether humanity will even have a soul.

This contest is taking place not only between nations but inside Germany as well, where the real German soul is being threatened by the growing influence of Americanism. To prevail, Germany must have recourse to poetry and the poetic. Only the poet can ground and authenticate a people in the fatherland. The true poet

engages in this task not according to the romantic idea of creating by and for himself *ex nihilo,* but according to a deeper searching and listening. In this listening,
the poet discovers the nation's real historical destiny. Heidegger cites Hölderlin:
"We are nothing; what we strive for is everything." Striving in this poetic sense is
made almost impossible under the reigning influence of the American understanding of the world: "Where the sought after becomes a mere object for discovery, it is then already something for the museum and thus something that is given
up and lost—an object for Americans. The surrender of the German essence to
Americanism has already gone so far as on occasion to produce the disastrous effect that Germany actually feels herself ashamed that her people were once considered to be 'the people of poetry and thought.'"[48]

But Heidegger does not foreclose all chance of renewal, speaking instead of the
possibility that "fate" may send a saving "happening" or "event." Yet even then
Germany may not be in a position to see or accept it, so much has its soul been corrupted by Americanism: "Even then no one will pay attention to the Happening,
as long as 'poetry and thought' are merely considered as things of 'culture' and as
long as culture is merely considered as something for entertainment and edifica-
tion—things in which the 'Americans' for decades have been the exemplars." If
Germany is to be able to receive the happening, it must reject the American model,
pushing it back, as Heidegger says, to the other "hemisphere."[49]

In Martin Heidegger's America we find a restatement, with some refinements
and curious reversals, of the themes of the eighteenth-century European natural
historians. For the Count de Buffon and Cornelius de Pauw, America represented
the extreme form of degeneracy, where everything becomes physically deformed.
For Heidegger, the degeneracy is no less marked, although it is spiritual rather than
biological, at least until the point where Americans begin their genetic transformation of plants, animals, and finally themselves. The deformation Heidegger depicts also assumes a different form. For Buffon and de Pauw, it consisted in a corruption into a smaller size, where everything becomes shriveled and stunted; for
Heidegger, it is a distortion in the direction of the mass, the uniform, the monstrous, and the grotesque.

I leave it to literary theorists, who are experts in the matter of symbols, to pon-
der the significance of this change of imagery. No doubt they can detect layers of
meaning that escape the ordinary political analyst. I will confine myself only to
the surface observation that this change bespeaks a shift from an attitude of contempt to one dominated by fear. The Third Reich, in this version, cannot ignore
America. In one respect, is this not a fulfillment of Publius' hope to humble the
"arrogant pretensions of the European . . . and teach that assuming brother mod-

eration"? Even more, is it not a vindication of political science and its effort, in behalf of the real "origin of the West," to save mankind from one of its worst despotisms?

The Spiritual Crisis: Is There a Way Out?

Heidegger's account of history presents an inexorable movement that culminates in the present crisis of the modern age. Is there, however, no escaping this fate, or no epoch in history beyond the present one? Did Heidegger see no role either for a political movement or for philosophy in promoting a reawakening? These questions have preoccupied popular intellectual commentary on Heidegger's thought and dominated the two important interviews he gave in his later years.[50] Any serious effort to understand his response must take account of the symbolic America and how it functions in his system.

America for Heidegger operates on two different levels: on one, it serves as the sign of liberal democracy in an analysis of alternative political regimes; on the other, it is a rhetorical device, in a new political-cultural discourse, that is designed to repulse the reader and thereby help to promote a spiritual reawakening. These two uses of America correspond to the two basic modes of thought that have been identified in Heidegger's political philosophy. One mode is referred to as voluntaristic, metaphysical, or self-assertive; the other is described as anti-, non-, or postmetaphysical, or as a posture characterized by "tranquil detachment" or "releasement."

There is in Heidegger scholarship a great controversy about the status of these two modes of thought. According to one group, which includes Jacques Derrida and Hannah Arendt, these modes capture a decisive discontinuity between an earlier period, which culminated in Heidegger's active political engagement in behalf of the Nazis in 1933–1934, and a later period that began just thereafter, when he abandoned political involvement and any idea that thought could construct reality.[51] In this interpretation we have, as it were, an early, "bad" Heidegger, who tried to play a direct political role, and a later, "good" Heidegger who moved beyond this to a more detached, postmodern stance. Other scholars dismiss this idea of a significant change of direction. As Jürgen Habermas observed in 1953, "The appeal changes, but the structures of meaning preserve their continuity over the decades of his development."[52] In this view, Heidegger's voluntaristic mode can be found in the later period as well as in the early 1930s. The apparent shift to a more antimetaphysical mode in the later period was no more than a tactical move, begun by Heidegger himself and continued by his partisans, to sanitize his involvement with Nazism and to prepare for a rebuilding of his reputation after the Allied victory.

It is sufficient here, without entering into this controversy, to outline the two modes of thought in order to indicate how America operates inside each one. Heidegger's voluntaristic or metaphysical mode, in which he emphasized an important role for political action, culminated during the period when he served as rector of the University of Freiburg and actively supported the Nazis. At this time he thought that a political program, guided by thought or philosophy, could lead the way to a spiritual reawakening. Heidegger would himself lead that reawakening, both by transforming the university's mission and plan of study and by influencing the political direction of National Socialism. His hope, as one German commentator has described it, was "den Führer führen" (to lead the Führer).[53] In 1933 Heidegger delivered a speech that illustrates his activist posture: "University study must again become a risk, not a refuge for the cowardly. . . . The new courage must accustom itself to steadfastness, because the battle for the institutions where our leaders are educated will continue for a long time. It will be fought out of the new Reich that Chancellor Hitler will bring to reality. A hard race [*Geschlect*] with no thought of itself must fight this battle, a race that lives from constant testing and that remains directed toward the goal to which it has committed itself."[54]

Heidegger's voluntarism was still very much in evidence in his 1935 lectures, *An Introduction to Metaphysics,* which contain his famous reference to the "inner strength and greatness of the movement." Although Heidegger left no doubt of the directing position that thought or philosophy would have to occupy in any positive political movement, he nevertheless saw the problem of modern times as being partly played out on the stage of politics. Philosophy, he argued, should assume a guiding role, working in and through a political transformation of Europe and, specifically, the German people, to effect a renewal: "We have related the question of being to the destiny of Europe, where the destiny of the earth is being decided. . . . [Germany] is the most metaphysical of nations. We are certain of this vocation, but our people will only be able to wrest a destiny from it if within itself it creates a resonance, a possibility of resonance for this vocation, and takes a creative view of its tradition."[55]

In Heidegger's nonmetaphysical mode of thought, which developed some time thereafter, he rejected the idea that philosophy could play a directing role in society and abandoned support for any program of collective political action. Philosophy and metaphysics, rather than being the source for an awakening or salvation, are now presented as impediments to renewal. The word "metaphysics," which Heidegger had previously employed in a positive way, is now used in an almost pejorative sense.[56] Metaphysics needs to be "overcome," as he indicated by the title of one of his most famous late essays, "Overcoming Metaphysics." In this nonmetaphysical mode, Heidegger insisted that real thinking, which he alternatively referred to as poetic thinking, genuine thinking, the other thinking, or meditative thinking, does not function to build programs or produce things: "Philosophy will not be able to effect an immediate transformation of the present condition of the world. This is true not only of philosophy, but of all merely human thought and endeavor." What occurs in history is nothing that man can directly control, either by his will or his thought. Instead, everything is in the hands of fate or of the gods. "Only a god can still save us," he declared, and we have no certainty that a god will ever come.[57] We can only wait.

Heidegger's meditative thinking cannot, however, be characterized as simply passive. He does not adopt an attitude of indifference to what happens, nor does he assume that smug posture of all-knowing detachment, sometimes called irony, that has come to characterize one strain of his postmodernist followers. Heidegger's postmetaphysical mode was always in earnest and, in its own way, very much engaged. After all, it was Heidegger who asked, "What task is reserved for thinking at the end of philosophy?" His response, while it affirms in one sense a passive posture, also leaves the door open to something more: "The thinking in question remains unassuming because its task is only of a preparatory, not of a founding character. It is content with awakening a readiness in man for a possibility whose contour remains obscure, whose coming remains uncertain." Although thought itself cannot directly change things, everything nevertheless may depend on whether man takes the action of keeping the "other thinking" alive, of "awakening a readiness," and of "preparing a site." A renewal "will not be granted to men by the benevolence of Being without the action of their questioning and thinking."[58]

It is likewise misleading to view Heidegger's nonmetaphysical mode as entirely apolitical. He developed what, for want of a better term, may be called a "cultural-political" project in which he folded the political realm into poetic or meditative thinking. The claims made in behalf of such thinking are at once modest and monumental. Meditative thinking can produce an "indirect, but not a direct effect . . . that can, as it were, causally change the condition of the world." Heidegger reinterprets the meaning of "political" to refer, not to the struggle over power and justice, but to man's encounter with the fundamental questions. The site of this encounter, he contends, captures the original Greek meaning of the polis, and he approvingly repeats Plato's famous formula, in *The Republic*, that there will only be continuing disaster until either philosophers become rulers or rulers become philosophers.[59] This formula works perfectly for Heidegger, on the assumption that philosophy no longer means philosophy in the traditional sense, but poetic or meditative thinking, and that ruling no longer means ruling in the traditional sense, but a slow process of changing consciousness. The political has vanished as an autonomous realm that shapes history and has been absorbed by aesthetic, post-philosophic thought.

The distinction in Heidegger's thought between the voluntaristic and the non-metaphysical prepares the ground for the two ways in which he uses the image of America. In his voluntaristic mode, he treats the traditional topic of regime analysis, using America as the representative of liberal democracy. Although he addresses here a conventional subject, he does so in a most unconventional way. Regimes are classified and judged not by the usual criteria of their standard of justice and their claim of who should rule but by whether (or how) they assist man in having a genuine encounter with Being. For the modern period, this means that Heidegger discusses regimes in terms of how they deal with man's situation at the point of the completion of metaphysics.

There is a practical reason, Heidegger insisted, for this highly theoretical starting point. The decisive factors that influence the modern world, down to the basic character of all political systems and the nature of international relations, derive from technological thinking. Beginning the study of politics with technology allows one to analyze the essence of political life "without having to take account of the transformations that history might observe among different peoples and continents"—in short, without having to deal with the myriad details and contingencies with which political analysis ordinarily concerns itself.[60] These differences wash out, so to speak, in the face of the control of man exercised by technological thinking.

But Heidegger seemed to be far less interested in the effects of Being on politics than in the effects of politics on Being.[61] He was seeking above all a positive political program, if one could be devised, that would help to transform man's mode of thinking in a way that would enable him to get control of, or to overcome, technological thinking. It is here that one can begin to speak of a kind of regime analysis in Heidegger's thought. The articulation of a positive political program is necessarily connected to the form of government and the question of who should rule. A positive program suggests putting power into the hands of those able to address the question of man's mode of thinking or at any rate into the hands of those who could be guided, knowingly or unknowingly, by such knowledge. Although no general regime *type*—a monarchy, tyranny, or liberal democracy, for example—can assure this result, there may be certain forms that inhibit or enhance the possibility.[62]

To put Heidegger's regime analysis into its most simplified form, political regimes in modern times are of two kinds. On one hand are regimes that preclude any possibility of developing a constructive encounter with technology, and on the other are regimes that offer at least a chance of providing for such an encounter. This is the only distinction that really matters. In his 1935 reference to the pincers surrounding Europe, Heidegger placed the two modern systems of Communism and liberal democracy into the first category. He continued thereafter to hold this position, certainly in regard to liberal democracy. In a 1966 interview, he was asked whether Americanism could be classified as one of the systems ruled by technology. Responding in the affirmative, he went on: "It is for me today a decisive question how the age of technology can be coordinated with a political system and which political system that can be. I have no answer to this question. I am not convinced that it is democracy."[63] Liberal democracy seemed to him too weak a system to confront technological thinking. Democracy can be likened to a kind of gang tyranny that turns power over to those already molded by the numbing mindlessness of technological society. Democracy "requires that everybody be left to his own opinion. But mere popularity is a slave of contingency."[64] Citing Nietzsche's view of democracy as a "degenerate regime form," Heidegger at points seemed to ally himself with revolutionary conservatives in thinking that the crisis of modern technology needed to be addressed by a decisive principle of leadership that was democratic only in the sense of engaging the mass of people.[65]

Some commentators, going back a step further, have tried to examine the political implications of Heidegger's existentialist philosophy in *Being and Time*. Although that work does not treat politics explicitly, the existentialist emphasis on authenticity and resoluteness in making decisions strongly implies a critique of liberal democracy that corresponds to the revolutionary conservatives' attack on the softness and weakness of the bourgeoisie. Existentialist analysis helps to prepare the ground for a claim that only the strong and daring should rule. According to Hans Jonas, a famous philosopher and a student of Heidegger, existentialism placed a premium on risk and on embracing the dangerous alternative. Heidegger's contempt for the moderation of liberal democratic procedures and his support of the Nazis in 1933 are thus plausible conclusions from his existentialist categories: "In Hitler and in National Socialism and in the new Departure, in the will to begin a new Reich, even a thousand-year Reich, he saw something he welcomed. . . . He identified the decisiveness (of the Führer and the Party) with the principle of decisiveness and resoluteness as such."[66]

Whatever the implications of Heidegger's early existentialism, his contention that liberal democracy could not control technology rested on his historical argument that liberal democracy was itself a product of, and hence necessarily captive to, technological thinking.[67] Liberal democracy cannot be part of the solution when it is part of the problem. Heidegger eventually broadened his argument to include all modern isms, which he came to see as products of technological thinking. Even to conceive of the political problem and its solution in terms of instituting a general regime type (or ism) represented a false way of thinking, for in the very act of defining the political question in terms of a choice of isms, one has already subordinated the particular thing (a people with its destiny) to an abstract category or general idea (such as liberalism or Communism). There can be no hope for renewal when this abstract way of thinking holds sway.

A positive political solution, if one is to be found, must proceed on a different level altogether than that of a general regime type or ism. It must emerge out of a way of thinking that rejects universals and defines the political problem in terms of particulars—in terms of the function or destiny of distinct peoples and the encounter of each people with Being. In the view of one commentator, Heidegger's preferred world order envisaged a "reemergence of rootedness in closed, tradition-dominated wholes, which would eventually become confronted by a plurality of like constituted communities. . . . A revitalized Germany would require its neighbors likewise to seek their roots and accede to their history."[68] These "wholes" or communities are formed, not by the philosopher-ideologue instituting a modern ism nor by the modern statesman-founder acting under the guidance of a science of politics, but by the poet or postmetaphysical thinker. As Heidegger noted, "The truth of the existence of a people is originally founded by the poet."[69]

The regime that offers at least a chance of opening the way to an encounter with technology must be a kind of non- or antitype that insists on the primacy of a particular nation's destiny. The only regime that Heidegger analyzed in this connection was fascism and in particular German National Socialism. (I refer to *German National Socialism* because Heidegger was less interested in the general attributes of a regime than the particular characteristics of a movement that was fashioning a path for the German people.) Only German National Socialism, as he said in 1966, attempted "to achieve a satisfactory relationship of man to technology."[70] National Socialism was the only political option that held any potential for promoting a reawakening. In 1945 Heidegger had noted, "I was then [in 1933] absolutely convinced that an autonomous collaboration of intellectuals would lead to an examination and a transformation of numerous elements of the national socialist movement, in order to put this movement in a position to contribute in its way to an overcoming of the disarray of Europe and the spiritual crisis of the West."[71] Heidegger even suggested that others were guilty of irresponsibility in opposing the Nazis in 1933: "What would have happened and what would have been prevented, if, around 1933, all capable forces had set out, in secret cohesion, to slowly purify and moderate the 'movement' that had come to power?" Or as he reportedly complained to Karl Lowith in 1936, "If these gentlemen [the intelligentsia] hadn't been too refined to get involved, then everything would have been different."[72]

As matters turned out, Heidegger acknowledged, the Nazi movement was not properly guided and did not realize its potential, forcing him at some point into what he called "spiritual opposition" to the regime. In Heidegger's postwar presentation, there was thus the National Socialism that might have been and the National Socialism that actually was. What Heidegger does not specify is the content of the National Socialism he wanted; for a long time, most commentators assumed that his preference must have been for a kinder and gentler democratic variant. Today, however, many believe that Heidegger wished to follow a more radical course than even Hitler did. In any case, as Heidegger explained after the war, the Nazi regime was not saved from the weak thinkers who preached, among other things, their metaphysics of biologism. Nazism evolved into a regime that was no different from democracy or Communism in its relation to technology and its conception of Being. Far from being the antidote that Heidegger hoped for, Nazism became technologism's captive: "From the point of view of the history of metaphysics," Heidegger observed in 1944, "Communism, Americanism, and National Socialism were identical." Or again (in 1945): "Today everything is a part of this reality [technology], whether it is called communism, or fascism, or world democracy."[73]

By 1944, therefore, Heidegger's position was that all of the major modern regimes—fascism and Nazism no less than Communism and liberal democracy—could be placed in the same category. In a still more general (and provocative) statement of this thesis, he argued in *A Letter on Humanism* that all contemporary regimes were expressions of the same humanism, which is the original ism from which all other isms have derived. Modern thought or technology culminates—equally, one might say—in the American founding, the Communist terror, and the policy of the Final Solution. Heidegger is reliably reported to have stated that "as for its essence, modern mechanized agriculture is the same thing as the production of dead bodies in gas chambers and extermination camps, the same thing as the blockade and reduction to starvation of a country, the same thing as the construction of hydrogen bombs."[74] Except perhaps for its brutal frankness and clarity, it is difficult to understand why Heidegger's most ardent philosophical adherents should have been shocked by this statement, as it follows his core method of assessing regimes according to their relation to Being or technology rather than to their relation to, say, a principle of justice. Among the different regimes of modern times, Heidegger admitted after 1944 to only one difference: Communism and liberal democracy are intrinsically flawed, whereas Nazism was flawed only as it turned out, not as it might have been.

Few issues of modern scholarship have provoked more commentary and polemics than the attempt to determine when, why, and to what extent Heidegger came to distance himself from Nazism. Heidegger's own account from after the war was that his break came early, by the mid-1930s, and that his opposition was principled and substantial. Accepting this claim has allowed Heidegger's defenders to try to present his record in a more sympathetic light. His support for National Socialism, they say, can be considered as an early and temporary misjudgment, mitigated by the fact that the National Socialism of 1933 was not the same as that of 1936. This account was adopted by many French existentialists and Marxists after the war. It was echoed by Hannah Arendt in 1969, when, on the occasion of Heidegger's eightieth birthday, she noted that "he was young enough to learn from the shock of the collision, which drove him back to his inherited abode after ten short hectic months thirty-five years ago, and to settle what he experienced in his thinking."[75]

Others regard this version of events as nothing more than an elaborate apologetic. According to the German historian Hugo Ott, "Heidegger's political past was disguised, minimized, until it appeared insignificant, even glossed over with decorative epithets describing Heidegger's supposed attitude of resistance after the short episode of his rectorate." In this view, Heidegger's so-called spiritual opposition was not a philosophical break at all; he was merely forced into a factional opposition when he lost favor with some in the party and had to give up his position as rector at the university. For a certain time, in fact, he still hoped to make a political comeback. Moreover, whatever Heidegger's personal views may have been, he continued to support the regime until a German defeat became evident. As late as 1942, he was still speaking of how one might best conceive the "knowledge of and valuation for the historical uniqueness of national socialism." He is quoted as saying in a lecture, "These two men, Hitler and Mussolini, who have, each in essentially different ways, introduced a countermovement to nihilism, have both learned from Nietzsche. The authentic metaphysical realm of Nietzsche has, however, not yet been realized."[76]

I mention this controversy here not because I wish to take sides but because many of the quotations I have used come from Heidegger's postwar account of his activities, which contain many of his major statements about technology and America. Some may be concerned that my approach inadvertently concedes too much to the apologetics on Heidegger's behalf, but it does not appear to me that, even with Heidegger's own presentation of the events, there is much that proves attractive.

In his postmetaphysical mode of thought, which dominated his pronouncements after World War II, Heidegger abandoned an explicit advocacy of a political program or regime and turned instead to the cultural-political project of "preparing the ground" for meditative thinking. Without any viable political movement or regime to which he could attach his thought, other than an informal alliance with the Marxist-existentialist Left, he had to rely on his own arms, and the only instrument at his disposal for executing his project was his own discourse. America in this mode functioned as the major rhetorical weapon.

It is characteristic of Heidegger's writing that the style is designed to be of a piece with the message. In accordance with his emphasis on the particular encounter, he often directly addresses his argument to a particular audience—to those who are situated in a particular setting or context. The group addressed is the relevant "we" or "us" of his discourse. Who this "we" or "us" consists of is subject to different interpretations. In its broadest dimension, I suppose, it is modern man at the point of crisis. In a narrower sense, it is, as he often says, "we Germans" or "we Europeans." Every "we" or "us" has, by implication, a "they" or "them" who is excluded. At the heart of Heidegger's rhetorical strategy is the technique of building the solidarity of one's own group by pitting it in a struggle against someone or something else. Man needs an enemy to maintain his spirit.[77]

America is that enemy, and its threat is both external and internal. The internal threat is the most insidious. America embodies all that is the worst in us, all that must be purified. America is the demonic, the thing inside us that is slowly stripping us of any spiritual quality. But although it is inside us, America does not fully possess us. We are not yet fully Americanized. The horror at being so possessed together with the hope of a possible escape is the spur designed to summon us to action. The rhetorical work that America performs should now be clear. The task of "preparing the ground" requires an action, in the form of an effort to resist the forces that bind us to the way of technology. That action needs a site. It must be undertaken by someone somewhere, and presumably not just by an individual but by an individual in relation to a community. It will be undertaken by "us" acting against "America." "Us" is sometimes "we Europeans" or "we Germans of the Fatherland."[78]

Heidegger frequently commented on a verse from Hölderlin: "Where danger lies, there too grows the chance for salvation."[79] This verse expressed a theme of his later philosophy which corresponds to one of the most powerful narrative archetypes implanted in the Western consciousness. Man is seen as moving ever more deeply into danger, with each successive disaster—World War I, World War II, the Cold War—being only the point of departure for a still greater calamity. But there is an end to this succession of crises, and the final catastrophe is America. The final catastrophe is nevertheless the basis for hope, for the worst danger opens the way to the "chance for salvation." Although salvation depends on something beyond our control—on fate—man still has a role to play. He must prepare himself for the awakening by adopting the "other thinking," which emerges in and through "us" thinking against America. Salvation begins in our revulsion at a place where human beings are no longer human and where the possibility of an awakening no longer exists. By showing us America, Heidegger summons us to that awakening.

It is tempting in these highly abstract discussions to dismiss the idea that Heidegger's America bears a connection to the United States. Yielding to this temptation, however, only allows that connection to become all the stronger, because the symbol is freely permitted to perform its subtle function of connecting an idea to a concrete thing. On the basis of Heidegger's own aesthetics, there is reason to think that a focus on the particular thing is what he had in mind. Pure poetic representationalism—viewing things as representing something else—is a kind of metaphysical thinking that implies a world of defined essences. That is a world that must now be overcome. Genuine poetry aims to escape metaphysical thinking and return us to a world of particular things. On the assumption that Heidegger was following his own rules, America is no "mere" symbol. America, I am afraid, is itself.[80]

Even though the average American is unlikely to have studied any of the works of Martin Heidegger or, for that matter, to have even heard his name, Heidegger's thought, often as filtered through the writings of legions of intellectuals, has exercised a profound influence on the actual world. We therefore cannot afford to ignore how his America has affected our vital interests. By "we," I mean of course we Americans and liberal democrats concerned with the well-being of the United States and the prospects for liberty in the modern world. From this admittedly parochial perspective, our concern should center on three legacies that Heidegger's symbolic America has bequeathed us.

First, if we take a step back to the recent Cold War, Heidegger's America lent support to the widespread "equivalency thesis," which said there was no essential difference between the Soviet Union and the United States. They were simply the two "superpowers." As this thesis was elaborated by many in Western Europe, the developed world was seen as divided into three types of regime: Communism, liberal capitalism (Americanism), and a third way of social democracy that was being created in some Western European nations. Western Europe's task—supported by enlightened segments inside America—was to promote this third way, which alone offered the prospect for human development. Even many who acknowledged, when pressed, the qualitative distinction between Americanism and Soviet Communism often found petty reasons for adopting an attitude of a "plague on both your houses," which amounted in practice to an endorsement of the equivalency thesis. Had this thesis prevailed among the major governments of Western Europe—as it very nearly did—the outcome to the Cold War might well have been different. Thanks, however, to the stand of a few thinkers and political leaders, enough resistance to this thesis was maintained until Communism collapsed in Europe. At that point, there followed the usual deathbed conversions. The bankruptcy of Communism suddenly became evident to "everyone"—which now included those who had recently soft-pedaled Communism's tyranny—and "everyone" further agreed that, whatever minor differences might separate America from the Western European democracies, they had been engaged all along in a common struggle against the same enemy.

Now that a decent interval has passed since the collapse of Communism, a second legacy of Heidegger's America has reemerged in many intellectual circles. Many argue that the conflict all along was never really about political regime forms—that is, about Communism versus liberal democracy—but about something much more fundamental: the struggle between "spirit" and technologism, between something "deep" and something homogenizing. With the diversion of the Cold War behind us, it is possible to focus on the real threat to humanity. That threat is the barren and empty humanism found in America. The real war for the soul of humanity has only just begun.

The third and final legacy of Heidegger's America is found in a way of thinking about politics that denies autonomy to the political realm and offers no place for political science. The political realm is squeezed between the pincers of a new historicism (*Seinsgeschichte*) and a passionate aestheticism. According to historicism, political life as we know it has been subsumed under the historical movement of thought. What governs the world is nothing accomplished at the level of politics—none of the struggles among regimes and the wars between tyranny and freedom that once seemed to matter so much. Instead, the world is governed by the mysterious movement of Being. A philosophy that is supposed to have turned our thinking away from universals and back to specifics has somehow managed to exclude political phenomena in the form that they have always presented themselves to those acting in politics. According to aestheticism, when we do look for intellectual guidance in political affairs, it comes not from political actors schooled in political science but from a new species of artists, poets, and literary critics who take their bearings from postmetaphysical philosophy and literary criticism.[81] As the creator of this new way of thinking, Martin Heidegger has sought to provide the modern world with a new language and poetry in which America has become a preeminent symbol of despair. America is the house of Being from which we now must try to escape.

9

★ ★ ★

America as the End
of History

Alexandre Kojève is a name few Americans recognize. Born in Russia in 1902, Kojève studied in Berlin after the Russian Revolution and settled in Paris in 1932. His one major work, *An Introduction to the Reading of Hegel,* published in 1947, is not even a book in the ordinary sense but a compilation of lectures from a course Kojève taught periodically between 1933 and 1939 on Hegel's *Phenomenology of the Spirit.* A second edition of the book appeared in 1968 in which Kojève added one footnote, now well known in the philosophical world, that presents his haunting and ironic vision of America.[1] Notwithstanding his limited written legacy, Kojève has had a profound impact on modern philosophy. His seminar in Paris was attended by a Who's Who of the future giants of French intellectual life, and it revived Hegelian philosophy as a serious alternative in modern thought. Kojève has been called the "big secret of French philosophy," the force whose thinking "dominated France between 1945 and 1970."[2]

If Kojève's name is unfamiliar to most Americans, his central concept, the end of history, has virtually become an intellectual cliché. It was popularized in 1989 by Francis Fukuyama in a widely read article, "The End of History?" which he followed up with a modestly named book, *The End of History and the Last Man.*[3] Updating Kojève's argument, Fukuyama identifies the end of history with the collapse of Communism and with the recognition of only one legitimate principle of rule: the liberal view, with its center of power in America. As well known as this argument may be in intellectual circles, the typical American will most likely have encountered it not in Fukuyama's writings but in the Hollywood movie *Star Trek VI: The Undiscovered Country.* According to the film's director, the idea to dramatize this theme came from Leonard Nimoy (perhaps better known as Spock, the

214

character he has played in the *Star Trek* television show and feature films), who urged "making a movie about the Berlin wall coming down in outer space." At one point in the film, the theme of the end of history is explicitly invoked when Captain Kirk poignantly declares: "Some people think that the future means the end of history. Well, we haven't quite run out of history yet."

In a meticulous analysis of Captain Kirk's thought, the critic Paul Cantor has observed that Kirk's spirited defiance of the "end" is tragically belied by his own actions.[4] The film's plot revolves around the long-standing conflict between the United Federation of Planets, with its progressive governing principles of equality, tolerance, and pluralism, and the Klingon Empire, with its backward principle of cultural and racial particularity. (As one Klingon puts it, "You haven't experienced Shakespeare till you've read him in the original Klingon.") What happens in the film, to make a long story short, is that through the strategy and bravery of Kirk and his crew on the starship *Enterprise,* the federation defeats the Klingons, who are then pacified and integrated into the federation's hegemony on the federation's terms, as one group among many. The federation now becomes a universewide state respecting the principle of equality. Captain Kirk fights for the goal contained in the end of history but certainly not for any idea of the end itself. Herein lies the Kirkian dilemma, aptly described by Cantor: "The members of the *Enterprise* crew are in the process of putting themselves out of business. . . . Their heroism—especially Kirk's heroism—is necessary only while the United Federation of Planets has powerful enemies like the Klingons." Whatever misconception Kirk may have labored under is no reason for condemnation, for, as Kojève and Hegel note, such world-historical figures as Caesar, Napoleon, and Kirk need not be fully conscious of the plan of history that they each serve.

In light of the situation prevailing in the universe at the end of *Star Trek VI,* the actors who played in the movie drew the inevitable conclusion and declared that it would be the last film in the series. No other option was open. Because all people living in the federation are satisfied with the new state, no serious political conflict can develop and no life-or-death cause can arise. *Star Trek VI* is the last picture show because the essential story of intelligent life's history in the universe has not only been completed but also recorded and understood (in the movie series itself). This being the case, nothing significant is left to be said. To claim that history is at an end thus does not mean, as some might think, that life stops or that everything is completed in a cosmic catastrophe. Another movie could be made— say, one with a retired Captain Kirk vacationing on a starship cruise to far-off planets and awakening early every morning for low-impact aerobic workouts on the main deck. But the kind of real drama that existed before—a struggle to achieve something valuable against a formidable, possibly deadly enemy—is no longer possible.

Allowing, of course, for some slippage along the way from Hegel to Hollywood, Kojève's end of history is not entirely dissimilar from the scenario just depicted, nor are some of the dilemmas it poses. Kojève's account of human history, which he also calls the final philosophy, is based on telling the story of man's step-by-step progress toward the final state: "The universal and homogeneous state brings all humanity together (at least that which counts historically) and overcomes or suppresses all particularities (nations, social classes, family). . . . Accordingly, wars and revolutions are henceforth impossible."[5]

What, one may wonder, does the end of history have to do with America? Just this: for Kojève the symbol of this end state is America, and living at the end of history is equated with the American way of life. Americans are the exemplars of the "animals" (or, in another version, the "automata") who inhabit the earth in the posthistorical era.[6] To understand how America acquired this distinction, one must consider the role of human thought and philosophy in history.

Philosophy and History

Kojève identifies his philosophy as one of realism. He focuses only on the actual or the this-worldly, dismissing as idle chatter any discussion of a metaphysical realm "out there." What counts is what is and what happens—what man has done and the record of his existence. The account of history in its entirety is the full or final philosophy.

Even before the articulation of the final philosophy, when history is still running, philosophy plays an actual or this-worldly role. Ideas are the prime moving force of history: "History appears as a continual series of actions guided more or less directly by the evolution of philosophy." To speak of philosophy in this way may at first seem remarkably "academic," as if Kojève thinks that polite discussions and scholarly conferences are the warp and woof that determine events. But nothing could more misstate his intention. When Kojève refers to thought guiding history, he means thought that vies to be made concrete—thought that can become an ideology or a project. Thought that does not vie to become a project dies. Thought becomes "true" only by becoming actual, for philosophic conflicts can never be resolved merely by discussion: "If one leaves it at *talking,* one will never succeed in definitively 'eliminating' the contradictory or, consequently, the contradiction itself." Philosophic disputes are settled insofar as certain ideas become actualized by being put into practice, "by winning on the historical plane of active social life where one argues by acts of Work (against Nature) and of struggle (against men)."[7]

The true is the result. Ideas that win are thereby proven to be true, whereas those that lose are thereby irrelevant or false. The one caveat to this formulation is that one can discover which ideas are true only when the end of history can be glimpsed. Before then, an idea that seems to have lost out may yet come back to win the day.

Kojève uses Hegelian language to describe this competition among ideas. Each philosophic idea or project, because it is designed to change or refute things, represents a "negation" or a plan of action against the existing order. It is an idea of what could be, but is not yet. To realize itself, it must change or modify what exists. History "is nothing more than a permanent revolution, since it progresses by a series of negations of the existing order." Or, as he states it more polemically, "every action . . . is a sin [in reference to the existing order]. But the sin may be pardoned. How? By its success. Success absolves the crime, because success is a new reality that exists."[8] Kojève, then, is clearly not moving in a kinder and gentler realm of "academic" philosophy, where such terms as "eliminate" and "crime" tend to be used as metaphors. He does not shy away from bold and bloody events; on the contrary, he seems to find satisfaction in them. Truth is won not necessarily in the proverbial (but bourgeois) marketplace of ideas but often on the battlefield and at the guillotine.

To say that philosophic ideas govern the movement of history does not mean, however, that philosophers themselves normally try to lead armies or rule nations. Philosophers generally lack the time to become generals or statesmen (although they sometimes do become involved as advisers); if they tried to perform these roles, they would be unable to philosophize and would have nothing to offer those acting in politics. In fact, philosophers are generally too pressed for time even to put their ideas into a form that can be understood or used by political actors. They accordingly leave it to a "constellation of intellectuals" to bring their ideas down to a level where, when conditions are ripe, the ideas can be taken up and made into political programs. Intellectuals are thus mediators who stand between the philosophers and the politicians. Kojève proposes what amounts to an "invisible hand" of historical movement that coordinates the activities of the producers of ideas (philosophers), the middlemen (intellectuals), and the consumers (tyrants and statesmen). What Adam Smith had done for economics, Alexandre Kojève tries to do for history as a whole: "It is history that attends to 'judging' (by 'achievement' or 'success') the deeds of statesmen or tyrants, which they perform (consciously or not) as a function of the ideas of philosophers, adopted for practical purposes by intellectuals."[9]

The idea of the end of history is coupled with another theme that is equally, if not more, fantastic: the disappearance of man. Kojève speaks of these two events together—the "disappearance of man at the end of history"—because they are really names for the same thing. Hegel, Gobineau, Nietzsche, Spengler, and Heidegger had adumbrated this concept, but Kojève gives it its most arresting formulation.

In Kojève's account, the disappearance of man is not the result of a nuclear war or biological catastrophe. From the point of view of the natural biological order, nothing has changed. After man has disappeared, there continues to be a creature which, in its biological form, is no different than man, having the same external appearance and the same number of chromosomes. But man properly speaking— an agent who acts on or against the world, who opposes himself to something else to negate it and thus to forge something new—ceases to exist, and "an animal of the species of *Homo sapiens*" takes his place. This animal will do many of the things man once did, or at any rate analogous things. It will practice a kind of art, but in the way that "spiders weave their webs." It will construct edifices, but after the fashion of "birds building their nests." It will engage in discussion, but in the manner of the "'discourse' of bees." It will perform musical concerts, but these will resemble the noises of "frogs and cicadas."[10] It will be content in the way that animals are content but not happy, as only humans can be.

In 1947, when the first edition of his *Introduction to the Reading of Hegel* was published, Kojève considered the end of history and the disappearance of man to be something "not unthinkable as a perspective on the future, albeit a future more or less near." But a few years later, after a trip to America, he concluded that the "end of History in the Hegelian-Marxist sense was not something yet to come, but is already present." Its outline was visible in America: "The American way of life is the type of life proper to the post-historic period and that the presence today of the United States in the World prefigures the future 'eternal present' of humanity in its entirety. Thus the return of man to an animal nature appeared no longer as a possibility still to come, but as a certitude already present."[11]

Kojève's assessment of the quality of life at the end of history is tinged with ambiguity. Ever the realist who eschews ordinary value judgments, Kojève nonetheless seems almost obliged to see the end state as something positive. History comes to an end because it fulfills man's deepest longing: the desire for recognition. In the universal and homogeneous state, all men have achieved their equal rights and thus a kind of satisfaction. Struggle ceases, wars and bloody revolutions end, material goods are abundant, and security is guaranteed. With man no longer "against" anything, the animal-creature who takes his place—the American—lives contentedly in his "eternal present."

Still, there is a negative undertone to this happy picture. I am not referring to the disappearance of human beings, which may after all seem unfortunate only to us, given our prejudice, certain ecologists excepted, in favor of our own species. Rather, I have in mind the mild contempt Kojève seems to betray when likening music, art, and thought to the activities of frogs, spiders, and bees—although, in fairness to these creatures, their expressions in these areas do not always compare unfavorably to contemporary human productions. Kojève's description of the posthistorical political regime also at times has a sinister quality that is highly reminiscent of some of the themes of Michel Foucault: "In the final state there are naturally no human beings in our sense of an *historical* human being. The healthy automata are 'satisfied' (sports, art, eroticism, etc.), and the 'sick' ones get locked up. . . . The tyrant becomes an administrator, a cog in the 'machine' fashioned by automata for automata."[12]

The end of history brings another result that one might have thought would cause Kojève regret: an end to philosophy. Philosophy, which up to now has been the cause of all negating action and thus progress, not only will have been completed but will no longer be necessary. Nothing more will need to be negated. The completion of philosophy, which Kojève calls "wisdom," comes on the eve of the end of the historical process, when the shape of history can be seen in its entirety. It is then that man (perhaps only one man or a few men) becomes conscious of and can finally articulate the meaning of all that has happened. The completion of philosophy is at one and the same time an acknowledgment of the disappearance of man and a precondition for it.[13] Yet even in this case, Kojève remains formally nonjudgmental. He makes only one brief concession in the face of what looks to be this most extreme of all tragedies: he notes that Hegel, on his discovery of the end in 1802, fell into a deep depression that lasted five years and that paralyzed his mental forces. But the truth being what it is, Hegel managed to overcome his bout of "hypochondria," after which he set about the task of writing—philosophically, as one might now say—the final philosophy.[14]

Kojève concluded that history had already ended, at just about the time that the leaders in the United States and the Soviet Union were preparing their respective populations for the ensuing struggle of the Cold War. Evidently, the great ideological conflict between liberal democracy and Communism was not significant from a philosophic point of view, as the end in either case was the same: a universal homogeneous state.[15] Hegel was correct. History had ended with him, with the Battle of Jena in 1806—that is, with the triumph of the principles of the French Revolution. It perhaps took a longer time than Hegel thought for these revolutionary principles to work themselves out, but the delay of more than a century that included two world wars was a mere detail: "What has occurred since [the Battle of Jena] has been no more than an extension in space of the revolutionary-universal power actualized in France by Robespierre-Napoleon." All of the major isms and movements since 1806—liberalism, Communism, anticolonialism, even (in a certain way) Nazism, along with both world wars and presumably the Cold War as well—have gone in the direction of furthering the principles of the French Revolution and the Enlightenment.

Modern political development follows the program of the political "party" of the French Revolution. That party may have different factions (Communism and liberalism today), but all factions seem to be members in good standing. America, or liberal capitalism, appears to be the strongest and the most representative of modernity, as the revolutionary principle has gone further in America than in Europe. Thus if America is different from Europe, it is so only in the sense that it is more fully Europeanized than Europe. From this perspective, Europe is today behind America, although heading in the same direction.[16] America is apparently also more progressive than the Communist nations of the Soviet Union and China: "From a certain point of view, the United States has already achieved the final stage of Marxist 'communism,' in view of the fact that practically all members of a 'society without classes' could from henceforth appropriate for themselves all that seems good without having to work more than their hearts tell them." Kojève believes that his empirical observations bear out this theoretical contention: "Several trips of comparison (between 1948 and 1958) to the United States and to the Soviet Union gave me the impression that if the Americans only appear as rich Chinese and Soviets, it is only because the Chinese and Russians are merely Americans who are poor, even though they are now ever more on the way to increasing wealth."[17]

Kojève made one last modification of his thesis, on which I will not dwell here. In 1959, following a trip to Japan, he saw that there was an alternative to the American way of life at the end of history. This would be the practice of a pure formalism, or "snobbism," of the kind represented in aspects of Japanese art and culture. Kojève saw this principle as more efficacious than the Western one and foresaw that the contact between Japan and the world would lead not to a Westernization of Japan but to a "'Japanization' of the West."[18]

Almost everyone who encounters the idea of the end of history reacts with a profound sense of sadness and horror, followed by an urge to resist. It is not surprising, for example, that many of Hegel's followers refused to see themselves as being at the end, acknowledging only that they were near it; and they proceeded to create parties or ideologies to interpret and direct the final act. The human impulse to resist the end often holds true, paradoxically, even for those who appear to favor the goal of the end state. As one commentator has observed, "There will always be men (*andres*) who will revolt against a state which is destructive of humanity or in which there is no longer a possibility of noble action or of great deeds."[19] The theme of an end of history thus seems to be able to serve as a sustaining human project only as long as it is something one is struggling to achieve. Once the goal is in sight or has been achieved, it immediately loses all its luster. The ideal suddenly turns into a nightmare.

It is in the face of this human reaction that the uniqueness of Kojève's position becomes apparent, for he has no such reaction—his philosophy, in fact, excludes it. His realism holds that thought describes what has happened and what must be. Knowledge of the entire human story is wisdom. In setting out the characteristics of the end state at the end of history, wisdom leaves no room for a program or a project. The end is really the end. Unlike Heidegger, Kojève issues no call for action and no plea for an awakening. Any such gesture would be gratuitous and unphilosophic.

The position that thinking can do nothing more (because there is nothing more to be done) is so extraordinary—so inhuman—that one might surmise that it represents an elaborate rhetorical strategy designed to provoke a reaction. Readers will be moved to resist Kojève's conclusion (Captain Kirk's defiant "we haven't quite run out of history yet"), which in turn will give rise to a new project to negate the end of history. In such an interpretation, Kojève's America, no less than Heidegger's, is something to be eliminated or overcome—only Kojève can never say so. His silence is the key to his strategy. Like comedy's perfect straight man, Kojève can never yield to the temptation to signal that he is anything other than perfectly serious. He must refrain even from that last remaining postmodernist conceit, signaling by wink or knowing gesture, that "we"—"the sophisticated"—are aware of the "joke." Ingenious as this interpretation is, it remains by definition unprovable, and Kojève never gives even the smallest hint that the real Kojève is anyone but the literal Kojève whom we read.

The impulse to deny the sincerity of Kojève's position—and here I admit to going in circles—stems from a human, perhaps all too human, inability to fathom so stark a realism. Not even Kojève's most famous follower, Francis Fukuyama, was able to live up to Kojève's rigorous standard. After boldly proclaiming what no international relations theorist had ever proclaimed, Fukuyama at the last moment wavers in his insistence that history has ended and appeals to his reader to take some action to restart it. Kojève himself never suffered from this human weakness but unflinchingly followed his philosophical premise to its conclusion.

Although Kojève's end state of America recalls previous thinkers' images of degeneration or desolation, he never speaks of America as being anything other than the result of progress. To be sure, "progress" for Kojève has a peculiar signification. It means not something higher or better but something that serves to move man forward to the end state: "The universal and homogeneous state is 'good' only because it is the *last*."[20] America is also the most ethical state, because ethics from this point of view "prescribes that one do everything that leads to . . . and condemn everything that impedes . . . progress toward 'the universal and homogeneous state.'" This approach supplies Kojève's writing with its distinct tone. Whereas Heidegger's America provoked anger and prompted a sense of urgency (even if Heidegger conceded we might need to wait "three thousand years" before we are prepared for a renewal), Kojève's America is designed to elicit a more bemused response. The end state is more comic than tragic. With history at an end and "nothing more to do," all that remains for the thinker is the detached role of an "ironic culture critic."[21]

The Kojève-Strauss Dialogue

Although many consider Kojève's end state too fantastic to be believed, his general historicist position—that man is the contingent product of his environment—enjoys widespread acceptance. This position directly challenges America's central intellectual contribution: a political science predicated on the existence of a structure or nature to the political world and on the assumption that the choice of a political future can, within a circle traced by destiny, depend on man's own decisions, assisted by reason. In Kojève's account, no place is left for political science as an intellectual discipline that can help to guide political life. That space has been occupied by History.

Thanks either to fate or to a natural human capacity to grasp perennial problems, a voice has always emerged to respond to the threats to political science. This task, which was assumed by Publius at the end of the eighteenth century and by Alexis de Tocqueville in the nineteenth century, fell in the twentieth century to Leo Strauss (1899–1973). Strauss was a theorist who left Germany in 1932 and eventually emigrated (as Alexander Hamilton had done) to America, where he first taught at the New School for Social Research in New York (1938–1949) and later joined the political science department at the University of Chicago (1949–1967). With Strauss, therefore, the defense of political science returns once again to the United States.

Despite their great philosophical differences, Strauss and Kojève were close friends from the time they both lived in Paris in the 1930s. In the years afterward they carried on a lively correspondence, mostly in German, which has recently been translated. The exchange shows the great esteem the two men held for each another. In one letter, Kojève speaks of writing an article in which he had used deep textual analysis, a well-known characteristic of Strauss's writing; he then playfully describes himself as having "publicly appear[ed] as a faithful Strauss disciple."[22] It would surpass all permissible bounds, even of irony, to call Kojève a "Straussian," a label that many academics and journalists pejoratively apply to anyone whom they suspect of being influenced by Strauss; but Kojève did tell Strauss that "except for yourself and [Jacob] Klein I have not yet found anyone from whom I could learn something."[23] For his part, Strauss paid Kojève the high compliment of sending some of his students, among them Allan Bloom and Stanley Rosen, to study with Kojève in Paris.

The exchange between Kojève and Strauss appears in a book entitled *On Tyranny,* which came about in a peculiar fashion. In 1948, Strauss published an essay on Xenophon's dialogue "Hiero." At Strauss's request, Kojève agreed to review the work. That review soon grew into a full-length essay of its own, and at Strauss's urging the two men decided that Strauss's original work, together with Kojève's essay and a reply by Strauss, should be published together under one cover.[24] Despite its disjointed format—part classical text, part commentary, part debate—the book has been widely celebrated and contains what George Grant, the well-known Canadian political theorist, called the "most important controversy in contemporary political philosophy."[25]

Strauss's original commentary—in his own words, a "detailed analysis of a forgotten dialogue"—would seem a perfect candidate for an audience of classical scholars. Yet Strauss addresses the work to "political scientists," and he opens by claiming the practical purpose, based on the model of classical political science, of developing a body of knowledge about how to avoid tyranny and how to establish free regimes. In 1948, faced with the prospect of a world that could indeed come under the grip of tyranny, Strauss had written: "We are forced to wonder how we could escape from this dilemma. We reconsider therefore the elementary and unobtrusive conditions of human freedom."[26]

One of the conditions for maintaining freedom, Strauss argues, is the existence of a genuine discipline of political science, without which the battle against tyranny cannot be successfully waged. Yet political science has had its foundation undercut by the development of modern thought, which has assumed two basic forms: positivism and historicism. Positivism in social science, which disallows value judgments of any kind, has missed the most important fact about our current situation: "When we were brought face to face with tyranny—with a kind of tyranny that surpassed the boldest imagination of the most powerful thinkers of the past—our political science failed to recognize it." Far more influential than positivism is historicism, which Strauss considered to be "not just one philosophical school among many, but a most powerful agent that affects more or less all present-day thought."[27] Whereas positivism had merely failed to recognize tyranny, historicism was helping to promote it.

Strauss placed a wake-up call to political scientists, asking them to recover the classic function of their discipline. He did so initially by appealing over the heads of positivism and historicism to the palpable "experience" man has had with modern tyrannies. Such an experience, Strauss suggested, is something man continues to be able to grasp, notwithstanding the influence of certain theories overlaying and distorting our perception of the world. But experience, although it can sometimes serve as a check on misleading abstractions, is no substitute for a systematic body of knowledge or science. Strauss offers his interpretation of Xenophon's text as a way of helping to recapture an understanding of the phenomenon of tyranny: "One cannot understand modern tyranny in its specific character before one has understood the elementary and in a sense natural form of tyranny which is premodern tyranny."[28]

Modern tyranny, although it is related to premodern tyranny, is thus something new. Premodern tyranny was based on the rule of a tyrant who desired to be loved and to enjoy the fruits of power; modern tyranny is essentially the rule in behalf of an ideology (although the biographies of many of the modern tyrants reveal surprisingly strong "premodern" motivations). Modern tyranny thus presupposes the existence of modern science, of technology, and of the basic idea of conquering nature to implement the ideology—all the characteristics that Heidegger (with whom Strauss had studied) grouped under the label "technology" and under the symbol "America." The shape of this new tyranny was frightening to contemplate: "We are now brought face to face with a tyranny which holds out the threat of becoming, thanks to 'the conquest of nature' and in particular human nature, what no tyranny ever became: perpetual and universal." Strauss saw the danger of tyranny as extending beyond its harder political forms to a softer variant that might develop by means other than a dramatic seizure of political power: "Confronted by the appalling alternative that man, or human thought, must be collectivized either by one stroke and without mercy or else by slow and gentle processes, we are forced to wonder how we could escape from this dilemma."[29]

Strauss at this point offered Kojève what amounted to an invitation to respond, which Kojève could hardly refuse: "The manifest and deliberate collectivization or coordination of thought is being prepared in a hidden and unconscious way by the spread of the teaching that all human thought is collective independently of any human effort directed to this end, because all human thought is historical."[30] Historical or historicist thought, far from innocently recording what is and what must be, was itself causing the homogenization of man and thought. Without ignoring the importance of technology, Strauss nevertheless attributed the immediate problem not to the scientific way of knowing things but to historicism; and contrary to the historicists' claims of being the first to escape the grip of the modern scientific view, Strauss argued that they had in fact intensified its ends, presumably in ways that might have been avoided.[31] Those who promoted a historicist way of thinking must bear responsibility for preparing the ground for the spread of tyranny.

Historicist thought in its most developed form, according to Strauss, rests on a philosophy of history. A philosophy of history is different from history itself, which is an inquiry that tries to understand the past as it was. In contrast, a philosophy of history begins with a built-in presupposition about the character of reality. It proceeds on the basis that the meaning and purpose of existence are worked out and revealed inside of time. Not nature or human nature but a historical account of man's odyssey from beginning to end reveals the essential meaning of all things. This kind of account Strauss refers to as History (as distinct from history, the inquiry into the past as it actually occurred). Because History contains a full view of reality, its properties—for those few who prefer such abstract language—can be expressed in terms of a metaphysical formula. Historicism rests on the hypothesis that "'Being creates itself in the course of history,' or that the highest Being is society and history, or that eternity is nothing but the totality of historic time."[32] Kojève's philosophy is one of the supreme statements of this view, though there are of course other versions as well.

Philosophies of history leave no place for political science. Kojève confirms this point by replacing any kind of regime analysis—any discussion of the merits and qualities of different political systems—with an analysis of what promotes or impedes progress toward the end state. A political system is "good" insofar as it progressive. Strauss's attempt to revive political science therefore involved contesting the historicist hypothesis, at least to the extent of showing that it was not the only possible starting point for human thought, but one alternative among others. Challenging historicism, Strauss realized, would be a difficult undertaking, so strong was its grip on the modern mind. To free thinkers from historicism would be akin to liberating them from a "second cave," one deeper even than the original cave described by Plato. Whereas the first cave was fashioned from "natural" prejudices, the second resulted from a layering of ideas that had thrown a thick cover over all natural phenomena.[33]

One method Strauss adopted to confront historicism was to prepare a genealogy of the concept of historicism, or a history of History. This inquiry indirectly served a philosophical purpose by showing that the development of historicism, rather than being a product of pure philosophy, owed far more to political strategy and to accident than most have thought. At its birth, which occurs in Kant's essay "Idea for a Universal History," the element of strategy was already apparent in Kant's presentation of History as a kind of modern myth to promote the realization of Enlightenment principles. Because "sovereigns and their agents" are ever in search of "fame," they can be expected to do what they think will bring them recognition. An idea of History that postulates the eventual triumph of Enlightenment principles may therefore induce these leaders to work for this result.[34] But the real boost to historicist thinking came partly by accident, in the political struggle over the French Revolution, when conservatives discovered in historicism an instrument for attacking revolutionary ideas. Historicism's first major practical effect was thus not to promote the Enlightenment project (as Kant had proposed) but to oppose it. Such is the cunning of historicism. Strauss then went on, in a story I need not recount here, to trace the twists and turns in the growth of historicist thought until the advent of "radical historicism" in his time.

Nothing in this genealogy disproved the premise on which historicism rested. But by showing historicism's less than solid foundation, Strauss sought to open the door to a consideration of other alternatives. His approach was designed to shift the discussion from an automatic appeal to history to a discussion of the philosophical argument for historicism, where the case on its behalf was far from conclusive. For when it came to metaphysical formulae, it seemed no more plausible to accept the historicist hypothesis ("Being creates itself in the course of history") than the nonhistoricist hypothesis ("Being is essentially immutable in itself and eternally identical in itself"). It is questionable in any case how far Strauss thought such abstract formulations, without reference to the important experiences of political life, would take us. The final sentence of *On Tyranny,* which undoubtedly refers to Heidegger, notes the consequences that befell those who "did nothing but speak of Being" and would not consider independently the political question of tyranny.[35]

Strauss tried to demonstrate the utility or truth of a nonhistoricist political analysis by showing its payoff in the understanding of political phenomena. He put the idea of a human nature to work in his discussion of classical tyranny as portrayed in "Hiero" and then in his critique of the supposed finality of Kojève's end state, pointing out that human inequalities could not assure the full mutuality of recognition and thus the universal satisfaction of which Kojève speaks.[36] Strauss also indicated how a concept of the world's structure—an "eternal and immutable order within which history takes place"—can support the idea that the political realm is a component of reality endowed with an importance of its own.[37] Man's concern with the character of political life and his capacity to grasp the significance of basic political alternatives—above all freedom versus tyranny—are not expressions of contingent facts, any more than the existence of man himself is a contingent fact. Strauss was critical of any philosophy or conception of the whole that denied a place for the political as a distinct and independent part of reality, for without considering the place and status of the political realm inside the whole of existence, the whole itself cannot be understood.[38]

Because we live in a world in which chance and human freedom play a role, Strauss insisted there can be no pure historical inevitability and thus no "realism" in the sense that Kojève understood the word. Human beings possess a degree of freedom and therefore can alter trends. Any statement about the future cannot be purely deterministic, if only because it can provoke a human reaction that will change the predicted result: "Under no circumstances can we avoid the question as to whether the probable future order is desirable, indifferent or abominable. In fact, our answer to that question may influence the prospects of the probable future order becoming actually the order of the future."[39] None of this meant that man should imagine that he possessed total freedom of action. Strauss called for a careful study of each historical situation within which man lives in order to understand in each context the best possible result, and even then certain results might be beneath man's dignity. The openness of history to chance means that alternatives that look like lost causes might, as a result of a courageous stand on their behalf, one day rise to live again.[40]

The character of history also helps to define the kind of knowledge political science seeks and the way in which it can guide society. Because of the role chance plays in history, the main objective of political science is not to try to predict exactly what will occur inside history, but rather to offer statements of what is more or less likely to result, assuming certain conditions and the adoption of certain measures. This kind of knowledge has in principle the character of being helpful to those who act in political life. Furthermore, because the conditions in any two situations are never the same, political science cannot by itself supply an infallible guide to action. It cannot be plugged in, turned on, and expected to work automatically. It is meant to be an aid or tool, to be used by statesmen and citizens together with their own judgment and prudence to deal with the challenges of an always changing agenda.[41] Political science serves as a supplement to, but never as a total replacement for, the practice of the political actor's own art.

The Two Legacies of Leo Strauss

Given the broad themes Strauss addressed, many intellectual historians refer to him not as a political scientist but as a political philosopher. (If it were not for the periodic tirades that charge Strauss with being so extremely conservative as to defend constitutional government, some analysts might even overlook his concern with politics altogether.) But a review of Strauss's work shows that he practiced a great deal of standard political science and paid very close attention to the fate of the discipline that claimed this name. This said, it is also true that, compared to the two other major defenders of political science of the past two centuries—Publius and Tocqueville—Strauss devoted less time to analyzing institutional arrangements and more time to investigating philosophical issues.

There is no doubt, then, that one part of Strauss's concern was with philosophy proper and with questions about what he calls "the whole." His inquiries in this realm often took him far afield from political matters, into the examination of such large themes as reason versus revelation and the nature of the philosophic way of life. And even some of his discussions of political things proceed more from the perspective of philosophy than from that of political science. A well-known instance is Strauss's examination of "philosophical politics," which refers to the relation between philosophy and politics treated from the viewpoint of how philosophy as an enterprise can be protected and maintained. Here Strauss contrasts the problem that philosophy encountered in ancient and medieval times, when it had to be protected from the "closed" character of politics and hence from charges of impiety and undermining customary ways, with the very different problem that philosophy faces in modern times. In the modern era (from the seventeenth century on), philosophy itself has changed from a predominantly contemplative activity to a politicized instrument and a weapon that has aimed to remake the world.

This role for philosophy and the success it has enjoyed paradoxically pose a greater risk for philosophy than it experienced in premodern times. A universal tyranny grounded in philosophy can now turn against philosophy and conceivably stamp it out forever. This was the somber note on which Strauss ended the English version of *On Tyranny*: "Thanks to the conquest of nature, . . . the Universal tyrant . . . has at his disposal practically unlimited means for ferreting out, and for extinguishing, the most modest efforts in the direction of thought. Kojève would seem to be right for the wrong reason: the coming of the universal and homogeneous state will be the end of philosophy on earth."[42]

Given Strauss's interest in such questions, it is understandable that one part of his legacy in academia today should be found in the area of philosophy (including philosophical politics). But his concern for philosophical issues never implied a disinterest in "ordinary" political philosophy and political science. (By ordinary political philosophy I mean the inquiry into the nature of the best regime and the ranking of regimes accordingly; and by political science I mean the inquiry, guided by political philosophy, into the factors that preserve and destroy different regimes.) Strauss approached these disciplines in a public or political spirit, with his primary objective being to search for knowledge to improve political life, not to contribute to the greater awareness or joy of the thinker. And even where Strauss addressed broad issues of intellectual history, his main purpose was often to assist political science. Just as he sometimes treated political issues from the perspective of protecting philosophy, so he sometimes treated philosophical issues from the perspective of protecting political life. The character of the times and situation in which he lived dictated this approach. Political science was under threat from the dominant, philosophically generated way of viewing the world, and it could be rescued only if a space could be reopened for it inside modern thought. A political scientist, even if that were all Strauss wished to be, was compelled to become philosophical and to practice a critical account of the prevailing philosophical tradition.

Opening a space for the practice of political science, then, is the second legacy of Leo Strauss. If Strauss himself lacked the time to develop a complete political science for the modern era, he surely pointed the way. Others influenced by Strauss continued his efforts to recover the tradition of political science, pursuing this inquiry by studying the thought of America's founders and of Alexis de Tocqueville and by analyzing the policies and actions of some of the great statesmen of our age; and they began to apply traditional or constitutional political science to the study of contemporary politics. This approach has influenced parts of the academic discipline of political science, and it has helped to reinstate elements of political science, both inside and outside the academy, as a guide for governing and legislating. Constitutional political science is certainly not the dominant approach today—far from it—but it has been actively at work now for more than a quarter-century, above all in the United States and France, and it has played no small part in this generation in the struggles of freedom against tyranny. It is certainly true that today political science displays more of the characteristics of its classical function than it did when Strauss began to write. What then looked like a lost cause for political science has been partly rescued by his last-ditch effort.

For those who have benefited from this second legacy, the task today cannot be limited to rehearsing previous arguments. The theoretical challenge of maintaining a place for political science inside modern thought necessarily changes as the character of the intellectual threats to it change, and the enterprise of constructing a functioning political science is different from that of mounting a theoretical defense of its role, however much these two depend on each other. Every theoretical defense is tied in some measure to what it seeks to modify or to combat—in the way, for example, that Strauss's own discussion of the waves of modern thought (which was designed in part to help combat historicism) emphasized almost to the point of distortion the controlling power of philosophical ideas over human affairs. A political science proper must proceed by other techniques and other means, focusing more on the independent influence of political factors and paying attention at times to the autonomy of political things. Important as the great themes of philosophy may be—and I am including here the unfolding of the idea of modern liberty in the thought of philosophers, the emergence of the Enlightenment, and the crisis of modernity—they do not make up the totality of causes that constitute political life. These ideas never by themselves founded a regime, fought a war, or made a political decision. Political life as we know it has never been a mere creation of some philosophical project. It is shaped as well by the thoughts and acts that emanate from inside the political realm—from previous facts of history, from the acts and thoughts of statesmen and citizens, and from the play of events. There is always a political realm, which is not just a theoretical possibility but an omnipresent reality. And it is for political philosophy and political science to insist on the existence of this realm, protecting its relative autonomy from the incursions of overbearing theorizing and promoting an approach to the study of politics that begins from political phenomena.

The two legacies of Leo Strauss, although clearly different, are not polar opposites dividing North from South or, for that matter, East from West. From the perspective of philosophy, it is clear that a consideration of political things is necessary for exploring questions about the whole. This inquiry becomes attenuated to the extent that it ignores political life or treats the political realm merely as a laboratory for the sake of philosophy. From the perspective of political science, the political good cannot be calculated without considering what promotes the human good. Not only is philosophy indispensable to investigating the human good, but also the practice of philosophy itself is clearly among the highest of human activities. From a more political perspective, the health of the souls of an important part of society, ideally a part that will have some influence on its governance, cannot be achieved except with the aid of philosophy. If statecraft is soulcraft, there is also a sense in which soulcraft is statecraft.

Alexandre Kojève introduced into contemporary discourse the ideas of the end state and the disappearance of man at the end of history. Both concepts are represented in his thought by the symbol of America. Kojève's America, although no doubt intended in part as a literary device, cannot help but have important real-world consequences; for if we follow Kojève's premise that the "deeds of statesmen or tyrants" are, consciously or not, always a function of the "ideas of philosophers, adopted for practical purposes by intellectuals," then it follows that even the most extravagant of a philosopher's ideas risk becoming part of the actual world that governs us.[43] Kojève cannot, and would certainly not wish to, exempt his own thinking from the logic of his own system.

Whether, therefore, intellectuals choose to view America in its less threatening form as a nation of contented frogs, spiders, and cicadas disguised as human beings or in its more sinister form as the land of soulless automata exercising in jogging suits, the symbol of America is sure to be exploited by some demagogue or tyrant and used to America's detriment. To rescue America from this fate, it must be freed from the control of this symbol. An ironic political science is needed for an ironic world.

10

★ ★ ★

America as Postmodern

Jean Baudrillard, author of the widely read travelogue *America* (1986), is a prominent figure in contemporary French intellectual life. He has written no fewer than ten books, most of which deal with themes that may loosely be called postmodernist. Among his most important works are *The System of Objects,* in which he develops some of the concepts of the semiologist Roland Barthes, and *Forgetting Foucault,* in which he turns on the master he had followed for years, committing the intellectual ritual murder known as deconstruction. Although Baudrillard may be unfamiliar to most Americans, those who move within postmodernist circles are well aware of his exploits. The *New York Times* described him as a "guru for many seeking to grasp the quintessence of modern life," while the authors of a leading American survey of postmodern thought call him the "'talisman' of the new postmodern universe [and] *the* supertheorist of a new postmodernity."[1] Baudrillard also enjoys a considerable following in Germany, where many of his works have been translated and where in 1995 he received the prestigious and highly remunerative Siemens Media-Art Prize.

Why a thinker of Baudrillard's stature, a supertheorist at the apogee of a brilliant literary-philosophic career, should trouble himself to write a travel guide on America is hard to figure. Admittedly, it was not uncommon in previous centuries for major thinkers to write travelogues—both Montesquieu and Goethe, for example, wrote books about Italy. But these works appeared in an era when few had the means for making long voyages to distant places and when most of the reading public had no way, except through such books, to satisfy its curiosity about foreign lands. Today, conditions have changed dramatically. International travel is now commonplace, at least for the wealthy and for intellectuals; the cinema churns out vivid images of modern life, especially of America; and the publishing industry produces scores of travel guides, from Fodor's to Michelin's (*Rouge* and *Vert*). All in all, these changes would seem to make a travelogue by a philosopher-intellectual a dubious undertaking—unless, of course, a guide on America is something more than a traditional guide, and a postmodern intellectual is something other than a traditional thinker. If the United States is not just a country but an image of life at the end of history, and if the contemporary intellectual has nothing else to do but amuse himself with sophisticated commentaries, then a travel guide on America might be just the thing for today: a new kind of "philosophy," for light reading to be sure.

These are precisely the claims Baudrillard makes in *America*. Baudrillard had journeyed to America not so much to visit the United States itself as to see the face of modernity: "America is the original version of modernity, . . . and Americans make up the ideal material for an analysis of all the variants possible of the modern world." America is history's final stop, the "utopia achieved." And it is, I suppose, the modern intellectual's role—"duty" would be too strong a word—to capture and present this utopia, not with the aim of changing anything (earnestness of purpose now being passé), but with the simpler purpose of interpreting and appreciating it, much in the way that the modern literary critic plays with a text. As befits a guru, Baudrillard provides the classic definition of his activity. The "postmodern," he writes, is "characteristic of a universe where there are no definitions possible. . . . It has all been done. . . . It has destroyed itself. It has deconstructed its entire universe. So all that are left are the pieces. *Playing with the pieces—that is postmodern.*"[2]

What does Baudrillard mean by calling America a "utopia"? Two major characteristics earn it this description. First, in a modest departure from Kojève's analysis wherein Americans are likened to animals, Baudrillard describes them more gently as "savages" or "primitives." This formulation is in no sense intended as any kind of moral judgment, much less a criticism; it is used benignly to depict Americans simply as they are. In Baudrillard's view, Americans live their lives blissfully unaware of their condition, as if they were precivilized primitives; they lack depth or culture and possess no sense of the past. America, "with its space, its technological refinement, its brutally innocent conscience, is the only existing primitive society."[3]

The second characteristic of utopia is a bit more complicated, as it involves an ever so paradoxical relationship between the name and the thing, or the copy and reality. What is truly modern or utopian about America is that the real America is no longer "real" in the commonsense understanding, but rather a copy: "What is necessary is to enter into the fiction of America, into America as fiction; besides it is in this sense that America dominates the world."[4] It is just this quality—namely, a capacity to make copies without disdaining the copies as mere copies—that defines the modern primitive (and that accounts for the paradoxical coexistence of advanced technology and primitive consciousness). When the image becomes as real as the real thing, true modernity or postmodernity has been achieved.

To illustrate this point, Baudrillard studies the images and fictions of contemporary America, taking the view that these are more real than the real America. What typifies the American is his naive ability to create copies or images through such means as the cinema and modern advertisement, without being paralyzed by the intellectual "problem" of contrasting the real and the artificial. In America, life copies image as much as image copies life: "In America, the cinema is true because . . . the whole mode of life is cinemagraphic: life is cinema."[5]

Here, then, is the modern utopia, the destination of Baudrillard's now famous trans-Atlantic journey. Yet, the postmodernist universe never being quite what it seems, room must be left for a certain amount of irony and play, on the understanding that every concept is subject to a double entendre. The American utopia, it turns out, is not exactly what it seems: "They [the Americans] achieved there a utopia, they are achieving an anti-utopia: that of unreason, of deterritorialization, of indeterminacy of subject and language, of the neutralization of all values, and of the death of culture."[6] Evidently, then, we have to explore the "dialectic" of "utopia-nonutopia" in order to understand America.

Baudrillard's America

In *America,* Jean Baudrillard has come close to realizing what is manifestly his uppermost purpose: to produce a sophisticated book. *America* is a work filled with wit and esprit, written in a lively style that flouts academic conventions. It moves in staccato flashes that parallel the cinemagraphic "reality" of its subject. Themes taken from high culture (Tocqueville's *Democracy in America,* for example) are interspliced with references to pop culture (lyrics from a pop song by Michael Jackson, for instance). Form and content are fused into a single whole, so that one can hardly separate the *signifiant* from the *signifié.*

Few readers would forget Baudrillard's account of the New York City Marathon, where he observes some seventeen thousand joggers pounding away on the pavement in order to fill up the emptiness of their lives and provide tangible proof to themselves that they exist. Baudrillard contrasts the oddly private and self-centered character of the contemporary event with the public, political purpose of the original race: "'We won' sighed the one Greek of the Marathon and then expired. 'I did it!' gasps the marathon runner, exhausted and crawling on the grass of Central Park."[7] Baudrillard concludes by noting the amazing fact that more joggers participated in the New York City Marathon than soldiers fought at the Battle of Marathon.

Better still is Baudrillard's remarkable description of campus life at the University of California at Santa Cruz. After presenting his first impression of the university—as a utopia in a spectacular natural setting, with proud claims of academic freedom and a splendid summer-camp atmosphere—he goes on to reveal his darker second thoughts. Paradise begins to disintegrate, slowly devolving into a sinister hell of "overprotection," both natural and social. Baudrillard finds himself trapped in the ultimate prison, forced to breathe the stultifying fresh air of the ocean breezes rather than the liberating tobacco smoke of a Left Bank café.[8] Santa Cruz resembles nothing so much as No Exit, a kind of Panatopia on the Pacific.

Given these unflattering characterizations of two great American institutions, it would be easy enough to charge Baudrillard with having written an anti-American screed. The book often reads like one, for Baudrillard cribs almost every element of Heidegger's negative symbolic or metaphysical America, improving on it by using the literary genre of the travelogue, which enables him to connect each metaphysical criticism of America to an aspect of everyday American life that he has supposedly observed. But to charge Baudrillard with having written a diatribe would be unfair; one must remember that he is being ironic.[9]

It is this irony that explains the ostensibly unfriendly comments, as these do make up a large part of the book. Baudrillard claims, for example, that Americans have no sense of history. America "exorcises the question of origins, she does not cultivate the origins or the mythical authenticity, she has neither a past nor a founding truth." America is characterized by a rootlessness that manages to blot out the past by "living in a perpetual simulation, a perpetual presence of signs." Or else Baudrillard defines the "distinctly American miracle" to be "that of the obscene." Obscene here does not refer to pornography but to a general "tastelessness" (*fadeur*) that characterizes the artificial paradises Americans have tried to construct, especially in the suburbs. (Baudrillard told the *New York Times* that he was entranced by the "inspired banality" of America.) Or, Baudrillard also maintains, America is a mass society where quantity is what counts: "Americans view the numeric and statistical as a fortunate incitement . . . of the happy accession of the majority." America is the "only country where the quantitative is exalted without apology."[10] Or, finally, Baudrillard evokes the idea of America as the land of the living dead—a theme suggested to him by the omnipresent smiles on the faces of nearly everyone he meets in California. The smiling American initially delighted Baudrillard, but after a while the cheerful countenances began to drive him to near madness: "Smile if you have nothing to say, and don't hide above all that you have nothing to say. Show spontaneously the void, the profound indifference of your smile. . . . Illustrate the zero-degree of joy and pleasure, smile, smile!"[11] Baudrillard relents only a bit from this biting criticism to acknowledge that "though Americans are lacking entirely in identity, they nevertheless have fine teeth."[12]

One could mention other points where Baudrillard gives at least the impression of hostility toward America. For example, there are his remarks about Americans' tendency to obesity (when, that is, they are not either indulging their passion for bodybuilding or suffering from anorexia), or his observation that Americans are superficial, or his claim that Americans are devoid of any aesthetic sense. But such charges are mere bagatelles. The fact that Baudrillard calls Americans fat, dumb, and uncultured is surely no reason to think that he is anti-American.

To be guilty of genuine anti-Americanism—if anti-Americanism be a crime—Baudrillard would have had to approach America not just with an attitude of intellectual superiority but with condescension as well, and he would have had to call for action of some sort against America, if not politically then at any rate culturally. But Baudrillard is innocent of both charges. The evidence is conclusive. On the first count, Baudrillard does not deny, of course, that Europeans are intellectually superior to Americans, for to assert the contrary would be disingenuous. It is acknowledged by nearly every thinker (above all, as he correctly points out, by American intellectuals) that, unlike Americans, Europeans "possess the art of thinking about things, of analyzing them, and of reflecting on them." But observing the fact of intellectual superiority is not the same thing as condescension, and Baudrillard is never condescending. On the contrary, he argues that European intellectual superiority is a worthless anachronism: "We [Europeans] philosophize about a whole host of things, but it is here that they take shape. . . . It is the American mode of life, that we judge naive or devoid of culture, that gives us the completed picture of the object of our values."[13]

European intellectuals only discredit themselves by their anti-Americanism. They are contemptuous, for example, of the easy familiarity with which Americans treat each other and with the equality of status accorded to almost everyone: "This easiness can appear to us as vulgar or common, . . . [but] it is our affectation that is ridiculous."[14] Or European intellectuals go on and on about the absence of culture in America, but it is they, with their obsession about cultural heredity and their insistence that everything be judged in cultural terms, who are foolish. The genuinely postmodern thinker is one who has moved beyond this kind of anti-Americanism. She is one for whom disgust has given way to fascination and for whom American primitivism is not an object of disdain but of appreciation.

Baudrillard's criticisms of European intellectuals apply even more to their

American counterparts, who can best be described as would-be Europeans. For Baudrillard the American intellectual is a sad, even pathetic figure—a lonely character without a country, wandering in a land where neither thought nor culture plays any formative role. Baudrillard gives the American intellectual scant attention, other than to take him gently to task for his overwrought efforts to ape the European intellectual.[15] Americans are mistaken when they believe that they can think like Europeans. They cannot, and, poor things, they should not try. They would do much better to content themselves with being the primitives that they are, devoting themselves (as now, incidentally, many do) to their institutes of pop culture or media studies. Fortunately for America, however, the intellectuals manage to do little harm. Cloistered in their academic paradises, they leave the formation of culture to the real postmoderns working in cinema and advertising.

Baudrillard is, if anything, even less guilty of the second charge of anti-Americanism. He refuses to take the side of "Europe" and advocates no program, at least in *America,* for an intellectual reawakening to transform American culture or politics. Baudrillard is so far from this position that when it comes to any judgment between the Old World and the New, he almost always pronounces himself in favor of the New. If there is any hint of political voluntarism in his thought, it seems to be in the direction of trying to make Europe more like America, rather than the reverse.

We are accordingly spared those boring sermons, so fashionable today, about how "American" (that is, the English language) is polluting all the European tongues. Linguistic penetration, of course, may well be a serious problem; but if it is, Baudrillard at least cannot be counted among those who think it can be solved by Americans apologizing for their language or trying to restrict its use. One may add here that, apart from merely expecting that everyone should speak English, Americans have never been terribly imperialistic about their language. The same cannot be said, of course, of the French, who according to James Wilson made "laudable attempts toward establishing a universal language" in the eighteenth century.[16] The paradox is that those in France who complain loudest about American linguistic imperialism have not yet apologized for when the French-speaking Norman kings forced thousands of French words into the English language, forever diluting its character, or for when French was the obligatory language of the courts and polite society throughout Europe.[17]

Baudrillard's preference for America derives above all from his belief that America is the wave of the future. As there is no standard of natural right, the only standard is simply what is: success absolves almost any crime. American primitivism means power: "America has the power of in-culture. . . . The future power lies with peoples without origins, without authenticity, and who will know how to exploit that situation to the limit." This power manifests itself concretely not so much in military might or in economic strength or even in the appeal of an idea of rights and freedom, but in the capacity to project copies or images: "All myths of modernity are American."[18]

Baudrillard attributes the modernity and power of America to her primitive mind-set. To be modern, one must be able to fashion reality according to one's will, even to the extent of accepting copies as real. One must believe in the immanence of things here and now and must have the confidence to construct a utopia. These are ideas that European thinkers conceived but that Europeans have been incapable of putting fully into effect. Americans can. America is thus the fulfillment of Europe, the end point of the Old World's development. The European will understand nothing of his "own history or of the end of his own history" if he cannot appreciate that the "barbarism" and "power" of American primitivism represent the culmination of his own principles.[19]

The European's strange hesitancy in the face of modernity and inadequacy when compared with the American's boldness can be traced to the effects of the American and French Revolutions. The French Revolution—which is also, according to Baudrillard, the European Revolution—created a gap between the here-and-now and some ideal of the transcendent pictured in history, ideology, or an idea of Nature. This dualism has ever since immobilized the European by erecting a kind of standard against which he acts or seeks to create. He is self-conscious of quality and therefore helpless. Culture paralyzes. The American Revolution, in contrast, promoted the idea of building a reality in this world. America, Baudrillard asserts, skipped over nineteenth-century thought. Americans can therefore create unself-consciously in this world without experiencing the difficulty that comes from searching for the "authentic." There is not even an American equivalent for *Angst*. Americans are not burdened by taste or by standards. To the primitive's way of thinking: "Disneyland, there, that's authentic; the movies, TV, there that's real!"[20]

It is for this theme of what is or is not real that Baudrillard is apparently most recognized today. "The importance of Baudrillard for society," Bryan Turner has observed, "lies in the fact that he has attempted to address the peculiar problems of postmodern culture in contemporary society and has developed a unique style for its analysis."[21] One of these problems is clearly that odd sense that any thinking person experiences today in observing so much copying and image making; one can only wonder sometimes what exactly *is* the real thing. Early in the twentieth century, a principal objection to America was the ersatz quality of its way of life—the charge, in Rilke's words, that everything here is a "copy" or a "sham article." With Baudrillard this problem becomes less a fault than a great theme, perhaps even the central reality, of our time. Baudrillard treats this theme under the heading of what he calls the "simulacrum" or "hyperreality."

One of the first to explore this theme in detail was not Baudrillard but Umberto Eco in a wonderful essay, "Travels in Hyperreality," written in 1975. In his search to understand one facet of modern life, Eco came to America to "take a journey into hyperreality, in search of instances where the American imagination demands the real thing, and, to attain it, must fabricate the absolute fake." Eco spent much of his time, naturally, in California, which—as some Californians have observed—stands as a symbol in relation to America somewhat as America stands in relation to Europe. Eco, of course, visited Disneyland, which is a whole park of hyperreality. The high point of his journey, however, was the visit to the Palace of Living Arts in Buena Park, Los Angeles. There, the customer can see three-dimensional wax replicas of classic works of art, including the Mona Lisa, the display of which offers the added benefit of depicting Leonardo da Vinci in the process of creating her. The experience at the wax museum provided Eco with his central thesis: "The Palace's philosophy is not 'We are giving you the reproduction so you want the original,' but rather 'We are giving you the reproduction so you will no longer feel any need for the original.'"[22]

Baudrillard makes much the same discovery. In *Simulations,* a work published in 1981, Baudrillard describes the epiphany he experienced at Disneyland: "Disneyland is presented as imaginary in order to make us believe that the rest is real, when in fact all of Los Angeles and America surrounding it are no longer real, but of the order of the hyperreal and of simulation. . . . Disneyland is a deterrence machine set up in order to rejuvenate in reverse the fiction of the real." What was a facet of modernity for Eco becomes the core of the whole of the postmodern for Baudrillard, who has made the world to resemble his text. There are so many similarities between the insights and even the phrasing of Baudrillard and those of Eco (although Baudrillard never mentions Eco) that one sociologist has wondered why no one has compared Eco's *Travels in Hyperreality* with Baudrillard's work.[23] Indeed, the parallels are so uncanny that it seems we are experiencing a real simulacrum—Baudrillard's copy of Eco—and are uncertain whether we are reading Umberto Baudrillard or Jean Eco.

This is certainly not the first instance in which Baudrillard engages in wholesale literary simulation. His presentation of the American way of life, as I have noted, duplicates almost perfectly the symbolic America sketched by Heidegger. But in this case Baudrillard differentiates himself from his source. He takes that patented postmodern next step and turns everything back on itself by posing as America's champion, not her adversary. Whereas Heidegger spoke ominously of a world in crisis and of a last, desperate chance for redemption by overcoming America, Baudrillard revels in the triumph of American primitivism as he speeds along a Los Angeles freeway, convertible top down, shouting, "Forget Heidegger, forget Foucault!" In any event, resistance to America is futile. To overcome America by an act of intellectualized will or by a program of philosophy or politics is out of the question. Thought no longer has this role or office in the modern world. It was that bourgeois Marx who dreamed of using thought to change the world. Until now philosophers have only changed the world; the point, however, is to play with it. For Baudrillard, there is no unhappy ending, no epoch beyond the present, no "catastrophe." He is beyond anti-Americanism.

Postmodernism and Reaganism

Near the end of his journey, with a literary tour de force within his grasp, Baudrillard unexpectedly succumbs to the temptation to preach. The object of his animus, unfortunately, is just the target one would expect from a conventional analysis from a conventional intellectual: Baudrillard cannot stand Ronald Reagan. This reaction is curious and even unjust. Reagan, of course, possesses every credential that Baudrillard set for the American model. After all, who better than Reagan has mastered the postmodernist techniques of advertising and image creation? Who better than Reagan was the archetype of the primitive?

Baudrillard acknowledges these points, which only makes his turn against America's great actor-president all the more mysterious. Reagan's success, Baudrillard complains, comes at the expense of America's "victims." Reaganism hides poverty and racism, and conceals the genocide of the Indian. Somehow, too, Reaganism suppresses all memory of the assassination of John F. Kennedy, and it is the suppression of this memory "on which at bottom is founded the present reign of Reagan."[24] (It took Oliver Stone to unpack the connection.) The fixation on Kennedy leads Baudrillard to his final *gaucherie*: "Reagan has obtained through his smile a consensus far superior to that which any of the Kennedys might have obtained through thought or through political intelligence."[25] A half-century of sometimes anguished, sometimes ironic postmodern philosophy has left us with this one great truism: every Kennedy is more intelligent than Ronald Reagan.

One can only wonder why so bold a thinker would suddenly change from enfant terrible to enfant banal. Was he perhaps attempting to ingratiate himself with American postmodernist thinkers, who, despite all the bluster about their anti-essentialism, toe a fairly orthodox ideological line? If this was his gambit, however, he managed to show only how deeply he underestimated the pull of the symbolic America on American postmodern intellectuals. They could not be bought off so easily. At an international conference on Baudrillard's thought, held in 1989 in Montana, two American postmodernist theorists risked a criticism of *America* on the following grounds: "He [Baudrillard] hangs out in southern California and concludes that the United States is a 'realized Utopia.' He fails to see, however, the homeless, the poor, racism, sexism, people dying of AIDS, oppressed immigrants, and fails to relate any of the phenomena observed . . . to the conservative political hegemony of the 1980s. . . . Baudrillard's erasure of the fundamentality of sexual and racial differences is highly insensitive and even grotesque. Most blacks and people of color experience virulent racism in the United States. . . . Most blacks do not achieve the media fame and wealth of Michael Jackson and cannot easily mix racial and sexual features in new configurations."[26]

Postmodern Politics

With Baudrillard we reach the end point in the fabrication of the symbolic or metaphysical America, where America has been fully transformed from a country into a trope or a fiction. America is a vast literary playground where sophisticated thinkers exercise their wit and practice their ironic aerobics. Baudrillard draws a parallel—in this instance without even a hint of irony—between his voyage to America and that of his countryman Alexis de Tocqueville. Both came to America, Baudrillard tells us, to see the face of modernity. But there, I must say, all similarities end. Tocqueville came to study the real America and to aid the cause of freedom by restoring political science as the guiding discipline of modern politics. Baudrillard came to observe the "copy" of America and to "discover that one can exult in the liquidation of all culture and rejoice in the consecration of in-difference."[27] For Tocqueville, the sociological fact of modernity was important, but it marked not the end of his analysis but the beginning. He treated modernity as a circumstance or condition and proceeded to elaborate a new political science for a new world. For Baudrillard, no such step is even contemplated. The sociological fact of postmodernity is all there is, and describing it becomes the whole of his enterprise.

Embedded in Baudrillard's sociology is nevertheless a clear political line. It is one guided not by political analysis but by certain categories and assumptions that derive from postmetaphysical thinking. As far removed as Baudrillard's jargon of the "consecration of in-difference" may seem from politics, we live today in an intellectualized world where all manner of ideas from art, philosophy, and literary criticism have managed to insinuate themselves into the real political world. Nor has this occurred by accident. For well over a half-century, America discourse has promoted an aesthetic or literary approach to political thinking, with artistic or literary criteria vying to take the place of political criteria. Baudrillard's work follows in this tradition. Is it reasonable, after all, to suppose that the symbol of America, so long employed to carry a political message, should now suddenly have lost all of its political overtones and become an anemic cultural icon? In the playful world of postmodernism, nothing is as innocent as it seems.

The political object of America discourse remains in fact what it has always been: a project to transform or overcome liberal democracy. There are different variants of this project. The kinder and gentler versions call for replacing our current order with a nominally more democratic and tolerant society devoted to fostering diversity and difference. The harder and more revolutionary versions spoken of now in some philosophical circles aim at the destruction of America and the West. And there is everything in between.

Some of the kinder and gentler variants derive from a line of thought that applies the ideas of anti-essentialism or of the method of deconstruction to political society. These philosophies, it seems, are expected to serve as the basic grounding for political life, on the premise that what is good for the intellectual life must somehow be good for political life as well. Philosophical or literary logic transfers directly into politics.

The elaboration of this view is found in the works of Baudrillard's famous compatriot Jacques Derrida. Derrida, who uttered the oracular phrase "Deconstruction is justice," is a difficult writer to decipher, lacking the wit, the charm, and above all the brevity of Baudrillard.[28] In spite of numerous stays in the United States, Derrida has not written very much on America. On one occasion, in fact, he passed up the perfect opportunity—I would even say the obligation—to do so. In 1976 he was invited to give a series of lectures at the University of Virginia to commemorate the bicentennial of America's founding and was asked by the university to compare the Declaration of Independence and the Declaration of the Rights of Man. Derrida accepted the invitation but declined to address the topic, remarking, "It is better that you know right away: I am not going to keep my promise." Derrida went on to devote his lectures to Nietzsche instead.[29]

Still, Derrida did make a few comments about Jefferson and the Declaration, referring to the general question of who may act, and in the name of whom, when a nation or institution is founded. Beginnings, when no authority or tradition is yet established, are at once delicate and decisive moments when something new is being created. But it was not so much the political as the literary aspects of origination that interested Derrida, as if what holds for the creation of a new literary genre must hold for the establishment of a new political regime. In contrast, for America's founders it was the political aspects of the problem of origination that demanded attention, and they never suggested that the logic of political innovation was the same as that for literary innovation. Because of the dangers in acting beyond or outside established authority, the founders thought it was unwise to encourage movement into a revolutionary situation for "light and transient causes." And once embarked on this course, it is important to circumscribe authority as clearly as possible by citing natural law, in order to avoid the falling into an open sea of revolution and counter-revolution.

Although Derrida did not treat political questions directly in 1976, he turned to some of them in *Force of Law* (1994). His focus here was not on revolutionary moments but on the opposite situation of established authority and tradition. The problem in this case is that once laws exist, many issues become closed off or circumscribed, and injustices get locked in. Because justice is never fully realized by law, law should be put under question and deconstructed. In the context of modern societies Derrida is concerned in particular with achieving liberation for various minorities and for animals. But in this admirable search for justice and liberation (although not liberty), he avoids confronting one of the first questions of political science: what are the things needed to keep a society together? An ongoing deconstruction of laws cannot take place without putting law as such into question, with all the consequences that might follow. Of course, in a nation of literary critics and philosophers, this consideration could be disregarded, and law could be supported by the voice of ironic thinking. But a "nation of philosophers," *The Federalist* reminds us, is an impossibility, so even the most rational government "will not find it a superfluous advantage to have the prejudices of the community on its side."[30]

The harder version of postmodern politics revives the notion that the Enlightenment will not just fade away, slowly ironized out of existence, but that it will need to be killed off. It may come as something of a surprise that Baudrillard has emerged as a leading exponent of this second version. What he covers up by irony in *America,* he exposes with frankness in *The Gulf War Never Took Place* (1991). In this book, Baudrillard reminds us of the awful character of the modern Western technological idea, which aims to control, homogenize, order, and dominate. A view of Being always determines the political realm. The West, with America at its center, is a vast despotism that practices a "consensual integrism (of Enlightenment, of rights of man, . . . of sentimental humanism) that is just as ferocious as

that of any tribal religion or primitive society." This project is all the more ominous because it is on the verge of being realized, with the West and America succeeding in "ordering" everything.[31]

For this project to be stopped, fate will have to send us a force strong enough
and hostile enough to destroy America. Only a god can save us. Meanwhile, we—
meaning we intellectuals—must do our part by preparing the ground. Just as Heidegger once took up a blunt political instrument to try to subdue the liberal project, so Baudrillard does not shy away from an anti-Western fundamentalism—or
from anything else—to overcome America today. Baudrillard concludes *The Gulf
War Never Took Place* by citing Heidegger's favorite line from Hölderlin: "There
where the danger grows, grows also that which saves us." So radical a view is outside the mainstream of postmodern thought today, which generally stops short of
such extremes. Still, to dismiss this radical wing would be a mistake, for if philosophy eventually works its way into politics, it will likely follow its boldest expression. Unfortunately for America, not the tendentious tracts on the politics of
difference but the daring attacks of Jean Baudrillard may represent postmodernism in its most resolute form.

Conclusion

Before me on my desk lies a pile of opinion poll data and anecdotal information on how different peoples around the world think about the United States. My original plan was to feature this material in a study of mass and elite public opinion on America in several foreign countries. What I quickly realized, however, was that such an inquiry would be premature. What I had to investigate first was the origin and development of the symbol of America, which has shaped much of the thinking about this country for the past two hundred years. Opinion about America has largely been an artifact of this symbol, if not always directly for the public at large, then at any rate for large segments of the intelligentsia.

The symbolic America was conceived as part of a project that is hostile to the Enlightenment, to liberal democracy, and to political science. America has carried much of the burden for promoting this message, and never more so than today, when the United States has achieved a prominent position in the world. As a symbol America is identified with images that represent at best simple half-truths and at worst grotesque caricatures of the real character of American life. But for those who employ this discourse, accuracy is irrelevant: America is a prop for carrying on a different discussion. In order for the symbol to bear its theoretical weight and to perform its function, America must be a certain way, whether it truly is so or not.

In tracing the development of this symbol, I sometimes found it impossible not to be indignant about a project meant to inflict so much harm on the United States. And I was saddened to observe how this discourse has spread to these shores, infecting the thinking of so many of our own intellectuals and contributing to a loss of confidence in our principles. Moved by these sentiments, I undertook the task of trying to recapture control of our own name. I did so not with the intention of defending everything American (for an unreflective patriotism can be almost as harmful as a reflexive hostility to one's country), but with the aim of removing the prejudices that prevent us from clearly assessing our situation. For a long time, however, I could not settle on the best way for going about this task. I seemed to be at a disadvantage, for in my discipline of political science, we have few means for rivaling the inventive narratives and charming paradoxes created by the literary critics and philosophers who have fashioned the symbolic America.

In order to meet this challenge, I considered for a time adopting some of the techniques of writers in these disciplines, as many of them are known to be masters of the art of unmasking traditional symbols. For some, indeed, this is their central vocation. "The job facing the cultural intellectual," Edward Said has written, is "to show how all representations are constructed, for what purposes, by whom, and with what components."[1] I thought that nothing could be more helpful to my own purpose than following the example of such thinkers, employing their techniques to deal with a representation that they have found expedient to leave untouched.

Two methods from these disciplines stood out as most promising. One might best be called, for want of an adequate English term, the hieroglyphics of literary criticism. This name struck me as appropriate when I opened up a work by Jacques Derrida, whose ideas helped to lay the foundation for the modern politics of difference. On many pages of Derrida's text, in the place of the written word in its usual form, one finds what looks at first glance to be markings like those seen on the coffins of ancient Egyptian mummies. But closer inspection reveals that these odd signs are nothing more than ordinary words (in French) printed with large Xs superimposed on them. Thus one passage of Derridean text reads (one need not bother, really, with the meaning): "The formal essence of the sign can only be determined in terms of presence. One cannot get around that response, except by challenging the very form of the question and beginning to think that the sign ~~is~~ that ill-named ~~thing~~, the only one that escapes the instituting question of philosophy: 'What is . . . ?'"[2]

Derrida refers to this technique of crossing out words as writing *sous rature* (under erasure). It apparently originated not with Derrida but, as far as I have been able to discover, with Martin Heidegger's essay "On the Question of Being," where Heidegger places the key term *Sein* (to be) under an X or what he called a *Zeichen der Durchstrichung* (a sign of striking through).[3] Writing sous rature, as Derrida explains, allows one to deal with an insoluble problem connected with the use of language. Because all signs or concepts of language are constructed, they are therefore in some sense arbitrary; at the same time, however, we need language in order to communicate. Writing under erasure enables us to be conscious of this problem, for in a sense we both have a word and do not have a word. (Incidentally, the founders agonized over the similar difficulty that "no language is so copious as to supply words and ideas for every complex idea, or so correct as not to include many equivocally denoting different ideas."[4] But not having available to them the modern technique of writing sous rature, they were forced to make do with the cruder method of trying to explain, by successive refinements, the meaning of the words they used.)

For a time, I was so impressed with this technique that I thought of applying it in this study: each time a cultural intellectual used the word "America" in his narrative, I would place it sous rature. With this device I could remind readers of how arbitrary or constructed is this symbol. Yet as effective as this tactic would have been, I hesitated to adopt it, thinking that there was an excess of refinement in taking something I knew to be real, and to which a rational attachment is in every sense justified, and questioning its very existence. Nor could I prevent myself from thinking that the use of this technique would amount to a desecration of my country. Would it be right, for example, to print the Pledge of Allegiance with "America" written sous rature? Or, setting aside considerations of rightness (for many do not subscribe to them), would it not at least be imprudent to "depriv[e] the government of that veneration . . . without which perhaps the wisest and freest governments would not possess the requisite stability"?[5]

So, rejecting this method, I turned to a second and more fashionable technique employed by these writers: "Other discourse." Other discourse, I discovered, is linked directly to the philosophical problem identified in writing sous rature. In the interpretation of any word or sign (it is said), one reading can become "privileged," thus having the effect of marginalizing alternative readings, which then become "Other." However this may be, it is the transference of Other discourse from the philosophical to the political realm that accounts for its broad appeal to intellectuals today. In the political use of this discourse, certain nations, races, or groups are said to be the Hegemon (or Oppressor) with the power to control the situation, while those excluded merit the distinction of being the marginalized Other. The purpose of this discourse is not, of course, primarily to describe the current power relationship, but to subvert and reverse it. The Other is converted into a valorized object while the Hegemon becomes a figure of obloquy.

In view of America's military and economic prowess today, it is readily understandable why many in the world wish to label America the Hegemon and avail themselves of a discourse that might weaken the United States. Such tactics are to be expected in the conduct of international affairs, where some nations have interests and purposes at odds with those of a great power. But the symbol of America arose long before the United States acquired its current status. Setting aside the immediate political situation, therefore, and focusing on the realm of intellectual ideas, it is hard to see how anyone could justify counting America as the Hegemon. Just the opposite is the case. In literature and philosophy, one nation stands out during this period for the abuse to which it has been subjected. Of no other country today could one say the things routinely charged against America without being accused of something far worse than cultural insensitivity. Can one imagine, for example, a famous intellectual calling the people of Zimbabwe "obese" or those of Ecuador "idiotic" or those of Cambodia "uncultured" and yet withal still being accorded the highest accolades?

There would be every ground, therefore, for viewing America as the marginalized figure of modern intellectual life and the veritable Other of our era. By availing myself of Other discourse, I could no doubt have achieved much for America, just as those who daily use it accomplish so much for their various clients. It would have been possible to browbeat the bearers of the new intellectual orthodoxies into halting their relentless attacks on America, compel students to open their ears to the founders' muffled "voice of reason," and force university administrators and faculty to end the privileged status of cultural and gender studies and reinstitute real American studies, including traditional political science. Yet once again, after due reflection, I decided to forgo this strategy, tempting as it was. I saw that any compensation this rhetoric might win for the abuses America has suffered would be more than offset by the harm it would do to Americans' pride and spirit. To single out America as the Other would mean abandoning the noble project of vindicating the honor of the entire human race. I knew, for example, that I could not employ this technique without violating the self-evident truth that Americans were created equal to everyone else—no more hegemonic, but certainly no more marginalized either.

So, forsaking the weapons used by the purveyors of symbolic America, I decided that the only way to proceed was by using a straightforward language that appealed to my readers' reason and good sense. Shunning all pretense and literary embellishment, I resolved to present the case for the real America to a world that I hoped was not yet so overcome with the sense of irony that it could not weigh candidly a few simple observations. So it was that I tried first to show that the abandonment of political science as the intellectual guide for political actions would be a dangerous error. Each time in the past that an alternative discipline took the place of political science, either reducing politics to the subpolitical (for example, natural history) or elevating politics to the suprapolitical (for example, the movement of History), the result was disastrous. Although we do not yet know all the consequences that will follow from the latest substitution of literary disciplines for a political approach, there is every reason here, too, to fear the worst.

I tried next to demonstrate that our fascination with the emergence of modernity or postmodernity constitutes a form of reductive sociologism. It is perhaps true—at least virtually everyone seems to think so—that America is the most modern nation in the world, the place where modernity is daily working itself out. But modernity is a condition or circumstance—no less, but also no more. It is the circle of fate in which we operate. Political science has never been content to stop its inquiry at the point of describing a historical circumstance, but it has always continued on to ask how different political regimes can address that circumstance inside particular societies and around the world. Have we become so absorbed in our postmodernity that we have forgotten that humans have always lived inside a modernity? Were America's founders any less conscious of acting in new times, under new conditions? Was Tocqueville any less mindful of writing for a new age? Yet, for all that, none of them abandoned political science for intellectual history or cultural commentary. Our modernity, many like to think, is qualitatively different from their modernity. But each modernity is unique, and experience offers no reason to think that our time is the first to have obviated the need of dealing with the human predicament at the political level.

I then tried to show the fallacy involved in the criticism made today against America as the symbol for the Enlightenment. The attack today on the Enlightenment, which is so much a part of modern philosophy and cultural studies, is all very interesting, perhaps even largely merited; but it is also misplaced in its use of America. It has given rise to the following syllogism, which, whether stated or unstated, undergirds contemporary America discourse: the Enlightenment is totalitarian; America is a quintessential part of the Enlightenment; America is therefore totalitarian. Unlike many who offer this syllogism, I have no quarrel with the use of reason. But consulting facts is also a part of reason, and the most elementary study of history teaches that political science as it was reintroduced at the time of America's founding produced one of the most profound criticisms of the excesses of abstract ideological thought. By what sort of perverse logic would one wish to group together the best hope for mankind with a doctrine that would doom the world to despotism?

Finally, I tried to address a broader but vaguer indictment, which asserts that our civilization (designated the West, or sometimes America) is responsible for the horrors that have occurred in the twentieth century. This charge is difficult to challenge, because it appeals to an inchoate sense of guilt that aims to put the accuser on a higher moral plane. But for those who set emotion aside, it will be seen that this charge rests on the questionable assumption that civilization is the unit that moves history. On this view it follows that political phenomena and a specifically political field of action have no claim to being a primary cause of human destiny. No wonder, then, that those who have adopted this premise have usually dismissed all talk of essential differences among regimes, placing them instead on the same plane. But for all the intellectual confidence that accompanies the assigning of causality to civilization, few in fact have examined this unit or whole to determine if it deserves all the attention. Might not the correct unit be something "above" our civilization—say, human nature and the human race? We could then all be horrified at what we have done to one another. Or perhaps the relevant unit is something "below" civilization, which is the political regime. The different regimes could then be assigned the degrees of responsibility and culpability they deserve.

I know, of course, that all these units somehow play a part. Surely the human race is involved, and here we are answerable to one another and to God. Civilization, too, has a role, and we are responsible on this score for what we contribute to the ideas that influence the mores and ways of thinking in all of our societies. But our destiny is also shaped at the level of political life, in the actions and decisions taken by different political regimes. We are most plausibly accountable here. And it is just here that we should look to rediscover the real America.

Notes

Introduction

1. Henry de Montherlant, *"Le chaos" et "La nuit"* (Paris: Gallimard, 1963), 265. Translation of Jean-Philippe Mathy, *Extrême-Occident* (Chicago: University of Chicago Press, 1993), 18.

2. *L'Amérique dans les têtes,* ed. Denis Lacorne, Jacques Rupnik, and Marie-France Toinet (Paris: Hachette, 1986).

3. Roland Barthes, *Le degré zéro de l'écriture* (Paris: Seuil, 1972), 16.

4. Bernard Lewis, "The Roots of Muslim Rage," *Atlantic,* September 1990, 52. Lewis has traced the Islamic view of America to "intellectual influences coming from Europe," especially German philosophy, "which enjoyed a considerable vogue among Arab and some other Muslim intellectuals in the thirties and early forties."

5. Mathy, *Extrême-Occident,* 17.

6. Walter Lippmann, "Stereotypes," in *Public Opinion* (New York: Free Press, 1966), 53–68.

7. The quotations from Cau and Gallo are cited in Alan Riding, "Only the French Elite Scorn Mickey's Debut," *New York Times,* 13 April 1992, A1, A13. For an analysis of French attitudes toward Disney, see Peter Guerlain, "Qui diabolise Mickey?" *Esprit,* June 1992, 160–168; and Shanny Peer, "Marketing Mickey: Disney Goes to France," *Tocqueville Review* 13, no. 2 (1992): 127–142. The expression "Trojan Mouse" is from Peer's article.

8. The Adorno-Benjamin exchange is in Walter Benjamin, *Gesammelte Schriften,* ed. Rolf Tiedemann and Herman Schweppenhäuser (Frankfurt: Suhrkamp Verlag, 1977), and is discussed in Laurence Rickels, *The Case of California* (Baltimore: Johns Hopkins University Press, 1991); Jean Baudrillard, *Simulacre et simulation* (Paris: Galilée, 1981), 25–26.

9. Martin Heidegger, "Hölderlins Hymne 'Der Ister,'" in *Gesamtausgabe* (Frankfurt: Vittorio Klostermann, 1975), 53:86; Martin Heidegger, "Die Zeit des Weltbildes," in *Holzwege* (Frankfurt: Vittorio Klostermann, 1957), 103; Heidegger, "Hölderlins Hymne," 53:179.

10. Edward Said, *Culture and Imperialism* (New York: Knopf, 1994), 298.

11. Iris Marion Young, *Justice and the Politics of Difference* (Princeton: Princeton Uni-

versity Press, 1990), 98, 99; Max Horkheimer and Theodor Adorno, *Dialectic of Enlightenment* (New York: Continuum, 1995), 6.

12. Young, *Politics of Difference,* 99, 111.

13. Joyce Appleby, "Recovering America's Historic Diversity: Beyond Exceptionalism," *Journal of American History* 79 (September 1992): 430, 420, 429. The pejorative epithet "founderism" does not come from Appleby, who is one of the foremost scholars of the founding, but from Stanley Fish, who used the term to characterize the position I took in a speech delivered at Michigan State University in May 1992.

14. Charles Baudelaire, "Edgar Poe: Sa vie et ses oeuvres," introduction to Edgar Allan Poe, *Histoires extraordinaires,* trans. Baudelaire (1857; reprint, Paris: Hachette, 1980), iii.

15. Jean Baudrillard, *La Guerre du Golfe n'a pas eu lieu* (Paris: Galilée, 1991), 90.

16. Letter of John Adams to James Lloyd, 29 March 1815, in *The Works of John Adams* (Boston: Little, Brown, 1856), 10:148.

17. Richard Rorty, *Contingency, Irony, and Solidarity* (Cambridge: Cambridge University Press, 1989), 82–83.

18. For America's founders, as for most people in the late eighteenth century, "science" and "philosophy" were synonyms. My distinction is a nineteenth-century one, but it is useful for modern readers.

19. James Wilson, speech at the Pennsylvania Ratifying Convention, 11 December 1787, in Jonathan Elliott, ed., *The Debates in the Several State Conventions on the Adoption of the Federal Convention* (New York: Burt Franklin, 1974), 2:527.

20. Octavio Paz, "América en plural y en singular," *Vuelta* 194 (January 1993): 11.

21. The description of Vespucci's theft comes from the abbé Guillaume Thomas François Raynal's *History of Two Indies* (1770) and is cited in a letter from Benjamin Rush to James Madison, 27 February 1790, *The Letters of Benjamin Rush,* ed. L. H. Butterfield (Princeton: Princeton University Press, 1951), 1:539.

The theft to which Raynal refers was not entirely of Vespucci's making. According to Kirkpatrick Sale, in his journals Vespucci took credit for discovering South America in 1497, a year when he was at home in Europe. The earliest use of Vespucci's name to describe the New World territories occurred in 1507, when a mapmaker named Martin Waldseemüler used a latinized version of Vespucci's first name to describe the southern continent. Although Waldseemüler corrected his mistake in his revision of 1513, the error had taken hold. In 1538, the mapmaker Gerardus Mercator first used the word "America" to refer to the northern continent. See Kirkpatrick Sale, *The Conquest of Paradise* (New York: Knopf, 1990), pp. 215–216.

22. Johann Wolfgang von Goethe, "The United States," in *Amerika: Im Spiegel des Deutschen politischen Denkens,* ed. Ernst Fraenkel (Cologne: Westdeutscher Verlag, 1959), 108; Joseph Horowitz, *Wagner Nights: An American History* (Berkeley: University of California Press, 1994), 22; Glenn Plaskin, *Horowitz* (New York: William Morrow, 1983), 216, 217. Wagner frequently threatened to emigrate to America, sometimes merely as a way of letting off steam, at other times as a way of pressuring his patrons to increase their support. A more typical view of America came in one of King Ludwig's responses to Wagner's threats: "Your roses will not grow in America's sterile soil, where selfishness, lovelessness, and Mammon hold sway" (Horowitz, *Wagner Nights,* 23). Rachmaninoff was referring to the Disney film *Mickey's Opry House,* in which Mickey plays the famous prelude. By this time,

however, Rachmaninoff had become thoroughly Americanized. After leaving Russia during the 1917 Revolution, he came to America and eventually settled in Beverly Hills, where he socialized with Walt Disney.

23. Almost all the intellectual historians who have surveyed this topic support this conclusion. See especially C. Vann Woodward, *The Old World's New World* (Oxford: Oxford University Press, 1991); Rickels, *Case of California*; Paul Hollander, *Anti-Americanism* (Oxford: Oxford University Press, 1992); and Antonello Gerbi, *The Dispute of the New World* (Pittsburgh: University of Pittsburgh Press, 1955).

24. John Dewey, *Reconstruction in Philosophy* (Boston: Beacon Press, 1948), 130.

25. Alexander Hamilton, James Madison, and John Jay, *Federalist* no. 40, in *The Federalist Papers,* ed. Clinton Rossiter (New York: New American Library, 1961), 254 (hereafter cited as *Federalist,* followed by the number of the paper and the page number).

26. Thomas Jefferson, query 6, *Notes on the State of Virginia,* in *The Portable Thomas Jefferson,* ed. Merrill Peterson (New York: Penguin, 1975), 102–103 (hereafter cited as *Notes*); *Federalist* no. 11, 91.

Chapter 1: America as Degeneracy

1. This point is discussed in Gilbert Chinard, "Eighteenth-Century Theories on America as Human Habitat," *Proceedings of the American Philosophical Society* 91, no. 1 (1947): 27–57.

2. These characterizations of the views of the New World are taken from Leo Marx, *The Machine in the Garden* (London: Oxford University Press, 1964), 36–45.

3. *Notes*, query 6, 90.

4. This history of the term "anthropology" is confirmed by a number of modern scholars, and it fits with the approach of many late-eighteenth-century and early-nineteenth-century thinkers who called the part of natural history that treated man "ethnology" or "anthropology." See Michèle Duchet, introduction to Georges Louis Leclerc, the Count de Buffon, *De l'homme,* ed. Michèle Duchet (Paris: Maspero, 1971), 7–36; this work, which is hereafter cited as *De l'homme,* is a single-volume edition of selections from the various editions of Buffon's forty-three-volume work. See also Michèle Duchet, *Anthropologie et histoire au siècle des lumières* (Paris: Maspero, 1971), and Jacques Roger, *Buffon: Un philosophe au jardin du roi* (Paris: Fayard, 1989), 223–247. The history of the development of anthropology is told by Duchet in *Le partage des savoirs* (Paris: La Découverte, 1985). In 1788 Alexandre Chavannes defined the term in its modern sense. Buffon did not favor the term, but the subject matter and method he developed in his study of man under the general rubric of natural history became the foundation of anthropology.

5. Cornelius de Pauw, *Recherches philosophiques sur les Américains: Mémoires intéressants pour servir à l'histoire de l'espèce humaine,* 3 vols. (1770; reprint, Upper Saddle, N.J.: Gregg Press, 1968) (hereafter cited as *Recherches*). The book's subtitle—*Important Notes Toward a History of the Human Species*—indicates de Pauw's broader scientific interest in the question of the unity and diversity of man.

6. Chinard, "Eighteenth-Century Theories," 45.

7. The controversy was named after the title of Gerbi's *Dispute of the New World.* Among

the important New World respondents not from the United States was the Mexican Francesco Clavigero, author of *Storia antica del Messico* (1780–1781), which was written and first published in Italian.

8. *Federalist* no. 1, 33.

9. Jefferson uses the name *Homo sapiens Europaeus* in his discussion of Buffon and the degeneracy thesis (*Notes*, query 6, 99); the name actually derives from Linnaeus, not Buffon. Publius' quotation is from *Federalist* no. 11, 90.

10. *Recherches* 3:115–116, 105–118.

11. The only English-language essay on de Pauw I have found is Henry Ward Church, "Corneille de Pauw and the Controversy over His *Recherches philosophiques sur les Américains*," *Publications of the Modern Language Association of America* 51 (March 1936): 178–206. Other discussions of de Pauw's influence can be found in the works cited here by Chinard, Gerbi, and Martin. In French, Duchet's *Le partage des savoirs* devotes an interesting chapter to de Pauw's account of America.

12. Chinard, "Eighteenth-Century Theories," 35. Duchet argues for the influence of de Pauw on Hegel, showing certain similarities of their argument and language (*Le partage des savoirs,* 117–118).

13. The article was written in 1890 by John Clark Ridpath, a DePauw University history professor, and is discussed in Church, "Corneille de Pauw." I am deeply indebted to Professor Baughman, who checked the archives at DePauw University in order to disprove that Cornelius and Washington Charles were related. What remains a mystery is why Ridpath invented this narrative.

14. *Recherches* 1:3–4, 3:6, 1:iii–iv.

15. *Recherches* 1:12, 1:7, 1:8; Louis Dumont, *Mémoires sur la Louisiane* (Paris, 1753), 1:103.

16. *Recherches* 1:5, 1:5, 1:26, 1:122–123; Church, "Corneille de Pauw," 187; *Recherches* 1:5, 1:57.

17. *Recherches* 1:13, 1:13; John Varner and Jeannette Varner, *Dogs of the Conquest* (Norman: University of Oklahoma Press, 1983), xiv.

18. *Recherches* 1:13, 3:10, 1:28. In the eighteenth century, a low rate of population growth was widely viewed as a sign not only of disease but also of poverty and misery. Adam Smith expressed the accepted view: "The most decisive mark of the prosperity of any country is the increase in the number of inhabitants" (*An Inquiry into the Nature and Causes of the Wealth of Nations* [Oxford: Oxford University Press, 1993], 69).

19. *Recherches* 3:10; John Bertram and Peter Kalm, *Histoire naturelle et politique de la Pensilvanie* (Paris, 1768), cited in *Recherches* 3:10 (Kalm's other writings on America, which had appeared in Swedish editions beginning in 1753, are discussed in Chinard, "Eighteenth-Century Theories," 34–36); *Recherches* 3:227; cited in Church, "Corneille de Pauw," 187; Abbé Raynal, *Histoire philosophique et politique des établissements et du commerce des Européens dans les deux Indes,* 4 vols. (Amsterdam, 1770), cited in Jefferson, *Notes,* query 6, 101 (in later editions of his work, Raynal exempted North America, but not South America, from this criticism).

20. Jefferson later recognized de Pauw as the originator of the thesis but had only contempt for his writings: "Paw," as he identifies him, was nothing but a "compiler from the works of

others; and of the most unlucky description; for he seems to have read the writings of travellers only to collect and republish their lies. It is really remarkable, that in three volumes, . . . it is scarcely possible to find one truth" (Jefferson to Chastellux, 7 June 1785, in *The Papers of Thomas Jefferson,* ed. Julian Boyd [Princeton: Princeton University Press, 1950], 8:185).

21. Chinard, "Eighteenth-Century Theories," 36.

22. Ernst Cassirer, *The Philosophy of the Enlightenment* (Princeton: Princeton University Press, 1968), 77. For a similarly favorable judgment of Buffon's importance, see Michel Foucault, *Les mots et les choses* (Paris: Gallimard, 1966), 137–176.

23. The attacks on de Pauw appear in a 1777 addendum to "The Varieties of the Human Species," in which Buffon defends some of the Indian tribes, notably those in Mexico and Peru, from de Pauw's criticisms.

24. Edwin Martin, *Thomas Jefferson: Scientist* (New York: Henry Schuman, 1952), 184–191, catalogues the items Jefferson sent to Buffon and the lengths he went to in assuring their safe passage to France. Dumas Malone, *Jefferson and the Rights of Man* (Boston: Little, Brown, 1951), 98–102, recounts that Jefferson sent to Buffon a copy of Jefferson's *Notes* together with a large panther skin, as the latter disproved one of Buffon's points about the cat species on the two continents.

25. Cited in Gerbi, *Dispute of the New World,* 17; Martin, *Thomas Jefferson,* 157; Gerbi, *Dispute of the New World,* 30.

26. *The Writings of Thomas Jefferson,* Memorial Edition, ed. Andrew Lipscomb (Washington, D.C.: n.p., 1905), 18:170; Bristed, *Resources of the United States,* cited in Martin, *Thomas Jefferson,* 210.

27. Jefferson's translations of passages from Buffon appear in Chinard, "Eighteenth-Century Theories," 30–31.

28. These translations of Buffon are from Martin, *Thomas Jefferson,* 159; Chinard, "Eighteenth-Century Theories," 30; and (the last seven quotations) Martin, *Thomas Jefferson,* 159. The last seven quotations are from Jefferson, *Notes,* query 6, 94–95.

29. Marvin Harris, *The Rise of Anthropological Thinking* (New York: Thomas Crowell, 1968), 85.

30. Man, according to Buffon, is the "only animated being on whom Nature has bestowed sufficient genius . . . to survive and multiply in every climate of the earth." As Chinard notes, Buffon sharply distinguished the American savages, who passively accepted their natural surroundings and readily adapted to natural conditions, from the European colonists, who made every effort to become the masters of nature ("Eighteenth-Century Theories," 32).

31. Roger, *Buffon,* 50–51. "Natural physics" is Roger's term, not Buffon's.

32. Cited by Jefferson in *Notes,* query 6, 87.

33. De Pauw pointed out in his defense that many of his subjects, such as the condition of the Indian when America was first discovered, could never have been observed firsthand. Indeed, his overall focus—the condition and variety of humankind over history—was not observable by any one person. A scholar always had to rely on others' accounts, which then must be subjected to a method that discounts fabricated reports or predetermined conclusions.

34. Buffon's understanding of a species—and its difficulties—are discussed by Ernst

Mayer in *The Growth of Biological Thought* (Cambridge: Harvard University Press, 1982), 260–265.

35. Because climate, an important cause, is also the result of both meteorological factors and physical attributes, climate is also partly an effect. In Buffon's analysis, physical features are affected by the age of the continent, making the newness of the New World a cause of its climate. This theory affected Buffon's attitude toward the New World: things deteriorate in the New World because of its climate, but the New World as a whole is maturing and hence gradually improving. For de Pauw, the two continents are the same age; there is accordingly no historical excuse for the poorer climate of the New World, and no natural process of improvement can be expected.

36. Harris, *Rise of Anthropological Thinking,* 85; *De l'homme,* 271, 320.

37. *De l'homme,* 320–321.

38. *De l'homme,* 321, 317; *Recherches* 1:175–207.

39. Chinard, "Eighteenth-Century Theories," 30; *Recherches* 3:206; *De l'homme,* 319. For the ranking of the Indian below the black, I rely on their general descriptions; for Buffon, see *De l'homme,* 282–283, and for de Pauw, see *Recherches* 3:49.

40. Jacques Roger, "Science and Definitions of Man," in *"Les droits de l'homme" and Scientific Progress* (Washington, D.C.: Smithsonian Institution, Office of Interdisciplinary Studies, 1989), 20; Roger, *Buffon,* 244, 245.

41. "UNESCO Statement by Experts on Race Problems" is printed in Ashley Montagu, *Race, Science, and Humanity* (New York: Van Nostrad, 1963), 172–178. Among those who signed the text were Montagu and Claude Lévi-Strauss. The statement attacks the racialist theories that had guided much thinking in philosophy and social science in the previous century and that had culminated in Nazism.

42. A century earlier, some argued that indigenous beings in the New World were not humans but a different species of animal.

43. Those today who take the view that mankind is a composite of different species do not correlate this fact to differences among racial or ethnic groups. Still, the fear that this position may open the door to a kind of modern-day polygenesis has led some to try to discredit it.

44. Harris, *Rise of Anthropological Thinking,* 85.

45. This point is also argued by Tzvetan Todorov, *Nous et les autres* (Paris: Seuil, 1989), 111–139.

46. Cited in Martin, *Thomas Jefferson,* 208.

47. *Recherches* 1:25–26.

48. *Recherches* 3:129. By the publication of the third volume, however, de Pauw is not so certain that future improvement is impossible. He also discusses the tremendous changes in climate that took place over the ages in Europe, and one wonders why he did not think that the same could occur in America (3:61–66).

49. Jefferson to Le Roy, 13 November 1786, *Writings of Thomas Jefferson* 5:463–472.

50. *Recherches* 1:iv, v, vii.

51. *Recherches* 1:88, 1:89, 3:7.

52. See "Of Cannibals," in *The Complete Essays of Montaigne,* trans. Donald Frame (Stanford: Stanford University Press, 1976), 150–159.

53. *Recherches* 1:vii, 18–19.

54. *Recherches* 1:xi.

55. Church, "Corneille De Pauw," 188.

Chapter 2: American Responses to the Degeneracy Thesis

1. See Benjamin Franklin, *An Historical View of the Constitution and Government of Pennsylvania* (Philadelphia: Olmstead and Power, 1812).

2. Benjamin Franklin, "Those Who Would Remove to America" (1782), in Edwin Martin, *Thomas Jefferson*, 201.

3. *Notes,* query 6, 98–99.

4. *Notes,* query 6, 101–102.

5. Washington to the Marquis de Lafayette, 28 May 1788, *The Writings of George Washington,* ed. John Fitzpatrick (Washington, D.C.: United States Printing Office), 29:506–507.

6. *Notes,* query 6, 101.

7. Cited in Martin, *Thomas Jefferson,* 226.

8. *Notes,* query 14, 186.

9. *Federalist* no. 54, 337–338.

10. *Notes,* query 18, 215.

11. Benjamin Rush, "An Address on the Slavery of the Negroes in America" (1773), in *The Anti-Slavery Crusade in America* (New York: Arno Press, 1969), 23–24. Incidentally, the same "hard" side is also curiously evident in Jefferson's later statement *opposing* a plan to emancipate immediately: "We have the wolf by the ears, and we can neither hold him nor safely let him go" (Jefferson to John Holmes, 22 April 1820, *Writings of Thomas Jefferson* 15:249). In this instance, Jefferson argued that the moral action was incompatible with a prudent action that ensures preservation; indeed, there seemed no longer to be any moral course that was prudent.

12. *Notes,* query 14, 186.

13. *Notes,* query 14, 193.

14. The final version of Jefferson's *Notes* drops this sentence, but not the basic idea.

15. *Notes,* query 6, 104; *Notes,* query 14, 192.

16. *Notes,* query 14, 193, 191. Jefferson twice hedges on the question of polygenesis, at any rate in regard to blacks. He does so in the quotation cited here and also in the preceding section, where he discusses "blacks, whether originally a distinct race, or made distinct by time and circumstance" (192). The second formulation differs from that of Buffon, who does believe that people are made distinct by time and circumstance. In the case of the Indians, Jefferson follows Buffon in holding that they derive from Asians who came across the Bering Strait and that the Eskimo descend from the Greenlanders and the Lapps. But when it comes to black people, Jefferson goes well beyond Buffon in arguing the distinctness of the race. Buffon emphasizes the gradation of colors, which finally reaches the sharper hues. Jefferson does not speak of gradations of white merging into black. Nor can one overlook the fact that what Buffon sees as having a certain beauty, Jefferson finds to be ugly.

17. *Notes,* query 14, 193. Jefferson credits the idea of each species or gradation "moving up" the chain by way of the sexual instinct of the male. Thus the "Oranootan" will prefer black women over the females of his own species, and the black male will presumably pre-

fer white females (187). Jefferson argues that this natural or instinctual preference ought to be regulated by man's "effort" to maintain distinctness and gradation (193).

18. *Notes,* query 14, 193; Jefferson to Edward Coles, 25 August 1814, *Portable Thomas Jefferson,* 546.

19. Jefferson's plan for relocating black Americans is discussed by John Miller, *Wolf by the Ears* (New York: Free Press, 1977), 269–272.

20. For an example of this kind of history, see Paul Finkelman, "Jefferson and Slavery," in *Jeffersonian Legacies*, ed. Peter Onuf (Charlottesville: University Press of Virginia, 1993), 181–221.

21. See Finkelman, "Jefferson and Slavery," who writes that "Josiah Nott, Samuel Cartwright, and Samuel Morton apparently learned their science from him [Jefferson]" (186). I discuss this school of anthropology in Chapter 5. Admittedly, the categories of natural history do not account for why Jefferson placed the black rather than the Indian in the lowest position, but this point changes nothing essential in my discussion.

22. David Walker, *One Continual Cry: David Walker's Appeal to the Colored Citizens of the World, 1829–1830,* ed. Herbert Apathecker (New York: Humanities Press, 1965), 90, 91.

23. The view that Jefferson's argument strengthened slavery is held by many historians, including John Hope Franklin, *Race and History* (Baton Rouge: Louisiana State University Press, 1989), and William Stanton, *The Leopard's Spot* (Chicago: University of Chicago Press, 1960). The damage done to natural rights is discussed in Joyce Appleby, "Jefferson and His Complex Legacy," in *Jeffersonian Legacies,* ed. Peter Onuf (Charlottesville: University Press of Virginia, 1993), 1–16. Appleby believes that Jefferson virtually finished off natural rights as a vital force in ending slavery in America: "It is not surprising that the antislavery movement that finally led to abolition came from America's Evangelical Christians who spoke the language of sin and damnation, not that of natural rights" (11).

24. *The Notes on the State of Virginia* is explicitly taken up and criticized in *Federalist* no. 49.

25. In support of the view that Jefferson changed his mind, the letters most frequently cited are Jefferson's responses to Benjamin Banneker, a black mathematician and astronomer, and to Bishop Henri Grégoire, a French writer who had refuted Jefferson's views by providing case studies of black intellectual accomplishments. Miller, *Wolf by the Ears,* 776–779, discusses these letters and demonstrates that in fact they reflected no change in Jefferson's position. Banneker was one case only, and Jefferson's admiration of his intellect was highly qualified. As for Grégoire's work, Jefferson admitted (to others) his doubts about the project and about Grégoire's competence to execute a genuinely scientific study.

26. Jefferson to Hopkinson, 1 August 1787, in Martin, *Thomas Jefferson,* 183.

27. I am using the phrase "moral causes" in its eighteenth- and nineteenth-century sense to refer to those causes that derive from within human beings and are in principle under human control. A typical expression of this meaning is found in John Bristed's *Resources of the United States of America*: "The character of nations is formed, not by *physical,* but by *moral* causes and influences, as government, religion, and education" (cited in Martin, *Thomas Jefferson,* 210).

28. *Federalist* no. 11, 90–91.

29. *Federalist* no. 49, 315. *The Federalist* not only teaches the need for rhetoric but also illustrates the sentiments that are most appropriate to a republican government.

30. *Federalist* no. 15, 110.

31. *Federalist* no. 14, 104.

32. *Federalist* no. 2, 37; *Federalist* no. 15, 110.

33. These different methods are discussed in *Federalist* nos. 1, 38, and 49.

34. Hamilton to Marquis de Lafayette, 6 January 1799, *Selected Writings of Alexander Hamilton,* ed. Morton Frisch (Washington: American Enterprise, 1985), 455.

35. For a discussion of what makes a people, see especially *Federalist* no. 2.

36. *Federalist* no. 85, 527.

37. Hamilton to John Jay, 14 March 1779, *Papers of Alexander Hamilton* (New York: Columbia University Press, 1961), 2:17–18. One of the most important sources of both the demand for and the acceptance of equal rights for black Americans has been the participation of blacks in the American armed forces.

38. *Federalist* no. 15, 111.

39. *Federalist* no. 34, 208; *Federalist* no. 6, 56, 59.

40. *Federalist* no. 6, 59.

41. See "UNESCO Statement," 172–178.

42. Martin Heidegger's *Letter on Humanism* (1947) was the work that did the most to inaugurate the postmodern attack on humanism.

Chapter 3: America in the Mirror of France

1. Alexis de Tocqueville, *Oeuvres,* ed. André Jardin (Paris: Gallimard, 1991), 1:1219.

2. Friedrich von Schlegel, *The Philosophy of History,* trans. James Burton Robertson (London: Henry Bohn, 1859), 453.

3. The other and more common name for the group was the *constitutionnels.* See Durand Echeverria, *Mirage in the West: A History of the French Image of American Society to 1815* (Princeton: Princeton University Press, 1957), and C. Bradley Thompson, "The American Founding and the French Revolution," in *The Legacy of the French Revolution,* ed. Ralph Hancock and L. Gary Lambert (Lanham, Md.: Rowman and Littlefield, 1996), 109–150.

4. Cited in Marie-Christine Granjon, "Sartre, Beauvoir, Aron: Les passions ambiguës," in *L'Amérique dans les têtes,* 145, 152. The views of Sartre and Beauvoir on America were not entirely negative, but the more the two fell under the thrall of Marxist thought, the more critical their comments became.

5. *Federalist* no. 14, 104.

6. Georg F. Hegel, *Philosophy of Right,* trans. T. M. Knox (London: Oxford University Press, 1967), par. 347; see also par. 345. When Hegel wrote these words, the "world" that he had in mind referred to only part of the globe. But, as he well foresaw, there would come a time—and that time has now arrived—when the "world" refers to almost everyone, i.e., to informed opinion everywhere.

7. Paul Berman, "French Revolutions," *New Republic,* 27 June 1994, 39.

8. Georg F. Hegel, *Philosophy of History* (New York: Dover, 1956), 86.

9. Alexis de Tocqueville, *Democracy in America,* ed. J. P. Mayer, trans. George Lawrence (New York: Harper and Row, 1969), vol. 1, pt. 1, chap. 8.

10. Chateaubriand, *Mémoires d'outres-tombe* (Paris: Brodard et Taupin, 1973), 1:276.

11. Pierre Manent, "La Révolution Française et le libéralisme français et anglais," paper presented at conference entitled "The French Revolution," Harvard University, Cambridge, Mass., April 1989. Manent excludes from this generalization certain of the military leaders of the revolutionary period, the foremost being Charles-François Dumouriez, whose merits were beyond doubt.

12. Antoine-Nicolas de Condorcet, *Esquisse d'un tableau historique* (Paris: Masson et Fils, 1822), 208.

13. *Federalist* no. 14, 104; *Federalist* no. 1, 33.

14. Emmanuel-Joseph Sieyès, *What Is the Third Estate?* trans. M. Blondel (London: Frederick Praeger, 1963), 117.

15. *Federalist* no. 28, 178.

16. *Federalist* no. 6, 59.

17. Alexis de Tocqueville, *Souvenirs* (Paris: Robert Laffont, 1986), 765.

18. Alexis de Tocqueville, *L'Ancien régime et la révolution* (Paris: Robert Laffont, 1986), 1037, 1036.

19. Stendhal, *Le rouge et le noir* (Paris: Garnier, 1963), 293. Tocqueville himself at times shared this spirit: "There are undertakings that only the French nation is in a condition to conceive, magnanimous commitments that she alone dares to make. Only France could wish to embrace, at a certain moment, the common cause of humanity and wish to do battle for it" (from the half-completed second volume of *The Old Regime and the Revolution*; a translation of this passage may be found in Alexis de Tocqueville, *The European Tradition and the Correspondence with Gobineau,* trans. and ed. John Lukacs [Gloucester, Mass.: Peter Smith, 1968], 87).

20. Antoine-Nicolas de Condorcet, *Sketch for an Historical Picture of the Progress of the Human Mind,* trans. June Barraclough (1795; reprint, New York: Noonday Press, 1955), 147.

21. *Federalist* no. 51, 322. For a full-length treatment of this issue, see Christian Lerat, "La première constitution de Pennsylvanie: Son rejet à Philadelphie, ses échos en France," in *Le discours sur les révolutions,* ed. Jean-Louis Seurin, Christian Lerat, and James Ceaser (Paris: Economica, 1991), 2:111–134.

22. *Federalist* no. 1, 33.

23. Augustin Cochin's explanation of the revolutionary process provides a rational account for Joseph de Maistre's earlier view of how the Revolution was guided by providence. According to de Maistre, "It was not men that made the Revolution, it was the Revolution that made use of the men" (*Considérations sur la France* [1797; reprint, Geneva: Slatkine, 1980], 34).

24. The debate between Boutmy and Jellinek, which is well known to students of French thought, is discussed in Jean-Louis Seurin, "Célébrations et éclipses de la déclaration des droits de l'homme et du citoyen de 1789," in *Le discours sur les révolutions,* ed. Jean-Louis Seurin, Christian Lerat, and James Ceaser (Paris: Economica, 1991), 2:61–97. Boutmy's thesis of the minimal influence of the American Revolution has few adherents today.

25. *The Papers of George Washington,* ed. W. W. Abbot et al., Presidential Series (Charlottesville: University Press of Virginia, 1987), 2:175.

26. *Federalist* no. 10, 79.

27. Condorcet, "On the Influence of the American Revolution," in *Condorcet: Selected Writings,* ed. Keith Michael Baker (Indianapolis: Bobbs Merrill, 1976), 145.

28. Stendhal, *Le rouge et le noir,* 6.

29. There are many antecedents to Burke's ideas (in particular some of David Hume's writings against John Locke and certain parts of Montesquieu's work), but it was Burke's *Reflections on the Revolution in France,* as well as some of his other speeches against the French Revolution, that defined the broad outlines of conservatism.

30. For a treatment of these issues, see Philippe Beneton, *Le conservatisme* (Paris: Presses Universitaires de France, 1988). For an instructive essay on de Maistre, see Isaiah Berlin's "Joseph de Maistre and the Origins of Fascism" in Berlin, *The Crooked Timber of Humanity* (London: John Murray, 1990), 91–174.

31. Joseph de Maistre, *Oeuvres complètes* (Geneva: Slatkine, 1979), 1:67, 72 (cited hereafter as *Oeuvres*).

32. *Oeuvres* 1:68.

33. *Oeuvres* 1:74.

34. *Oeuvres* 1:72, 71.

35. *Federalist* no. 38, 232–233, 234; *Oeuvres* 1:87.

36. *Oeuvres* 1:88.

37. *Oeuvres* 1:87.

38. Edmund Burke, *Works,* Bohn's British Classics (London: Bohn, 1854–1859), 2:25, 2:16, 1:464.

39. Russell Kirk, introduction to Albert Jay Nock, *Mr. Jefferson* (Delavan, Wis.: Hallberg, 1983), xxx.

40. Jefferson to John Cartwright, 5 June 1824, in Jefferson, *Writings* 16:44.

41. Hamilton, "The Farmer Refuted," 23 February 1775, in *Selected Writings,* 21.

42. See Zoltan Harastzi, *John Adams and the Prophets of Progress* (New York: Grosset and Dunlap, 1964), 246, 247. See also Hamilton's 1794 essay on the French Revolution in his *Selected Writings,* 413–416.

43. Hamilton, *Selected Writings,* 414; the quotation is from an article by Hamilton dated 1794 and printed in French in *Vue d'Amérique: La Révolution Française jugée par les Américans,* ed. Simon Newman and Jean-Pierre Dormois (Paris: Franc-Empire, 1989), 178. I have been unable to locate the original in English; the translation in the text is my own.

44. Condorcet, *A Commentary and Review of Montesquieu's Spirit of the Laws,* cited in Thompson, "American Founding," 131.

45. *Federalist* no. 37, 228. Compare this to Condorcet's remark that a "being foreign to our species . . . would study human society as we study the beavers and the bees" (*Selected Writings,* 6).

46. *Federalist* no. 45, 289.

47. *Federalist* no. 31, 194.

Chapter 4: America as a Racial Symbol

1. George Stocking, *Race, Culture, and Evolution* (New York: Free Press, 1968), 40. See also Smedley, *Race in North America: Origin and Evolution of a Worldview* (Boulder, Colo.: Westview Press, 1993), 256.

2. For a survey of contemporary extremist groups in America, see Raphael Ezekiel, *The Racist Mind* (New York: Viking, 1995).

3. Barthes, *Le degré zéro,* 16.

4. Michael D. Biddiss, *Father of Racist Ideology: The Political and Social Thought of Count Gobineau* (New York: Weybright and Talley, 1970), 3.

5. For a discussion of the Bayreuth group, see Biddiss, *Father of Racist Ideology,* 256–260. For a systematic treatment of the effects of Gobineau on Renan and Le Bon, see Todorov, *Nous et les autres,* 113–196.

6. Gobineau's admirers appear to be conservative sympathizers of the old nobility, and they see Hitler as a crass populist having nothing in common with the refined thought of Gobineau. For a discussion of those adopting this view, see John Lukacs, ed. and trans., *The European Revolution and Correspondence with Gobineau* (Gloucester, Mass.: Peter Smith, 1968), 185–186 (hereafter cited as *Correspondence*).

7. Hitler's main objection to Gobineau was his fatalism or unwillingness to act to reverse racial decay: "How can we arrest racial decay? Must what Count Gobineau says come true?" Hitler clearly preferred the thought of Richard Wagner, Gobineau's friend, because Wagner envisaged that the decay could be reversed (Hermann Rauschning, *The Voice of Destruction* [New York: Putnam, 1940], 229).

8. Biddiss, *Father of Racist Ideology,* 19.

9. Biddiss, *Father of Racist Ideology,* 108. For Gobineau's claim of his family's links to the Vikings, see *Correspondence,* 180.

10. Gobineau argued that Aryans had spread throughout most of the globe. See Arthur de Gobineau, *Essai sur l'inégalité des races humaines,* ed. Hubert Juin (Paris: Pierre Belfond, 1967), 869 (hereafter cited as *Essai*). Gobineau's association of race with class rather than nation appears to have drawn on the seventeenth-century views of Henri de Boulainvilliers.

11. Biddiss, *Father of Racist Ideology,* 19.

12. *Correspondence,* 274–275. Hannah Arendt traces the origin of Gobineau's thought, noting that French racialist thinking tended to divide the nation, whereas German racialist thinking, which adopted the nation or dominant ethnic group as the core of the "race," operated to unify the nation (Arendt, *Origins of Totalitarianism* [New York: Harcourt, 1951], 45).

13. Gobineau's *Essay on the Inequality of the Human Races* is divided into four books: the first two were published in 1853, the second two in 1855. I will be quoting mostly from the French edition. Part of Gobineau's *Essay* is translated in *Gobineau: Selected Political Writings,* ed. Michael Biddiss (New York: Harper and Row, 1970).

14. *Correspondence,* 183.

15. *Essai,* 70. The theme that a civilization is the most important whole or unit comes from Hegel and Guizot, both of whom Gobineau carefully studied.

16. *Essai,* 39–40.

17. *Essai,* 856; Gobineau to Tocqueville, 20 March 1856, *Correspondence,* 285.

18. *Essai,* 42.

19. *Essai,* 40.

20. Hannah Arendt, *The Origins of Totalitarianism,* 2nd ed. (New York: Meridian Books, 1958), 171; *Essai,* 58, 58–59.

21. *Essai,* 66.

22. *Essai,* 67.

23. *Essai,* 67–68.

24. *Essai,* 105, 182, 182.

25. *Essai,* 205, 205–206, 208, 206–207, 207.

26. The *Essai* frequently cites the British natural historian James Pritchard, who wrote *Natural History of Man* (London, 1848), as well as the work of such American anthropologists as Samuel Morton, who had extensively researched cranial measurements (*Essai,* 127–129). From letters written during this period, we know that Gobineau was interested in Buffon and Gustave Flourens (see, e.g., Gobineau to Tocqueville, 29 April 1852, *Correspondence,* 219–222).

27. *Essai,* 133.

28. *Essai,* 145, 864. Any effort to determine the truth of man's origins, Gobineau believed, was designed more to satisfy idle speculation than to instruct judgment.

29. Benjamin Rush, *Essays: Literary, Moral, and Philosophical,* ed. Michael Merange (Schenectady, N.Y.: Union College Press, 1988).

30. At one point, however, Gobineau does suggest that there is doubt about the future physical survival of man when all men have become half-breeds (*Essai,* 871).

31. *Essai,* 180.

32. As Michael Biddiss comments, "Long before Spengler and Toynbee, Gobineau saw historical movement in terms of the cyclical rise and fall of those quasi-organic civilizations [listed in] the first book of the *Essay*" (*Gobineau,* 25).

33. *Essai,* 30.

34. *Essai,* 817–819.

35. *Essai,* 818.

36. *Essai,* 819.

37. For his sketch on America, Gobineau borrows much of his content—indeed, much of his phraseology—from his two most influential teachers: Tocqueville and Hegel. He relies most heavily on Tocqueville's *Democracy in America,* vol. 1, chap. 10 ("Three Races That Inhabit the United States"), and Hegel's introduction to *The Philosophy of History.* Even with these considerable debts, Gobineau's argument is very much his own and in the end is most noteworthy for its disagreements with Tocqueville and Hegel.

38. *Essai,* 842.

39. *Essai,* 844.

40. *Essai,* 847.

41. *Essai,* 848–849.

42. *Essai,* 848.

43. *Essai,* 852–853. Later Gobineau comments on the emigration of Asians into California.

44. *Essai,* 854.

45. *Correspondence,* 186.

46. Biddiss, *Gobineau,* 204–206.

47. Gobineau to Tocqueville, 15 January 1856, *Correspondence,* 275.

48. Gobineau to Tocqueville, 20 March 1856, *Correspondence,* 284–285.

49. *Essai,* 870; Gobineau to Tocqueville, 15 October 1854, *Correspondence,* 248.

50. *Essai,* 870–871.

51. Hegel, *Philosophy of History,* 87, 88. In the introduction to this volume, its translator and editor, Carl Friedrich, criticizes Kojève's interpretation of Hegel and argues that Kojève

failed to consider *Philosophy of History*. Kojève's view is based on a reading of Hegel's *Phenomenology of Spirit*.

52. Alexandre Kojève, *Introduction à la lecture de Hegel,* ed. Raymond Queneau (Paris: Gallimard, 1968), 437.

Chapter 5: From Ethnology to Multiculturalism

1. Rauschning, *Voices of Destruction,* 68, 69 (Hitler made these comments in 1933); Louis-Ferdinand Céline, *Les beaux draps* (Paris: Nouvelle Editions Françaises, 1941), 33.

2. See, for example, Stephen Gould, *The Mismeasure of Man* (New York: Norton, 1981). Pat Shipman, in *The Evolution of Racism: Human Difference and the Use and Abuse of Science* (New York: Simon and Schuster, 1995), describes the hostile reactions encountered by postwar scientists conducting valid inquiries into hereditary differences, and she shows that in these instances the condemnations were based not on scientific reasons but on political ones.

3. *Essai,* 127–129.

4. James L. Cabell, *Testimony of Modern Science to the Unity of Mankind* (New York: Robert Carter, 1859).

5. Historians of the University of Virginia will know that Cabell Hall is named for Joseph Cabell, James's uncle and Jefferson's friend. But it was James who contributed more to the university and to the furtherance of scientific knowledge.

6. Henry Patterson, foreword to Josiah C. Nott and George Gliddon, *Types of Mankind* (Philadelphia: Lippincott, 1854), xxxii–xxxiii (hereafter cited as *Types*).

7. Josiah C. Nott, appendix to Arthur de Gobineau, *The Moral and Intellectual Diversity of Races* (American edition, 1856; reprint, New York: Garland, 1984), 463.

8. One of the acknowledged shortcomings of craniology, or the comparative study of skulls, was the limited number of cases for certain races. In what Nott considered to be an ingenious effort to overcome this sampling problem, he surveyed haberdashers, asking them to send him the hat sizes of their clientele, broken down according to race; his data appear in his appendix to Gobineau's *Moral and Intellectual Diversity,* 470.

9. Nott, appendix, 464.

10. For a discussion of the American school, see Smedley, *Race in North America,* 234–246, and James Bilotta, *Race and the Rise of the Republican Party, 1848–1865* (New York: Peter Lang, 1992), 1–72.

11. Cited in Eric McKitrick, ed., *Slavery Defended* (Englewood Cliffs, N.J.: Prentice-Hall, 1963), 136–137.

12. Nott, appendix, 506.

13. *Types,* 375; cited in Smedley, *Race in North America,* 239.

14. *Types,* 68; see also 405, 407. The authors add, "The 'improvements' among Americanized negroes . . . are due solely to those ultra-ecclesiastical amalgamations which . . . have deteriorated the white element in direct proportion that they are said to have improved the black" (260).

15. Nott, appendix, 479. Nott's definition is from Jourdain's *Dictionary of Terms of the Natural Sciences.*

16. *Types,* 7. Nott is citing here, approvingly, Luke Burke's definition of ethnology.

17. *Types,* 50–52. Nott allows that a certain kind of philanthropy might argue that "no race has a right to enslave or oppress the weaker." But such general propositions as these could not help societies where, as in the American South, the institution of slavery already existed. In these cases, insisting on the unity of the human race becomes "fanaticism"—an effort to determine practice by "groundless hypotheses [rather than] by experience, sound judgment, and real charity" (52).

18. William Sumner Jenkins, *Pro-Slavery Thought in the Old South* (Chapel Hill: University of North Carolina Press, 1935).

19. Cited in Jenkins, *Pro-Slavery Thought,* 277.

20. McKitrick, *Slavery Defended,* 2.

21. McKitrick, *Slavery Defended,* 126.

22. Different versions of Stephens' speech appear in different works, and we have no single definitive text. I have relied mostly on Henry Cleveland, *Alexander H. Stephens* (Philadelphia: National Publishing, 1866), 721, with a few phrases from Edward McPherson, ed., *The Political History of the Great Rebellion* (Washington, D.C.: Philp and Solomons, 1865), 103–104. For Harry Jaffa's conclusion, see his *Equality and Liberty* (New York: Oxford University Press, 1965), 160.

23. Ashley Montagu, *Man's Most Dangerous Myth: The Fallacy of Race* (New York: Columbia University Press, 1942), ix.

24. See Montagu, *Race, Science, and Humanity,* 172–178.

25. Charles Murray, interview by Michael Jackson, *Larry King Live,* Cable News Network, 1 November 1994; Richard Herrnstein and Charles Murray, *The Bell Curve* (New York: Free Press, 1994), 297.

26. Herrnstein and Murray, *Bell Curve,* 313, 314.

27. Herrnstein and Murray, *Bell Curve,* 315, 287.

28. Rauschning, *Voice of Destruction,* 229, 230.

29. See Richard Wolin, *The Heidegger Controversy* (Cambridge: Massachusetts Institute of Technology Press, 1993), 62.

30. The first volume of Spengler's *Decline of the West* was published in 1917; in the second edition, which appeared in 1923, he added several passages about the United States. The second volume was published for the first time in 1922.

31. The encounter between Spengler and the Nazis is recounted in Walter Struve, *Elites Against Democracy* (Princeton: Princeton University Press, 1973), 271.

32. I am indebted to John Farrenkopf for bringing to my attention Spengler's treatment of Americanism. For an overview of Spengler's later works, see Farrenkopf, "The Transformation of Spengler's Philosophy of World History," *Journal of the History of Ideas* 53 (1991): 463–485.

33. Oswald Spengler, *Man and Technics,* trans. Charles Francis Atkinson (London: Allen and Unwin, 1932), 64–65, 64, 92. I will refer to this book in the text as *Man and Technology,* translating *Die technik* as "technology." For citation purposes, however, I will use Atkinson's title of *Man and Technics.*

34. Oswald Spengler, *The Year of Decision* (New York: Knopf, 1934), 202.

35. Spengler, *Year of Decision,* 219; cited in Struve, *Elites Against Democracy,* 272; Spen-

gler, *Year of Decision,* 200. Spengler held that the Germanic and the Celtic groups were part of the same race (73).

36. Spengler, *Man and Technics,* 91.

37. Spengler, *Year of Decision,* 71, 70.

38. Adolf Hitler, *Mein Kampf* (New York: Houghton Mifflin, 1939), 399. Hitler admired America partly for its technological development. This theme can be traced to the treatment of America by such writers as Moeller van den Bruck, discussed in Chapter 7.

39. Hitler, *Mein Kampf,* 658.

40. Rauschning, *Voice of Destruction,* 68, 69.

41. Alfred Rosenberg, *Der Mythus des 20. Jahrhunderts* (Munich: Hoheneichen-Verlag, 1933), 668–670.

42. Rauschning, *Voice of Destruction,* 69.

43. Special representation for the "oppressed and disadvantaged" is called for in Young, *Politics of Difference,* 187.

44. Charles Taylor, *Multiculturalism and the Politics of Recognition,* ed. Amy Gutmann (Princeton: Princeton University Press, 1992).

45. Bazon Brock, "Die Kultur zivilisieren," *Der Spiegel* 16 (1995): 216–218.

46. The quotation is from Chokwe Lumumba, the current leader of the New African People's Organization. In a close parallel to a scenario that Tocqueville predicted for race relations in America, Lumumba claims for New Africa a territory comprising Louisiana, Mississippi, Alabama, Georgia, and South Carolina (see his "Notfalls Bürgerkrieg," *Focus* 24 [July 1995]: 228). Today few minorities in America call for independent states, partly because their populations are dispersed across the country, making territorial separation difficult, if not impossible. Blacks, for example, are a minority in all fifty states.

47. Amy Gutmann, introduction to Charles Taylor, *Multiculturalism and the Politics of Recognition* (Princeton: Princeton University Press, 1992), 3.

48. In the United States, the scientists' postwar reaction against racial distinctions was not matched in the political and legal arenas until the dismantling of legal segregation in the 1960s.

49. Franz Boas, *The Mind of Primitive Man* (New York: Macmillan, 1938), 195.

50. The groups often lumped together as Asian Americans do share certain qualities and sometimes face similar prejudices; in fact, Asians were once legally designated and discriminated against in America. Beyond this, however, the multiculturalist theorists' invention of the single category and the category's subsequent application in law have created powerful incentives for Asians to organize as a single culture.

51. Georg F. Hegel, *Reason in History,* trans. Robert Hartman (New York: Macmillan, 1988), 64.

52. Taylor, *Multiculturalism,* 25, 26.

53. Young, *Politics of Difference,* 59.

54. The Whitney Museum's multicultural exhibit included a videotape made in 1992 that shows Rodney King, a black man, being beaten by four Los Angeles policemen, who are white; the videotape, made by a bystander named Holiday, was replayed many times in the media and was introduced as evidence when the policemen were tried. In the words of the museum's curator, "There's a long history of art showing us something about the world, and

the Holiday tape adds a new dynamic to that tradition." Incidentally, the same "art" dealer who supplied the King tape to the Whitney Museum also offered Timothy Goldman's videotape from the 1992 riots in Los Angeles; Goldman's footage shows a white truck driver being pulled from his truck and beaten by three black men. The curators decided against using this videotape, evidently judging that it lacked a comparable artistic "dynamic" (Suzanne Muchnic, "King Beating Footage Comes to the Art World," *Los Angeles Times,* 10 March 1993, F8).

55. Young, *Politics of Difference,* 98, 99; Cornel West, *The American Evasion of Philosophy: A Genealogy of Pragmatism* (Madison: University of Wisconsin Press, 1989), 208.

56. The identification of culture and race was originally an invention of the founder of Third World ideology, Franz Fanon, who therefore becomes an important forebear of multiculturalism. This point is discussed by Charles Taylor, *Multiculturalism,* 65, and Thomas Pangle, *The Ennobling of Democracy* (Baltimore: Johns Hopkins University Press, 1992), 79.

57. Said, *Culture and Imperialism,* 314, 301, 282–336.

58. Said, *Culture and Imperialism,* 303; Young, *Politics of Difference,* 98, 99, 111; Richard Sennett, "The Identity Myth," *New York Times,* 30 January 1994, D17. For a call for a multicultural history, see Appleby, "Recovering America's Historic Diversity," 419–431.

59. Martha Minow, "Justice Engendered," *Harvard Law Review* 101 (1988): 10; Mari Matsuda, "Looking to the Bottom: Critical Legal Studies and Reparations," *Harvard Civil Rights–Civil Liberties Law Review* 22 (1987): 326.

60. William Weaver, "Antifoundationalism, Feminism, and the Temptations of Theory," Ph.D. diss., University of Virginia, 1993, 18.

61. Richard Rorty, "Feminism and Pragmatism," *Michigan Quarterly Review* 30 (Spring 1991): 231, 236–237; Seyla Benhabib, "Epistemologies of Postmodernism: A Rejoinder to Jean François Lyotard," in *Feminism/Postmodernism,* ed. Linda Nicholson (New York: Routledge, 1990), 124.

Chapter 6: Racialism Versus Political Science

1. Alexis de Tocqueville, *Democracy in America,* ed. J. P. Mayer, trans. George Lawrence (New York: Harper and Row, 1969), 115 (hereafter cited as *DA*). I exempt here some of Tocqueville's state papers from his tenure as foreign minister of France, which must be treated in a different fashion. *The Federalist* stands somewhere between Tocqueville's general theoretical writings and papers of state (which, of course, many of the founders also wrote). *The Federalist,* although tied to a specific context, is also quite consciously a more general attempt at political science; it goes so far in this direction that it often signals which of its arguments are more "case specific" and which more general in character.

2. *DA,* 146.

3. For a discussion of nineteenth-century political science and the racial aspects of Francis Lieber's thought, see James Farr, "From Modern Republic to Administrative State," in *Regime and Discipline,* ed. David Easton, John Gunnell, and Michael Stein (Ann Arbor: University of Michigan Press, 1995), 131–167.

4. *DA,* 12.

5. Tocqueville, speech of 2 April 1853, *DA,* 147.

6. Tocqueville often cited *The Federalist* in *Democracy of America*. He called it a "fine book, and though it especially concerns America, it should be familiar to statesmen of all countries" (*DA,* 115). But as it happened, *The Federalist* was not much studied in the nineteenth century. In Germany, according to Ernst Fraenkel, it was rarely mentioned until the historian Heinrich Von Treitschke discussed it in *Amerika im Spiegel des Deutschen politischen Denkens* (1864; reprint, Cologne: Westdeutscher Verlag, 1959), 24. It appears that *The Federalist* began to be studied seriously in Europe only in the late twentieth century, helped in part by various conferences and celebrations connected to the American bicentennials in 1976 and 1987.

7. *Correspondence,* 16.

8. Tocqueville to Gobineau, 7 November 1853, *Correspondence,* 227, 229.

9. Tocqueville to Gobineau, 24 January 1857, *Correspondence,* 308–309.

10. Tocqueville to Gobineau, 30 July 1856, *Correspondence,* 291.

11. Tocqueville to Gobineau, 22 July 1854, *Correspondence,* 244.

12. Tocqueville to Gobineau, 20 December 1853, *Correspondence,* 231.

13. Tocqueville began writing *The Old Regime and the Revolution* in 1853 and published it in 1856.

14. Tocqueville to Gobineau, 20 December 1853, *Correspondence,* 232.

15. Tocqueville to Gobineau, 8 January 1856, *Correspondence,* 270.

16. The adjective "weak" comes from the passage near the end of *Democracy in America,* where Tocqueville refers to deterministic theories as "false and cowardly doctrines which can only produce feeble men and pusillanimous nations" (*DA,* 705). The word "self-pitying" comes from a letter to Gobineau (20 December 1853, *Correspondence,* 232). The "doctrine of fatalism" is discussed in the chapter entitled "Some Characteristics Peculiar to Historians in Democratic Centuries," *DA,* 493–496.

17. Gobineau to Tocqueville, 17 November 1853, *Correspondence,* 229. Compare this forecast with the "predestined circle" Tocqueville discusses in *Democracy in America* (705).

18. Gobineau to Tocqueville, 17 November 1853, *Correspondence,* 229.

19. Tocqueville to Gobineau, 22 October 1843, *Correspondence,* 211; Gobineau to Tocqueville, 20 March 1856, *Correspondence,* 285.

20. Gobineau to Tocqueville, 20 March 1856, *Correspondence,* 286.

21. Tocqueville to Gobineau, 17 November 1853, *Correspondence,* 227; Gobineau to Tocqueville, 20 March 1856, *Correspondence,* 285.

22. Gobineau to Tocqueville, 20 March 1853, *Correspondence,* 286. Although happy for the recognition, Gobineau was also a bit ambivalent about it, for he was aware that portions of his work were included and others omitted in order to serve certain political purposes.

23. Tocqueville to Gobineau, 30 July 1856, *Correspondence,* 294; Tocqueville to Gobineau, 14 January 1857, *Correspondence,* 305.

24. Tocqueville to Gobineau, 20 December 1853, *Correspondence,* 232.

25. Tocqueville to Gobineau, 30 July 1856, *Correspondence,* 294.

26. *DA,* 310.

27. *Correspondence,* 221–223. Tocqueville also points out a passage where Flourens' *disproves* one of the elements of supposed difference among the races—an element which Voltaire had relied on to prove his idea of polygenesis and which Jefferson also had noted.

28. Tocqueville to Gobineau, 24 January 1857, *Correspondence,* 305.

29. Tocqueville, "Discours prononcé à la séance publique annuelle de l'Académie des Sciences Morales et Politiques," 3 April 1852, in Tocqueville, *Oeuvres* 1:1216. ("Race" here is used to refer to the human race and is synonymous with "species.")

30. Tocqueville to Gobineau, 24 January 1857, *Correspondence,* 310. Incidentally, Raymond Aron, one of those who has sought to keep political science alive in the twentieth century, has been much taken by this dialogue. See Raymond Aron, *In Defense of Political Reason,* ed. Daniel Mahoney (Lanham, Md.: Rowman and Littlefield, 1994), 175–177.

31. The slaveholders had created a "spiritualized despotism" in seeking to keep slaves from wishing to break their bonds (*DA,* 361). In addition, there was the original extremity of the situation in which blacks in America found themselves torn from their native civilization, transplanted to another continent, and then treated in the most humiliating and unnatural way: "The Negro hardly notices his ill-fortune. . . . The habit of servitude has given him the thoughts and ambitions of a slave; he admires his tyrants even more than he hates them and finds his joy and pride in servile imitation of his oppressors" (*DA,* 317). But notwithstanding even this degree of spiritual subjugation for the black slaves in America, Tocqueville foresaw that the future of the South would be marked by black rebellion against white rule.

32. *DA,* 309. Tocqueville did acknowledge, however, that extreme and powerful regimes may be able to undo man's natural inclinations, as was the case with the tyranny of whites over blacks in America (*DA,* 317). Yet even there, he predicts, slavery will one day end, so unnatural and hard is the regime that maintains it (*DA,* 361–363).

33. *Correspondence,* 169–170 (a quotation from Tocqueville's proposed second volume of *The Old Regime and the Revolution*).

34. *DA,* 615.

35. *DA,* 228–229.

36. This is the suspicion of Michael Biddiss (*Father of Racist Ideology,* 57–58).

37. In *Democracy in America,* Tocqueville used the term "race" in a number of different ways and not always with precision. It refers sometimes to the basic color groups, sometimes to subsets of the basic groups, and sometimes to generically different peoples. Indeed, in the brief, five-page conclusion that closes the first volume of *Democracy in America,* Tocqueville uses the term "race" no fewer than seven times.

38. *DA,* 325; see also 326–327.

39. This is why Tocqueville sometimes puts "civilized" in quotation marks (see, e.g., *DA,* 28–29).

40. *DA,* 410.

41. Tocqueville's treatment of the Anglos is a case in point. They brought something with them; in the case of the Puritans, it was a particular political-religious view that emphasized citizenship and participation.

42. De Maistre, *Oeuvres* 1:68.

43. Tocqueville observed, "While the French exercise no healthy influence on the Indians, the English were always strangers to them" (*DA,* 329–330).

44. *DA,* 318.

45. *DA,* 227.

46. Tocqueville never says that hereditary differences must fall along racial or ethnic lines.

The problem of even exploring this hypothesis appeared to him very difficult, at any rate among white Europeans, as so much intermixing had occurred long ago. Among the basic color groups, the differences were obviously greater and apparently more original. But here no one had made the case for the hereditary source of qualitative differences.

47. *DA,* 317, 342. The black seems a "stranger" to the white, "hardly recognized as sharing the common features of humanity." Part of the reaction Tocqueville describes in this passage is presumably a natural one; but part of it is a reaction formed already by virtue of the fact that the black has been brought here in a degraded state.

48. Henry Louis Gates, Jr., *Loose Canons* (Oxford: Oxford University Press, 1992), 36, 48, 50.

49. *DA,* 341.

50. *DA,* 342.

51. Tocqueville had set aside the question of race and slavery for most of *Democracy in America* in order to explore a general model of liberal democracy. He returned to it, at the end of volume 1, in the chapter "On the Three Races," in which he makes clear that race was *the* question of American politics.

52. *DA,* 358.

53. *DA,* 357. The chances for blacks to achieve a partial stalemate in the South would be enhanced, paradoxically, if the Union split up, for then the Southern whites could fight the blacks without the support of the Northern whites. The Southern whites in effect needed the North to prevail. The other possibility—the elimination of blacks from North America—was the mirror image, although on a much larger scale, of what Tocqueville foresaw for some of the Caribbean Islands, where the blacks would take the lion's share and whites would be forced out (*DA,* 357–358).

54. *DA,* 342, 357, 356, 360. Tocqueville pointed out, and Gobineau made much of the fact, that of all the European groups the Anglos were the least disposed to intermarrying with blacks, just as they were with Indians.

55. *DA,* 356.

56. Tocqueville to Gobineau, 17 November 1853, *Correspondence,* 228–229.

57. Tocqueville to Gobineau, 17 November 1853, *Correspondence,* 228.

58. Tocqueville to Gobineau, 17 November 1853, *Correspondence,* 228; Gobineau to Tocqueville, 13 November 1855, *Correspondence,* 268.

59. Tocqueville to Gobineau, 24 January 1857, *Correspondence,* 309.

60. *DA,* 110.

61. *DA,* 110.

Chapter 7: From America to Americanization

1. Otto Basler, "Americanismus: Geschichte des Schlagwortes," in *Deutsche Rundschau* (August 1930): 142.

2. Cited in Basler, "Americanismus," 144.

3. Cited in Basler, "Americanismus," 144.

4. The abbé Charles Maignen's book was entitled *Le Père Hecker: Est-il un saint?* It was translated into English (and softened somewhat in its anti-Americanism) and published as

Studies in Americanism; Father Hecker: Is He a Saint? Maignen published his attacks on Americanism in the magazine *La Vérité.* Maignen's quotations are from Felix Klein, *Americanism: A Phantom Heresy* (Cranford, N.H.: Personal Printing, 1951), 121, 122.

5. Cited in Klein, *Americanism,* 127.

6. Quotations are from Robert Cross, *The Emergence of Liberal Catholicism in America* (Cambridge: Harvard University Press, 1958), 194. See also the abbé Henry Delassus, *L'Américanisme et la conjuration antichrétienne* (Lille: Desclée, Du Brouwer, 1899).

7. Cited in Klein, *Americanism,* xxiv. The reference is to Pope Leo XIII, *Testem benevolentiae,* April 1899. This letter is discussed at length in Gerald Fogarty, *The Vatican and the American Hierarchy from 1870 to 1965* (Collegeville, Minn.: Glazier, 1982).

8. America was treated and interpreted mainly in the light of the French Revolution. After the French Revolution turned into a tyranny, there was an effort, most notably by Friedrich von Gentz, to contrast the American Revolution with the French Revolution in order to redeem the modern idea of freedom. For the most part, however, German thinkers looked to the classical Greek state for their idea of freedom. For early treatments of America in German literature, see Paul C. Weber, *America in Imaginative German Literature in the First Half of the Nineteenth Century* (New York: Columbia University Press, 1926); Hildegard Meyer, *Nord-Amerika im Urteil des Deutschen Schriftums zur Mitte des 19. Jahrhunderts* (Hamburg: De Gruyter, 1929).

9. Georg Wilhelm Friedrich Hegel, *Vorlesungen über die Philosophie* (Hamburg: Felix Meiner, 1955), 206; for English translation, see Hegel, *Philosophy of History,* 84.

10. Hegel, *Vorlesungen,* 206–207; for English translation, see Hegel, *Philosophy of History,* 84–87.

11. Woodrow Wilson, "The Study of Administration," *Political Science Quarterly* 2 (June 1897): 201.

12. Hegel, *Vorlesungen,* 209–210; for English translation, see Hegel, *Philosophy of History,* 86–87.

13. Johann Wolfgang von Goethe, "The United States," in *Amerika: Im Spiegel des Deutschen politischen Denkens,* ed. Ernst Fraenkel (Cologne: Westdeutscher Verlag, 1959), 108. According to Fraenkel, "The German image of America was first created not in the Classic period [i.e., in the late eighteenth century] but in the Romantic period" (*Amerika,* 19–20).

14. For a discussion of these two ideas of the nation, see the lecture by Ernst-Wolfgang Bockenforde, 4 May 1995, available from Carl Friedrich von Siemens Stiftung, Munich; and Anthony Smith, *The Ethnic Origins of Nations* (Oxford: Blackwell, 1986).

15. Nikolaus Lenau to Anton Schurz, 16 March 1832, in *Nikolaus Lenau: Sämtliche Werke und Briefe* (Frankfurt: Insel-Verrl, 1971), 2:161 (hereafter cited as *Sämtliche Werke*); Meyer, "Lied eines Auswandernden," in *Nord-Amerika,* 26.

16. Nikolaus Lenau to Joseph Klemm, 6 March 1833, *Sämtliche Werke* 2:214.

17. Nikolaus Lenau to Emilie von Reinbeck, 5 March 1833, *Sämtliche Werke* 2:210; Lenau to Schurz, 16 October 1932, *Sämtliche Werke* 2:207.

18. Lenau to Reinbeck, 5 March 1833, *Sämtliche Werke* 2:210; cited in Fraenkel, *Amerika im Spiegel,* 103–104; Schlegel, *Philosophy of History,* 110.

19. Lenau to Klemm, 6 March 1933, *Sämtliche Werke* 2:215–216.

20. Lenau to Klemm, 6 March 1933, *Sämtliche Werke* 2:216; Lenau to Reinbeck, 5 March 1833, *Sämtliche Werke* 2:213.

21. Heinrich Heine, "Jetzt wohin?" (1830), cited in Fraenkel, *Amerika im Spiegel* 106–107, 107.

22. Fritz Stern, *The Politics of Cultural Despair: A Study in the Rise of Germanic Ideology* (Berkeley: University of California Press, 1961), 131.

23. For treatments, see Walter Struve, *Elites Against Democracy: Leadership Ideals in Bourgeois Political Thought in Germany, 1890–1933* (Princeton: Princeton University Press, 1973); Jeffrey Herf, *Reactionary Modernism* (Cambridge: Cambridge University Press, 1984); and Kurt Sontheimer, *Antidemokratisches Denken in der Weimarer Republik* (Munich: Nymphenburger, 1962).

24. Friedrich Nietzsche, *Human, All Too Human,* trans. R. J. Hollingdale (Cambridge: Cambridge University Press, 1986), 365.

25. Nietzsche, *Human, All Too Human,* 132.

26. Friedrich Nietzsche, *The Gay Science,* trans. Walter Kaufmann (New York: Vintage Books, 1974), bk. 4, sec. 329, 258–259. For a few other references by Nietzsche to America, see *Nachgelassene Fragmente,* where he speaks of the American's "dullness" and passion for the "search for profit" (Friedrich Nietzsche, *Sämtliche Werke* [Munich: Deutscher Taschenbuch, De Gruyter, 1980], 9:357.

27. Nietzsche, *Gay Science,* 303.

28. Arthur Moeller van den Bruck, *Das dritte Reich* (Berlin: Der Ring, 1923).

29. Arthur Moeller van den Bruck, *Die Zeitgenossen* (Minden: J. C. C. Bruns, 1906).

30. Van den Bruck, *Die Zeitgenossen,* 13.

31. Sontheimer, *Antidemokratisches Denken,* 214.

32. Cited in Fraenkel, *Amerika im Spiegel,* 309. The "Taylor system" refers to the ideas of Frederick Taylor and his school of scientific management, known best for its time and motion studies. In the way these studies were interpreted in Germany, the human being is reduced to the status of a cog in a machine.

33. Sontheimer, *Antidemokratisches Denken,* 351.

34. Arthur Moeller van den Bruck, *Das Recht der Jungen völker* (Berlin: Der Nahe Osten, 1932), 166–168.

35. Spengler, *Man and Technics.* For the origin of the English word "technology," see Leo Marx, *The Machine in the Garden,* 149. Both Jacques Ellul (in French) and George Grant (in English) have used "technology" in this broader sense.

36. Spengler, *Man and Technics,* 10, 11.

37. Spengler, *Man and Technics,* 94.

38. Spengler, *Man and Technics,* 93, 94.

39. Spengler, *Man and Technics,* 94–95, 103.

40. Spengler, *Man and Technics,* 97.

41. Spengler, *Man and Technics,* 64, 92, 86.

42. Spengler, *Man and Technics,* 104.

43. Spengler, *Year of Decision,* 92.

44. Spengler, *Year of Decision,* 92, 100, 67.

45. Spengler, *Year of Decision,* 68.

46. Spengler, *Year of Decision,* 68–69.

47. Spengler, *Man and Technics,* xvi.

48. See Heidegger's testimony, "The Rectorate, 1933–1934: Facts and Thoughts," in Gunther Neski and Emil Kettering, *Martin Heidegger and National Socialism* (New York: Paragon House, 1969), 18. For the influence of revolutionary conservative thought on Heidegger's political ideas, see Pierre Bordieu, *L'ontologie politique de Martin Heidegger.* Bordieu's interview "Back to History" appears in *The Heidegger Controversy,* ed. Richard Wolin (Boston: Massachusetts Institute of Technology Press, 1993), 264–271. Heidegger devoted an important essay, "Zur Seinsfrage," to a discussion of Jünger's work and noted there the attention he had also paid to Spengler (Martin Heidegger, *Wegmarken* [Frankfurt: Vittorio Klostermann, 1978], 384). Heidegger had corresponded with Jünger, and Heidegger's understanding of technology and its role in the modern world was decisively shaped by Jünger (and perhaps Spengler), although Heidegger's final posture toward technology was somewhat different. For the influence of Spengler on Heidegger, see Michael Zimmerman, *Heidegger's Confrontation with Modernity* (Bloomington: Indiana University Press, 1990). Heidegger noted his own close reading of Spengler's *Man and Technology* in Martin Heidegger, "Parmenides," in *Gesamtausgabe* (Frankfurt: Vittorio Klostermann, 1957), 54:101.

Despite its recognized importance and great commercial success, *The Worker* has never been translated into English, probably because, as Water Struve has argued, its elusive and evocative language make it virtually untranslatable.

49. Jünger's picture appeared on the cover of *Die Zeit Magazin,* 17 March 1995, on the occasion of his one-hundredth birthday.

50. Christian Graf von Krockow, "Grübler, Deuter, Wegbererreiter," in *Die Zeit Magazin,* 17 March 1995, 24. Von Krockow quotes from a Jünger novel without providing a full citation.

51. Ernst Jünger, "Total Mobilization," in *The Heidegger Controversy,* ed. Richard Wolin (Boston: Massachusetts Institute of Technology Press, 1993), 130. The German text appears in Ernst Jünger, *Sämtliche Werke* (Stuttgart: Klett-Cotta, 1980), 7:119–142.

52. Jünger, "Total Mobilization," 137–138.

53. Herf, *Reactionary Modernism,* 104, from Jünger, *Der Arbeiter,* 213–214.

54. Herf, *Reactionary Modernism,* 90.

55. Herf, *Reactionary Modernism,* 86–87, 95.

56. Ernst Jünger, "Untergang oder neue Ordnung?" *Deutsches Volkstum* 15 (1929): 415.

57. Struve, *Elites Against Democracy,* 385, 388 (Struve's translation of the passages from Jünger's "Total Mobilization").

58. Max Weber, *The Protestant Ethic and the Spirit of Capitalism,* trans. Talcott Parsons (London: Routledge, 1992), 181.

59. Lawrence Scaff, *Fleeing the Iron Cage* (Berkeley: University of California Press, 1989); Ronald Takaki, *Iron Cages* (New York: Knopf, 1979).

60. This scholarship is surveyed and discussed in Bryan Turner, *Max Weber: From History to Modernity* (London: Routledge, 1992), which refers to works by Robert Eden, W. J. Mommsen, William Hennis, and Lawrence Scaff.

61. Weber, *Protestant Ethic,* 48, 49.

62. Weber, *Protestant Ethic,* 192, 198, 51.

63. Weber, *Protestant Ethic,* 181–182.

64. Max Weber, *Gesammelte Aufsätze zur Religionssoziologie* (Tübingen: J. C. B. Mohr, 1922), 1:204.

65. Weber, *Protestant Ethic,* 182.

66. "Steel encasement" is the translation found in W. G. Runciman, ed., *Max Weber: Selections in Translation* (Cambridge: Cambridge University Press, 1978).

67. Weber, *Gesammelte Aufsätze* 1:204; Weber, *Protestant Ethic,* 182.

Chapter 8: Katastrophenhaft

In citing Heidegger's works below, I use the following abbreviations: *HC* for Richard Wolin, ed., *The Heidegger Controversy* (Boston: Massachusetts Institute of Technology Press, 1993); *GA* for Martin Heidegger, *Gesamtausgabe,* 79 vols. (Frankfurt: Vittorio Klostermann, 1975); *MHNS* for Gunther Neski and Emil Kettering, *Martin Heidegger and National Socialism* (New York: Paragon House, 1969); "Seminars" for Martin Heidegger, "Four Seminars," in *Questions Three and Four* (Paris: Gallimard, 1976); and Martin Heidegger, "Nur noch ein Gott kann uns retten," *Der Spiegel,* 31 May 1976 (interview took place on 23 September 1966), hereafter cited as *"Spiegel* Interview."

1. The Left, far more than the Right, structured the development of postwar intellectual thought. For an overview of Heidegger's influence, see Henri Meschonnic, *Le langage Heidegger* (Paris: Presses Universitaires de France, 1990); Richard Wolin, "French Heidegger Wars," in *HC,* 272–300; and Joseph Cropsey, "The United States as Regime," in *The Moral Foundations of the American Republic,* ed. Robert Horwitz, 3rd ed. (Charlottesville: University Press of Virginia, 1986), 165–181.

By the "far Right" I mean not the procapitalist, proliberal groups but those who remain suspicious of or hostile to liberal democracy. (The procapitalist neoliberals have generally been pro-American and have had little or no patience for this kind of philosophy.) The radical Right, which has maintained a virulent strain of anti-Americanism, lost much of its respectability and has been able to win influence only with difficulty—sometimes by disguising its views, sometimes by joining the Left, and sometimes by making tactical alliances with proliberal forces.

Recently, a radical Right has reemerged in a few pockets in both France and Germany. Heidegger's thought has been directly connected to these groups. The views of Robert Faurisson, the historian who has denied the facts of the Holocaust and the gas chambers, were supported by Jean Beaufret, a friend of Heidegger who translated many of his works into French. Beaufret, who had fought in the resistance in France, continually vouchsafed for Heidegger and denied elements of Heidegger's activities in behalf of national socialism (*HC,* 282). Should the Right reemerge, a Heideggerianism of the Right would also reoccur.

2. "A Letter on Humanism," in Martin Heidegger, *Basic Writings,* ed. David Krell (New York: Harper and Row, 1977), 241. One of the first scholars to treat Heidegger's symbolization of America is Michael Allen Gillespie in *Hegel, Heidegger, and the Ground of History* (Chicago: University of Chicago Press, 1984), 131.

3. Martin Heidegger, *Einführing in die Metaphysik,* in *GA* 40:40–41, 48–49. I am relying substantially on Ralph Manheim's translation of this work, *An Introduction to Metaphysics* (New Haven: Yale University Press, 1959), 37, 45–46.

4. Martin Heidegger, "Hölderlins Hymne," in *GA,* vol. 53. This course contains many references to America.

5. The Marxism with which Heidegger envisaged this dialogue may well have been in Western Europe rather than in the Soviet bloc. For his openness to such a dialogue, see Heidegger, "A Letter on Humanism," in *Basic Writings,* 220–221.

6. Martin Heidegger to Herbert Marcuse, 20 January 1948, *HC,* 162–163.

7. I am referring here to sec. 27 of *Being and Time.* The leading English translation, by John Macquarrie and Edward Robinson (New York: Harper and Row, 1962), translates "das Man" as "they."

8. Martin Heidegger, "A Television Interview," with Richard Wisser (1969) in *MHNS,* 82.

9. Heidegger makes these points most clearly in the opening pages of *Das Ende der Philosophie und die Aufgabe des Denkens* (Tübingen: Max Niemeyer Verlag, 1968).

10. Martin Heidegger, *A Discourse on Thinking* (a translation of *Gelassenheit*), ed. John Anderson and Hans Freund (New York: Harper Torchbacks), 50.

11. Martin Heidegger, "Überwindung der Metaphysik" (Overcoming Metaphysics), in *Vorträge und Aufsätze* (Pfullingen: Neske, 1954), 80 (sec. 10); Martin Heidegger, "Seminars" (Thor, 1969), 457.

12. Heidegger, "Hölderlins Hymne," 53:86; Heidegger, *What Is Called Thinking?* 21.

13. Heidegger, *Nietzsche* (Pfullingen: Neske, 1961), 2:487; "*Spiegel* Interview," 214. Heidegger goes on to concede that in the United States there are some attempts, "here and there," to think otherwise, and he asks whether in any case anyone should discount the possibility that a genuine mode of thought might emerge in a place like the United States or China.

14. Heidegger, *Discourse on Thinking,* 45.

15. Heidegger, *Discourse on Thinking,* 51.

16. Martin Heidegger, *Holzwege* (Frankfurt: Vittorio Klostermann, 1957), 267.

17. Heidegger, "Seminars," 446; Heidegger, *The Overcoming of Metaphysics,* sec. 26, in *HC,* 86.

18. Heidegger, *Overcoming Metaphysics,* sec. 26, in *HC,* 84–85.

19. Heidegger, *Overcoming Metaphysics,* sec. 26, in *HC,* 84–85; Martin Heidegger, "Zur Seinsfrage," in *Wegmarken,* 388.

20. Heidegger, *Overcoming Metaphysics,* sec. 26, in *HC,* 84–85; Martin Heidegger, "Zur Seinsfrage," in *Wegmarken,* 388; Heidegger, "Seminars," 447.

21. Heidegger, *Discourse on Thinking,* 56. Heidegger makes the same point in "The Origin of the Work of Art," in *Holzwege,* 58, and in the concluding chapter of the Nietzsche volume, composed in 1944–1946. There he writes, "It may well be that blindness in the face of the extreme need of Being . . . is still more hazardous than the crass adventures of a merely brutal will to violence" (*Nietzsche,* ed. David Krell [San Francisco: Harper Collins, 1982], 4:247).

22. Heidegger, *Überwindung,* 94 (sec. 26).

23. Heidegger, "*Spiegel* Interview," 206.

24. Heidegger, *Neue Zürcher Zeitung,* 26 September 1959, in *Cahier de l'Herne: Heidegger* (Paris: L'Herne, 1983), 362.

25. For a treatment of Heidegger's relationship to modern ecologism, see Dominique Janicaud, "Face à la domination: Heidegger, le marxisme, et l'écologie," in *Cahier de l'Herne,* 449–477.

26. Martin Heidegger, "A Television Interview with Richard Wisser," in *MHNS,* 84.

27. Heidegger, "Hölderlin," in *GA,* 53:179. Heidegger strengthens this point later in the same work, asserting that Americanism stands not merely for an absence of a historical sense (*das Geschichtlose*) but of an antihistorical posture (*das Ungeschichtliche*).

28. Heinrich Petzet, *Encounters and Dialogues with Martin Heidegger,* trans. by Parvis Emad and Kenneth Maly (Chicago: University of Chicago Press, 1993), 101, 102.

29. Heidegger, *Holzwege,* 103.

30. Heidegger, *Introduction to Metaphysics,* 38, and "Seminars" (Zurich, November 6, 1951), in *GA* 15:438; 438.

31. Heidegger, *Introduction to Metaphysics,* 37–38.

32. Martin Heidegger, *Der Satz vom Grund* (Pfullingen: Neske, 1971), 203.

33. Martin Heidegger, *Hebel der Hausfreund* (Pfullingen: Neske, 1965), 26, 27.

34. *GA* 53:80.

35. Heidegger, "Brief über den 'Humanismus,'" in *Wegmarken,* 355; and *Die Technik und die Kehre,* in "Seminars," 313.

36. Heidegger, "Seminars," 456; *Overcoming Metaphysics,* sec. 26, in *HC,* 84.

37. Heidegger, *Holzwege,* 269.

38. *Holzwege,* 268; "Seminars" (Zähringen, 1973), 477.

39. Martin Heidegger, "Grundbegriffe" (summer semester lectures, 1941), in *GA* 51:92, 84.

40. Heidegger, "Seminars" (Thor, 1969), 457; Heidegger, "Seminars" (Zähringen, 1973), 476.

41. Heidegger's definition of a "Volk" as a group able to seize its history, usually through the aid of the poet, is articulated throughout the Hölderlin commentaries. The most rigorous discussions and definitions of the term are provided in the recently published *Beiträge zur Philosophie* (1989), in *GA* 65:42–43, 308–309.

42. Heidegger, "Hölderlins Hymne," 53:68.

43. Martin Heidegger, "Andenken, Erläuterungen zu Hölderlins Dichtung," in *GA* 52:34. See also Meschonnic, *Le langage,* 355.

44. See, for example, Zimmerman, *Heidegger's Confrontation,* and Philippe Lacoue-Labarthe, *La fiction de la politique* (Paris: Christian Bourgeois, 1987). The poetic commentaries include discussions not only of Hölderlin but also of Heraclitus and Parmenides.

45. Cited in Otto Pöggeler, "Heidegger's Political Self-Understanding," in *HC,* 217.

46. Martin Heidegger, *Heraklit,* "Der Anfang des Abendländichen Denkens," in *GA* 55:123.

47. Lacoue-Labarthe, *La fiction de la politique,* 27, and Meschonnic, 354–364. See also the discussion of Veronique Foti, *Heidegger and the Poets* (Atlantic Highlands, N.J.: Humanities Press, 1992), 45–59.

48. Heidegger, "Andenken," *GA* 52:134.

49. Heidegger, "Andenken," *GA* 52:37.

50. These were a television interview conducted by Richard Wisser on 24 September 1969 and the interview published in *Der Spiegel,* cited above.

51. See the writings of contemporary French Heideggerians Jacques Derrida and Philippe Lacoue-Labarthe as well as those of Hannah Arendt. The background for Arendt's comments, which were affected by her long personal relationship with Heidegger, is treated in Elz-

bieta Ettinger, *Hannah Arendt and Martin Heidegger* (New Haven: Yale University Press, 1995).

52. Cited in *HC,* 195. This position is similar to the one argued at length by Tom Rockmore, *On Heidegger's Nazism and Philosophy* (Berkeley and Los Angeles: University of California Press, 1992). Rockmore writes, "Although Heidegger's position changes, and although he abandons philosophy for thought beyond philosophy, he does not abandon, in fact he specifically maintains, the political role of his thought of Being" (187).

In a letter to *Die Zeit,* Heidegger indirectly commented on Habermas' argument, noting that his point in 1935 was that National Socialism was admirable because it was a symptom of the conflict between technology and man, a sign of the danger that all alternatives were now captives of technology (*MHNS,* xvii). See also Heidegger's letter, *GA* 40:232–233; the letter by Christian Lewalter, *Die Zeit,* 14 August 1953; and Heidegger's response, *Die Zeit,* 24 October 1953.

53. Pöggeler, in *HC,* 56. As some have described his goal or ambition, Heidegger hoped to cut Hitler off from certain currents within the party and to become himself the main intellectual source for the new Germany.

54. Martin Heidegger, "The University in the New Reich," speech of 30 June 1933, in *HC,* 45.

55. Heidegger, *Introduction to Metaphysics,* 42, 38.

56. See the change as found in the use of the word "metaphysics" in his lecture "Was ist Metaphysik?" delivered in 1929, and the afterword he added in 1943, which speaks of the "overcoming of metaphysics" (*GA* 9:303). But when one looks at how Heidegger used the word in each case, one realizes that the difference between these two usages is not as great as it may seem. Heidegger discusses the continuity of his meaning at the end of his Nietzsche lectures (see especially *Nietzsche,* ed. Krell, 4:250).

57. Martin Heidegger, "Was Heist Denken?" in Heidegger, *Vorträge und Aufsätze,* 143 ("Wir Denken noch nicht eigentlich"); "*Spiegel* Interview," 212; *Discourse on Thinking,* 46; "*Spiegel* Interview," 209.

58. Martin Heidegger, "The End of Philosophy and the Task of Thinking," in *Basic Writings,* 378–379; "*Spiegel* Interview," 214; Martin Heidegger, "A Greeting to the Symposium in Beirut in November 1974," in *MHNS,* 254.

59. "*Spiegel* Interview," 209. See also *GA* 53:105–106 and Heidegger's statement in "Logos": "Thinking changes the world" (*Vorträge und Aufsätze,* 229).

60. Heidegger, "Overcoming Metaphysics," sec. 26, in *HC,* 60–61.

61. See Reiner Schurmann, "Que faire à la fin de la métaphysique?" in *Cahier de l'Herne,* 449–476; Mark Blitz, *Heidegger's "Being and Time" and the Possibility of Political Philosophy* (Ithaca: Cornell University Press, 1981), 121–122.

62. One interpretation of the "positive program" calls for special attention: the idea, developed by Reiner Schurmann, that the only path to renewal is through a total destruction of the West. The positive program for now thus becomes, in ordinary language, the most negative one, the one that ensures a flight to complete barbarism and nihilism. This program would be Nazism.

63. "*Spiegel* Interview," 204.

64. Martin Heidegger, *Beiträge zur Philosophie, GA* 65:38. See also *HC,* 9.

65. Martin Heidegger, *Was heißt Denken?* (Tübingen: M. Niemeyer, 1954), 65; *HC*, 9. In general, Heidegger's comments on democracy, though sparing, closely track those expressed by Nietzsche.

66. Interview with Hans Jonas for Swiss radio, October 1987, in *MHNS*, 202–203.

67. See Heidegger, *Nietzsche,* ed. Krell, 4:21.

68. Gregory Bruce Smith, "Heidegger's Postmodern Politics?" *Polity* 24:1 (Fall 1991): 164, 167.

69. Martin Heidegger, "Hölderlins 'Germanien' und 'Der Rhein,'" in *GA,* 39; see also *HC,* 20n.16. For a later view, see *"Spiegel* Interview": "The only possibility of salvation left to us is to prepare for readiness, through thinking and poetry" (209).

70. *"Spiegel* Interview," 214.

71. Letter to the rector of the University of Albert-Ludwig, 4 November 1945. This account was intended to help Heidegger in his effort to maintain his position at the University of Freiburg, from which he was dismissed the next year after an investigation by French authorities. The letter was not published until 1983, but it circulated in translation in France, and its content became well known. Taken from the French translation that appears in *Cahier de l'Herne,* 394.

72. Heidegger, "The Rectorate," 19; Karl Lowith, "My Last Meeting with Heidegger in Rome, 1936," in *HC,* 142.

73. Georg Picht, "The Power of Thinking," in *MHNS,* 164 (Picht was one of Heidegger's students); Heidegger, "The Rectorate," 18.

74. Lacoue-Labarthe, *La fiction,* 58. Lacoue-Labarthe pronounces this formulation to be "scandalously insufficient," although he does not seem to abandon altogether Heidegger's main point about all modern regimes being expressions of a humanism.

75. Hannah Arendt, "For Martin Heidegger's Eightieth Birthday," in *MHNS,* 216. Arendt took Heidegger at his word in this matter partly because of her personal involvement with him in a long-lasting love affair. The story of how he shamelessly manipulated her emotions—and of how she allowed herself to be manipulated—is told in Ettinger, *Arendt and Heidegger.*

76. Hugo Ott, in *MHNS,* 134 (as Ott carefully summed up the matter, "Heidegger clearly presented his break and end to be more decisive than it was—and his opposition was less clear-cut" [xiv]); Heidegger, "Hölderlins Hymne," 53:106; Otto Pöggeler in *HC,* 17.

77. All that is, "is governed by struggle," in Lowith's recounting of a lecture Heidegger gave during this period (*HC,* 177). For Heidegger's comments on the centrality of struggle as "father of all things," see *Hölderlins Hymne "Germanien" und "Der Rhein,"* in *GA* 39:125–127.

78. Even after the war, when Heidegger spoke more often of the site of renewal as being Europe as a whole, he guarded a special place for Germany because of the "special inner relationship of the German language with the language of the Greeks and of her thought" (*"Spiegel* Interview," 217).

79. Cited in "Die Frage nach der Technik," in Heidegger, *Vorträge und Aufsätze,* 36. The line in German is "Wo aber Gefahr ist, wächst / Das Rettende auch."

80. Heidegger's discussion of the need for getting beyond poetic techniques and interpretations that rely on symbol and metaphor comes in the same short work that contains his most

extensive comments on Americanism: see "Hölderlins Hymne," 53:17–20. The point is not to dismiss an interpretation that relies on a symbolic reading of America in Heidegger's thought but to interpret Heidegger's own view of a symbolic reading.

81. I bring together here the "poet" and "thinker" without making a clear distinction between them, i.e., between Hölderlin and himself. In fact, there is finally no real difference as far as guiding politics is concerned. For support on this point, see *GA* 15:434. The statesman or founder—whom Heidegger once referred to in 1935 as a kind of artist—drops out altogether, to be replaced by the artist-poet and critic.

Chapter 9: America as the End of History

1. Alexandre Kojève, *Introduction à la lecture de Hegel*, ed. Raymond Queneau (Paris: Gallimard, 1968) (hereafter cited as *Introduction*).

2. This is the assessment of André Glucksmann cited by Michael Roth in "A Problem of Recognition: Alexandre Kojève and the End of History," *History and Theory* 24 (1985): 293. Similar appraisals of Kojève's importance are made by Allan Bloom in his foreword to *On Tyranny*, by Leo Strauss (Ithaca: Cornell University Press, 1968), vi–vii; by Stanley Rosen, *Hermeneutics as Politics* (New York: Oxford University Press, 1987), 91–92; and by Vincent Descombes, *Modern French Philosophy* (Cambridge: Cambridge University Press, 1983). Descombes argues that the entire pattern of French thought since the 1930s has followed a dialectic based on Hegel's thought, in which Hegelianism (as interpreted by Kojève) was set forth, accepted, and then rejected—but in a way that incorporated most of its categories. Among those who attended Kojève's course were Maurice Merleau-Ponty, Jacques Lacan, Raymond Aron, and Raymond Queneau.

3. Francis Fukuyama, "The End of History?" *National Interest* 16 (Summer 1989): 3–18; Francis Fukuyama, *The End of History and the Last Man* (New York: Free Press, 1992).

4. Paul Cantor, who teaches literature at the University of Virginia, has written extensively on modern wrestling and on various movies and television series. Cantor's (unpublished but widely circulated) seminal paper on *Star Trek* is entitled "Shakespeare in the Original Klingon: *Star Trek* and the End of History." Demonstrating in more ways than one that he takes quite seriously the notion of the end of history, Cantor has lectured on this topic in and around Virginia. All quotations in this and the previous paragraph are taken from Cantor's paper.

5. *Introduction*, 145.

6. "Animal" is the term Kojève used in his published writings. Now, thanks to Victor Gourevitch and Michael Roth, we have access to the correspondence of Kojève and Leo Strauss. In a letter written to Strauss on 19 September 1950, Kojève speaks interchangeably of "animals" and "automata," seeming to prefer the latter term. This letter and all other extant correspondence between Strauss and Kojève appear in the new edition of Leo Strauss, *On Tyranny*, ed. Victor Gourevitch and Michael Roth (New York: Free Press, 1991), 255–256 (hereafter cited as *On Tyranny*).

7. *On Tyranny*, 174, 184, 167, 168.

8. *Introduction*, 404, 95.

9. *On Tyranny*, 175–176, 176.

10. *Introduction*, 436. The reference to frogs must refer to a similar passage in Nietzsche's *Will to Power*, sec. 808, where Nietzsche speaks of the last men who practice art for its own sake and resemble the "virtuoso croaking of shivering frogs, despairing in their swamp."

11. *Introduction*, 436, 437.

12. Kojève to Strauss, 19 September 1950, *On Tyranny*, 255.

13. Kojève goes back and forth, it seems, about whether a new kind of posthistorical thought or philosophy will continue. At some points he seems to suggest that we have all become animals or automata, whereas at other points he seems to leave the door open for a passive kind of contemplation: "As for those who are not satisfied with their 'purposeless activity' (art, etc.), they are the philosophers (who can attain wisdom if they 'contemplate' enough)" (Kojève to Strauss, 19 September 1950, *On Tyranny*, 295).

14. *Introduction*, 443.

15. Kojève allowed that, depending on whether Russia or the West won, there would be a different "interpretation." In the first case, the interpretation would be described in "Russian," in the second case in "European." Kojève worked in behalf of the second alternative and was highly prescient in detecting some of the policies that promoted the European victory. See Kojève to Strauss, 19 September 1950, *On Tyranny*, 295–296.

16. Kojève follows Hegel in identifying the French Revolution rather than the American Revolution as the major revolutionary event of world history, but he interpolates or qualifies Hegel by treating the history of America as nothing really new, as merely a working out of European history.

17. *Introduction*, 436–437.

18. *Introduction*, 437.

19. *On Tyranny*, 209. See also Leo Strauss, *Natural Right and History* (Chicago: University of Chicago Press, 1950), 320.

20. Kojève to Strauss, 19 September 1950, *On Tyranny*, 255.

21. Kojève to Strauss, 29 October 1953, *On Tyranny*, 262; Victor Gourevitch and Michael Roth, introduction to *On Tyranny*, xiv.

22. *On Tyranny*, 304. Kojève's reference here is to his essay "The Emperor Julian and His Art of Writing," in Joseph Cropsey, ed., *Ancients and Moderns: Essays in the Tradition of Political Philosophy in Honor of Leo Strauss* (New York: Basic Books, 1964).

23. Kojève to Strauss, 29 March 1962, *On Tyranny*, 307.

24. *On Tyranny* was published first in 1954 in French and then a decade later in English.

25. George Grant, *Technology and Empire* (Toronto: House of Anansi), 181. For further commentaries, see Stanley Rosen, *Hermeneutics as Politics*; Michael Roth, *Knowing and History: Appropriations of Hegel in Twentieth-Century France* (Ithaca: Cornell University Press, 1988); and Robert Pippen, "Being, Time, and Politics: The Strauss-Kojève Debate," *History and Theory* 32 (1993): 138–161.

26. *On Tyranny*, 27.

27. *On Tyranny*, 23; Leo Strauss, *What Is Political Philosophy?* (Chicago: University of Chicago Press, 1959), 57.

28. *On Tyranny*, 23.

29. *On Tyranny*, 27.

30. *On Tyranny*, 27. Strauss does not claim that historicist thought was the first or original attack on traditional political science, which had already come under attack from the modern political science of certain philosophers. Historical thought, culminating in a philosophy of history, is for Strauss a further development or intensification of modern political science: "The concern with a guarantee for the realization of the 'ideal' led to both a lowering of the standards of political life and to the emergence of a 'philosophy of history'" (106).

31. *On Tyranny*, 106n.5.

32. *On Tyranny*, 212.

33. The "second cave" appears in Leo Strauss, "Besprechung von Julius Ebbinghaus: Uber die Fortschritte der Metaphysik," *Deutsche Literaturzeitung* 52 (27 December 1931): 2453. The image was called to my attention by a paper by Heinrich Meier, "The History of Philosophy and the Intention of the Philosopher: Reflections on Leo Strauss," presented at the University of Virginia, 18 November 1994.

34. Strauss, *Natural Right and History*, 316.

35. *On Tyranny*, 212. Strauss omitted this concluding sentence, which appeared in the French edition of *On Tyranny*, from the English versions. Gourevitch and Roth restore it. A clearer reference to Heidegger on this point may be found in Strauss, *What Is Political Philosophy?* 26–27.

36. *On Tyranny*, 69, 209–211. Without full mutual satisfaction, there would be no way to prevent history from beginning again; see Pippen, "Being, Time, and Politics," 158.

37. The full statement reads, "I assume, then, there is an eternal and immutable order within which history takes place, and which remains entirely unaffected by history" (*On Tyranny*, 212).

38. Strauss, *What Is Political Philosophy?* 24–27; Strauss, *Natural Right and History*, 78, 305–306.

39. Strauss, *What Is Political Philosophy?* 69. See also Strauss, *Natural Right and History*, 304–306.

40. Political actors must size up the general situation, mindful of the fact that it is their duty "to act virtuously and wisely in it" (Strauss, *What Is Political Philosophy?* 311). Still, a situation can be so bad that no practical political alternative is honorable. In a case of tyranny on all sides, Strauss commends an assertion of freedom almost for its own sake, as an act of nobility in the face of an implacable and seemingly triumphant evil. Yet even this kind of act may have a practical impact. It can "contribute greatly toward keeping awake the recollection of the immense loss sustained by mankind [and] may inspire and strengthen the desire and hope for its recovery" (*Natural Right and History*, 318).

41. Strauss, *Natural Right and History*, 320.

42. Strauss, *Natural Right and History*, 34; *On Tyranny*, 211.

43. *On Tyranny*, 176.

Chapter 10: America as Postmodern

1. James Markham, *New York Times*, 12 December 1988, A4; Steven Best and Douglas Kellner, *Postmodern Theory* (New York: Guilford Press, 1991), 111.

2. Jean Baudrillard, *Amérique* (Paris: B. Grasset, 1986), 151, 58, 194 (hereafter cited as *Amérique*); Jean Baudrillard, "Game with Vestiges," in *On the Beach* 5 (Winter 1984): 24 (emphasis added).

3. *Amérique,* 21.

4. *Amérique,* 58.

5. *Amérique,* 201. The American, as noted, is not conscious of this fact but "lives" it as a primitive. The European feels the disjunction between the thing and the copy and is uneasy with it. But the truly sophisticated thinker—he who is "modern or ultra-modern"—understands that the secret of modernity consists precisely in being able to grasp that which is artifice or representation and to see in the artifice something profounder or deeper than the real or the first image (139).

6. *Amérique,* 194.

7. *Amérique,* 44.

8. *Amérique,* 89–90.

9. I say Baudrillard "supposedly" came to America because one cannot be sure that his visit ever took place. Had he truly sought to focus on the "fiction" of America, he might have followed the *beau geste* of Chateaubriand, who wrote his famous travelogue about America without leaving France. Unfortunately for Baudrillard, however, I have met several persons, reliable witnesses all, who swear to have seen him in exactly some of the places he claims to have visited.

10. *Amérique,* 151, 23; *New York Times,* 12 December 1988, A44; *Amérique,* 173.

11. *Amérique,* 68. Incidentally, for those interested in allusions, the odd phrase "zero-degree" is a reference to a concept of Roland Barthes: the zero degree is a (final) stage in the evolution of literature, when literature is without signs and is, as it were, no longer literature.

12. *Amérique,* 68.

13. *Amérique,* 50, 195.

14. *Amérique,* 186.

15. *Amérique,* 157.

16. James Wilson, speech at the Pennsylvania Ratifying Convention, 2:17.

17. This does not count the times that French was imposed on the various linguistic minorities in France—for example, after the Revolution, when French was made the national language of instruction. Jacques Derrida apologizes for this injustice in *Force de loi* (Paris: Galilée, 1994), 47. He says little, however, about the liberating experience afforded by knowing a world language.

18. *Amérique,* 156, 152. Baudrillard also follows Kojève in suggesting that Japan possesses even more of this ability to reinvent itself than America does (162).

19. *Amérique,* 196.

20. *Amérique,* 208–209.

21. Bryan Turner, "Baudrillard for Sociologists," in *Forget Baudrillard?* ed. Chris Rojek and Bryan S. Turner (London: Routledge, 1993), 70–84.

22. Umberto Eco, *Travels in Hyperreality,* trans. William Weaver (San Diego: Harcourt Brace Jovanovich, 1983), 8, 18–19.

23. Jean Baudrillard, *Simulations,* 25; Chris Rojek and Bryan S. Turner, introduction to *Forget Baudrillard?* ed. Rojek and Turner (London: Routledge, 1993), x.

24. *Amérique,* 174.

25. *Amérique,* 69–70.

26. Best and Kellner, *Postmodern Theory,* 138–139.

27. *Amérique,* 123; Jean-Philippe Mathy, *Extrême-Occident,* 232.

28. Derrida, *Force de loi,* 35.

29. Jacques Derrida, "Declarations of Independence," *New Political Science* 15 (1986):7, reprinted from *Otobiographies* (Paris: Galilée, 1984), 14.

30. *Federalist* no. 49, 315. *Federalist* no. 49, which responds to a proposal by Jefferson to facilitate the rewriting of the Constitution, is one of the best treatments in political science of the dangers of deconstructing fundamental law.

31. Baudrillard, *La Guerre du Golfe,* 90, 100.

Conclusion

1. Said, *Culture and Imperialism,* 314.

2. Jacques Derrida, *Of Grammatology,* trans. Gayatri Spivak (Baltimore: Johns Hopkins University Press, 1974), 19.

3. Martin Heidegger, *Zur Seinsfrage* (On the Question of Being), in *Wegmarken.*

4. *Federalist* no. 37, 229.

5. *Federalist* no. 49, 314.

Index

Index